Triumph of the Lamb

Triumph of the Lamb

A Commentary on Revelation

Dennis E. Johnson

P&R PUBLISHING
P.O. BOX 817 • PHILLIPSBURG • NEW JERSEY 08865-0817

Unless otherwise indicated, Scripture quotations are from the *NEW AMERICAN STANDARD BIBLE®*. ©Copyright The Lockman Foundation 1960, 1962, 1963, 1968, 1971, 1972, 1973, 1975, 1977, 1995. Used by permission.

Italics in Scripture quotations indicate emphasis added.

Printed in the United States of America

Library of Congress Cataloging-in-Publication Data

Johnson, Dennis E. (Dennis Edward)
    Triumph of the lamb : a commentary on Revelation / Dennis E. Johnson.
       p.   cm.
    Includes bibliographical references and index.
    ISBN 0-87552-200-9
    1. Bible. N.T. Revelation—Commentaries. I. Title.
BS2825.53 J64 2001
228'.07—dc21

                                    2001021371

To Jane

Contents

Abbreviations

BAGD	Bauer, Arndt, Gingrich, and Danker, *A Greek-English Lexicon*
BDB	Brown, Driver, and Briggs, *A Hebrew-English Lexicon*
ExpT	*Expository Times*
HNTC	Harper's New Testament Commentary
ICC	International Critical Commentary
JETS	*Journal of the Evangelical Theological Society*
JSNT	*Journal for the Study of the New Testament*
LCL	Loeb Classical Library
LS	Liddell and Scott, A *Greek-English Lexicon*
LN	Loew and Nida, *Greek-English Lexicon*
LXX	Septuagint
NASB	New American Standard Bible (updated edition, 1995)
NCB	New Century Bible
NICNT	New International Commentary on the New Testament
NIGTC	New International Greek Testament Commentary
NIV	New International Version
NovT	*Novum Testamentum*
NRSV	New Revised Standard Version
NTS	*New Testament Studies*
P^{47}	Papyrus 47
TBST	The Bible Speaks Today
WBC	Word Biblical Commentary
WTJ	*Westminster Theological Journal*

Acknowledgments

My thanks go to the board of trustees of Westminster Theological Seminary in California for a study leave in the fall of 1997, during which I began writing on this project, and for the opportunity to teach our course General Epistles and Revelation from 1982 to 1997. I am also thankful to fine students who, early in my teaching of this course, "began to importune me," as Moses Stuart's had importuned him more than 150 years before, to help them to understand the Book of Revelation and to bring its divine message to Christ's churches. Their questions and our discussions have taught me much about this intriguing and practical New Testament book.

I am always thankful to God for our congregation, New Life Presbyterian Church (PCA) in Escondido, which is truly family to our family, even though our children—so young when we moved here in 1981—are grown up, married, and most scattered to far places. I am honored and humbled to work alongside the wise and grace-full elders whom the Lord has given to New Life, appreciative of our committed staff, and grateful in so many ways for our members. As a congregation and as a family we have gone through deep waters these days. This should come as no surprise in view of Revelation's realism about the church's struggles on earth. Through it all, though, we are seeing how our Lord makes good his promise of Isaiah 43:2. Encouraging responses from New Life people to my teaching on Revelation in our School of Discipleship and our evening worship have kept me motivated, and their prayers have kept me afloat.

Thanks also to other parts of the body of Christ who have asked me to teach on Revelation in Bible conference settings over the last several years: Rocky Mountain Community Church (OPC), Billings,

Montana; First Presbyterian Church (PCA), Kosciusko, Mississippi; and the Presbytery of Northern California of the Orthodox Presbyterian Church. Thanks also to Reformed Theological Seminary (Orlando) and New Geneva Theological Seminary for the invitation to teach their cosponsored course, Hebrews to Revelation, in Colorado Springs over three weekends in fall 1999.

Thanks to Barbara Lerch, P&R acquisitions editor, for her patience, prayer, and ongoing encouragement despite the deadlines I missed; and to the editorial staff of P&R Publishing for making this book better.

I want to express special thanks to two people who have had a special role in the writing and refining process. My colleague and friend Dr. S. M. Baugh inherited from me the General Epistles and Revelation course when Westminster in California invited me to move into the department of practical theology. Steve has brought to the course his expertise in ancient Greek, his special research interest in the social and religious history of Greco-Roman Asia Minor, and his wise and godly exegetical skills. He has kindly used the not-yet-complete typescript in the course, and he has read every chapter carefully, raising questions, suggesting improvements, and bringing to my attention helpful information that I would not otherwise have known. When you see his name in the footnotes, join me in thanking God for this good brother and faithful servant of Christ's Word.

My best friend on this earth, and my kindest and best editor, is Jane, who celebrated with me thirty years of marriage in June 2000. She has read every chapter for clarity and grammar, and she kept encouraging me that a book like this could help the church. Although the months since our nest pretty much emptied have been full of unexpected challenges for our church and our extended family, I thank God for the tranquility and delight of being at home with this lovely, loving, and wise woman. God has graced us with adult children who are loving and serving Jesus where he has dispersed them: Eric and Susanne (Oregon or Texas or elsewhere), Christina and Julien (California), Peter and Mandi (Georgia), and Laurie and Daniel (Florida). It is a special, high-intensity time in which we're all under one roof again! But it's also a special treat when calm recaptures our household and it's just the two of us.

CHAPTER ONE

Introduction:
A Strategy for Seeing

Wrestling with Revelation

In 1845 Moses Stuart saw his two-volume, 1,008-page *Commentary on the Apocalypse* brought to publication at last. In the preface he reported that, soon after his appointment to teach at Andover Theological Seminary in 1809, his students "began to importune" him to teach about the Book of Revelation.

> I commenced study of it, with a design to comply with their request. I soon found myself, however, in pursuing the way of regular interpretation as applied to other books of Scripture, completely hedged in. . . . I frankly told my Pupils, therefore, that I knew nothing respecting the book which could profit them, and that I could not attempt to lecture upon it. After still further examination, I came to a resolution, not to attempt the exegesis of the Apocalypse, until a period of ten years had elapsed, which should be devoted, so far as my other duties would permit, to the study of the Hebrew prophets. I kept my resolution. After this period had passed, I began, with much caution, to say a few things, in the Lecture-room, respecting the book in question. . . . In the process of time I began to go through the whole book. This I have done several times; and the present work is the result of these often repeated and long continued labors.[1]

1. Moses Stuart, *A Commentary on the Apocalypse,* 2 vols. (London: Wiley and Putnam, 1845), 1:v.

Perhaps few people today share Stuart's methodical and cautious patience, but no doubt many identify with his initial experience of the Book of Revelation: "hedged in" and understanding "nothing respecting the book which could profit" ourselves or others. His reminiscence well illustrates some of the challenges that this fierce New Testament book poses for its readers.

Revelation seems resistant and unresponsive to "the way of regular interpretation as applied to other books of Scripture." It is neither historical narrative like 1 Samuel, nor an epistle like Romans, nor a collection of laws (Leviticus), songs (Psalms), or wise aphorisms (Proverbs). Yet it speaks of historical events, opens as an epistle addressed to seven churches, is deeply concerned with covenant faithfulness (the central theme of biblical law), is punctuated with songs of praise and victory, and demands a mind of wisdom to unlock its secrets (see Rev. 17:9). The impression that Revelation speaks a foreign language when compared with the rest of the Bible is only partly true. Revelation's mode of communication has affinities not only with significant portions of the Old Testament prophetic literature, as Stuart implies, but also with Jesus' teaching methods in the Gospels (both apocalyptic sections such as Mark 13 and his use of imagery in parables) and some sections of the epistles. Revelation is, as its Greek title implies, apocalyptic—not in the modern sense of "catastrophic" but in the ancient sense of "unveiling, disclosing" in vivid, visual form the invisible realities and forces that drive and therefore explain the course of observable historical events. Most modern readers of the New Testament are not at home with ancient apocalyptic literature, so our sense of Revelation's alienness can make us feel hedged in, frustrated because this book doesn't deliver its message in the form to which we are accustomed, a form accessible to reading strategies that have proved tried and true elsewhere.

One way through the impasse, however, is to pay careful attention to Revelation's biblical precursors, "the Hebrew prophets." As Stuart recognized, the visions of Ezekiel, Daniel, Zechariah, and others provided not only a fertile field from which the images of Revelation have been harvested but also a genre—that is, a community or family of literature whose members are related to each other in style and therefore in the expectations evoked in readers.[2] We may marvel at Stuart's self-control. A decade seems a long time to postpone studying Revelation directly, to immerse one's heart and mind in its canonical antecedents. Nevertheless, such study of the prophets as well as other Old and New Testament precedents will repay our effort many times over, for, as Richard Bauckham has aptly said, Revelation is "the climax of prophecy"—bringing to consummate fulfillment the prophetic tradition of Israel.[3]

Stuart's repetitive teaching of the Book of Revelation, cautiously circling and recircling through the book in successive years of seminary instruction, points to one of the book's challenges and the way to meet the challenge. The challenge can be stated simply: You cannot understand any individual passage in Revelation unless you understand the book as a whole, but you cannot understand the book as a whole unless you understand its individual passages.

In one sense, this is a conundrum posed by any lengthy text. Each individual passage must be understood in its context, and one of the most relevant contexts for any sentence or paragraph is the whole document in which it is found. The document provides invaluable signals regarding its setting in life: the stage in the conversation between writer and audience in which a particular passage comes, their previous acquaintance, and their present questions or crises. It also helps us get our bearings with respect to genre, or the type of literature with which we have to do, the way in which this kind of literature uses language. Is it more metaphorical or literal, more direct or indirect, more formal or informal, organized thematically or chronologically? Understanding genre helps us choose a strategy for reading that is appropriate to a text of this type. Of course, close attention to the individual passages that make up a document may expand or revise our impression of its genre as a whole, since each passage makes its own contribution as part of the context of its neighbors in the document.

2. Tremper Longman III, *Literary Approaches to Biblical Interpretation,* Foundations of Contemporary Interpretation, vol. 3 (Grand Rapids: Academie Books, Zondervan, 1987), 76–83.

3. Richard Bauckham, *The Climax of Prophecy: Studies on the Book of Revelation* (Edinburgh: T & T Clark, 1993).

We need a general sense of how the book as a whole is delivering its message in order to get the point of its particular components, but our study of the components has to enrich, expand, perhaps correct the big picture with which we began. Although the image of a hermeneutical circle or spiral normally refers to the give-and-take between a modern interpreter's horizon or worldview and that of the biblical text,[4] one dimension of the circular or spiraling process of interpretation is the way in which a growing grasp of the document as a whole (themes, genre, structure, life setting, etc.) illumines our understanding of its individual passages and vice versa.

This paradoxical, circular principle of interpretation is even more crucial and even more difficult to apply when we come to the Book of Revelation. It is more crucial because the symbolic nature of the apocalyptic-prophetic genre to which Revelation belongs is susceptible to subjective flights of imagination in interpretation. Countless innovative connections have been drawn between Revelation's images and proposed referents in history. How do we sort out which of these are intended by God and which are the fruit of our hyperactive imagination? Many students of biblical prophecy adopt as a working principle a preference for a literal sense where such is possible. They believe that this principle provides an objective way to test the validity of our interpretation, anchoring it to the terra firma of the text rather than letting it float free, drifting in the breeze. Although, as we will see, applying the literal-where-possible maxim to prophetic literature is problematic, its inadequacy does not mean that Revelation is a wax nose, to be manipulated into any shape we choose. The process of sifting our impressions from what the text means is complex and challenging but not impossible. One check on exegetical flights of fancy is to pay attention to the interplay between specific passages and their context.

4. Anthony C. Thiselton, *The Two Horizons: New Testament Hermeneutics and Philosophical Description with Special Reference to Heidegger, Bultmann, Gadamer, and Wittgenstein* (Grand Rapids: Eerdmans, 1980). See especially chapter 11 on the thought of Gadamer regarding the distance and fusion of horizons (293–326). Grant R. Osborne, *The Hermeneutical Spiral: A Comprehensive Introduction to Biblical Interpretation* (Downers Grove, Ill.: InterVarsity Press, 1991), especially "Context," 19–40.

It is difficult in Revelation to maintain the rhythmic movement from context to text and back again for two reasons. Revelation's apocalyptic-visionary mode of speaking is foreign to many modern readers' way of thinking, so our minds quickly experience fatigue, like the bewildered exhaustion we feel when surrounded by people conversing in a language that we are only starting to learn. With intense effort we manage to pick out a word, a phrase, occasionally a whole sentence or a vague idea of the topic. But we miss more than we grasp, and the effort needed to pierce the veil of foreignness and hear the patterns that make meaning wearies us.

It is unlikely that anyone who has been a Christian for any length of time comes to Revelation as a blank slate, blissfully undecided about all matters pertaining to the form and significance of the book. Through teaching, preaching, or reading you have probably been exposed to one or more of the three perspectives on the thousand years spoken of in Revelation 20 and to one or more of the four views concerning the relationship between Revelation's visions and the events to which they refer. It is an advantage to begin reading with a pattern in mind, but if the paradigm is so deeply embedded in our minds that it cannot be corrected by what we find in particular passages, our framework may obscure rather than illumine the message.

For this reason I have departed from the common practice in books on Revelation, which typically place in their introductions a survey of the premillennial, postmillennial, and amillennial interpretations of Revelation 20 and of the preterist, historicist, idealist, and futurist approaches to the book. Instead of putting this discussion up front, tempting readers to choose sides at the outset, I have moved it to the end as an appendix. Readers who feel that they must know to which camp I belong before we study the text together can turn immediately to that appendix—but I would encourage you not to. Should we not first try to reach an understanding of Revelation's message, as inductively as we can from specific passages and their larger context, and then ask which label best fits what we have seen and heard?

Let us then follow in Moses Stuart's footprints, circling and recircling through Revelation with patience, expecting that each pass through its lush imagery will unveil new beauties as well as new connections between truths previously discovered. To begin the exploration, however, we do need some general sense of the terrain that lies before us. This chapter proposes seven principles, derived inductively from what Revelation says about itself and shows us about itself. These principles taken together provide a strategy for seeing what God intends to bring before the eyes of our hearts. A brief rationale for each principle is offered in order to show how it is rooted in the text. As we work through Revelation section by section, I invite you to judge whether these principles are keys that fit this New Testament treasury and unlock its riches.

Principles for Reading Revelation

Revelation Is Given to Reveal. Although we have noted Professor Stuart's commendable caution in approaching Revelation, we must not let ourselves be intimidated by the strangeness of its visions or the controversies that swarm, locustlike, around it. Our starting point should be confidence that God has given this book not to confuse, terrify, or divide his people but to give us light, to reveal to us the invisible forces and the secrets of his invincible plan that make sense of visible events and movements experienced by his church in the world. God's purpose for Revelation is disclosed throughout the prologue (1:1–3):

> The *Revelation* of Jesus Christ, which God gave Him to *show* to His bond-servants, the things which must shortly take place; and He sent and *communicated* it by His angel to His bond-servant John, who testified to the word of God and to the testimony of Jesus Christ, even to all that he saw. Blessed is he who reads and those who *hear* the words of the prophecy, and heed the things which are written in it; for the time is near.[5]

Each of the italicized words emphasizes that God's purpose for Revelation is not to confuse his servants or obscure our perception of his ways in the world but the reverse.

5. Unless otherwise noted, Scripture quotations are from NASB (updated edition, 1995).

"Revelation" represents the Greek word *Apocalypsis,* and hence some English versions and scholars speak of this book as the Apocalypse; this noun is cognate to a verb (*apokalyptō*) that speaks of the removal of a veil or other covering to disclose what lies behind it (see Matt. 10:26). Paul speaks of Jesus' second coming in visible splendor as "the revelation of the Lord Jesus Christ" (1 Cor. 1:7; cf. 2 Thess. 1:7).

The purpose of this revelation is "to show His bond-servants what must soon take place." The verb *show* (*deiknymi*) implies that the message of the book has been communicated to John in visible form, as the phrase "to all that he saw" makes explicit. There may also be a visual connotation to the Greek verb represented by "communicated" (*sēmainō*), which is distantly related to the Greek word for "sign" (*sēmeion,* Rev. 12:1, 3; 15:1).[6] We could capture the Greek play on words by translating the verb "signified," showing its kinship with "sign." This book discloses its message by impressing vivid, sometimes startling, pictures on our imaginations.

The beatitude pronounced on one who reads and "those who hear" and keep these prophetic words provides special encouragement to approach this book with the expectation that God intends to make its message clear to those who seek it. This blessing envisions the common situation in the early church, when copies of New Testament writings were extremely rare and literacy levels low in some regions and classes. The scene is of one reader standing in the congregation, reading Revelation aloud from start to finish, while the rest of the Christians ("those who hear") experienced its words only by hearing. The promise of blessing that opens Revelation may astonish our text-oriented minds, awash as we are in printed Bibles, concordances, com-

---

6. A visual element seems present in the other three uses of this Greek word in the Johannine literature: "But He was saying this [i.e., that he must be lifted up from the earth] to *indicate* the kind of death by which He was to die" (John 12:33); "to fulfill the word of Jesus which He spoke, *signifying* by what kind of death He was about to die" (John 18:32, referring to 12:33); "Now this He said [i.e., that Peter would be tied and taken where he did not wish], *signifying* by what kind of death he would glorify God" (John 21:19). G. K. Beale, *The Book of Revelation,* NIGTC (Grand Rapids: Eerdmans, 1999), 50–52, demonstrates that the wording of Rev. 1:1 alludes to Dan. 2:28–30, 45 LXX, in which *sēmainō* highlights the symbolic form of the king's vision of the great statue and the stone.

mentaries, and Bible-search software. How could anyone understand Revelation well enough to keep its words and receive its promised blessing without flipping pages back and forth, checking cross references, consulting concordances and commentaries? But God promises his blessing to people who experience the Book of Revelation by hearing it and who take its message to heart. This means that the besieged believers scattered throughout the cities of western Asia Minor (now Turkey) in the first century, who had not read it with their own eyes, could nevertheless understand the core of its message with sufficient clarity to respond to it as God desired and to receive from it the comfort, encouragement, and correction that God wanted them to receive—to be blessed (in the rich, biblical sense of blessing) through this word, this means of grace.[7]

Revelation Is a Book to Be Seen. John characterizes the message to which he bears witness as "the word of God and . . . the testimony of Jesus Christ," adding the important description, "even to all that he saw" (Rev. 1:2). The motif of what the prophet saw is so pervasive in Revelation (the verb appears fifty-two times with John as its subject) that it is easy to overlook. But this opening statement, which equates John's testimony to God's word and Jesus Christ with what he saw, shows that we must not ignore it. It indicates the book's genre and is therefore a guide to the reading strategy we must use if we are to see its message.[8] The visible, visionary mode of the message

7. They did have advantages in understanding that we do not. They knew, by living in their cities and their churches, more information about the culture and context to which Revelation was addressed than our most rigorous scholarship can discover at this distance of almost two millennia.

8. Readers with visibly challenged imaginations will do well to view the powerful illustrations in Jay E. Adams and Michael W. Carroll, *Visions of the Revelation* (Virginia Beach: Donning, 1991). Carroll, an elder in the Presbyterian Church in America, is a founder of the International Association of Astronomical Artists and has served as artistic consultant to the Reuben H. Fleet Space Theater and Science Center in San Diego, California. His paintings vividly dramatize the visions while showing respect for what John does not tell us and for the pervasive biblical disapproval of human attempts to portray God's being graphically (The Donning Co./Publishers, 184 Business Park Dr., Ste. 106, Virginia Beach, VA 23462).

is reemphasized in the prophetic commission given to John by the voice of the One like a son of man: "Write in a book what you see, and send it to the seven churches" (1:11). Revelation comes to us, as it came to the seven churches, in writing, but it is literature that paints for us the scenes that John has seen.[9]

Revelation is a book of symbols in motion. What John has seen in prophetic vision is the true character of events, individuals, forces, and trends, the appearance of which is quite different on the physical, sociocultural, observable plane. One of the key themes of the book is that things are not what they seem. The church in Smyrna appears poor but is rich, and it is opposed by those who claim to be Jews but are Satan's synagogue (Rev. 2:9). Sardis has a reputation for life but is dead (3:1). Laodicea thinks itself rich and self-sufficient, but this church is destitute and naked (3:17). The beast seems invincible, able to conquer the saints by slaying them (11:7; 13:7); their faithfulness even to death, however, proves to be their victory over the dragon that empowered the beast (12:11). What appear to the naked eye, on the plane of human history, to be weak, helpless, hunted, poor, defeated congregations of Jesus' faithful servants prove to be the true overcomers who participate in the triumph of the Lion who conquered as a slain Lamb. What appear to be the invincible forces controlling history—the military-political-religious-economic complex that is Rome and its less lustrous successors—is a system sown with the seeds of its self-destruction, already feeling the first lashes of the wrath of the Lamb. On the plane of visible history things are not what they appear, so Revelation's symbols make things appear as they are. Its surprising, paradoxical imagery discloses the true identity of the church, its enemies, and its Champion. Paradox is central to the symbolism. Not only are things not what they appear to be in history, but also typically their true identities as portrayed in the visions are the opposite of their appearance in the world.

The explicit identification of certain symbols makes plain this disparity between surface appearance and visionary presentation. The

---

9. William Hendriksen, *More Than Conquerors: An Interpretation of the Book of Revelation* (Grand Rapids: Baker, 1939), 50: "The entire book consists of changing scenes, moving pictures, active symbols. . . . It is, *as it were,* a 'sound-film'" (emphasis in the original).

seven stars that John sees in the hand of the Son of Man "are the angels of the seven churches," and the lampstands among whom the Son of Man walks "are the seven churches" (Rev. 1:20). The harlot dressed luxuriously in purple, scarlet, gold, and gems "is the great city, which reigns over the kings of the earth" (17:18), and the seven heads of the beast on which she sits "are seven mountains . . . and seven kings" (17:9–10). The fine, clean linen from which the wedding dress of the Lamb's bride is fashioned "is the righteous acts of the saints" (19:8). The dragon-serpent is "the devil and Satan" (20:2). In the physical world the church in Laodicea looks like a gathering of people, not a lampstand. The great city looks like a collection of buildings, streets, inhabitants, and social and commercial institutions, not a loose woman gaudily dressed. But the symbols show us something about the church, the great city, the bride, and the Enemy, revealing what does not appear to the naked eye. They display the true identity of these individuals and institutions with a vividness that could not be matched by merely conceptual description. The strength of symbolism is vividness, for often a picture is worth a thousand words.

The challenge of symbolism, however, is its ambiguity. All forms of metaphor, analogy, and simile place a demand on the reader to discern the precise point of comparison between two things that are dissimilar in many respects but alike in at least one. This is why Jesus exhorts those who hear his parables: "He who has ears, let him hear" (Matt. 13:9; Luke 14:35), a summons that is echoed in each of his letters to the churches of Asia (Rev. 2:7, 17, 29, etc.; see also 13:9). As the parable of the sower challenges its hearers to recognize in what sense a farmer scattering seed resembles and illustrates the coming of God's kingdom, so the symbols of Revelation demand eyes that see, ears that hear, and a heart that understands what links the image to its referent (cf. Matt. 13:13–16, alluding to Isa. 6:9–10). In introducing two of its significant symbols, the beast and the harlot, Revelation insists that wisdom is needed to see what the symbols say about the realities they portray (Rev. 13:18; 17:9).

The challenge of drawing the right connection between the symbol and its referent is complicated not only by the paradoxical juxtapositions of Revelation's symbolism but also by the application of multiple symbols, themselves apparently incompatible, to the same referent. John hears the promise that the triumphant Lion from Judah's tribe has authority to open the sealed scroll of God's purposes, but what he sees is a Lamb, standing though slain (Rev. 5:5–6). He hears the census of Israel's army, 144,000 sealed from destruction, but he sees an innumerable host from every nation, tribe, people, and tongue (7:4–14; 14:1–5).

The ambiguity intrinsic to symbolism helps to explain the diversity of interpretations that have been offered throughout the church's reflection on the Book of Revelation. Students of Scripture differ regarding the extent of the symbolism in the book, the criteria by which connections between symbols and their referents should be drawn, and the identification of the referents to which particular symbols point. Some have felt that in interpreting all biblical prophecy, whether in the Old Testament or in Revelation, the objectivity of the interpretive process and the historicity of God's acts could be safeguarded by assuming that prophetic speech should be interpreted literally where it can possibly be taken literally and symbolically only in texts that label images as symbolic or in which literalness yields an impossible or contradictory meaning.

In Revelation, however, a literal-where-possible mode of operation raises more problems than it solves. In the first place, the word *literal* is troublesome. It seems typically to be used to signify that the image in a prophet's vision corresponds physically to its historical referent. Hence, when God promises a regathering of Israel in his land, this promise must be fulfilled in a resettlement of physical descendants of the patriarchs in the physical land between the eastern shore of the Mediterranean Sea and the Jordan River. Or when God promises a rebuilt temple (Ezek. 40–48), this promise cannot find fulfillment in a "spiritual house" constructed of "living stones" who are people (1 Peter 2:5). But this usage of "literal" overlooks the fact that the literal meaning of a piece of language depends on what type of language it is, its genre. The literal meaning of symbolic language is the symbolic correspondence between the imagery of the language and the referent that it describes.[10]

10. Vern S. Poythress, "Genre and Hermeneutics in Rev 20:1–6," *JETS* 36 (1993): 41–42, points out that there are four levels of meaning to which we need

Second, signals embedded throughout the Book of Revelation make it manifestly clear that visionary symbolism is the dominant feature of the book's genre. Not even the strongest advocate of a literal-where-possible hermeneutic expects that when we see Jesus in his resurrection body, a double-edged sword will proceed from his mouth (Rev. 1:16) or that he will look like a Lamb with seven horns and seven eyes (5:6). Even when symbols are not labeled as such, we sense instinctively that when we step into this book we are walking in a world of symbols. What appears as a beast in John's vision is, as scholars of all schools recognize, a world kingdom or world ruler who will not look like the image in the vision, with ten horns and seven heads and resembling a leopard, bear, and lion all at once. If we are to follow an interpretive rule of thumb in reading Revelation, it should be that we take what John sees as symbolic where possible. What then will anchor our interpretation of this highly symbolic book to the meaning that God intends it to convey? One anchor is found in our third principle.

Revelation Makes Sense Only in Light of the Old Testament. Professor Stuart's example and Professor Bauckham's book title have suggested how important it is to recognize that Revelation presents itself as the climax of prophecy, drawing together images that pervade Old Testament prophetic visions and bringing them to fulfillment. The display of divine splendor that initiates John's prophetic call (Rev. 1; 10) has appeared before as prophets were commissioned to carry God's message from his council chamber (Ezek. 1; Dan. 9–10). The beast that emerges from the sea in Revelation 13 is a composite of the four beasts of Daniel 7, namely, the world kingdoms that oppress the saints until the Son of Man receives royal dominion from the

---

to pay attention in a book marked by visionary symbolism, such as Revelation. The first level is linguistic, or what the words, clauses, sentences, and paragraphs mean in the linguistic setting of Hellenistic Greek. The second is visionary: the visual experience of John that is portrayed and described in the language. The third is referential: the persons, forces, or events in history to which the images that John saw refer or point. The fourth is symbolical: what the visionary level of meaning, the images John saw in his visions, are revealing about the referential level, the persons, forces, events that the images symbolize.

Ancient of Days. The two witnesses of Revelation 11 are the two olive trees of Zechariah 4, "the two anointed ones who are standing by the Lord of the whole earth" (Zech. 4:14). The woes of judgment that fall on the harlot Babylon (Rev. 18) echo those that fell on Israel's ancient oppressors, Tyre (Ezek. 27) and Babylon (Jer. 51; Isa. 48).

Revelation's symbolic vocabulary is drawn not only from the thesaurus of the prophetic literature but also from other parts of the Old Testament. The tree of life in paradise at the dawn of biblical history (Gen. 2:9) reappears at the consummation (Rev. 2:7; 22:2). The ancient serpent whose murderous lie seduced the woman and plunged the world into floods of misery (Gen. 3:1) is seen again, waging war against the woman, her son, and her other children—but this time his doom is sure and his time is short (Rev. 12; 20). Plagues that struck ancient Israel's Egyptian oppressors (Exod. 7–12) strike the church's persecutors (Rev. 8:7, 10, 12; 9:3; 11:6; 16:13), so the church's exodus-deliverance is celebrated with the song of Moses and of the Lamb (Rev. 15:3; Exod. 15).

Although exact Old Testament quotations in Revelation are rare, allusion to Old Testament imagery is everywhere: Elijah and his nemesis Jezebel; Balaam, the prophet who masterminded the seduction of Israel; God's temple, served by his kingdom of priests, offering incense prayers on the altar, from which the fire of judgment falls, as on Sodom and Gomorrah; Israel the Messiah's mother; Israel the Lord's bride; Israel's twelve tribes, armed for holy war; God's winepress of wrath; the water of life, offered free of charge; Jerusalem, the city of God. Yet God does not cut and paste Old Testament images, unchanged, into the texture of John's visions. While remaining recognizable, they are modified and recombined into new configurations—as we would expect, since the sacrifice and resurrection of the Lamb have brought the warfare of the ages to a new phase and theater of operations. We dare not tackle the symbolism of Revelation without immersing our minds in the rich imagery of the Old Testament, but we also will pay attention to the transformation that these ancient pictures undergo as they are used to express the impending, climactic victory of the kingdom of God and of his Christ.

Numbers Count in Revelation. One aspect of the symbolism of Revelation is the use of significant numbers to signal the structure of John's visions to the listening congregation and to represent important concepts. Seven, ten, and twelve and some of their multiples are especially important.[11]

Seven is the number of churches to which the book is addressed and consequently the number of letters/proclamations addressed by the risen Christ through his Spirit to the churches. Though other New Testament writings show that churches existed in other cities of western Asia Minor when Revelation was given, these seven represent the churches of Jesus Christ generally, since their number, seven, symbolizes completeness. Likewise the Lamb's seven horns symbolize his complete power, and his seven eyes, his complete knowledge through the Spirit's presence in the whole world (Rev. 5:6). The scroll of the purpose of God for "the things which must soon take place" (1:1) is sealed with seven seals (5:1), and the visions associated with the Lamb's breaking of them structure the second major section of the book (6:1–8:2). The angels' sounding of seven trumpets structures the third major section (8:6–11:18), portraying providential disasters that span the time between Christ's comings. These disasters, though limited in scope, provide previews of the total destruction to be poured out in the seven bowls, limitless in scope and "last, because in them the wrath of God is finished" (15:1, 7; 16). We also read of seven heads, seven hills, seven kings, and the seven Spirits of God.

The number ten is significant in itself when it numbers the dragon's heads (Rev. 12:3) and those of the beast (= kings; Rev. 13:1; 17:12; cf. Dan. 7:7) or signifies a brief, ten-day period of affliction to be endured (2:10). More frequently, however, it appears in its multiples. It is cubed to one thousand to symbolize a vast number of years (20:2–7) or cubed and multiplied by twelve to portray the vast dimensions (12,000 stadia [roughly 1,380 miles[12]]) in all directions—length, breadth, and height—of the new Jerusalem (21:16). Or it is cubed and multiplied by twelve squared to symbolize the full registration of armed

11. In several visions the number four also has symbolic import.

12. Clearly symbolic, since the length of ancient Israel, Dan to Beersheba, in literal physical geography is less than 150 miles.

warriors in each of Israel's tribes, the sealed "bond-servants of our God" who are the Lamb's army, purified for holy war (7:4–8; 14:1–5). In even larger multiples (thousands of thousands = millions; myriads [ten thousand] of myriads = hundreds of millions) it symbolizes the countless hosts of heavenly worshipers who praise the Lamb (5:11–12).

Twelve is the number of the people of God, identified with the tribes of Israel (Rev. 7:4–8; 21:12) and with the apostles of the Lamb (21:14). The number twelve is therefore employed in the symbolic presentation of God's people as the heavenly Jerusalem to enumerate its structural features such as gates and foundations and to measure the thickness (144 cubits [12^2] = 216 feet) and the length, breadth, and height of its wall (12,000 stadia = 1,380 miles).

The symbolic use of numbers in Revelation is flexible. Readers unaccustomed to this flexibility are perplexed, for example, to read in the opening benediction: "Grace to you and peace, from Him who is and who was and who is to come; and from the seven Spirits who are before His throne; and from Jesus Christ" (Rev. 1:4–5). Does John propose to replace our triune understanding of God with a conception of one God in nine persons (Father, Son, seven Spirits)? Does he repudiate Paul's clearly trinitarian formula, "one Spirit . . . one Lord . . . one God and Father of all" (Eph. 4:4–6)? Some versions render the expression "sevenfold Spirit" (NIV margin), and this is accurate. The context of Revelation makes it clear that when John's description moves away from the apocalyptic imagery he inherited from Zechariah 4:10 to speak directly of the Referent to whom the imagery points, his language changes to singular: "I was in the Spirit in the Lord's day" (Rev. 1:10; cf. 4:2; 17:3; 21:10); "Hear what the Spirit says to the churches" (2:7, 11, 17, 29; 3:6, 13, 22; 22:17). John clearly knows that the Holy Spirit of God is one.[13] Why then does he speak of the seven Spirits of God? The number seven symbolizes the Spirit's fullness and completeness. He is pictured as the seven lamps burning before the One seated on the throne—fully, completely present with the Father in heaven (4:5). He is also pictured as the Lamb's seven

---

13. Zechariah also knows the unity of the Spirit, for in the same text that speaks of seven lamps (Zech. 4:3) and eyes (v. 10) is the promise, "Not by might nor by power, but by My Spirit, says the LORD of hosts" (v. 6).

eyes, "sent out into all the earth"—fully, completely present with the church, knowing each congregation's strengths and weaknesses, its outward pressures and its inward reality (5:6). Just as one image of the beast's seven heads can point to multiple referents, both seven hills and seven kings (17:9–10), so one referent, the Spirit, can be portrayed in multiple images, those of lamps and eyes.[14] When we recognize the symbolic significance of numbers and the flexibility of numerical symbolism in Revelation, we will get the message that the numbers are intended to convey without pressing for a literal connection between the numerical measurements in the visions and the temporal, spatial, or demographic dimensions of their referents.

Revelation Is for a Church under Attack. The violence of Revelation's visions have given children nightmares and offended the supposedly enlightened sentiments of adults. Johann Salomo Semler (1725–1791) contended that the humane reader cannot be blamed for finding the Book of Revelation "unpleasant and repulsive" in its descriptions of God's wrath on his enemies, for such visions conflict with the self-evident truth of "divine, all-inclusive love and charity for the restoration of men."[15] Such opinions, however, fail to understand the social and spiritual situation that Revelation addresses. Revelation is addressed to a church that is under attack. Its purpose, to reveal "things which must soon take place," is not to satisfy idle eschatological curiosity or feed a hunger for revenge but to fortify Jesus' followers in steadfast hope and holy living.

The seven beatitudes that punctuate the narrative promise God's blessing on those who keep Christ's word (Rev. 1:3; 22:7) even upon pain of death (14:13), who maintain purity in alert expectation of

14. Numbers also have a more complex symbolic function through an ancient practice called *gematria,* in which letters of the alphabet are assigned numerical value, making possible a code use of numerical sums to represent personal or national names. It appears that readers are signaled to use gematria to crack the code in Rev. 13:18, a possibility to which we will return. See Bauckham, *Climax of Prophecy,* "Nero and the Beast," 384–452.

15. J. S. Semler, *Treatise on the Free Investigation of the Canon* (1771–1775), quoted in Werner Georg Kümmel, *The New Testament: The History of the Investigation of Its Problems* (Nashville: Abingdon, 1972), 63–64.

Christ's return (16:15), who are invited to the Lamb's wedding feast (19:9), who have been beheaded for their faith and so share in the first resurrection (20:4–6) and share in the tree of life in the city of God (22:14). In these blessings we hear hints of the various forms of attack being launched against the church: persecution leading to martyrdom and seduction leading to defilement.

The church's struggle is also reflected in the promises made to the victor, the overcomer. Each letter to the seven churches in Revelation 2–3 closes with a promise "to him who overcomes," and generally these promises reach ahead to the final victory portrayed in Revelation 19–22: to eat from the tree of life, to escape the second death, to share Christ's authority over the nations, to be a pillar in God's temple, inscribed with God's name, and so on. The precise form that overcoming must take in each church depends on the particular challenge to faith and faithfulness that confronts each congregation, whether the attack comes in the form of a threat to unity, or in external persecution, or in syncretism with pagan belief and practice, or in complacent compromise with the materialism of the surrounding culture.

The church's ultimate enemy, the dragon, "the serpent of old, who is the devil and Satan" (Rev. 20:2), manifests the massive cunning symbolized in his seven heads (12:3) by attacking the church from within and without, through physical threat, spiritual deception, and material seduction. The visions of Revelation 12–19 symbolize these various avenues of assault as the beast from the sea (physical threat), the beast from the land (later called the false prophet; spiritual deception), and the harlot (material seduction). Though representing distinct forces by which the dragon seeks to separate the besieged bride from her triumphant Lord, these three form a devilish coalition in which the false prophet pours out lies to promote worship of the beast and the harlot rides on the beast and toasts the beast's victory with the martyrs' blood.

In response to these attacks, those who hold to "the word of God and to the testimony of Jesus" are called to endure and to stay pure. Because the enemy attacks ruthlessly, employing the intimidating force of Rome's armies and, by implication, the politico-military muscle of Rome's lesser successors, the people of Jesus must steel their hearts to endure persecution in persistent hope. "Here is the perseverance of the saints who keep the commandments of God and their faith in Jesus" (Rev. 14:12).[16] The call to perseverance is obeyed not through monastic withdrawal from the hostile surrounding culture but through evangelistic confrontation with the culture. Perseverance is therefore related to the call to be a faithful witness on behalf of Jesus. "I, John, your brother and fellow partaker in the tribulation and kingdom and perseverance which are in Jesus, was on the island called Patmos because of the word of God and the testimony of Jesus" (1:9). It was John's faithful testimony on behalf of Jesus that plunged him into the tribulation of exile on the prison-island Patmos. He is therefore an empathetic and credible witness to be sent by Jesus, the faithful witness (1:5; 3:14), to encourage and summon the churches to persevering hope and witness not in isolation from the world but in interaction with it.[17]

Because the serpent slips in subtly, luring Christ's bride away through plausible lies and pleasant compromises, the church must also overcome by staying pure. The white garments of the victors symbolize their victory over defiling temptation and consequently their fitness to enter God's temple as the kingdom of priests, to serve gladly in his presence (Rev. 3:4–5, 17–18; 22:14–15). Though their white linen presents a portrait of their righteous deeds (19:7–8), the purity that makes them presentable before the thrice-holy God is not their personal achievement but the result of the costliest of cleansers: "they have washed their robes and made them white in the blood of the Lamb" (7:14).

Our interpretation of Revelation must be driven by the difference God intends it to make in the life of his people. If we could explain every phrase, identify every allusion to Old Testament Scripture or Greco-Roman society, trace every interconnection, and illumine every mystery in this book and yet were silenced by the intimidation of public opinion, terrorized by the prospect of suffering, enticed by afflu-

16. See also commendations for and calls to endurance in the letters to the churches (Rev. 2:2–3, 10, 13, 19, 25; 3:8, 10).
17. On the theme of witness or testimony in the face of affliction, see also Rev. 1:2; 2:13; 6:9; 11:3, 7; 12:11, 17; 17:6; 19:20; 20:4.

ent Western culture's promise of "security, comfort, and pleasure,"[18] then we would not have begun to understand the Book of Revelation as God wants us to. The dragon's assault on the church comes in different forms and from different quarters in different times and places. In some parts of the world the attack comes head-on, through the persecuting violence of hostile governments or neighbors; in others the danger is insidious, a slow infection to numb the Body's discernment of error and weaken its immune system; in others the weapon is an appealing encouragement to enjoy the advantages of compromised conformity. But always, in every age and place, the church is under attack. Our only safety lies in seeing the ugly hostility of the enemy clearly and clinging fast to our Champion and King, Jesus.

Revelation Concerns "What Must Soon Take Place." Many of the time references in Revelation are puzzling and will require close attention in the chapters ahead: "ten days" (Rev. 2:10), "forty-two months" (11:2; 13:5), "one thousand two hundred and sixty days" (12:6), "a time and times and half a time" (12:14), "one thousand years" (20:2–7). One of the clearest, most literal time references, however, is the repeated description of the contents of John's visions as having to do with "things which must soon take place" (1:1). The prologue's call to hear and keep Revelation's message is reinforced with the motive: "for the time is near" (1:3).

Lest we suppose that some long delay or parenthesis lies unseen behind the scenes, between John's receiving of the visions and the events that the visions symbolize, the conclusion of the book returns to the opening motif of imminence with even greater clarity:

> And he said to me, "These words are faithful and true"; and the Lord, the God of the spirits of the prophets, sent His angel to show to His bond-servants the things which must soon take place. "And behold, I am coming quickly. Blessed is he who heeds the words of the prophecy of this book." (Rev. 22:6–7)

18. P. D. James, *The Children of Men* (New York: Knopf, 1993), 60, describing a culture devoid of hope and therefore devoid of conscience, responsibility, and compassion.

To this reprise of Revelation 1 is added an angelic instruction that plainly alludes to and contrasts with a command given to Daniel: "But as for you, Daniel, conceal these words and seal up the book until the end of time" (Dan. 12:4). Daniel's sealing of his book symbolizes that a long period of time—a major epochal change—will separate his receiving the prophetic revelation from the fulfillment of its predictions: "for these words are concealed and sealed up for the end time" (Dan. 12:9; cf. 8:26). John, by contrast, is commanded not to seal up the words of his prophecy, "for the time is near" (Rev. 22:10). The Lamb has broken the sealed scroll and unfurled previews of God's purposes for history not merely to comfort his people with the prospect of a long-distant relief, as Daniel's prophecy did for his contemporaries, but also to comfort John's first-century companions with the assurance that the coming months and years are firmly held in the Lamb's strong hand.

This announcement, which opens and closes Revelation, that the book concerns matters that were to occur "soon" (in contrast to Daniel's visions), is perplexing. Although scholarly opinion varies as to the date of Revelation, from as early as the 60s to the mid-90s, it is generally agreed that Revelation was written by the end of the first century. More centuries have elapsed between John's day and ours than between Daniel's day and the fulfillment of most of his prophecies. How then can John's book concern things that would occur soon from the perspective of the members of seven first-century churches in western Asia Minor? Or is our time so far beyond the horizon that Revelation for us can focus only as a window on the past, not addressing directly either our present or our future?

To this knotty and important question we will return, but for the present we need to give due weight to the interpretive value of this principle: Revelation gave first-century Christians insight into the purposes of God in their time. We can at least conclude, therefore, that interpretations of the visions that lie completely beyond the original readers' frame of reference are suspect. If we begin our inquiry with the assumption that God intended first-century believers to get the message of Revelation, we read its visions against the backdrop of Old Testament imagery rather than forcing them into the template of twenty-first-century technologies or politics. This principle also encourages us to understand Revelation in the context of the cultural and intellectual forces that were affecting the churches of first-century Asia: religious institutions, political structures, military conflicts, natural disasters, and even, perhaps, the symbolic vocabulary of Jewish apocalyptic literature or pagan myth. God is so much the sovereign of history that he can use every dimension of his people's experience to communicate his word.

The Victory Belongs to God and to His Christ. The introduction to Revelation in the pages that follow will fall far short of the detail contained in Professor Stuart's two massive volumes. But abundance of detail can confuse rather than clarify, if we lack a sense of the pattern in which each piece of the puzzle has its place. The next chapter will address questions of the pattern of the book as a whole, the structure of the visions and their interrelationships with each other. The most significant pattern to be grasped, however, is the movement from conflict to victory and the identity of the victors.

Revelation is a book permeated by worship and punctuated throughout with songs of praise and celebration.[19] Its worship not only extols God for his eternal attributes and creative power (Rev. 4:8, 11) but also especially celebrates God's redemptive triumph through the Lamb over the enemies that have threatened his church and challenged his supreme worthiness. Preeminently the scenes of worship and songs of praise celebrate the victory of Jesus the Lamb of God, the defeat and destruction of his and our enemies, the vindication of his martyrs, and the inauguration of the new heavens and earth (5:9–10, 12, 13; 7:10–12; 11:15–18; 15:3–4; 16:5–7; 19:1–7).

Though the enemies' might is portrayed in all its hideousness, Revelation's last word is not about the destructive power of the "prince of darkness grim" but rather about the joyful celebration of those re-

19. Readers' experience of hearing the worship in Revelation will be enriched by listening to great music based on the song texts in Revelation. In the classical tradition, the Revelation portions of Handel's oratorio *Messiah* are powerful despite their familiarity. In a more contemporary vein, I recommend Michael Card, *Unveiled Hope,* sound cassette/CD (Nashville: Covenant Artists/Myrrh, 1997).

deemed by Jesus, the Lord's Messiah. This hope motivates the suffering church to endure tribulation and the tempted church to remain a pure bride for her Groom.

Conclusion

This introductory chapter has identified some of the key interpretative principles that emerge from a careful observation of the literary genre to which Revelation belongs and from the way in which such works use language and imagery to convey their message. In the chapters to come we will put this strategy for seeing to the test as we work our way through the text of Revelation. To summarize our observations so far:

1. Revelation is given to reveal. It makes its central message so clear that even those who hear it can take it to heart and receive the blessing it promises.
2. Revelation is a book to be seen, a book of symbols in motion. Because the appearance of individuals and institutions in everyday experience often masks their true identity, Revelation is given in visions full of symbols that paradoxically picture the true identity of the church, its enemies, and its Champion.
3. Revelation makes sense only in light of the Old Testament. Not only the visions of such prophets as Ezekiel, Daniel, and Zechariah but also historical events such as creation, the fall, and the exodus provide the symbolic vocabulary for John's visions.
4. Numbers count in Revelation. Since numbers are used symbolically in Revelation, we must discern the meaning they convey rather than trying to pull them as numbers directly into our experience, measured by calendars and odometers.
5. Revelation is for a church under attack. Its purpose is to awaken us to the dimensions of the battle and the strategies of the enemy, so that we will respond to the attacks with faithful perseverance and purity, overcoming by the blood of the Lamb.
6. Revelation concerns "what must soon take place." We must seek an understanding that touches the experience of our broth-

ers and sisters in seven first-century congregations scattered in the cities of western Asia Minor. Revelation is not about events and hostile forces remote from their struggle.

7. The victory belongs to God and to his Christ. Revelation is pervaded with worship songs and scenes because its pervasive theme—despite its gruesome portrait of evil's powers—is the triumph of God through the Lamb. We read this book to hear the King's call to courage and to fall down in adoring worship before him.

Another important component of our strategy for seeing is to note the ways in which the structure of Revelation reveals the relationship of its various visions and texts, providing the framework in which the pieces fit together. In the next chapter we will examine the features of this framework that provide the big-picture view of the book's contents. We will also notice additional principles that emerge from the biblical text to guide us in connecting the visions to each other and to the realities that they symbolize.

CHAPTER TWO

Structure:
Framing the
Pieces of the Puzzle

Assembling jigsaw puzzles may seem a tranquil pastime, but it presents intense temptations to the serious puzzler. Almost to the end the puzzler struggles with the suspicion that the manufacturer ineptly failed to pack that one piece in a thousand that is needed to fill an odd-shaped hole. A more serious temptation, however, is to glance at the reproduction of the puzzle's design on the box-top lid—which is, in the minds of hard-core jigsaw enthusiasts, a shameful indulgence of weaker impulses akin to outright cheating, like consulting the answer key before doing our homework or sneaking a peek at the end of a mystery novel.

However, even the puzzler of impeccable integrity, who always does things the hard way, is savvy enough to look first for pieces that have one straight edge. After all, those straight edges usually mark the puzzle's outside boundaries, and fitting those pieces together provides a frame of reference for the detailed detective work that will make the irregular pieces mesh.

Although the Book of Revelation is a picture clear enough to bring blessing to its simple listeners (principle 1), it is also a puzzle complex enough to challenge the most rigorous researcher. We need all the help we can get as we try to fit its pieces together. We therefore do well, like experienced assemblers of jigsaw puzzles, to take note of straight-edge pieces that form its frame. In Revelation certain aspects of the text stand out as signposts and boundary markers, marking off its structure.

Beginning, Middle, End

At the broadest level, Revelation is composed of a beginning, a middle, and an end—a prologue (1:1–8), a body (1:9–22:9), and an epilogue (22:6–21).[1]

The prologue introduces the book's content and genres. With respect to content Revelation concerns "the things which must soon take place" (1:1), events that will affect the forces then threatening Christ's churches in western Asia Minor. With respect to genre Revelation is a book of prophetic vision ("all that he saw," 1:2; "the words of the prophecy," 1:3), but it is also an epistle. Revelation 1:4–6 contains four standard components of epistolary opening: identification of author (John) and recipients (the seven churches in Asia), followed by a greeting that extends divine grace and peace to the recipients ("from Him who is and who was and who is to come; and from the seven Spirits . . . and from Jesus Christ") and an expression of praise to God ("To Him who loves us . . . be the glory and the dominion for ever and ever").

The greeting and praise sections in the opening are expanded to foreshadow themes that will appear in the body. This expansion of some sections of a letter's opening has parallels in other New Testament correspondence, in which elaboration on the author (e.g., Rom. 1:1–6), recipients (1 Cor. 1:2; 1 Peter 1:1–2), greeting (Gal. 1:3–5), or doxology (Eph. 1:3–14) introduces themes to be discussed later. Here the expanded greeting (Rev. 1:4b–5a), pronouncing God's grace and peace on the churches, emphasizes God's eternal sovereignty over present, past, and future (anticipating 1:8; 4:8; cf. 11:17; 16:5); the Spirit's presence before the Father's throne (4:5; 3:1; 5:6); and Jesus Christ's faithful witness (3:14; 19:11), resurrection-victory (1:18), and

---

1. Richard Bauckham, *The Climax of Prophecy: Studies on the Book of Revelation* (Edinburgh: T & T Clark, 1993), 3–5, shows that Rev. 22:6–9 is both the conclusion of the body and the beginning of the epilogue. See my discussion below.

supreme dominion (11:15; 19:16). In other words, the supremacy of the triune God will be prominent in all that John will see and write thereafter. The expansion of the praise section (1:5b–6) continues the greeting's climactic focus on Jesus Christ, ascribing to him glory and dominion because of his redemptive work: moved by love, he "released us from our sins by His blood" (see 5:9; 7:14; 12:11), making us to be a kingdom and priests (5:10). This is "the Revelation of Jesus Christ" because he is not only its speaker but also its subject.

At the other end of the book, the epilogue (Rev. 22:6–21) returns to themes introduced in the prologue. God sends his angel "to show his bond-servants the things which must soon take place" (22:6, 16; cf. 1:1). The book's sixth benediction, like the first, is pronounced on the one who "heeds the words of the prophecy" (22:7, 9; cf. 1:3).[2] John identifies himself as witness of the prophecy (22:8; cf. 1:1, 4). The promise, "the time is near," also recurs (22:10; cf. 1:3). The divine self-designation (22:13) blends titles used by God the Almighty in the prologue ("the Alpha and the Omega," 1:8) with those used by Jesus in the opening vision ("first and last, beginning and end," 1:17; cf. 21:6), making plain the deity of the Son. And the epistolary closing, "The grace of the Lord Jesus be with all" (22:21), corresponds to the opening's pronouncement of grace and peace from the triune God (1:3–4).[3]

The epistolary structure of the prologue and epilogue reinforces the principle that Revelation is Jesus' public correspondence with his churches in first-century Asia. Its message addressed the challenges confronting their life of faith, just as 1 Corinthians spoke to the issues confronting the church in Corinth (meat offered to idols, sexual looseness, admiration for Greek rhetoric). The fact that Revelation is em-

---

2. Revelation's benedictions number a complete seven. The other five are pronounced on the dead who have died in the Lord (14:13), the one who remains awake (16:15), those called to the Lamb's wedding supper (19:9), the one who has a share in the first resurrection (20:6), and those who wash their robes and can eat of the tree of life and enter the city (22:14).

3. See Gal. 1:3–4; 6:18 for a Pauline example of the recapitulation of the opening benediction at the letter's close.

bedded in the experience of those early Christians of Asia Minor does not mean that it has nothing to say to us today. But it is only as we hear what Jesus' letter said then to them that we will see valid parallels to our trials in our time.

The body begins with the opening vision of "one like a son of man," who appears in blazing glory to commission John as prophet (Rev. 1:9–20). This scene introduces the reader and hearers to the visual mode of Jesus' message and to the symbolic significance of the images that John will record. The Son of Man interprets two images of the opening scene, the lampstands among which he walks and the stars that he holds (1:20). Many other features of this vision had already been invested with symbolic significance by their appearance in Old Testament prophecy.

The body closes with a vision of the new Jerusalem as "the bride, the wife of the Lamb" and the promise of uninterrupted joy in God for those who cling to the words of the prophecy (Rev. 21:9–22:9). Since this final vision discloses Christ's pure and peaceful bride in contrast to the beast's vile and violent harlot, the two women are introduced with words so similar that the parallel cannot be missed:[4]

> Then one of the seven angels who had the seven bowls came and spoke with me, saying, "Come here, I will show you the judgment of the great harlot who sits on many waters. . . ." And he carried me away in the Spirit into a wilderness; and I saw a woman sitting on a scarlet beast. (Rev. 17:1–3)

> Then one of the seven angels who had the seven bowls full of the seven last plagues came and spoke with me, saying, "Come here, I will show you the bride, the wife of the Lamb." And he carried me away in the Spirit to a great and high mountain, and showed me the holy city, Jerusalem, coming down out of heaven from God. (Rev. 21:9–10)[5]

4. Bauckham, *Climax of Prophecy,* 4–5.
5. The parallel and hence the contrast between the women revealed in these two visions is stressed again through unmistakable echoes at the close of each of these two sections:
    And he said to me, "These are true words of God." Then I fell at his feet to worship him. But he said to me, "Do not that; I am a fellow servant of

Thus the body opens with a vision of the heavenly Bridegroom, the Son of Man, and it closes with a vision of the heavenly bride, the new Jerusalem. Toward the end of the body are the contrasting visions of the judgment of the harlot Babylon (17:1–19:10) and the joy of the bride Jerusalem (21:9–22:9). Thus 22:6–9 is the climax of the body and the opening of the epilogue—a literary interweaving of themes characteristic of Revelation elsewhere. Between the portraits of these two women are visions that portray the last battle between their respective champions: the warrior Word of God, the church's husband, defeats and destroys the beasts and dragon, who had sustained the harlot (19:10–21:8). In this last battle scene the Word's fiery eyes and the sword proceeding from his mouth remind us of the opening vision of the Son of Man (19:12, 15; 1:14, 16). The body closes where it began: with Jesus and his protective love for his church.

The Title (1:1) and the Structure of the Body

The first verse not only announces its title, "The Revelation of Jesus Christ," but also traces a chain of transmission by which this Revelation has reached the church on earth. The transmission process involves four steps:

(1) God "gave" the revelation to Jesus Christ (to show his bond-servants);
(2) Jesus revealed it by sending it through his angel;
(3) The angel communicated it to John;

---

yours and your brethren who hold the testimony of Jesus; worship God. For the testimony of Jesus is the spirit of prophecy." (Rev. 19:9b–10)

And he said to me, "These words are faithful and true"; and the Lord, the God of the spirits of the prophets, sent His angel to show to His bond-servants the things which must soon take place. "And behold, I am coming quickly. Blessed is he who heeds the words of the prophecy of this book." I, John, am the one who heard and saw these things. And when I heard and saw, I fell down to worship at the feet of the angel who showed me these things. But he said to me, "Do not do that; I am a fellow servant of yours and of your brethren the prophets and of those who heed the words of this book. Worship God." (Rev. 22:6–9)

(4) John bears witness to all he saw, writing to the seven churches (1:2, 4).

Two steps in this process are dramatized in later visions, introducing major sections. The first step is portrayed in John's vision of the One seated on the throne and of the Lamb (Rev. 4–5). Heaven is opened and John is summoned to "come up" into the court of God, to be shown "what must take place after these things" (4:1). There John sees God seated on his throne, just as Old Testament prophets were commissioned in a visionary audience in God's heavenly court (Isa. 6; Ezek. 1; 1 Kings 22:19–22; Jer. 23:16–18). As in our dreams we sometimes know intuitively information that we've never been told, so in this revelatory vision John has the intuitive insight that the message he needs to see and deliver is written in a scroll that lies in the hand of the enthroned One. The scroll is sealed, and it seems that no one is worthy to break its seals and disclose its contents; John inexplicably grasps the dire implications of this lack, weeping bitterly (Rev. 5:1–4). Unless someone is found who exceeds the authority of the four living creatures and the twenty-four elders, the scroll will stay sealed, John's prophetic mission will be aborted, and God's blessing (1:3) will remain unclaimed by the embattled churches. John's sorrow is turned to joy, however, when he hears the announcement of the worthy Lion from the tribe of Judah, whom he sees to be a Lamb, standing though slain (5:5–6). The Lion/Lamb receives the scroll from the right hand of the enthroned One (5:7). Thus through John's eyes we see the first step in transmission: God has given the Revelation to Jesus Christ.

The third step is portrayed in the vision recorded in Revelation 10. John sees an angel descending from heaven, the court of God, resplendent in light and holding in his hand a little book, which is open. Scholars debate whether this open "little book/scroll" (*biblaridion* or, in some manuscripts, *biblidarion*) is the "book/scroll" (*biblion*) that had been taken and opened by the Lamb in Revelation 5–8. The interchangeability of these words in Revelation 10 ("little book" in 10:2, 9, 10; "book" in 10:8)[6] suggests that in Hellenistic Greek there was

---

6. There are further textual variations among ancient manuscripts of Revelation. In one early papyrus, P[47] from the third century, the original copyist appears to have

no great difference of meaning between the two.[7] There is good reason to conclude that the open scroll brought by the angel to John is the same scroll that the Lamb received from the Father—the Revelation of Jesus Christ. It now lies open, ready to be read (to be eaten and then spoken),[8] because the Lamb has broken its seals. Jesus Christ has sent his Revelation through his angel to his servant John.

Revelation 10 repeats and completes John's call to be Jesus' prophetic witness. Not only has John been caught up to God's heavenly court and made privy to the counsels of the One seated on the throne (4–5), but also he has been sent forth with the book of God's plan, opened by the Lamb and consumed by John to proclaim to the churches (10–11). The members of the heavenly court ("they") commission John to resume his prophetic proclamation: "You must prophesy again concerning many peoples and nations and tongues and kings" (10:11)—"again" because he has been prophesying by reporting the visions of the seals cycle and trumpets cycle, which flow from the enthronement scene in Revelation 4 and 5. John's call now leads directly into the heart of the drama revealed in the visions on Patmos (12–22): the cosmic conflict between God, the heavenly woman, and her son/groom and the dragon, the beasts, and the harlot. Everything that precedes Revelation 12 is preliminary to this central drama, preparing us to see our daily struggles as part of the great conflict of the ages. The appearance of the woman with child is a "great sign in heaven" (12:1) and marks a fresh starting point in John's narrative. The conflict envisioned in Revelation 12–22 sweeps across the span of redemptive history, from the sin- and curse-defiled garden sanctuary in which God promised a woman's seed to destroy the ancient serpent (Rev. 12:1; cf. Gen. 3:15) all the way to a new, pure, curse-freed,

---

written "book" (*biblion*) throughout Rev. 10. Another major manuscript, Sinaiticus (fourth century), has "book" instead of "little book" in 10:9–10.

7. For more detail in support of the identification of the "book" (Rev. 5) and the "little book" (Rev. 10), see the extensive discussion in Bauckham, *Climax of Prophecy*, 243–57.

8. The instruction to eat God's word and to speak it (Rev. 10:9) is derived from the prophetic commissioning of Ezekiel (Ezek. 2:8–3:3), just as the next command, that John measure the sanctuary (Rev. 11:1–2), echoes Ezekiel's later vision of the temple and its measurements (Ezek. 40–48).

city-sanctuary whose residents enjoy the tree of life (Rev. 22:2; cf. Gen. 2:9; 3:22–24).

The new beginning at Revelation 12:1 shows that the order in which John experienced and narrated the visions may be very different from the order in which the events symbolized occur. The events symbolized in Revelation 12:1–5 precede the churches' circumstances described in the letters of Revelation 2–3 and the events symbolized in the visions of Revelation 6–11. This chronological dislocation between vision order and historical order in Revelation 12 exemplifies a principle evident throughout Revelation. Although the book's dramatic sweep takes its hearers from the present (the churches' current trials) to the future (the reversal of the curse in the new Jerusalem), there is no necessary connection between the order of the visions and the order of the events symbolized in the visions. We misunderstand John's visions if we insist on seeing them as a chronologically arranged timeline of history.

The Command to Write (1:19) and the Content of the Body

Another early frame piece that orients us to the picture in the puzzle is the table of contents dictated by the Son of Man in the opening vision: "Therefore write the things which you have seen, and the things which are, and the things which will take place after these things" (Rev. 1:19).

Although this might appear to be a threefold list (things which you have seen, which are, and which shall take place afterwards), the first description includes the other two: Write "things which you have seen," namely, "things which are" (the present situation) and "things which shall take place after these things" (future trends and events). This is consistent with the way John equated "all [the things] that he saw" with "the word of God and the testimony of Jesus" in Revelation 1:2. John first describes the mode by which he received the revelation (he "saw" = prophetic vision). Then he indicates the content revealed (in 1:2, "the word . . . and the testimony"; in 1:19, "things which are, and things which shall take place").[9]

9. If "the things which you have seen" had referred to a distinct category of content rather than including the other two, the only thing that John would need to

So John must write his visions, which concern the present and the future. The present includes the situation of the seven churches, known by the Christ who walks among them and accurately diagnosed in his seven letters (Rev. 2–3). Each letter also contains a promise that is focused on the future, usually to be fulfilled in the new Jerusalem. Therefore the letters of Revelation 2–3 concern primarily the churches' present circumstances, but they also promise things yet future.

Revelation 4:1 marks a transition to the future, for when John is summoned into God's heavenly court, he hears the promise, "I will show you what must take place after these things." The echo of 1:19 is so unmistakable that we must infer that whereas the letters describe the present (2–3), what follows John's prophetic initiation in Revelation 4 and 5 (and 10–11) concerns what would be future from the standpoint of John's reception of the visions on Patmos. The fact that the events symbolized in the visions of Revelation 4–22 were future when John received the visions in the first century does not, however, tell us which of those events are future at our time, at the turn of the twenty-first century. Moreover, as we saw in Revelation 12:1–5, some visions narrated in Revelation 4–22 symbolize events that predate the present situation of the churches in Asia. The present trials confronting the Asian congregations were local expressions of the forces and figures symbolized as beast, false prophet, and harlot in the cosmic conflict section (12–22). So the visions of Revelation 4–22 concern primarily the "things which shall take place" in the future, but they also show the cosmic context of the churches' present struggle.

The Spirit of Prophecy

We have noticed that scenes portraying John's call to be a prophet (Rev. 4–5; 10–11) are markers that introduce major sections of visionary material in the body of Revelation. We have also observed the parallel introductions of the harlot Babylon and the bride Jerusalem (17:1; 21:9). The structural importance of these signposts is confirmed by the role of the Spirit in initiating John's visions.

---

write in that category would be the appearance of "one like a son of man" (1:12–16), since by Rev. 1:19 this is all that John had seen.

The body opens with John's reference to his exile to the island Patmos, a prison colony in the Aegean Sea, "because of the word of God and the testimony of Jesus" (Rev. 1:9). John "became[10] in the Spirit" on the Lord's day (1:10). This is a reference to prophetic inspiration, like Ezekiel's statements, "Then the Spirit lifted me up" (Ezek. 3:12), and "the Spirit lifted me up and brought me in a vision by the Spirit of God[11] to the exiles in Chaldea" (Ezek. 11:24). As a result of John's "becoming in the Spirit" he hears a voice like a trumpet, and when he turns to "see the voice," he is confronted with the stunning splendor of the Son of Man (Rev. 1:11, 13).

The other reference to John's "becoming in the Spirit" also marks his initiation into prophetic vision. The same trumpetlike voice summons John to "Come up here," and "immediately I [became][12] in the Spirit; and behold, a throne was standing in heaven, and One sitting on the throne" (Rev. 4:2). The phrase "I became in the Spirit" marks John's entrance into the state to receive prophetic visions from the Spirit of God. And its two occurrences mark the beginnings of significant cycles of prophetic material: the Son of Man and his seven letters to the churches (1:9–3:20); the enthroned One, the Lamb, the seven seals, and the seven trumpets (4:1–9:21; 11:15–18).

The prophetic role of the Spirit is also prominent in the visions introducing the two women, the harlot and the bride. As in Revelation 4:1, the prophet is summoned to "come" and transported in vision to a new "location" in order to view what he must record and reveal (17:1; 21:9). In both cases John is enabled to respond to the call to come only through the Spirit, for he recounts that the angel "carried me away in the Spirit" (17:3, 21:10). Again Ezekiel's visionary experience provides the background, for he reports that the Spirit "lifted

---

10. "I became" is preferable to "I was." The form is aorist indicative of *ginomai,* a verb that especially in aorist aspect usually indicates some sort of change in being or status. (E.g., Rev. 6:12: "there *was* a great earthquake; and the sun *became* black as sackcloth made of hair, and the whole moon *became* like blood." Each italicized word represents an aorist indicative form of *ginomai*.)

11. LXX, "in the Spirit of God" (*en pneumati theou*).

12. Again the verb is *ginomai* in the aorist indicative. NASB has "immediately I was in the Spirit."

34

him up" and carried him in vision to a new viewing point. For example, "and the Spirit lifted me up between earth and heaven and brought me in the visions of God to Jerusalem, to the entrance of the north gate of the inner court" (Ezek. 8:3; cf. 3:12, 14; 11:1, 24 [cited above]).

Richard Bauckham[13] and George Eldon Ladd see these four references to the Spirit ("I became in the Spirit," 1:10; 4:2; "he carried me in the Spirit," 17:3; 21:10) as the major sectional dividers in the macrostructure of Revelation. Ladd sees the body as composed of four visions: the glorified Christ and his seven letters (1:9–3:22); the heavenly throne, seals, trumpets, and bowls (4:1–16:21); Babylon, its judgment, and the final triumph and consummation (17:1–21:8); the heavenly Jerusalem (21:9–22:5).[14] This fourfold subdivision, however, although it is refreshingly simple and rooted in a specific feature of the text, glosses over the major turning point at the center of the book: John's reception of the scroll from the angel (Rev. 10–11) and the appearance of the Messiah's mother as the "great sign in heaven" (12:1), which opens the cycle that I have called cosmic conflict. The interconnections in Revelation may be so complex that one structural outline cannot do it full justice. Here we may have not a two-dimensional jigsaw puzzle but a three-dimensional Rubik's cube.

Sets of Seven

Although the possibility of finding multilayered structure in Revelation will make us suspicious of attempts to map the whole landscape using a single signpost, the most obvious and popular nominee for such an orienting landmark is the number seven. Four sets of seven (letters, seals, trumpets, bowls) provide the structure for major sections (2:1–3:20; 6:1–17 and 8:1; 8:6–9:21 and 11:15; 16). Is it not plausible that Revelation as a whole is structured by sets of seven—perhaps even seven sets of seven, a full sabbatical structure resembling Israel's calendar of weekly Sabbaths and sabbatical years?

13. Bauckham, *Climax of Prophecy*, 3–4.
14. George Eldon Ladd, *A Commentary on the Revelation of John* (Grand Rapids: Eerdmans, 1972), 14–17.

The visions associated with the seals, trumpets, and bowls are linked with each other in important ways. In each cycle the first four come together as a subgroup. The first four seals introduce four riders on horses of various colors, bringing disasters of various types (Rev. 6:1–8). The first four trumpets bring fiery judgments on four spheres affecting human life: land (source of vegetation), sea (source of fish and avenue of transportation), rivers and springs (sources of fresh water), and the sun, moon, and stars in the sky (sources of light; 8:6–12).[15] The first four bowls bring destruction on the same spheres in the same order: land, sea, rivers and springs, and the sun in the sky (16:2–9). Clearly there is a close connection between trumpets 1–4 and bowls 1–4.

The seven seals and seven trumpets, however, are grouped not only as four plus three but also as six plus one. The breaking of the first six seals is separated from the breaking of the seventh by an interlude vision concerning the protection of the people of God portrayed as 144,000 Israelites and as an innumerable international multitude (Rev. 7). Similarly the sounding of the first six trumpets is separated from the seventh by a major interruption, a set of visions portraying John's prophetic call (10) and the protection of the people of God portrayed as a temple and as witness prophets (11:1–13). These interludes, which impede the advance of the seal and trumpet cycles toward their climax, inject into the experience of hearing or reading the Book of Revelation a taste of the divine delay, which prolongs the time for repentance while it defers the martyrs' longed-for vindication: "How long, O Lord, holy and true, will You refrain from judging and avenging our blood on those who dwell on the earth?" (6:10).[16] In contrast

15. The last three trumpets are linked with each other as announcing the first, second, and third woes (Rev. 8:13; 9:12; 11:14), although the scene that opens with the seventh trumpet blast shows John not the final woe of rebels on earth but the joy of those who dwell in heaven (11:15–18). The last woe is the arrival of God's wrath in final, unrestrained judgment on his enemies—which is to say, the last trumpet contains within it the seven bowls of wrath, "which are the last, because in them the wrath of God is finished" (15:1), just as the seventh seal, when broken, was seen to contain the scene of the heavenly incense altar from which the seven trumpets were sounded (8:1–5).

16. Bauckham, *Climax of Prophecy,* 12: "These lengthy interruptions in the sequence of judgments *delay* the final, seventh judgment, and such delay would be

to the interludes that delay the cycles of seals and trumpets, nothing impedes the relentless outpouring of the seven bowls of wrath, for they are the last judgments on earth, completing the wrath of God (15:1). The seventh trumpet, which contains the bowls, signals the end of divine forbearance: "there will be delay no longer, but in the days of the voice of the seventh angel, when he is about to sound, then the mystery of God is finished" (10:6–7).

Postponing other comparisons between seals, trumpets, and bowls to a later discussion, we return to the question with which this section began: Since four clearly identified sevenfold cycles provide structure for major sections, could we not find three more—seven sets of seven? Or, since the final vision of the new Jerusalem portrays the eschatological fulfillment of Jubilee, should we perhaps look for eight sets of seven: seven focusing on the church's conflict in history, followed by an eighth portraying the new heavens and earth, when the curse is erased?

Various scholars have tried their hand at numbering the incognito sets of seven or otherwise detecting a sevenfold structure to the book as a whole. In *I Saw Heaven Opened*[17] Michael Wilcock sees the descriptions of an opening of heaven as the primary structural markers in the book, signaling the beginning of each new scene, which then unfolds in a sevenfold structure until the next opening of heaven occurs. The resulting structure of the body is a series of eight scenes:

(1) Son of Man and his letters to seven churches ("In the Spirit"), 1:9–3:22
(2) Vision of God and Lamb and opening of seven seals ("Door open in heaven . . . in the Spirit"), 4:1–8:1
(3) Incense altar and seven trumpets ("Silence in heaven"), 8:2–11:18

---

particularly felt in oral performance. They serve to incorporate the issue of the delay of judgment into the structure of the book."

17. Michael Wilcock, *I Saw Heaven Opened: The Message of Revelation*, TBST (Downers Grove, Ill.: InterVarsity Press, 1975). In later printings the subtitle and title are reversed.

(4) Cosmic conflict, in seven visions (marked by "I saw") ("Temple of God in heaven opened"), 11:19–15:4

(5) Pouring of seven bowls ("Temple in heaven open"), 15:5–16:21

(6) Babylon and seven words of doom on her ("Come, I will show . . . carried in Spirit"), 17:1–19:10

(7) Seven visions of ultimate reality ("I saw heaven opened"), 19:11–21:8

(8) Jerusalem and seven final revelations ("Come, I will show . . . carried in Spirit"), 21:9–22:19[18]

This proposal is sensitive to the clear sets of seven (scenes 1, 2, 3, 5) and to the four "in the Spirit" openings (scenes 1, 2, 6, 8) that indicate the initiation of prophetic visions. The resulting structure is eightfold rather than sevenfold, Wilcock suggests, because the sabbatical-year structure of seven times seven years leads up to the Jubilee year, which foreshadowed final and complete salvation—a fiftieth year, just beyond the seven times seven cycle of normal history. So also the last scene, revealing the bride of Christ, the new Jerusalem, shows the fullness of eschatological liberation in the complete eradication of sin and its curse—beyond the seven times seven cycle of history that leads up to Christ's return to defeat all enemies.

The question, though, is whether sections 4, 6, 7, and 8, in which John does not explicitly number seven items as "first, second, third," exhibit a seven-part structure. In scene 4, Wilcock identifies the preface "I saw" (*eidon*) as the marker that introduces seven "visions of cosmic combat" (13:1, 11; 14:1, 6, 14; 15:1, 2). But selecting this word as the structural key requires that the characters in Revelation 12— the heavenly woman, the birth of her son, the dragon, his defeat and ongoing warfare against the woman and her seed—must be all viewed as introductory to the sevenfold structure of the scene, since "I saw" does not introduce any of them. In scene 7 "I saw" is again supposed to be the signal of the scene's sevenfold structure (19:11, 17, 19; 20:1, 4, 11; 21:1); but "I saw" occurs nine times rather than seven. Conse-

18. Ibid., 15–18, 110–15.

quently two instances (20:12; 21:2) must be ignored to make the sevenfold structure come out right.[19]

Vern S. Poythress, recognizing the rich complexity of Revelation's visions, has proposed several distinct but complementary perspectives on the book's structure, employing the sevenfold motif in different ways. In one outline he proposes a sevenfold structure similar to Wilcock's, but he draws different boundaries in some sections, producing an outline consisting of seven sets of seven members each:

(1) Seven letters to churches, promising last things, 1:1–3:22
(2) Seven seals: messages of judgment, 4:1–8:1
(3) Seven trumpets, 8:2–11:19
(4) Seven symbolic histories, 12:1–14:20
(5) Seven bowls, 15:1–16:21
(6) Seven messages of judgment on Babylon, 17:1–18:24
(7) Seven last things, 19:1–22:21[20]

These sectional boundaries resemble Wilcock's until we reach the cycle of the judgment words on Babylon. Poythress finds seven messages of judgment in Revelation 17:7–18:24 and consequently sees this sixth section closing at Revelation 18:24. Wilcock hears seven words of justice, but the first begins as early as Revelation 17:1 and the seventh is not spoken until Revelation 19:6–8, followed by a brief word of affirmation (19:9–10). Then Poythress's seventh section (19:1–22:21) encompasses Wilcock's seventh and eighth sections, obviously using different textual indicators for the "seven last things": celebration, 19:1–10; battle, 19:11–21; elimination of evil, 20:1–10;

19. A further inconsistency occurs in scenes 6 and 8, where Wilcock categorizes the introductory "Come, I will show you" invitation in different ways in order to make each scene have seven members. In scene 6, "Come, I will show you" is the first of seven "words of justice" about Babylon (Rev. 17:1), but the corresponding "Come, I will show you" in 21:9 is the prelude to scene 8, followed by seven "final revelations" concerning the new Jerusalem.

20. Vern S. Poythress, unpublished series of structural and chiastic outlines on Revelation, especially "Heptadic Structure of Revelation" (Philadelphia: Westminster Theological Seminary, n.d.).

judgment, 20:11–15; heavens and earth, 21:1–8; city, 21:9–27; and paradise, 22:1–5.

More recently Poythress has published another outline in which a sevenfold structure commences with John's vision of the enthroned One and the Lamb (excluding the seven letters to the churches) and pertains to "cycles of judgment," followed by an eighth, "culminating act":

Cycle 1:   seven seals (4:1–8:1)
Cycle 2:   seven trumpets (8:2–11:19)
Cycle 3:   symbolic figures and the harvest = seven symbolic histories (12:1–14:20)
Cycle 4:   seven bowls (15:1–16:21)
Cycle 5:   judgment of Babylon = seven messages of judgment (17:1–19:10)
Cycle 6:   white horse judgment (19:11–21)
Cycle 7:   white throne judgment (20:1–21:8)
Culminating act: new Jerusalem (21:9–22:5)[21]

The first five cycles have an internal sevenfold structure, but Poythress does not make that claim for cycles 6 and 7 or for the "culminating" unveiling of the new Jerusalem.

The fact that Wilcock and Poythress, pursuing the same basic key to Revelation's structure, have arrived at different conclusions as to the structure of sections in which members are not numbered by John raises the suspicion that some sevenfold sets are the imports of commentators' creativity rather than indigenous to the text. Two additional factors should make us cautious about trying to decipher series of seven where John has not numbered them.

First, in Revelation 10:3–4, John hears seven thunders speak, a perfect introduction to a new series of seven. But the angel does not permit John to write what he has heard. G. B. Caird has suggested that this abortion in the unfolding of successive series of sevens emphasizes that the Lord is rushing to the relief of his persecuted church—dramatizing the promise of the angel, "there will be delay no longer"

21. Vern S. Poythress, *The Returning King: A Guide to the Book of Revelation* (Phillipsburg, N.J.: P&R Publishing, 2000), 60–63.

(10:6; cf. Luke 18:7–8).[22] If this view is correct, the Lord deliberately disrupts the sabbatical structure in order to stress the speed with which he will vindicate his church, encouraging endurance to the end.[23]

Second, we have noticed that Revelation is clear enough to bring blessing to those who hear it read aloud and keep what they hear (Rev. 1:3). Most first-century Christians would have experienced this book not by studying a manuscript for themselves but by hearing it read aloud by someone else. In oral delivery numbered sets of seven could help listeners keep their bearings. But it is hard to believe that, even in a more oral-aural culture than ours, hearers would recognize such common phrases as "I saw" as tacit text dividers and then keep mental count until the expected seventh occurrence arrived. Admittedly Revelation exhibits an intricacy of literary interconnectedness that could not be discerned on a first hearing. It is not accidental, for instance, that Revelation contains precisely seven beatitudes. Since these are not numbered in the text, it is unlikely that hearers could keep count as the book was read aloud from start to finish, but they would not need to keep a mental tally in order to get the message. For our purposes, this is the bottom line. Subtle, unmarked sevenfold structures may be embedded at various layers in the literary artistry of Revelation (hence Wilcock or Poythress may be correct in discerning a sabbatical macrostructure for the book as a whole and its individual sections), but the sevenfold structures that are essential to framing the puzzle will be those that are marked: letters, seals, trumpets, bowls.[24]

22. G. B. Caird, *A Commentary on the Revelation of St. John the Divine*, HNTC (New York: Harper & Row, 1966), 126.

23. Ibid., 126–27: "Other seers may depict human history as seven weeks of weeks, but not John; for him there are to be no more sevens but the last one. He is told to break in upon the sordid cavalcade of human sin and its ineluctable nemesis, because this is precisely what God himself has done. . . . 'If the Lord had not cut short the time, not a living creature could have escaped' (Mark xiii. 20)."

24. A third proposal to structuring Revelation in seven sections needs to be mentioned, though it does not rest its case on the four clearly designated sets of seven (letters, seals, trumpets, bowls), as do Wilcock and Poythress. R. H. Charles, *A Critical and Exegetical Commentary on the Revelation of St. John*, 2 vols., ICC (Edinburgh: T & T Clark, 1920), found that the body of Revelation, "apart from the Prologue and the Epilogue, falls naturally into seven distinct parts" (1:xxiv). He produced

Anticipation

A structural feature that at first seems disconcerting but in the long run proves illuminating is the element of anticipation. Symbolic figures and events that are to be disclosed in greater detail later in the

these "natural" divisions, however, by ignoring the explicitly marked sets of seven and by rearranging the text to correct what he perceived to be the inept editorial work of a "very unintelligent disciple" whose rearrangement of the prophet's material after John's death had muddled Revelation's structure and message from the end of the first century until . . . the work of R. H. Charles. "But unhappily the prophet did not live to revise his work, or even to put the materials of 20—22 into their legitimate order. This task fell, to the misfortune of all students of the Apocalypse, into the hands of a very unintelligent disciple . . . he was profoundly ignorant of his master's thought. If he had left his master's work as he found it, its teaching would not have been the unintelligible mystery it has been to subsequent ages; but unhappily he intervened repeatedly, rearranging the text in some cases, adding to it in others" (1:xii–xiii). Having corrected the structural blunders of the hypothetical disciple-editor, Charles identifies the seven sections of the body as

(1) Epistle opening and vision of Christ, 1:4–20;
(2) Occasion set forth in letters to churches, ch. 2—3;
(3) Vision of God and Christ, ch. 4—5;
(4) Judgments, 6:1—20:3;
(5) Millennial Kingdom, 20:4–10; 21:9—22:2, 14–15, 17;
(6) White throne judgment, 20:11–15;
(7) Everlasting kingdom, 21:1–8; 22:3–13, 16.

The collections of verses in sections 5 and 7 illustrate the extent to which Charles felt it necessary to rearrange the text to produce the "legitimate order" of the text, which neither the prophet nor his disciple had done (1:xxv–xxviii).

Although Charles expressed his solution with flair and extraordinary confidence, it is unconvincing for many reasons, among them that the "legitimate order" that he produced for 20:4–22:17 is hypothetical, as is the "ignorant disciple-editor" on whom Charles blames the puzzling features of Revelation. Even where Charles does not rearrange the text, his divisions separate sections that belong together (the vision of the Son of Man with his letters to the churches, Rev. 1–3; the vision of God and the Lamb with the seals of the scroll, Rev. 4–6). In other instances he combines sections that deserve to be recognized as distinct. He combines in one long section (6:1–20:3), generically characterized as "judgments," three series of sevenfold judgments (seals, trumpets, bowls), together with two proleptic visions of the martyrs in heaven (7:9–17; 15:2–4), one proleptic vision of the church triumphant on earth during the millennial kingdom (14:1–7), and other scenes. The disparity in size and diversity of contents between this large section 4 and the five-verse section 6 (white throne) damages the credibility of the whole structure.

42 ✍

book are often introduced briefly at an earlier point. A few examples establish the pattern.

John does not see the beast that emerges from the sea, the great persecuting power incarnated in John's day in seven-hilled Rome, until Revelation 13. But in Revelation 11 the two faithful witnesses, when they have completed their testimony, are slain by "the beast that comes up out of the abyss" that "will make war with them" (11:7, anticipating the wording of 13:7). The beast is mentioned before it is revealed. Likewise John does not see in lurid detail the sensuous and ruthless harlot Babylon until Revelation 17. As early as Revelation 14:8, however, Babylon's fall is proclaimed by an angel as a fait accompli.

When the Lamb breaks the sixth seal on the scroll, as early as Revelation 6:12–17, John sees the sun blackened, the moon reddened like blood, the stars fallen to earth, the sky split wide open, and an earthquake that shakes every mountain and island from its place. This scene is a preview of the dissolution of the whole order of the old creation, portrayed in detail in the visions of the seven bowls. This is the last and complete expression of God's wrath against the rebel world, plunging the beast's kingdom into utter darkness (16:10) and bringing the final earthquake that causes every island to flee and every mountain to disappear (16:20).[25]

These previews show that the order of John's narrative differs from the order of the historical events and developments symbolized in his visions. "Before and after" in the order of John's receiving visions, and even in the order of the narrative plot within a particular vision, do not necessarily mean "before and after" in the chronology of the history between Jesus' first and second comings.[26] Revelation exhibits an

---

25. My colleague S. M. Baugh has called my attention to the "inverted verbal parallelism" that links these two visions, noting that this stylistic convention for linking passages is frequent in Revelation:
   a   every mountain
      b   and island removed (6:14)
      b   every island flees
   a   every mountain is not found (16:20).
26. In contrast to this perspective, historicist and futurist approaches to Revelation (see appendix) often operate on the assumption that the order of the visions and their narration in Revelation reflects the chronological order of the fulfillment of Revelation's prophecies in history.

interlocking structure like a jigsaw puzzle, in which one section extends into neighboring pieces and sometimes replicates patterns encountered in a distant section of the book. Recognizing these instances of foreshadowing sensitizes us to the broader structural feature of repetition, or recapitulation.

Repetition

Repetition, or recapitulation, is used in two distinct ways in Revelation, although these two have not always been clearly distinguished by those who recognize its importance as an organizing principle in the book. Repetition in visions sometimes provides a second or third camera angle on the same person, historical event, or institution. However, repetition sometimes sends the signals that different historical events or ages participate in a common pattern that comes to expression at different points in the great cosmic conflict between God and Satan, Christ and the beast, the bride and the harlot.

We have already seen how repetition can provide different perspectives on the same person or time period: the "seven Spirits of God" are symbolized both in the seven lamps burning before the Father's throne (Rev. 4:5) and by the seven eyes of the Lamb "sent out into all the earth" (5:6). In the heart of the book multiple scenes provide windows on the events of a particular time period, variously measured as forty-two months (11:2; 13:5), 1,260 days (11:3; 12:6), or a time, times, and half a time (= one year, a pair of years, ½ year = 3½ years; 12:4; Dan. 7:25; 12:7).[27] The repetition of the time measurement suggests that the visions of the measured temple (Rev. 11:1–2), the two witnesses (11:3–13), the woman and the dragon (12:1–17),

27. Note the inversion or chiasm (repetition in reverse order) in the wording used to describe this period of time:
   a   42 months (11:2)
      b   1,260 days (11:3)
      b   1,260 days (12:6)
         c   a "time" (year?), (two?) "times," ½ "time" (12:14)
   a   42 months (13:5)
Note also the parallel between the 3½ "times" (= years) and the 3½ days that passed between the two witnesses' death and their resurrection in Rev. 11:9–11.

and the beast from the sea (13:1–10) have to do not only with the same time period but also with the same conflict, viewed from different perspectives: a temple protected within but exposed without, prophetic witnesses protected until their mission is accomplished, a mother assaulted yet protected in the desert, a beast waging victorious war on the saints. Later the repetition of terminology about the gathering of nations for "the war of the great day of God" (16:14–16) or simply "the war" (19:19; 20:8), will point to one, climactic last battle that will issue in the destruction of the beasts, their followers, and the dragon that animated them. God rewinds the videotape, in effect, and calls John to view the same drama from a different perspective.

Sometimes, however, the repetition that links one vision with another does not mean that the visions refer to the same time period. Some who have recognized recapitulation in Revelation have assumed that recapitulation of patterns functions only in the first way, providing differing perspectives on the same time span in the cosmic conflict, and have not seen this second type of recapitulation. William Hendriksen, whose sound insights in *More Than Conquerors* far outweigh his missteps, states as his first "proposition" for interpreting this book: "The Book of Revelation consists of seven sections. They are parallel: each spans the entire new dispensation, from the first to the second coming of Christ."[28] This approach, widely held throughout the history of reflection on Revelation, was harshly repudiated by R. H. Charles:

> Thus there is no need to resort to the theory of Recapitulation which from the time of Victorius of Pettau (circa 270 A.D.) has dominated practically every school of interpretation from that date to the present. So far is it from being true that the Apocalypse represents, more or less fully, under each successive series of the seven seals, the seven trumpets and the seven bowls, the same series of events, that the interpretation that it compelled to fall back on this device must be pronounced a failure.[29]

28. William Hendriksen, *More Than Conquerors: An Interpretation of the Book of Revelation* (Grand Rapids: Baker, 1939), 28–29.
29. Charles, *Commentary,* 1:xxiii.

Charles's objection has a valid point, which is tacitly acknowledged (it seems to me) in the nuancing Hendriksen introduced in his fourth proposition:

> The seven sections of the Apocalypse are arranged in an ascending, climactic order. There is progress in eschatological emphasis: the final judgment is first *announced;* then *introduced;* finally, *described.* Similarly, the new heaven and earth are described more fully in the final section than in those which precede.[30]

This qualification is a step in the right direction. The general movement of the narrative in Revelation as a whole is from the present status of the church militant to the future revelation of the church triumphant. The seven or however many sections do not simply replay the same story seven times over; rather there is "a climactic order," a "progress in eschatological emphasis."

Even this acknowledgment of increasing detail in concentration on the consummation, however, does not account for the blend of dissimilarity with similarity in sections that exhibit parallel patterns. For example, the spheres of human life and society affected by the judgments of the first four trumpets—land, sea, rivers and springs, sky (light source)—are identical to those affected by the first four bowls (Rev. 8:7–12; 16:2–9). Are these then two screenings from different camera angles of the same series of judgments, the same period of time? To say yes would be to overlook the crucial difference between the trumpet judgments and the bowl judgments. Every affliction that falls with the sounding of a trumpet (except the seventh) is restrained, circumscribed, less than universal: one-third of the earth and its trees are burned, one-third of the sea turned to blood and one-third of its crea-

30. Hendriksen, *More Than Conquerors,* 47 (emphasis in the original). Compare Robert H. Gundry, *The Church and the Tribulation* (Grand Rapids: Zondervan, 1973), 75: "The universally acknowledged Semitic style of Revelation favors the . . . view, according to which the seals, trumpets, and bowls will find somewhat concurrent fulfillment. For the sweeping summary of a complex of events with later regressions to add more detail is a well-recognized feature of narratival style in Semitic literature. Chronologically, the apocalyptic visions dart back and forth with a swiftness that sometimes bewilders our Western minds."

tures killed, one-third of the rivers and springs fouled, one-third of the heavenly lights darkened day and night. With the fifth trumpet, locusts arise from the abyss, forbidden to harm vegetation but permitted to torment—but not kill—human beings for a limited period of time. And with the sixth trumpet, riders come from the east to kill one-third of humankind. When the bowls are poured out, the judgment on each sphere is universal. There is no more delay, no more restraint. "In them the wrath of God is finished" (15:1). What then does the repeated pattern in trumpets 1–4 and bowls 1–4 tell us? The limited catastrophes symbolized in the trumpets are a bitter foretaste of the comprehensive judgment to come at the end, when the bowls are poured out. The trumpet judgments function not only to summon the Lamb's army to battle but also to sound a warning to his enemies. Yet the rebellious world does not respond with repentance (9:20–21). In interpreting repetition of wording and imagery, we need to give attention not only to the similarities but also to the differences between visions and vision cycles.

Structure of the Big Picture: A Working Proposal

In view of the structural markers we have surveyed, I propose that we piece together a frame such as the following to guide us as we seek to assemble the rest of the puzzle:

Prologue (1:1–8)
  A. *Title, chain of transmission, promise of blessing (1:1–3)*
  B. *Epistolary opening (1:4–6)*
  C. *Announcements about and by the coming King (1:7–8)*
Body (1:9–22:9)
  A. *"The things which are": Christ is with his churches and knows their conflict (1:9–3:20)*
    1. Vision of the Son of Man ("I became in the Spirit") (1:9–20)
    2. His seven letters to the churches (2:1–3:20)
  B. *"The things which shall take place after these things": Christ will defeat and destroy his enemies (4:1–22:9)*
    1. Scroll opened: Current and coming woes, precursors of the end (4:1–11:18)

a. *Vision of the One on the throne and the Lion/Lamb ("I became in the Spirit") (4–5)*

b. *The Lamb opens seven seals: instruments, rationale, and climax of current and coming woes (6:1–8:1)*

INTERLUDE: Sealing of Israel, worship by the nations (7)

c. *Vision of the incense altar (8:2–6)*

d. *Sounding of seven trumpets: current and coming woes sound warnings, prefiguring coming wrath (8:7–9:21, 11:14–18)*

2. Scroll delivered: The cosmic conflict of the ages (10:1–22:9)

a. *Vision of angel with scroll, seventh trumpet, open temple (10:1–11:19)*

INTERLUDE: Temple measured, witnesses killed but victorious (11:1–13)

b. *The combatants revealed ("a great sign . . . another sign") (12–14)*

   i.   **The mother, her child, and the dragon (12)**
   ii. **The beasts (13)**
   iii. **The Lamb and his army (14:1–5)**
   iv. **Announcements and harvests (14:6–20)**

c. *The end of God's wrath (15–16)*

   i. **Seven angels of the last plagues ("another sign") (15)**
   ii. **Seven bowls: the last plagues (16)**

d. *The harlot's judgment ("Come, I will show you . . . he carried me away in the Spirit") (17:1–19:10)*

e. *The last battle ("heaven opened") (19:11–20:10)*

f. *The end of the first creation and arrival of the new creation (20:11–21:8)*

   i. **The last judgment—"first things" ended (20:11–15)**
   ii. **The new heaven and earth—"all things new" (21:1–8)**

g. *The bride's glory ("Come, I will show you . . . and he carried me away in the Spirit") (21:9–22:9)*

Epilogue (22:6–21)

A. *God sent his angel; "I am coming quickly," so **blessing** is promised to the one who keeps the prophecy (22:6–9)*

B. *"I am coming quickly," so the **book** must not be sealed and **blessing** is promised to those who wash their robes; Jesus has sent his angel (22:10–16)*

C. *The Spirit and the bride invite the thirsty to come and petition the Lord Jesus to come; the **book** must not be altered; "I am coming quickly" (22:17–20)*

D. *Epistolary benediction (22:21)*

CHAPTER THREE

Vision:
The Son of Man among His Churches
(1:7–20)

Focus beyond the Surface of the Page

The Magic Eye craze passed just as I was getting the hang of it. This computer-generated pop art, pioneered in Japan and the United States, appeared in the 1990s as posters in mall art stores, then books, post-cards, and other novelty items.[1] To the uninitiated the conversation of the illuminati clustered before a display window, staring intently at a poster, may sound mystical:

"Do you see it?"

"No, all I see is the pattern on the surface."

"Look behind the surface . . . try to focus beyond . . ."

"Not quite, almost . . . ah! Oh, yes! There it is—dolphins frolick-ing under the sea, coming right out of the picture toward me! Oh, the 3–D is absolutely beautiful!"

The three-dimensional effect is astonishing (trust me, I'm one of the illuminati), but neither mysticism nor magic is involved. It seems that computer graphics can torque slightly a repeating-design pattern

---

1. N. E. Thing Enterprises, *Magic Eye: A New Way of Looking at the World* (Kansas City: Andrews and McMeel, 1993), 3.

on a page and so deceive our sense of perspective into seeing three-dimensionally another pattern hidden within the design that first meets the eye. The trick is to focus your vision not on the surface of the page but at a focal point beyond, behind, beneath the surface picture until the hidden picture emerges before your eyes. (In this game we the far-sighted, whose eyes no longer focus on things close at hand anyway, have the edge on the 20/20 population.)

The Magic Eye phenomenon provides a parable for Christian thinking about the world: to see the pattern that counts, you have to focus beyond the surface, to see the shape of deep realities not accessible to the casual observer. Like everyone else, Christians spend much of every day with eyes and minds focused on the surface of things—details about deadlines, delays, dollars, dress, food and shelter, going and coming, work and recreation, politics and more. Attending to everyday issues is necessary and right, but our hearts long to see the big picture, the meaning that lies behind the details. The Revelation shown to John unveils this deep pattern beneath the surface of history. How appropriate that before all else John sees the One who makes sense of history on a grand scale and of our experience!

We need to see Jesus—to meet his blazing eyes of heart-searching holiness, to wake up at the trumpet blast of his voice, to respond to his jealous demand for exclusive and passionate loyalty. Shocked insensible by the impact of his splendor, we need then to hear his words of compassionate comfort, quelling our fears and quickening our hopes. Every congregation, whatever its struggle at its post on the battlefront, needs to fix its eyes on Jesus, the pioneer and perfecter of faith (Heb. 12:2). Therefore Revelation begins with a vision of the glory of "one like a son of man" who died but lives forever, walking among the churches and holding them in his hand. For this reason in the letters that flow from this vision Jesus identifies himself in terms of what John has seen and heard in his overpowering encounter with the glorious Son of Man.

The Coming King (1:7–8)

The prologue closes with the announcement of the coming of the King (Rev. 1:7), who then proclaims his name to be the Alpha and

Omega (1:8). These announcements about and from the coming King form a bridge from the doxology (1:5b-6) to John's first vision on Patmos (1:9–20). The doxology mentioned Christ's death ("released us from our sins by His blood") and his royal authority ("to Him be the glory and the dominion forever"). The announcements of 1:7–8 likewise mention his death ("those who pierced Him") and his triumphant rule ("coming with the clouds"). The opening vision will again speak of Jesus' death ("I was dead") and his resurrection and authority ("I am alive forevermore, and I have the keys," 1:18).

The first announcement promises the King's coming "with the clouds," so that "every eye will see Him, even those who pierced Him; and all the tribes of the earth will mourn over Him." This announcement blends Daniel 7:13 ("coming with the clouds") with Zechariah 12:10, 12 ("they will look on Me whom they have pierced; and they will mourn"), with a touch of Genesis 22:18 and Genesis 26:4 ("all the nations of the earth").[2] Daniel was shown "one like a Son of Man" coming with clouds to the Ancient of Days amid his heavenly court, to receive endless dominion over all peoples and languages (Dan. 7:13–14). In Daniel's vision the direction of the Son of Man's "coming with clouds" was into heaven, toward God's throne, where authority was given to him (Dan. 7:14, 27; cf. Matt. 28:18). Jesus uses Daniel's wording in the same way, to speak of his resurrection and ascension "with the clouds" to the Father's right hand, to be invested with universal authority as the victorious Messiah (Mark 8:38; 14:62; Matt. 16:27; 26:64; Luke 9:26; cf. Acts 1:9).[3] Mark 8:38 and Mark 14:62 imply not only that the Son of Man's coronation will occur within the lifetime of Jesus' contemporaries but also that some of them, including his opponents (Mark 14:62), will see evidence of his exaltation. Some scholars believe that this visible coming of the Son of Man, evoking the lament of his enemies, was fulfilled in the

2. Richard Bauckham, *The Climax of Prophecy: Studies on the Book of Revelation* (Edinburgh: T & T Clark, 1993), 319. Dan. 7:13 and Zech. 12:10, 12 are blended also in Jesus' Mount of Olives discourse on things to come (Matt. 24:30).

3. R. T. France, *Jesus and the Old Testament: His Application of Old Testament Passages to Himself and His Mission* (Downers Grove, Ill.: InterVarsity Press, 1971), 139–48.

destruction of the temple and Jerusalem in A.D. 70.[4] Another view is that the lament expresses repentance for having pierced the Christ, which is produced by the proclamation of his gospel.[5] Jesus also used the language of Daniel's vision to describe his coming as Son of Man at the end of the age, to execute the last judgment (Matt. 19:28; 25:31–46).

Which coming of the Son of Man with clouds is promised in Revelation 1:7—his coming to the Father to receive all authority at the ascension, his coming to Jerusalem in the judgment of 70, or his coming to judge the world at the end of history? Revelation affirms that Jesus has come to the Ancient of Days and been given all authority. His right to open the scroll shows this (Rev. 5).[6] But the statement in Revelation 1:7, "He is coming with the clouds," is a promise for the future, as the future tense of the verbs ("they will see . . . they will mourn") makes clear.

Nor was this promise/threat fulfilled in Jerusalem's destruction by Roman forces commanded by Titus.[7] This view must insist that Revelation was written very early, before 70, but so early a date of composition is problematic.[8] Moreover, this view limits the scope of the lament to first-century Palestinian Jews, "all the tribes of the land," rather than "the tribes of the earth." But to limit the lament ethnically, geographically, and temporally is to obscure the passage's allusion to God's promise of international blessing to and through Abra-

---

4. Ibid., 142; David Chilton, *Days of Vengeance: An Exposition of the Book of Revelation* (Fort Worth: Dominion, 1987), 64–66.

5. Bauckham, *Climax of Prophecy,* 322: "Daniel 7:13–14 portrays not simply the parousia, but . . . the transfer of sovereignty over the nations of the world to Jesus, the 'one like a son of man,' as the one who exercises God's rule. The conflated quotation suggests that the kingdom of God will come, not so much by the destruction of the nations, as by their repentant acknowledgement of God's rule over them."

6. Compare Rev. 12:5: "And she gave birth to a son, a male child, who is to rule all the nations with a rod of iron; and her child was caught up to God and to His throne."

7. So Chilton, *Days of Vengeance,* 66.

8. G. K. Beale, *The Book of Revelation,* NIGTC (Grand Rapids: Eerdmans, 1999), 4–27, surveys arguments for both the early date (pre-70) and the later date (mid-90s) of composition; he concludes in favor of the later date, during Domitian's reign.

ham (Gen. 22:18). The circle of mourners will include not just Israel but also the Gentile nations.[9]

Although John does not specifically identify this coming, it is probably the second coming of Jesus Christ, as the later echoes seem to confirm (Rev. 22:7, 12, 20). Nevertheless, because Jesus lives and rules now, the visible second coming ("every eye will see him") will be foreshadowed even now by his interventions in his congregations and his imposition of providential judgments in the world at large. The announcement of Revelation 1:7 has a simple but profound point: the One who was pierced in rejection (John 19:34, 37) has been invested with supreme authority, and his appearance will strike deep sorrow to the hearts of his tormentors from all the tribes and nations of the earth.

The Lord identifies himself in Revelation 1:8, proclaiming his name.[10] Alpha and Omega are the first and last letters of the Greek alphabet, so this name signifies that the speaker stands sovereign over both ends of history and everything in between. "Alpha and Omega" will be joined to "the beginning and the end" in 21:6, and both pairs will be combined with "the first and the last" in the epilogue (22:13). "The first and the last" is the title claimed by the Son of Man in the opening vision (1:17). In Isaiah's prophecies the Lord calls himself the first and the last to sum up his supremacy over the idols (Isa. 41:4). The idols that tempted Israel in Isaiah's days were recent novelties, not the ancient Creator: "I am the first, I am also the last. Surely My hand founded the earth, and My right hand spread out the heavens" (Isa. 48:12–13). Nor can the idols compete with the Lord by contesting his control of the future: "I am the first and I am the last, and there

9. Later in Revelation the singular "every tribe" (corresponding to "all the tribes" in 1:7) describes a multiethnic, multiracial multitude, either the company of the faithful (5:9: "You . . . purchased for God with Your blood men from every tribe and tongue and people and nation"; 7:9) or the company of the rebels (11:9; 13:7: "authority over every tribe and people and tongue and nation was given to [the beast]").

10. Compare the self-identification of the covenant Lord at the opening of the Ten Commandments (Exod. 20:2) and in ancient Near Eastern treaties. M. G. Kline, *Treaty of the Great King: The Covenant Structure of Deuteronomy* (Grand Rapids: Eerdmans, 1963), 14.

is no God besides Me. Who is like Me? . . . Let them declare to them the things that are coming and the events that are going to take place" (Isa. 44:6–7). All three pairs—Alpha and Omega, beginning and end, first and last—proclaim God's eternal and invincible rule over history. The idols were not there at the beginning, nor will they last to the end. They did not give the universe its existence, nor can they manipulate its destiny. They cannot be trusted and need not be feared. The Lord is God from start to finish.

He is the One who ever lives ("who is") and who therefore exercises control over the whole sweep of history, from its dawn (Alpha, "who was") to its sunset (Omega, "who is coming"). His self-identification here alludes to the Lord's disclosure of his name to Moses at the burning bush, for his name, "I am," in Exodus 3:14 was translated "he who is" in the Septuagint, the ancient Greek version of the Old Testament.[11] The future component of God's self-designation does not merely affirm his perpetual life but rather promises his arrival to save: he is "the one who is to come" to rescue and rule, not merely "the one who will be" into eternity.[12] Likewise, the "I am" who met Moses at the burning bush declared that he had "come down" to deliver his people from Egypt (Exod. 3:8).

11. Jesus' reference to himself using "I am" alluded to the Hebrew text of Exod. 3:14, so it provoked charges of blasphemy and the threat of execution (John 8:58–59). See Dennis E. Johnson, "'I Am': Intimations of Eternity in John's Gospel," in *The Gospels Today: A Guide to Some Recent Developments,* ed. Malcolm J. Robertson III and William L. Lane, New Testament Student, vol. 6 (Philadelphia: Skilton House, 1990), 132–49.

12. The "he who is and who was" are forms of "to be" (*eimi*), but the third name is a present participle of "to come" (*ho erchomenos*) rather than a future form of "to be" (*ho esomenos*). Confirmation of the interpretation of "the one who comes" as having local instead of mere temporal significance is found in the fact that the threefold formula, "who is and who was and who is coming" is found in Rev. 1:4, 8; 4:8; whereas in 11:17 and 16:5 the last element is omitted: "who is and who was." Why the change? Because sounding of the seventh trumpet in 11:15 has heralded the coming of God: "The kingdom of the world has become the kingdom of our Lord and of His Christ. . . . We give You thanks, O Lord God, the Almighty, who are and who were, because You have taken Your great power and have begun to reign." Thanks to S. M. Baugh for this insight into the spatial rather (or more) than temporal significance of "the one who is coming."

It may look to the beleaguered churches of Asia Minor as if their fate lies in the hands of a beast that has been given "authority over every tribe and people and tongue and nation" (Rev. 13:7). In fact, however, in contrast to their ever-living Lord, the beast "was, and is not, and is about to come up out of the abyss" only for the purpose of going to destruction—a has-been, lacking reality in the present and to appear in the future only for the sake of disappearing forever (17:8). So ephemeral an enemy cannot harm those who stand under the protection of him "who is and who was and who is to come, the Almighty."

One Like a Son of Man (1:9–20)

John is a microcosm of the church, a brother of his hearers who shares with them a threefold treasure: "the tribulation and kingdom and perseverance which are in Jesus" (Rev. 1:9). "Tribulation" has been loaded with unique and horrifying baggage by the eschatological speculations through church history. In the New Testament it usually refers, as it does here, not to a distinct period of apocalyptic trauma as popularly perceived but to the distresses common to Christian experience: "In the world you have tribulation, but take courage; I have overcome the world" (John 16:33).[13] The New Testament also speaks of a "great tribulation" (Matt. 24:21; Rev. 7:14)—one unparalleled in the history of the world, before or after (Mark 13:19). But John's focus here is on the fact that his experience of tribulation, far from being extraordinary, was one that he shared with all the churches: to follow Jesus faithfully is to suffer affliction (see 2 Tim. 2:12).

Christians also share together in "the kingdom," for they have been made into a kingdom (Rev. 1:6; 5:10). But we are not only subjects of Jesus' kingdom, under his authority (Col. 1:13). We are also sharers of Jesus' royal authority (Rev. 5:10), seated with him at God's right

---

13. See also Acts 14:22: "Through many tribulations we must enter the kingdom of God." "And not only this, but we also exult in our tribulations, knowing that tribulation brings about perseverance" (Rom. 5:3). "[God] who comforts us in all our affliction so that we may be able to comfort those who are in any affliction with the comfort with which we ourselves are comforted by God" (2 Cor. 1:4). "I know your tribulation and your poverty (but you are rich)" (Rev. 2:9).

hand (Eph. 2:6) and heirs of his coming kingdom (James 2:5). Our participation in Jesus' royal power is symbolized in the iron scepter and the throne that he will share with those who overcome (Rev. 2:26–27; 3:21). Our Champion is a king with many diadems upon his head and a sharp sword proceeding from his mouth, to smite and rule the nations (19:12, 15). But the churches' participation in Jesus' royal power now lies largely hidden, veiled behind all-too-visible affliction, poverty, and "little power" (2:9; 3:8).

Because the tribulation that characterizes our present often obscures the kingdom that is our future, the family of God must share, finally, perseverance. Persistent endurance connects present suffering to future hope, as Paul says:

> For I consider that the sufferings of this present time are not worthy to be compared with the glory that is to be revealed to us. For the anxious longing of the creation waits eagerly for the revealing of the sons of God. . . . For in hope we have been saved, but hope that is seen is not hope; for who hopes for what he already sees? But if we hope for what we do not see, with perseverance we wait eagerly for it. (Rom. 8:18–19, 24–25)

Jesus commends congregations at Ephesus, Smyrna, Thyatira, and Philadelphia for perseverance in the face of opposition and pressures to conform (Rev. 2:2–3, 9–10, 19; 3:10). Later visions also will be punctuated by Christ's summons to perseverance (13:10; 14:12).

This threefold partnership in affliction, dominion, and endurance brought John to Patmos "because of the word of God and the testimony of Jesus." Patmos was a small island in the Aegean Sea, about forty miles west of the coast of Asia Minor and sixty-five miles from Ephesus, the nearest city. An old and widespread tradition said that Patmos had a penal settlement in which inmates worked stone quarries. There is archaeological evidence that islands in Patmos's part of the Aegean were used by local governors to exile socially disruptive individuals.[14] This apparently was John's experience, because wherever the words "the word of God and the testimony of Jesus" appear

14. G. B. Caird, *A Commentary on the Revelation of St. John the Divine,* HNTC (New York: Harper & Row, 1966), 21–23; Colin J. Hemer, *The Letters to the Seven*

in Revelation, they are associated with the suffering of Jesus' faithful witnesses (e.g., 6:9; 12:17; 20:4). Although John's testimony has not meant martyrdom, his exile is one form of the affliction that he shares with the family of God.

When the Spirit brings John into a state of prophetic vision, John's first sensation is not a sight but a sound: "I heard behind me a voice like the sound of a trumpet" (Rev. 1:10). The trumpet blast signaled the Lord's descent to meet Moses at Sinai (Exod. 19:16, 19; 20:18), and it was later associated with the Lord's entering his temple (Ps. 47:5). Trumpets called the troops to battle and the congregation to worship. The sound of the *shofar,* the ram's-horn trumpet, on the Day of Atonement every fiftieth year signaled liberation of God's people and land (Lev. 25:8–10). Poet-composer Michael Card captures this dimension of the trumpet voice heard by John: "Jesus is our Jubilee. In his voice we hear the trumpet sound that tells us we are free. He is the incarnation of the year of Jubilee."[15]

John will compare this voice with "many waters" (Rev. 1:15), echoing Ezekiel's description of the sound made by the wings of the living creatures who bore God's chariot throne, "like the sound of abundant waters as they went, like the voice of the Almighty" (Ezek. 1:24; cf. 43:2). Jesus' voice is the voice of the Almighty.

When John turns to "see the voice," the visible attributes of the Speaker overwhelm him. He sees first seven golden lampstands, later to be interpreted as symbols of the Asian churches (Rev. 1:11–12, 20). The order in which we see this vision is intentional. Before we see the speaker, we see that he is "in the middle of the lampstands," present with his churches.

Among the lampstands is "one like a son of man" (Rev. 1:13). The simile is drawn from the vision of Daniel 7, already alluded to in the announcement "he is coming with the clouds." This night vision granted to Daniel in the first year of Belshazzar's reign is a rich treasury from which the imagery of John's visions will be drawn. Daniel

---

Churches of Asia in Their Local Setting, JSNT Supplement 11 (Sheffield: JSOT Press, 1986), 27–29.

15. Michael Card, "Jubilee," *In the Beginning,* sound cassette (Brentwood, Tenn.: Birdwing Music/Sparrow, 1989).

saw four beasts rising from the sea, one like a lion, one like a bear, one like a leopard, and one dreadful beyond description—mighty world empires arrogantly resisting God and oppressing his people.[16] Then he saw the heavenly court of the Ancient of Days, radiant with flaming purity and glory, "and behold, with the clouds of heaven one like a Son of Man was coming, and He came up to the Ancient of Days. . . . And to Him was given dominion, glory, and a kingdom, that all the peoples, nations, and men of every language might serve Him" (Dan. 7:13–14). The interpretation that follows identifies the four beasts as "four kings," and the "one like a Son of Man" represents "the saints of the Highest One" (Dan. 7:18, 27). The message of this vision seems parallel to Nebuchadnezzar's earlier dream of the statue and the stone, which predicted four successive kingdoms, beginning with Neb-uchadnezzar's Neo-Babylonian Empire and climaxing in the time of the fourth kingdom, when "the God of heaven will set up a kingdom which will never be destroyed" (Dan. 2:44). The speaker who commissions John to write is the "one like a son of man" who received from the Ancient of Days the eternal kingdom on behalf of the saints.

Other aspects of the speaker's description exhibit the impact of Old Testament imagery on John's visionary experience, but also the newness of the revelation that he receives. Images drawn from different Scriptures or, even more confusing, different figures in the same prophetic vision are brought together to describe the Son of Man. He wears a robe that reaches his feet and a sash, like the ancient high priest in the tabernacle (Exod. 28:4; 29:9). Jesus, who consecrates God's kingdom of priests from all the nations, is the high priest who represents his church before the Father (Rev. 1:5–6; 5:9–10). His floor-length robe also resembles that of the angelic scribe in Ezekiel's vision, whom God commands to mark his faithful people before judgment sweeps through the city (Ezek. 9:3–6). Here is One fit to stand in God's presence and to protect the righteous, even amid raging storms. The Son of Man's golden sash, flaming eyes, glowing feet, and radiant face all reflect the splendor of the "man" who appeared to

16. We will reflect in chapter 8 on the implications of the fact that the beast emerging from the sea in Rev. 13:1 is a composite of the four beasts in Daniel's vision.

Daniel, sent by God to reveal the future destiny of the people of God (Dan. 10:5–21). Heavenly messengers shine with the glory of the God who sent them from his light-filled court, and the face of this Son of Man is "like the sun shining in its strength."

But John also sees that the Son of Man's "head and his hair were white like white wool, like snow." Like "coming with clouds" and "one like a son of man," this description comes from the vision of Daniel 7, but in Daniel's vision the One whose hair was white "like pure wool" was not the Son of Man but the Ancient of Days (Dan. 7:9). We might infer that this merely indicates that Christ reflects the glory of the One who sent him. God's messengers are images of his splendor as they emerge from heaven to do his will on earth, but the white hair of the Son of Man says more than this. In the symbolic vocabulary provided by Daniel's vision, John sees "one like a son of man" who is distinguished from and identified with the Ancient of Days— a mysterious combination but consistent with the fact that he lays claim to the title "the first and the last" (1:17), by which God proclaimed his divine eternity (Isa. 41:4; 44:6; 48:12). The Son of Man is God, infinite in wisdom and holiness.

From the mouth of the Son of Man proceeds a sharp two-edged sword. God's servant says in Isaiah 49:2: "He has made My mouth like a sharp sword." The word of God spoken by the servant will conquer everything that opposes the rightful King, whether the heart's errant intents (Heb. 4:12; Eph. 6:17) or the world's rebellious individuals (Rev. 19:15; cf. 12:5). In the cosmic conflict that lies below the surface and behind the scenes of daily life, the Son of Man is a warrior and judge, fulfilling the two primary purposes for which Israel first sought a king: "There shall be a king over us, that we also may be like all the nations, that our king may judge us and go out before us and fight our battles" (1 Sam. 8:19–20). Although Saul failed to demonstrate either wise justice or courage in battle, David exemplified the king as bold warrior and Solomon, the king as wise judge. Yet David and everyone in his dynasty fell short of David's poetic profile of the perfect ruler (2 Sam. 23:1–7)—until Jesus, the Son of Man, who is supremely wise in judgment and fierce in battle.

Jesus reveals himself to John in the language of prophetic symbolism, not in a literal description of his resurrection body as he now sits at God's right hand. We are not to think that the glorified body in which Jesus ascended to heaven now has a sword in place of a tongue, snow-white hair, or a face so overpowering with physical light that it cannot be viewed with joy by the pure in heart (see Matt. 5:8; Rev. 22:4). The symbols seen by John in the vision reveal not what Jesus looks like but what he is like—his identity as the searcher of hearts, full of consuming holiness and boundless wisdom, the perfect priest standing for his people before the Father, the perfect king defending them against the devil by his invincible Word. Revelation's visions show us how things are, not how they look to the physical eye.

The radiance and purity of the Son of Man are overwhelming: "when I saw Him, I fell at His feet as a dead man" (1:17). Daniel's reaction to a similar vision was the same:

> As soon as I heard the sound of his words, I fell into a deep sleep on my face, with my face to the ground. Then behold, a hand touched me and set me trembling on my hands and knees. . . . When he had spoken to me according to these words, I turned my face toward the ground and became speechless. . . . "O my lord, as a result of the vision anguish has come upon me, and I have retained no strength." (Dan. 10:9–10, 15–16)

Isaiah's woeful sense of defilement in the presence of "the King, the LORD of hosts" (Isa. 6:5) and Paul's fall to the roadway before Jesus' blinding light (Acts 9:4) show the sheer shock that mere mortals experience when confronted by the holy One of Israel. If the experience of biblical prophets is any measure, being slain in the Spirit is anything but pleasant![17] Worship that recognizes the presence of Christ's Spirit with his people does not need to be humorless, but it

17. It was even more unpleasant for Ananias and Sapphira, who were literally slain by the Spirit for trying to deceive him, showing contempt for his omniscience and his consuming purity (Acts 5:1–11). For a discussion of this unusual New Testament miracle of judgment, see Dennis E. Johnson, *The Message of Acts in the History of Redemption* (Phillipsburg, N.J.: P&R Publishing, 1997), 80–82.

will be serious, trembling as his laser searches and cleanses our stained hearts, even as we relish the refreshment of his friendship.

The Son of Man's touch and comforting words restore John's composure, again like Daniel's experience (Rev. 1:17; Dan. 10:10, 18). In addition to being "the first and the last," Jesus calls himself "the living One," for although he was dead, he now lives forever and ever. In the vision of Revelation 4–5 John will hear the heavenly court giving glory, honor, and thanks to the One seated on the throne "who lives forever and ever" (4:9). God's life is the solid rock on which solemn oaths are founded, so the oath of the strong angel who stands on earth and sea will be secured "by Him who lives forever and ever" (10:6; cf. Deut. 32:40; 1 Kings 17:1). By his death and return to life Jesus has acquired the keys of death and Hades. His ignominious defeat on the cross has proven to be his glorious victory over the ancient serpent, "the accuser of our brethren" (Rev. 12:10). The keys of death and the grave, now held by Jesus the ever-living Son of Man, make concrete the fact that his investiture with eternal dominion, shown to Daniel in the night visions, has occurred through his death and resurrection.

The Son of Man radiates heat and light: eyes like flames, feet like bronze heated to a glow, face blazing like the sun shining full strength. His luminous appearance is reflected and miniaturized in the seven stars that he holds and the seven lampstands that surround him. The lampstands belong to the imagery of ancient Israel's sanctuary, for in its outer chamber, the holy place, stood a golden lampstand with seven flames giving light to the priests who served the Lord there daily (Exod. 25:31–37). They symbolize the churches on earth, scattered across western Asia Minor (Rev. 1:19). Jesus, the holy One of God, is present among them and knows their situation more truly than they do. The appearance of the churches as golden lampstands also signals their calling, to reflect the light of God's heavenly court into the present darkness on earth. The seven lampstands (*luchniai*)[18] surrounding the Son of Man correspond on earth to seven lamps (*lampades*) that John will see in heaven (4:5). Since those later lamps picture the Spirit's presence with

---

18. This word also describes the "two witnesses" of John's later vision (Rev. 11:3–13), which draws on the imagery of Zechariah's vision of a seven-flamed lampstand, supplied by two olive trees, "the two anointed ones" (Zech. 4:14).

the Father, these lampstands call the churches to reflect the Spirit's presence on earth, in their communities. The letters will show them how.

The stars in Jesus' right hand are "the angels of the seven churches" (Rev. 1:20). Following the key that we have used for the lampstands (= churches), we might infer that if the stars are the symbols, the angels are their literal referents. But who are these angels? The key to their identity lies in the fact that each of the letters is addressed not to the church that is in each city but "to the angel of the church that is in" each city. The Greek word *angelos* can be applied to human messengers (Mark 1:2; Matt. 11:10; Luke 7:24–27; 9:52; James 2:25). Therefore some say that the messengers of the churches are seven people who will carry copies of the book to the seven congregations. The order in which the churches are listed and the geography of their locales imply, however, that one messenger would carry one original copy from city to city in a circuit from Ephesus north along the coast through Smyrna to Pergamum, then inland to Thyatira and south through Sardis and Philadelphia in the interior to Laodicea. Moreover, if the angels are merely messengers delivering the book to the churches, why does Jesus address his encouragement and rebukes to these mail carriers rather than to the churches?

Others believe that each church's angel is its pastor, whom Jesus holds responsible for the church's spiritual condition. This is more plausible, but it still faces two objections. Angels elsewhere in Revelation are always God's superhuman messengers, consistent with the word's usual meaning in the rest of the New Testament.[19] And, although in the letters Jesus usually addresses each angel as a single individual, he sometimes switches to plural forms of "you" in addressing the angel of a church. Some of these plural forms refer to subgroups within a congregation (2:10, 14, 15, 20–22, 24), but others refer to the congregation as a whole ("that you [pl.] will be tested," 2:10; "among you [pl.]," 2:13).[20]

Probably Jesus is evoking in John's mind the picture of guardian an-

19. Rev. 1:1; 5:2, 11; 7:1–2, 11; 8:2-12 (angels sounding seven trumpets); 10:1–10; 12:7, 9 (Satan's); 14:6, 8–10, 15, 17–19; 15–16 (angels with seven bowls); 17:1, 7; 18:1, 21; 19:17; 20:1; 21:9, 17; 22:6, 8, 16.

20. David E. Aune, "The Form and Function of the Proclamations to the Seven Churches (Revelation 2–3)," *NTS* 36 (1990): 186 n. 16.

gels charged with protecting the people of God and bringing his messages to them, such as the angel sent to Daniel, who reports having been delayed by "the prince of the kingdom of Persia" for twenty-one days from the time that God had heard Daniel's prayer (Dan. 10:12–13). (Both holy angels and demons are creatures, and their powers, though greater than ours, are limited. The fact that an evil spirit associated with the pagan kingdom Persia obstructed this holy angel's mission in no way compromises the comprehensive power of God to achieve his will, as Nebuchadnezzar eloquently testified when restored to sanity [Dan. 4:34–35].) But again in John's vision we see a slight modification on the Old Testament motif. Technically the angel of each church is not literally an angel—that is, a distinct spiritual being charged with the welfare of the church. Rather, the angel is the church, viewed from the perspective of Christ's control over his churches: the stars are in his hand.[21] It is challenging to think of the stars symbolizing angels, who in turn symbolize the churches, from the standpoint of their control by the authoritative hand of Jesus.[22] But it is more problematic to consider the letters as addressed literally to angels, for this reason: the "individual" addressed as "you" in most letters is a mixture of faithfulness and sin. Scripture gives us no reason to suppose that unfallen angels are anything but holy in motive and action, so the flaws identified in the letters are flaws not in holy angels but in human churches, as everyone instinctively recognizes. Stars and lampstands both speak of the churches as reflecting the light of their King, but the lampstands highlight his presence and the stars emphasize his protective possessiveness. The glorious Son of Man, who lives among his congregations and holds their lives in his hand, has something to say to each of them.

21. Aune (ibid., 185) speaks of "the author's unique literary device of addressing each proclamation to an *angelos,* who functions as the *alter ego* of the Christian community."

22. This two-layered symbolism has parallels elsewhere in Revelation. In Rev. 17, for example, John sees a woman who is labeled "Babylon" (17:4–5). In fact, however, Babylon is symbolic of another, unnamed city, "the great city, which reigns over the kings of the earth" (17:18) and rests on seven mountains (17:9)—clearly recognizable as Rome. Moreover, the interpretation of the vision makes clear that the city is viewed not as a geographical site in which residences, shops, roads, and public buildings are constructed but as a center of political and economic power and influence.

CHAPTER FOUR

Letters:
The Son of Man
Speaks to His Churches
(2:1–3:22)

West Coast Churches

West Coast churches face a variety of challenges. Their environment is anything but friendly to vibrant Christian faith. Some churches, located in self-sufficient, affluent communities, are tempted to pursue personal peace and a comfortable lifestyle, relying on their financial resources for security. Others are stained by the scandal of sexual immorality. Some are stigmatized by their community as aloof and intolerant of other viewpoints. After all, the populace and politicians of the West Coast, finding it expedient to cultivate the favor of power-brokers in the distant capital, show their loyalty to the system through a civil religion unencumbered by personal convictions.

Some churches are experts in doctrinal precision, but amid the theological wars they have lost the capacity to care for hurting people. Others are unclear about where to draw the line that defines the essentials of the gospel as they adapt their message to the culture in order to reach out to or fit in with non-Christians. Some churches are all image and no reality, lacking spiritual vitality despite an impressive array of activities. Others are a tiny minority struggling to hold on in the midst of a community that ignores or despises them.

These West Coast churches sound stereotypically twenty-first-century Californian, don't they? In fact, however, this is a sketch of the situation, strengths, and weaknesses of the West Coast churches in Asia Minor in the first century, to which Jesus addressed his Revelation through John. Laodicea was an affluent community, and Christians there were tempted to pursue personal peace and a comfortable lifestyle, relying on their financial resources. Churches in Pergamum and Thyatira were stained by the scandal of sexual immorality in their midst. The church of Smyrna apparently was stigmatized by outsiders. The cities of Asia Minor competed eagerly for the honor of being temple warden by building shrines to the glory of emperors who had provided financial subsidies from imperial treasuries and who were said to be divinized after death. In Asia Minor, crossroads between east and west, the worship of rulers had a long history, and Roman political pragmatism exploited this tradition in the civil religion of the imperial cult.[1]

The Ephesian church was full of experts in doctrinal precision, for which Jesus praised them, but in the theological wars they had fought they had lost the capacity to love imperfect people. The churches in Pergamum and Thyatira were unclear about where to draw the line that defines the essentials of the gospel as they tried, by any and all means, to connect with non-Christians, maintain standing with powerful trade guilds, and fit in with the culture. The church in Sardis was all image and no substance, lacking spiritual life despite an impressive array of activities. The Philadelphian church was a tiny minority struggling to hold on in the midst of a community that despised them.

---

1. Emperor worship was motivated by political expedience, not profound religious conviction. In Asia Minor, far from Rome, it had more surface plausibility than in the empire's capital, where the Caesars' behavior was better known. Roman cynicism about the apotheosis (transformation into deity) of emperors after death comes to humorous expression in a satirical piece attributed to Seneca and bearing the pun-laden title "The Apocolocyntosis" (transformation of a pumpkin) or "The Deification of Claudius the Clod." *Petronius: The Satyricon, and Seneca: The Apocolocyntosis*, trans. J. P. Sullivan (New York: Penguin, 1977), 207–23.

Seven churches, different in so many ways from one another. Seven churches, similar in so many ways to the churches in which we live and serve Jesus. What one thing do all these churches need to fortify them against the enemy's frontal assaults, to make them savvy to his subtle stratagems, and to make them loyal to God and compassionate toward their oppressors? They need to hear Jesus' voice. His voice comforts our weak and wounded hearts, diagnoses our diseases, shatters our dreams of ease here and now, and calls us forward to the consummation of his victory in the new Jerusalem. His voice addresses us today in his letters to the seven churches of Asia, for each letter is what the Spirit says to all the churches.

The Template of the Letters (2–3)

The letters follow a standard template, with eight components: address ("to the angel of the church in"); command to write; "thus says" (NASB: "says this") formula; identification of the speaker; description of the church's situation, introduced by "I know"; call to repentance or faithfulness, reinforced by threat or promise; summons to hear; and promise to the victor.[2] Some of these elements warrant special attention before we survey the letters individually.

The command to write and the "thus says" formula make each letter both a written and a spoken communication. The command to write echoes instructions already recorded (Rev. 1:11, 19). The "thus says" (literally, "such things says X") formula often appears in the Greek version of the Old Testament in the expression "thus says the LORD," which introduces prophetic oracles (e.g., Amos 1:6, 9, 11).[3] The same formula introduced the edicts of Persian kings. For example, the edict of Cyrus authorizing the reconstruction of Israel's temple begins, "Thus says Cyrus king of Persia" (2 Chron. 36:23).[4] David E. Aune comments,

---

2. David E. Aune, "The Form and Function of the Proclamations to the Seven Churches (Revelation 2–3)," *NTS* 36 (1990): 184.

3. Ibid., 187–88.

4. Ibid., 189. The LXX rendering of "thus says" is *tade legei,* as in the letters of Rev. 2–3. Aune also cites Esdr. 2:3; Jud. 2:5; Esth. 3:13; and extrabiblical Persian documents.

John has used this form to create prophetic proclamations issued by the King of kings and Lord of lords to his subjects. John has consciously employed the form of the royal or imperial edict as part of his strategy to emphasize the fact that Christ is the true king in contrast to the Roman emperor who is both a clone and tool of Satan.[5]

The identification of the speaker in each letter repeats a characteristic introduced in the first chapter, especially the opening vision of the Son of Man (Rev. 1:9–20). Christ identifies himself to each church in terms appropriate to the congregation and its struggle. The church at Ephesus must repent of lovelessness, lest its lampstand be removed by the One who walks among the lampstands (2:1, 5). The suffering church at Philadelphia needs to see its Savior as holding not only death's key but also David's key, giving his church "an open door which no one can shut" (3:7–8; cf. 1:18).

The description of the church's situation is the heart of each letter. Introduced by the preface "I know," it shows the implication of the Son of Man's position "in the middle of the lampstands" (Rev. 1:13). Because he is not an absentee Ruler but one present with his churches, he knows their deeds, tribulation, poverty, love, faith, service, and perseverance. For five of the seven, Jesus' description begins with commendation for their faithfulness. For three of these five, however, Jesus' commendation is balanced with rebuke, introduced by "but I have against you." The churches in Smyrna and Philadelphia receive no rebuke but only encouragement to endure. Jesus' "I know" in the letters to Sardis and Laodicea introduces his negative evaluation of these churches, whose appearance belies reality. Sardis is reputed to have life but is dead, while Laodicea, thinking itself affluent, cannot see its real destitution.

The summons to hear refrain ("He who has an ear, let him hear what the Spirit says to the churches") is as invariable as the "thus says" formula. Both imply that Revelation's message is received by an audience through hearing and taking its words to heart (cf. 1:3). This

---

5. Ibid., 204. John would insist that the strategy behind the "thus says" formula originated not with himself but with the Son of Man, who dictated these letters as divine oracles and royal edicts.

refrain echoes Jesus' challenge to those who heard his parables (Mark 4:9, 23). Like parables, John's visions speak in symbols that demand decoding, and this calls for a humble openness to receive the Word and meditate on its meaning. All the churches must listen to all the letters, for each message to a particular congregation is what the Spirit says to the churches in general. These seven churches of Asia Minor represent the totality of Christ's churches, scattered across the world and over time, and their problems are symptomatic of those confronting churches in all times and places.

The promises to the victor point forward to Revelation's closing visions of the victory of the Word/Lamb and the presentation of his bride. Those who overcome will share in Christ's iron-scepter authority over the nations and his royal throne (Rev. 19:15; 20:4, 11). He will protect them from the second death (20:6). They will have a place in the temple, the new Jerusalem (21:2–3), where they will eat from the tree of life (22:2). Purity in the face of temptation and persistence in the face of oppression are motivated by the hope of the new heavens and earth, in which we will see his face and he will wipe every tear from our eyes.

Two principles of organization dictate the order in which the seven churches are addressed. On the one hand, the order is simply geographical: the letters come in the order of the route to be followed by a courier bearing this precious message from Ephesus, the closest major city to Patmos, northward along the coast through Smyrna to Pergamum, and then turning inland to Thyatira and proceeding southward on the interior road network through Sardis and Philadelphia to Laodicea. On the other hand, the order also reflects a thematic arrangement. This thematic organization is signaled by the reversal of the order of the summons to hear and the promise to the victor beginning with the middle letter in the seven, the letter addressed to Thyatira. The letters are grouped in two triads, with the longest of the seven, Thyatira, serving as the hinge between the triads. In the first triad (Ephesus, Smyrna, Pergamum) the summons to hear precedes the promise to the victor; in the central letter (Thyatira) and the second triad (Sardis, Philadelphia, Laodicea) the order of these two elements is reversed. Within each triad the central letter (Smyrna,

Philadelphia) contains commendation without rebuke, reference to opposition from those who falsely claim to be Jews, and the promise of a crown. The opening and closing letters of the second triad (Sardis, Laodicea) are those in which the dominant tone is rebuke.[6]

The variation of content from one letter to the next shows that Jesus knows the diverse situations of his congregations, but the call to hear what the Spirit says to the churches shows the unity of the church throughout the world.

Ephesus: Discernment without Love (2:1–7)

Ephesus was famous for its temple dedicated to Artemis, the virgin huntress of Greek mythology.[7] The temple's extensive land holdings and banking reserves established its economic dominance in Ephesus and its environs. Miniature terra cotta copies of the goddess's image found throughout the Mediterranean region suggest that the temple was a magnet of religious tourism (see Acts 19:23–41). Ephesus was a center of learning with an impressive library, and it was a center of occult arts. Ancient writers mention so-called Ephesian letters, papyri containing magical incantations (see Acts 19:13–20).[8] If there was any city in which the church needed spiritual discernment, it was Ephesus.

Discernment is the very quality for which Jesus commends the Ephesian church: "you cannot tolerate evil men, and you put to the test those who call themselves apostles, and they are not, and you have found them to be false" (Rev. 2:2). "Yet this you do have, that

6. Albert Vanhoye, *Structure and Message of the Epistle to the Hebrews,* Subsidia Biblica 12 (Rome: Pontifical Biblical Institute, 1989), "Excursus: A Concentric Structure in the Apocalypse," 41–44.

7. It has been speculated that when Artemis worship traveled east to Asia Minor, the image of the goddess as virgin huntress was replaced by fertility themes associated with indigenous Asian goddesses, but archaeological and literary evidence seems to discredit this theory. See S. M. Baugh, "A Foreign World: Ephesus in the First Century," in *Women in the Church: A Fresh Analysis of 1 Timothy 2:9–15,* ed. Andreas J. Köstenberger, Thomas R. Schreiner, and H. Scott Baldwin (Grand Rapids: Baker, 1995), 13–52, especially 28–32.

8. Philo *Symposiaca* 7.5; Clement of Alexandria *Stromateis* 5.8.46.

you hate the deeds of the Nicolaitans, which I also hate" (2:6). The apostle Paul had urged the elders of this church to exercise discernment, recognizing that "from among your own selves men will arise, speaking perverse things, to draw away the disciples after them" (Acts 20:30). Later he left Timothy at Ephesus to "instruct certain men not to teach strange doctrines, nor to pay attention to myths and endless genealogies" (1 Tim. 1:3–4). Paul's protectiveness had borne good fruit. The Ephesians refused to tolerate counterfeit apostles and other purveyors of deceit. The church's intolerance was as politically incorrect in the midst of ancient pluralism as it would be today;[9] but it reflected Jesus' intolerance of poisonous lies and of liars who prey on his sheep (Acts 20:29). Jesus shares this church's hatred of the Nicolaitans' deeds.

In the letter to Pergamum (Rev. 2:14–15) the Nicolaitans are compared with Balaam, who, after failing to pronounce a prophetic curse against Israel, recommended to King Balak of Moab a different strategy to defeat God's people: estrange them from their divine Protector by luring them into immorality and idolatry (Num. 25; 31:16). This is the threat—using the same weapons, sex and idolatry—that the Nicolaitans posed for the churches of Asia Minor. But the church at Ephesus saw through their ruse, reacting with holy hatred.[10]

"The One who holds the seven stars, . . . who walks among the seven golden lampstands," (Rev. 2:1) does, however, find a serious

---

9. Robert L. Wilken, *Remembering the Christian Past* (Grand Rapids: Eerdmans, 1995), 27–28: "The oldest and most enduring criticism of Christianity is an appeal to religious pluralism. . . . In the face of what he took to be Christian exclusivism, Symmachus defended a genial toleration of differing ways to the divine. . . . [Even earlier] in Porphyry's view, it was arrogant for Christians to think that men and women have had access to God only since the coming of Christ. 'No teaching,' he writes, 'has yet been established which offers a *universal* way for the liberation of the soul'" (emphasis in original).

10. The Christians at Ephesus were also noteworthy for their "wearying toil" (*kopos*), which had not caused them to "grow weary" (*kopiaō;* 2:3), and for their perseverance in response to sufferings. Even though the Ephesians "cannot endure evil men," they "have endured for [his] name's sake" (the Greek verb is *bastazō* in both clauses). Their endurance is in response to persecution (2:3–4; cf. John 15:21; Acts 5:41).

flaw in this hard-working, tireless, enduring, discerning, truth-loving, lie-hating congregation: "I have this against you, that you have left your first love" (2:4). This "first love" was a height from which the church had fallen and to which it must return if its lampstand was not to be removed (2:5). Is Jesus rebuking their loss of love for himself, a waning of the devotion that characterizes new converts? In Jeremiah 2:2–3 the Lord reminds Israel of their honeymoon in the wilderness, calling his bride to the exclusive love she had for him then. But Jesus' rebuke to Ephesus is not like Jeremiah's accusation against Israel, for Jeremiah contrasts Israel's early love for the Lord to her later adultery with idols (Jer. 2:4–13). Idolatry is not the Ephesian church's problem. In other churches Jesus will identify classic symptoms of declining love for himself: idolatry (= adultery), lukewarm self-reliance, and tolerance of error. He finds none of these symptoms in Ephesus.

It is therefore more likely that the first love lost in Ephesus was love for other people. The noun *love* appears in Revelation only here and in Jesus' commendation of the church at Thyatira, where one pair of qualities, "love and faith," is made concrete in a second pair, "service and perseverance" (Rev. 2:19). As perseverance under persecution demonstrates faith, so service shows love. Jesus had predicted that persecution would tempt people to apostatize, to betray others, or to withdraw from others in suspicious hatred; and that false teaching would mislead others. Attacked on all sides, "most people's love will grow cold" (Matt. 24:10–12). An embattled church, surrounded by enemies, can turn inward in self-protection and suspicion. The remedy is a repentance that involves doing "the deeds you did at first" (Rev. 2:5). This command confirms the focus of first love on other people, for in John's writings the proof of love is found in deeds of service to others (1 John 3:16–19). Paul also had emphasized the balance of truth and love that makes the church grow (e.g., "speaking the truth in love," Eph. 4:15). Having heeded the apostles' emphasis on truth, this church had slipped off balance by neglecting love. Unless corrected, the loss would prove lethal to the church's light-bearing mission in its city.[11]

11. G. K. Beale, *The Book of Revelation*, NIGTC (Grand Rapids: Eerdmans, 1999), 230–31, argues that the first love now lost by the Ephesians was neither for Christ

Jesus' last word to Ephesus, however, is not threat but promise: the victor will eat from the tree of life in the paradise of God (Rev. 2:7). In this first letter the painful memory of paradise lost (Gen. 3:22–24) is transformed into hope, as the promise points ahead to the tree of life in the new Jerusalem, bearing a different crop each month and healing the nations through its leaves (Rev. 22:1–2). The great temple of Artemis at Ephesus was built on the site of an ancient tree-shrine, and the image of the date palm symbolized the goddess and her city, Ephesus.[12] But Jesus excels Artemis, for he promises to those who overcome, through truth expressed in love, access to a tree that yields endless delight and eternal life.

Smyrna: The Riches of Poverty (2:8–11)

Paradox is vivid in the letter to Smyrna, one of Jesus' two blameless churches. The Smyrnan Christians are poor, yet they are rich. Their opponents claim to be Jews but are Satan's synagogue. The victor who is faithful to the extremity of death is promised a crown of life and safety from the second death. This promise is secured by the One who is Israel's eternal refuge ("first and last," echoing Isa. 44:6; 48:12) and yet is also the suffering savior who "was dead, and has come to life" (Rev. 2:8).

Suffering and faithfulness fit the church that lives in a city such as Smyrna. The city's name was identified with mourning through association with the embalming spice, myrrh (Greek *smyrna* in John 19:39; Matt. 2:11), and through a legend that the poet Homer had died there.[13] Smyrna was proud of its history of faithful loyalty to political and military allies, most recently to Rome, marked as early as

---

nor for one another but for the world that needs the gospel witness (hence the reference in this letter to the churches' role as lampstands). Since believers' love for each other is integral to the church's witness to the world (John 17:21–23), there seems no need or warrant for distinguishing these two objects of love from each other in Rev. 2:4.

12. Colin J. Hemer, *The Letters to the Seven Churches of Asia in Their Local Setting,* JSNT Supplement 11 (Sheffield: JSOT Press, 1986), 44–47.

13. Ibid., 58–59, 64, citing Plutarch *Sertorius* 1.3 for the legend about Homer.

195 B.C. by the construction of Asia Minor's first temple dedicated to Rome's expanding power.[14]

The Smyrnan church's tribulation and poverty resulted from physical and economic assaults, which will be symbolized in the beast that attacks the saints and makes submission to his "mark" the condition for enjoying the prosperity of his evil empire (Rev. 13:7, 16–17). This church's affliction was instigated by slanderous accusations brought by "those who say they are Jews and are not, but are a synagogue of Satan" (2:9; 3:9). Though ethnically descended from Israel's patriarchs, the opponents' actions show that they are not God's people but Satan's synagogue. God shows covenant faithfulness to families through the generations, but in the last analysis the people of God are defined Christocentrically, not genealogically. The issue is not birth from the flesh but birth from the Spirit (John 3:6), just as the circumcision that marks God's people is not a fleshly surgery but a cleansing of the heart by the Spirit (Rom. 2:28–29; cf. Phil. 3:2–3). Gentiles, once not a people, have been called to become "a chosen race, a royal priesthood, a holy nation, a people for God's own possession" (1 Peter 2:9–10; 1:18). Titles that once set Israel apart (Exod. 19:5–6) now belong to all who belong to Jesus, who abide in him as branches in the true vine, bearing fruit pleasing to the Father (John 15:1–8; Isa. 5:1–7). Although the apostles often were welcomed initially by the Jewish communities of the dispersion (Acts 13:5, 15–42; 14:1; 17:2, 10–11; 18:4), in one city after another their message of a crucified Messiah and his welcome to pagans apart from circumcision led to expulsion from the synagogue (e.g., Acts 13:44–45; 18:12–13; cf. Heb. 13:12–14). In a culture that prized social stability and viewed new religious movements as political threats, Christians pushed out from the umbrella of established Judaism would be exposed to suspicion from neighbors and intimidation by local officials.

Imprisonment awaited the church at Smyrna, but Jesus assures his faithful ones that the tribulation will be brief, a mere "ten days" (Rev. 2:10).[15] Roman authorities used incarceration not for long-term con-

14. Ibid., 70–71.
15. "Ten days" had functioned as a brief period of "testing" of a different sort for Daniel, Hananiah, Mishael, and Azariah in the Babylonian court (Dan. 1:12–16).

tainment but for short-term custody of those awaiting trial or the sentence of death.[16] Since Jesus' prediction of coming affliction closes with the exhortation "Be faithful until death," the release that he promises after the "ten days" may not be a return to freedom on Smyrna's streets but something better: martyrdom—the apparent defeat that is, paradoxically, the supreme victory. The "crown of life" is the laurel wreath that honors the triumphant athlete when the contest is completed (1 Cor. 9:25; James 1:12; cf. 2 Tim. 4:6–8). It also has overtones of royal authority (Rev. 4:4, 10; 6:2; 12:1; 14:14). The Smyrnan martyrs are a preview of the host of martyrs, slain for the testimony of Jesus and God's word, who share in the first resurrection and enjoy Christ's protection from the second death (2:11; 20:4–6).

Pergamum: Steadfast in the Shadow of Satan's Throne (2:12–17)

To the church at Pergamum Jesus identifies himself as "the One who has the sharp two-edged sword" (Rev. 2:12). This should have special relevance to a church that, though withstanding persecution from without, had condoned the infection of Nicolaitan error within. If the church does not repent and fulfill its disciplinary responsibilities, Jesus will come and "make war against them with the sword of My mouth" (2:16).

Pergamum had once been the capital of the Roman province of Asia, but Caesar Augustus had made Ephesus the center of the financial and administrative functions for the province. The city had a temple dedicated "to the divine Augustus and the goddess Roma" (built in 29 B.C.),[17] another temple and related medical college dedicated to Asklepios the Savior (patron god of healing, symbolized by a serpent), and an enormous altar to Zeus the Savior on the city's highest point. Any of these idolatrous monuments—certainly the three in combination—

16. Hemer, *Letters,* 78.

17. Long before the Romans arrived, Pergamum had institutionalized the worship of its rulers: Attalus I (ruled 241–197 B.C.) took the divine title *savior,* and his son Eumenes II (197–159 B.C.) referred to himself not only as "savior" but also as "god" (Hemer, *Letters,* 82).

would justify Jesus' pronouncement that this church dwells "where Satan's throne is . . . where Satan dwells" (2:13). In this hostile environment the church receives Jesus' praise for holding fast to his name and not denying their faith in him, "even in the days of Antipas, My witness, My faithful one, who was killed among you" (2:13). The congregation had tasted martyrdom, for Antipas had paid the ultimate price to maintain his testimony, and in so doing he became a reflection of his Master, the preeminently "faithful witness" (1:5; cf. 1 Tim. 6:12–13). The circumstances of Antipas's death are veiled in mystery, but it was apparently related to the presence of "Satan's throne" in the city. The persecution of Christians instigated by the emperor Nero in the 60s was limited to Rome and its environs. Three decades later Domitian conferred upon himself the title "Our Lord and God,"[18] but even then no empirewide policy mandated the execution of Christians. Nevertheless those steeped in Rome's civil religion, especially Asians accustomed to deified monarchs, would view with suspicion anyone who declined to honor the emperor as Lord and God. Such simmering suspicion could boil over into mob violence or arbitrary bureaucratic decisions to teach such troublemakers a lesson in loyalty. When Satan flexed his strength on the site of his throne, silencing Antipas's witness by bloodshed, the church stood fast.

While standing against Satan's frontal assault, however, the church had let a dangerous enemy slip through the back door: the Nicolaitans. During Israel's wilderness wanderings, God had prevented the prophet Balaam from cursing the Israelites (Num. 22–24), so Balaam found a subtler avenue of ambush, advising Balak to send Moabite women to seduce Israelite men into sexual immorality and idolatry. By alienating Israel from the Lord, Balaam lured God's people into a defeat greater than Moab could have inflicted. The Lord warred against Israel through a plague, and twenty-four thousand died (Num. 25:1–9). The women of Moab "caused the sons of Israel, through the counsel of Balaam, to trespass against the LORD in the matter of Peor, so the plague was among the congregation of the LORD" (Num. 31:16). Now

18. Suetonius *Domitian* 13, cited in Jürgen Roloff, *The Revelation of John: A Continental Commentary* (Minneapolis: Fortress, 1993), 9.

the Nicolaitans at Pergamum were replicating Balaam's strategy, luring Christians into sexual and spiritual infidelity (Rev. 2:14).

Confusion regarding food sacrificed to idols and appropriate sexual conduct was widespread among early Christians who had converted from paganism. The church at Corinth, across the Aegean Sea from Asia, needed instruction on sexual issues (1 Cor. 5:1–13; 6:12–7:41) and on food offered to idols (8:1–11:1). Although the food's having been offered to idols doesn't defile it (8:4–7; 10:25–26), the social context can turn the innocent act of eating into serious sin, either by sending mixed signals (8:7–13; 10:23–33) or even by sharing "the table of demons" at banquets in honor of pagan deities (10:14–22). With respect to meat offered to idols, Paul issued the terse command, "Flee idolatry" (10:14), just as he had commanded, "Flee immorality" (6:18). Dabbling with idolatry or immorality denies that we belong to Jesus, our jealous husband who tolerates no rivals (6:13, 19–20; 10:22).

Only some at Pergamum adhered to the Nicolaitan error, but the whole church must repent (Rev. 2:16). This repentance would mean exercising church discipline, refusing to tolerate Nicolaitan teaching. The church and its leaders must confront the Nicolaitans, as Paul instructed Timothy: "with gentleness correcting those who are in opposition; if perhaps God may grant them repentance leading to the knowledge of the truth, and they may come to their senses and escape from the snare of the devil" (2 Tim. 2:25–26). If they do not, "I am coming to you quickly, and I will make war against [the Nicolaitans] with the sword of My mouth" (Rev. 2:16). Not all of the promises and threats of Jesus' coming in Revelation refer to the second coming. Here Jesus is not saying that his bodily return to earth will come soon if the Nicolaitans fail to repent but will be postponed if they turn around. Rather, since he already walks among the lampstands, he will "come quickly" by intervening in the church's life through his providential control of events and the work of his Spirit to call the Nicolaitans to account. When the Corinthian church abused the Lord's Supper, the result was illness and death in the congregation. Those providential instruments of discipline were motivated by Christ's love and directed to their good, "so that we may not be condemned with the world" (1 Cor. 11:30–32). Some similar visitation of purifying judgment would sweep through the church at Pergamum, unless church discipline and repentance ensued.

In Pergamum the victor is the believer who not only stands fast in the face of external pressure "where Satan's throne is" but also resists temptations to conform for the sake of personal convenience. Jesus promises hidden manna and a white stone, on which is written a name known only to the recipient (Rev. 2:17). Manna was the bread of heaven that nourished Israel in the desert; and Revelation portrays the church's life between Christ's ascension and his return as a sojourn in the wilderness, in which God sustains it (12:6, 14–17). Moses had shown that the manna pointed beyond itself, teaching that "man does not live by bread alone, but man lives by everything that proceeds out of the mouth of the LORD" (Deut. 8:3; Matt. 4:4). Jesus announced that the manna pointed to his sacrificed body as the true "bread out of heaven" (John 6:32–35, 48–51). Though the church's circumstances seem as desolate as a desert, Jesus sustains it by his word, revealing himself.

The white stone points to the climax of the church's pilgrimage. In the ancient world white stones were used for various purposes,[19] but in Revelation the name that the stone bears is more important than the connotations of its color. The name is known only to the recipient, just as the name of the Word of God, who rides a white horse, is known only to himself (Rev. 19:12–13). The name is a shared secret between the Lord and the recipient, blending mystery and disclosure. The victor's "new name" could be his transformed identity in Christ, as the renaming of Abram to Abraham and of Simon to Peter signaled their transformation by God's power and grace. To the one who holds fast his name (2:13) Jesus gives a new name, to mark us as his property and to reshape our identity to fit his perfection: "For those whom He foreknew, He also predestined to become conformed to the image of His Son, so that He might be the firstborn among many brethren" (Rom. 8:29).

19. Hemer, *Letters,* 96–102, documents among the uses of white stones: tokens signifying a juror's vote to acquit, admission to entertainment events, honorable discharge from gladiatorial combat, or initiation into the worship of Asklepios, and magical amulets bearing divine names.

Thyatira: Love without Discernment (2:18–29)

"The longest and most difficult of the seven letters is addressed to the least known, least important, and least remarkable of the cities."[20] Not only is the letter to Thyatira the longest, but it is also the centerpiece of the seven. The city was insignificant, but Jesus' words and actions in the church there had something of central importance to teach all his churches.

Thyatira had been a military outpost on the western border of the kingdom of Seleucus, who ruled from Antioch in Syria. Located in the middle of a broad valley, Thyatira was an easy target for capture, so it had changed hands repeatedly in the ebb and flow of eastern Mediterranean politics between Alexander's death and the rise of Rome. Lacking religious and political significance, Thyatira's identity was molded by commerce and manufacturing industries, each dominated by a trade guild dedicated to a patron god or goddess. Among the trades most in evidence in the archaeological remains are metalworking and the dying of fabrics. Lydia, who became a believer at Philippi in Macedonia, was an exporter of purple cloth from Thyatira (Acts 16:14). The influence of the economic sphere of life, exemplified in the trade guilds, challenges the church's fidelity.

Jesus identifies himself to this church as "the Son of God" (Rev. 2:18). This title alludes to Psalm 2:7–9, as does the promise that the victor will share his authority over the nations, ruling them with a rod of iron (Rev. 2:26–27). Jesus' burning holiness is manifest in "eyes like a flame of fire" and feet like burnished bronze.[21] This church needs to meet the searching gaze of those flaming eyes, for its naive abdication of the responsibility to discern has made it necessary for Jesus to show "that I am He who searches the minds and hearts" (2:23).

The church at Thyatira is strong in love and faith, in service and perseverance (Rev. 2:19). Thyatira is strong not only where other churches are strong (persevering faith, 2:2–3, 13) but also where the Ephesian

---

20. Ibid., 106.
21. Thyatiran bronze workers no doubt could envision the appearance of Jesus' feet "like burnished bronze" (Rev. 2:18), "when it has been caused to glow in a furnace" (1:15).

church is weak: in love demonstrated in service (2:5).[22] Whereas Ephesus needed to return to its "first deeds," Thyatira had so grown in faith and love that its recent deeds had excelled those done at first.

The flaw in the Thyatirans' growing faith and love was naïveté, a lack of discernment that took people at face value rather than putting them to the test of truth. Jesus says to the church at Thyatira, "I love your love, but I hate your tolerance." The target of their tolerance and Jesus' disapproval is a woman whom Jesus calls Jezebel. This is not her real name, any more than Balaam had taught the Nicolaitans or the harlot of Revelation 17 is Babylon, the Chaldean capital on the Euphrates. The Thyatiran prophetess, however, is working the same mischief in the first-century church that Jezebel, princess of Sidon and wife of Ahab, had worked in Israel centuries earlier. The ancient Jezebel wielded her influence to seduce Israelites into Baalism (1 Kings 16:30–33; 2 Kings 9:22, 30–37). So also this prophetess is seducing Jesus' servants to "commit acts of immorality and eat things sacrificed to idols" (Rev. 2:20). Despising the gospel of Christ because it is so simple and so public, leaving no secrets hidden from the uninitiated, the prophetess promised insight into "deep things," which Jesus labels Satan's deep things.

The combination of sexual immorality and food sacrificed to idols may suggest a setting of trade-guild banquets, held in honor of the guild's patron deity, especially in a city as dependent on manufacturing as Thyatira was. To opt out of such events, in which social and business purposes blended, would mean forfeiting social acceptance and risking economic loss. Perhaps among the deep things disseminated by the prophetess was the insight that bodily behavior is spiritually insignificant, so that those in the know could participate in idolatrous guild feasts, and even their sensual excesses, with spiritual impunity. Such a Jezebel was more dangerous to Jesus' servants than a military oppressor, because her secrets drive a wedge between God's people and the Lord.

The prophetess is a local expression of the harlot Babylon, who is to appear in Revelation 17. As the harlot seduced kings, nations, and merchants to commit adultery with her (17:2, 4; 18:3), so Jezebel's

22. Genuine love will be shown in action, not merely in words (1 John 3:17–18).

devotees in Thyatira are "those who commit adultery with her" (2:22). As the harlot's fall would cast her lovers into grief (18:9–11), so Jezebel's fall will entail tribulation for her paramours (2:22). Like the harlot, the Thyatiran prophetess advocated an adultery that was sexual and spiritual. How convenient, in a city dominated by trade guilds, for a prophetess to reveal the deep secret that Christians need not suffer loss by refraining from the guilds' immoral and idolatrous celebrations! The harlot offers the profits of participating in the economy that flows from Rome. Her siren song sounds sweet, but in her chalice is the blood of Jesus' witnesses (17:6). Materialism, no less than persecution, is the serpent's weapon of war against Christ's church.

Jesus had warned Jezebel and given her time to repent. But Jezebel had not seen that God's patience should produce not complacency but repentance (Rom. 2:4; 2 Peter 3:9). Jesus had given the church time to show real love to this Jezebel, her "lovers," and her "children"[23] by refusing to tolerate her deception. But this church, commended for love, had failed to speak the hard truth in love (Eph. 4:15). Church discipline and Jesus' demand of exclusive loyalty looked narrow to the pluralistic culture of the Hellenistic world, as it does in our tolerant and relativistic day; but church discipline, when pursued with biblical motives and methods, expresses Jesus' love for his bride.

Though the congregation has failed to discipline Jezebel, Jesus will not let spiritual adultery go unchecked. Because her opportunity for repentance is past, Jesus will cast the prophetess on a bed of sickness, her paramours into great anguish, and her children to death (2:22–23). He will teach a vital lesson not to the Thyatiran church alone; rather, "all the churches will know that I am He who searches the minds and hearts" (2:23). The echo of the Lord's words to Jeremiah is clear: "I, the LORD, search the heart, I test the mind, even to give to each man

23. Her children are not her physical offspring, executed for their mother's sins (Ezek. 18), although God would be right to treat the sin-stained human family thus (2 Sam. 12:14–23). In the symbolic vocabulary of Revelation, Jezebel's children are her adulterous lovers, who, when she has secured her grip on their hearts, become so enmeshed in her corruption that their identity becomes inseparable from hers— as the "children" of the heavenly woman (= the people of God) are the members of the people of God viewed as individuals (Rev. 12:17; cf. 2 John 1; 4).

according to his ways" (Jer. 17:10). Through insignificant Thyatira Jesus will show all churches that he does not tolerate undiscerning tolerance, which invites the Serpent's venom into his Body.

The victor who shares Jesus' intolerant love will share Jesus' messianic authority as the enthroned Son of God of Psalm 2 (Rev. 2:26–27). Though Thyatira had been a pawn in the tug of war of regional politics, Jesus promises to Christians in this town a share in his authority over the nations. "He will rule them with a rod of iron" describes Christ, the warrior Word of God in Revelation 19:15; but here it describes the victor with whom Jesus shares his power. Then Jesus promises something even better: "I will give him the morning star" (2:28). In a vision Balaam had seen a star emerging from Jacob, a scepter rising out of Israel to crush Moab (Num. 24:17). The star-scepter symbolized a warrior king, who identifies himself in Revelation: "I, Jesus, have sent My angel to testify to you these things for the churches. I am the root and the descendant of David, the bright morning star" (Rev. 22:16). Jesus promises his people not merely dominion but a better treasure, a deeper joy: himself.

Sardis: False Name and True (3:1–6)

Sardis was a city with a golden past and misplaced security. The gold in Sardis's past was reputed to extend back to King Midas of Phrygia, who, as the story went, "rid himself of the Golden Touch by washing it off in the springs of Pactolus," a stream near Sardis that had gold dust in its silt.[24] Later Sardis was the capital of King Croesus, whose wealth was also legendary.[25] Croesus' reign ended, however, with an event notorious as an example of misplaced security. As the forces of the Persian Empire pushed westward, Cyrus and his troops caught Croesus' army by surprise in the field of battle and then besieged Sardis. The fortress of Sardis was surrounded on three sides by sheer cliffs, so apparently impregnable that "to capture the acropolis of Sardis" became a maxim for achieving an impossible feat.[26] Herodotus recounts,

---

24. Hemer, *Letters,* 130–31.
25. Ibid., 131–32.
26. Lucian, cited in Hemer, *Letters,* 256 n. 20.

however, that on the fourteenth day of the siege a few Persian troops climbed the cliff at a point "where no guard was stationed, for there was no fear that it would ever be captured at that place, for the acropolis is sheer and impregnable there."[27] The city fell quickly into Persian hands. Ancient commentators blamed Sardis's tragic fall on "a lack of vigilance in its defenders."[28] Though the story was well known, the church in Sardis had not heeded the lesson of Croesus' misjudgment.

Jesus diagnoses this church's problem as a contradiction between name and reality. Though it had a "name" (= reputation) for being alive, this church was dead. At least, it was all but dead, for some remnant of life hung on by a thread, keeping hope barely alive (Rev. 3:2). Some "names" (= persons) in the church had maintained pure devotion to Jesus, walking in undefiled garments through a polluted society in anticipation of the promise of walking with Jesus in white wedding garments (3:4–5; cf. 19:8). Nevertheless the dominant tone of Jesus' words to Sardis is somber warning to a slumbering church.

The letter pinpoints no specific cause of sleep unto death. No Nicolaitans were luring Christ's servants in Sardis into immorality and idolatry. No Balaam-like prophet or Jezebel-like prophetess misled the unwary. Although Sardis is known to have had a strong Jewish community and vibrant paganism (the city's patroness goddess was Cybele), the letter mentions no external sources of intimidation, social rejection, or persecution, such as other churches encountered from Satan's throne or Satan's synagogues. Nevertheless this church was spiritually unconscious. Jesus' repeated exhortation to "wake up" and his threat to break in on the congregation's comatose comfort "like a thief" show that Sardis had lost consciousness of Jesus' future return and its present implications (Rev. 3:2–3). The sleeping majority had also forgotten grace received in the past and the motivation for purity that grace supplies (3:4).[29] Sardis had forgotten that it is engaged in spiritual, holy war. Jesus' summons to "wake up" has mili-

---

27. Herodotus 1.84, cited in Hemer, *Letters,* 132.

28. Hemer, *Letters,* 133.

29. Pure garments symbolize hearts cleansed from defiling guilt by the Lamb's blood (Rev. 7:14) but also upright actions that flow from hearts freed from sin's enslavement (19:8).

tary overtones not only in view of Sardis's sad history but also in the term's use elsewhere in the New Testament (1 Peter 5:8; cf. Matt. 24:42; Eph. 6:18).

Jesus calls himself "he who has the seven Spirits of God and the seven stars" (Rev. 3:1). The seven Spirits of God are God's one Spirit, who is limitless, knowing all, present everywhere, and almighty. In Revelation 5 John will see the Spirit symbolized as the Lamb's seven eyes, which "are the seven Spirits of God, sent out into all the earth" (5:6; cf. Zech. 3:9; 4:10). The Son of Man who sees his churches also holds their identity (stars/angels) securely in his hand. This church has underrated Jesus' present knowledge and therefore faces a shocking awakening at his coming.

Repentance, for Sardis, means awakening: a return to consciousness about their danger and a remembrance of "what you have received and heard," the gospel and the grace it conveys (Rev. 3:3). In the parables of his sudden return Jesus promised that those who remain vigilant, like slaves awaiting their master's unpredictable arrival, will receive the master's good pleasure and hospitality (Luke 12:35–38); but he also warned that his return would surprise the unwary like a burglar's intrusion (Luke 12:39–40). His "thief in the night" simile permeates New Testament teaching (1 Thess. 5:2–4; 2 Peter 3:10; Rev. 16:15). Since we cannot predict the time of Jesus' coming, those not living in constant preparedness will be caught off guard.

The pure garments of Sardis's faithful few foreshadow the white robes they will wear to the wedding (Rev. 3:4–5). This link between purity in the present and white robes in the future shows that the life motivated by hope is shaped by the goal for which we wait. Because victors hope for white wedding garments, they strive for purity here and now. "We know that when He appears, we will be like Him, because we will see Him just as He is. And everyone who has this hope fixed on Him purifies himself, just as He is pure" (1 John 3:2–3).

Jesus not only clothes his pure ones but also knows them by name. The majority in Sardis had a name for being alive although they were dead, but Jesus assures his minority that he knows their names truly and has inscribed them permanently in his book of life (Rev. 3:5). This citizen-register of the people of God is mentioned throughout the Old Testament, often to show that physical descent from the fathers does not guarantee access to the final assembly that will celebrate God's glory and grace eternally (Deut. 32:32–33; Ps. 69:28; Dan. 12:1). Erasure from God's book was the curse prayed by Jews on apostates, including the "Nazarenes" who followed Jesus.[30] But Jesus asserts that his victors' names will never be erased from the book. Only for those whose names are in this book will the last judgment mean joyful vindication rather than shameful destruction (Rev. 20:15), and only these may enter the new Jerusalem (21:27). How can the mere appearance of one's name in the book of life counterbalance the damning evidence contained in the books of our deeds (20:12)? This book belongs to the Lamb who has been slain in sacrifice for those listed in it (13:8). "Schindler's List" was, as the accountant Stern rightly said, life itself to the Jews rescued from Nazi death camps as they were registered to work in Schindler's factories; and their rescue cost Schindler dearly. But the drama of his courage and cunning pales beside the price paid for each name inscribed in the Lamb's list of life: their robes are whitened by the blood of the Lamb (7:14).

Jesus will speak the victor's name as well as writing it indelibly (Rev. 3:5). In the Gospels Jesus assured those who would confess him before men that he would confess them in the presence of his Father and his angels (Matt. 10:32; Luke 12:8). We glimpse this mutual confession on earth and in heaven, when Stephen, having borne his witness about Jesus, sees heaven opened and the Son of Man standing as witness at God's right hand (Acts 7:56).

Philadelphia: An Open Door (3:7–13)

Sardis and Philadelphia suffered widespread damage from an earthquake during the reign of the emperor Tiberius (A.D. 17). Although Sardis was closer to the epicenter, Philadelphia experienced destruc-

---

30. The twelfth of the Eighteen Benedictions used in synagogues each Sabbath from the end of the first century said: "For the renegades let there be no hope, and may the arrogant kingdom soon be rooted out in our days, and [may] the Nazarenes . . . perish . . . and be blotted out from the book of life and with the righteous may they not be inscribed." C. K. Barrett, *The New Testament Background: Selected Documents,* rev. ed. (1987; San Francisco: Harper & Row, 1995), 211.

tive aftershocks for years afterwards.[31] Roman historians noted the disaster relief granted to Philadelphia in the form of forgiveness from annual tribute and other subsidies.[32] In gratitude for imperial aid the leaders of Philadelphia erected a huge monument to Tiberius and renamed their city Neocaesarea, "Caesar's new city." The newly rebuilt city took a new name to honor its imperial patron and rescuer,[33] but Philadelphia's economic weakness slowed its recovery from the earthquake's devastation and prolonged its dependence on Rome.

To the church in Philadelphia, as to Smyrna, Jesus speaks commendation without rebuke. As in Smyrna, the challenge confronting the Philadelphian church was external opposition from those in the Jewish community who, instead of embracing Jesus the Messiah, had rejected him, proving to be not true Jews but a synagogue of Satan (Rev. 3:9; 2:9). Both of these churches lacked needed resources: the Smyrnan church was poor, and the Philadelphian church had only little power (3:8). Yet each held fast its confession despite adversity. "You have kept the word of My perseverance" (3:10). Despite pressure to renounce their allegiance, the Philadelphian believers had not denied Jesus' name (3:8).

"He who is holy, who is true" speaks to this church (Rev. 3:7). A similar Greek construction in 3:14 means "the faithful and true Witness," so perhaps here we should render Jesus' title "the true holy One." The fire and light radiating from the Son of Man in the opening vision symbolized divine holiness. Jesus alludes to the Old Testament title of Yahweh, the holy One of Israel. In Isaiah 60:14 God promises that his people's oppressors will bow at their feet and acknowledge that they are "the city of the LORD, the Zion of the Holy One of Israel." Likewise, Jesus the true holy One will bring opponents to bow at the church's feet and confess that she is the Lord's beloved (Rev. 3:9; cf. Isa. 43:4).

31. Hemer, *Letters,* 155.
32. Tacitus 2.47.3–4; Suetonius *Tiberius* 48.2; Dio Cassius 57.17.8; Strabo 13.4.8 (Hemer, *Letters,* 154).
33. Hemer, *Letters,* 157. Several decades later "under Vespasian . . . the city took the imperial epithet 'Flavia.' . . . It was a great honour for a city to be permitted to assume such titles, and they bound it closely to the imperial service" (157–58).

The emphasis in Jesus' self-designation falls on the fact that he holds "the key of David," having unchallengeable authority, so that what he opens none can lock and what he locks none can open. In the opening vision the Son of Man held the keys of death and Hades, signifying his right to unlock the grave and release its captives (Rev. 1:18). Here we see his authority over entrance to the messianic kingdom as the royal heir of David (cf. Isa. 22:22). "Those who say they are Jews and are not" may have claimed that the Christians at Philadelphia are locked out from the people of God; but Jesus, not they, holds David's key, the key to the kingdom.

Jesus has put an "open door" before his church by unlocking it with David's key (Rev. 3:8). Many commentators interpret this open door as an opportunity for mission and evangelism, since Paul uses the image in this way (1 Cor. 16:9; 2 Cor. 2:12; Col. 4:3). The context, however, shows that the open door before the Philadelphians is the door into the kingdom of God, which cannot be shut against them even when the "synagogue of Satan" repudiates them. The victor in Philadelphia will enjoy permanent access to God's presence as a pillar built into the structure of God's sanctuary, never to leave his holy presence (Rev. 3:12). The next open door that John will see is the door into heaven, through which John will enter to see the One seated on the throne and the Lamb (4:1). Because Jesus holds David's key, no one can lock Jesus' people out of the city-sanctuary of God.

Yet the door to the Father, which Jesus has opened, is related to our witness. Jesus promises an open door into heaven to those who have kept his word, and he promises that their word of witness will bear fruit even in their enemies. Jesus' words, "I have given [NASB: "put before"] you an open door," are echoed in the next verse, "Behold, I am giving [NASB: "will cause"] some of those from the synagogue of Satan."[34] Since only some of those from Satan's synagogue are given to the church, to bow and confess Jesus' love for it, this promise does not focus on the final, comprehensive vindication of Christ and his own. In that day every knee will bow and *every* tongue confess his lordship (Phil. 2:10–11), and believers will share his do-

---

34. The repetition of the verb *didōmi* is hard to replicate in a natural English translation.

minion (Matt. 19:28; Rev. 2:26; 1 Cor. 6:3). Here, however, Jesus describes a closer, grace-filled foretaste of that day, in which the humiliation of his enemies becomes their salvation. In Isaiah's prophetic imagery the Gentiles were to be saved as they came to bow at Israel's feet and to confess, "Surely, God is with you, and there is none else" (Isa. 45:14; cf. 49:23; 1 Cor. 14:25). Now the tables are turned: It is the multiethnic church to whom Jews will bow, confessing that here alone can the love of Israel's holy One be found. This is how Paul expected his mission to the Gentiles to work: Christ's mercy, extended to the Gentiles in the gospel, evokes envy among Jews, who by God's severe mercy are regrafted by faith into the tree of God's covenant (Rom. 10:19–11:32).

Jesus will reciprocate the Philadelphians' keeping. They have kept his word, and he will keep them "from the hour of testing, that hour which is about to come upon the whole world, to test those who dwell on the earth" (Rev. 3:10). What is this hour? Three features stand out. First is its brevity. In contrast to longer time periods of which we hear later—3½ days, 42 months, 1,000 years—one hour points to a brief time of trauma. Second is its targets. Although its scope is the whole inhabited world,[35] it focuses on "those who dwell on the earth," namely, God's human enemies, who murder the martyrs (6:10; 11:10), worship the beast (13:8), and get drunk on the harlot's wine (17:2). Third is its restraint. Jesus will "keep" his people from this hour of trial. How he will do so is not disclosed. Given Revelation's penchant for paradox and the fact that God promises to protect his church not from suffering but from apostasy, we should not assume that Jesus will keep believers from this trial by removing them from the scene or shielding them from pain.

---

35. John's word is not *gē,* which can mean either "earth" or "land (of Palestine)," but *oikoumenē,* which designates the whole scope of the earth to which human settlement and civilization had reached, or sometimes the whole scope of the Roman Empire (e.g., Luke 2:1). Later in the verse he does speak of "those who dwell on the earth (*gē*)." The interchangeability of *gē* and *oikoumenē* is one indication of the inadequacy the preterist interpretation that limits Revelation's prophecies of judgment to the devastation of Jerusalem and the "land" of Judea, culminating in 70 (e.g., David Chilton, *Days of Vengeance: An Exposition of the Book of Revelation* [Fort Worth: Dominion, 1987]; Kenneth L. Gentry, *Before Jerusalem Fell* [Tyler, Tex.: Institute for Christian Economics, 1989]).

Jesus had prayed, "I do not ask You to take them out of the world, but to keep them from the evil one" (John 17:15). Whatever the hour of trial entails, Christ's people know that no one can snatch us from the almighty hands of Jesus and his Father (John 10:28–29) and that nothing can separate us from God's love (Rom. 8:39).

Unlike his announcement to Pergamum (Rev. 2:16), Jesus' proclamation to Philadelphia, "I am coming quickly" (3:11), is not contingent on the church's response to his warning. The promise here looks beyond his providential interventions throughout history, focusing instead on that final coming of which all others are precursors.

Jesus' promise to the victor blends these present and future dimensions of his protective possessiveness. He will write on the victor "the name of my God, and the name of the city of my God, the new Jerusalem, . . . and My new name" (Rev. 3:12). Although the city of Philadelphia briefly became "new city of Caesar" in tribute to the emperor's patronage, the church in Philadelphia forever bears the name "new city of God." In the new Jerusalem God's servants "will see His face, and His name will be on their foreheads" (22:4). But victors already bear God's name as a seal that shields them from his coming wrath (7:3; 14:1).

Laodicea: The Poverty of Riches (3:14–22)

Laodicea was the most prominent of the three cities of the Lycus Valley, the other two being Colosse and Hierapolis. It was a major center of trade and transportation, located at a crossroads on the highway that reached from Mesopotamia across Asia Minor to the Aegean Sea. Significant features of the city were its robust economy, its medical college, and its water.

Although it sustained major damage from an earthquake in A.D. 60, Laodicea, unlike Philadelphia, declined disaster relief from the emperor. Instead, the Roman historian Tacitus records, "In the same year, Laodicea, one of the famous Asiatic cities, was laid in ruins by an earthquake, but recovered by its own resources, without assistance from ourselves" (*Annals* 14.27.1).[36] Laodicea was a prominent center

---

36. Translation by John Jackson in Tacitus, *Annals,* LCL (Cambridge: Harvard University Press, 1969).

of banking and commerce, and after the earthquake some of its wealthy citizens funded the construction or reconstruction of such public structures as a stadium, a gymnasium, heated and covered walkways and baths, and massive new city gates and towers.[37] Laodicea was also known for textile production, especially black woolen products.

Among its cultural assets was a medical school founded by Zeuxis, a disciple of Herophilus of Chalcedon, "a leading dogmatic physician of the third century BC, who is known to have written on ophthalmology."[38] Ancient sources mention a Phrygian powder that was used to make eye salve, and the medical school at Laodicea was probably involved in developing this and other pharmaceuticals. With its banks, its medical center, and its textile industry, Laodicea hardly seemed to be "poor and blind and naked" (Rev. 3:17).

Laodicea's location in the Lycus River basin was strategic for trade and transportation but far from ideal from the standpoint of a city's need for usable water. Hierapolis, on a plateau some six miles north, had hot springs known for their medicinal value. Colosse, ten miles to the east, received cool, pure drinking water from a nearby mountain stream. Laodicea had neither. The water of the Lycus River was and is "turbid with white mud" and "nauseous and undrinkable."[39] Remains of an aqueduct suggest that water may have been channeled from hot springs five miles south of the city.[40] For a city so affluent in financial resources and self-sufficient in civic spirit, Laodicea ironically lacked a basic resource, water to drink.

The city's self-sufficient affluence was mirrored in the church, which Jesus rebukes for its boast, "I am rich, and have become wealthy, and have need of nothing," and for its blindness to its destitution (Rev. 3:17). This is the only church about which Jesus has nothing good to say. Even Sardis had a few undefiled Christians (3:4), but to the church in Laodicea Jesus must express his love in unmitigated reproof and dis-

---

37. Hemer, *Letters,* 194–95.

38. Ibid., 196.

39. Ibid., 189, citing E. J. Davis, *Anatolica,* (London, 1862), 77; and W. M. Ramsay, *Cities and Bishoprics of Phrygia,* 2 vols. (Oxford: Clarendon, 1895–97), 1:215.

40. Hemer, *Letters,* 188, citing M. J. S. Rudwick and E. M. B. Green, "The Laodicean Lukewarmness," *ExpT* 69 (1957–58): 176–78.

cipline (3:19). As in Sardis, so in Laodicea Jesus mentions no coercion or seduction from pagan idolatry, imperial cult, or synagogue. Nor does he identify a particular theological or ethical threat from within. But Laodicea's boast in its wealth reveals how thoroughly seduced this church has been by the harlot Babylon, who enriches the earth's merchants with her immoral wealth (18:3) and boasts, "I sit as a queen and I am not a widow, and will never see mourning" (18:7). What Jesus finds repugnant—as repugnant as the city's tepid, polluted, nauseating water sources (3:16)—is the church's superficial complacency, resting on the delusion that fiscal affluence will insulate it from need. Laodicea's hallucinations of wealth are symptoms of potentially terminal "affluenza."[41]

The Laodicean church's true situation was not as it seemed, so it needed "the Amen, the faithful and true Witness" to tell it the hard truth (Rev. 3:14). The epistolary doxology had spoken of Jesus as "the faithful witness" (1:5). His reliability in attesting the truth is especially relevant to a church so blinded by smug self-deception. Jesus is uniquely reliable because he is "the Amen," the firm One who fulfills all of God's promises and threats (2 Cor. 1:20). Jesus is also "the Beginning of the creation of God." Paul's letter to the Colossians (also intended indirectly for Laodicea, Col. 4:16) called Christ the "beginning" as the originator and ruler over all creatures great and small (Col. 1:15–18). In Revelation "the beginning," with its complement "the end," expresses the eternity of God, who stands sovereign over history's whole span as "the Alpha and Omega, the first and the last, the beginning and the end" (Rev. 22:13; cf. 21:6). Jesus calls himself "the Beginning" to shame their self-reliance and to turn them to his inexhaustible resources.

---

41. "Affluenza" was coined to describe a late-twentieth-century North American syndrome. Anne Soukhanov defines it as "an array of psychological maladies such as isolation, boredom, passivity and lack of motivation engendered in adults, teenagers and children by the possession of great wealth." And it is "an unhappy condition of overload, debt, anxiety, and waste resulting from the dogged pursuit of more" (John de Graaf, producer of the public broadcasting documentary *Affluenza*). Michael Good, "Affluenza's Gonna Get You," *KPBS on Air* 29, 11 (September 1997): 14–15.

Laodicea's repentance must be expressed in zeal (Rev. 3:19), which will come only when they discover their destitution and Jesus' sufficiency. Jesus' advice is paradoxical: When you see how poor you are, then I counsel you to "buy from me gold refined by fire . . . and white garments . . . and eye salve to anoint your eyes" (3:17–18). How can paupers buy such precious commodities? Jesus echoes the divine Marketer who spoke through Isaiah: "Ho! Every one who thirsts, come to the waters; and you who have no money come, buy and eat. Come, buy wine and milk without money and without cost" (Isa. 55:1). This transaction is not a conventional purchase, for only those who cannot pay may partake. Everything we need must be the free gift of the Beginning of God's creation. Only he can clear our sight, cover our naked shame (Gen. 3:7, 21; Rev. 16:15), and make the poor rich (Matt. 5:3; Luke 1:52–53; James 2:5).

Jesus' sharp rebuke is tough love (Rev. 3:19), "for whom the LORD loves He reproves, even as a father corrects the son in whom he delights" (Prov. 3:12; cf. Heb. 12:6). Jesus' reproof is his warning knock on the door, summoning those with "ears to hear" to jump to attention as servants ready to greet their Master on his return (Rev. 3:21). As Jesus' warning of his coming "like a thief" had alluded to his teaching in Luke 12:39–40, so here his standing at the door and knocking looks back to the same context: "Be like men who are waiting for their master when he returns from the wedding feast, so that they may immediately open the door to him when he comes and knocks" (Luke 12:36). In Luke 12 and in Revelation 3 the stress falls on the privilege of awaiting servants who heed his knock and welcome his entrance: the master will serve dinner to his servants (Luke 12:37) and will dine with them (Rev. 3:20). This dinner is the marriage supper of the Lamb (19:9). Jesus' knock is not that of a homeless traveler, standing outside the locked door of a human heart, seeking shelter.[42] Rather, he is the

---

42. Richard Bauckham, *The Climax of Prophecy: Studies on the Book of Revelation* (Edinburgh: T & T Clark, 1993), 108: "A reference to the parable [of the watchful servants, Luke 12:37–38] eliminates the difficult image of Christ the guest. He is, on the contrary, pictured as the master whose servants are expected to be ready to open to him at his return. The house is his own in which he graciously and remarkably (cf. Luke 17:7–8) condescends to dine with his servants."

master of the house, and he will burst through the door in sovereign judgment (James 5:9). The Laodiceans cannot avert his arrival by ignoring his knock, but their response to his warning will determine whether his entrance brings them the joy of the banquet or the exposure of their shame.

Along with the Master's table fellowship, the victor will share his messianic rule, sitting with him on his throne, even as Jesus in victory shares the Father's throne (Rev. 3:22). Again the promise to the victor pulls our hopes ahead to the new Jerusalem in which "the throne of God and of the Lamb will be" (22:3). The imagery of sharing Jesus' throne corresponds to the earlier promise that the victor will share Jesus' iron scepter (2:26–27). Only those who see through the pseudo-riches being hawked by the harlot and who heed the knock of the faithful Witness will share Jesus' throne.

Conclusion

The seven churches of Asia belong to their first-century setting, but they are also case studies in the conflict that confronts all churches in all the world at all times. Their specific struggles in their time and place—institutionalized worship of the state through the cult of the emperor, pluralistic relativism of pagan polytheism, economic pressures to religious compromise in trade guilds, social ostracism and random harassment from pagan and Jewish quarters, love lost amid theological conflict and external adversity, complacency amid accommodation and affluence—are symptomatic of the strategies by which the enemy continues to assault the church. These forces will be pictured in horrifying vividness in the visions to come: a many-headed dragon summoning from the sea a many-headed monster; a second monster emerging from the land to deceive and coerce earth's inhabitants; and a harlot decked out in luxury and drunk on the blood of Jesus' martyrs.

The church under attack needs not only to see the splendor of our King but also to hear his imperial edicts, assuring us that he knows our situation, probing and exposing our subtle alliances with the enemy, and lifting our sights to the city that is the destination of our pilgrimage. Not only does Jesus walk among the churches (Rev. 2:1), but also he is coming to the churches—in two senses. To some he threatens a coming that will intrude into their present life in history with severe mercy and loving discipline. If they will not repent, he will come to remove a church's candlestick or to wage war against the Nicolaitans. These comings, which occur through Christ's providential rule and the Spirit's work, are real visitations by the risen Lord with real effects in the church's life and witness in the world, even though they are not that final coming in which "every eye will see Him, even those who pierced Him" (1:7). To other churches Jesus' promised coming is that bodily, glorious appearance from heaven that will bring the church's life and witness in the world to a climax. That will be an arrival so public that none can ignore it. The promise of this coming must motivate the faithful to hold fast what they have "until I come" (2:25; 3:11). Though distinct in timing and visibility from each other, Jesus' providential comings *in* history and his final coming at the end of history are related. His comings to purify his church foreshadow his coming to purge his creation of all who defile it.

Jesus' final promise to the victor reminds us that he is the Victor par excellence over the dragon: "I will grant to him to sit down with Me on My throne, as I also overcame and sat down with My Father on His throne" (3:21). The conflict in which West Coast churches are engaged is so severe that our only hope of victory is the presence of Jesus the Victor.

CHAPTER FIVE

Scroll Opened:
The Lamb Is Worthy
(4:1–5:14)

From Oz to Awe

The movie made from Frank L. Baum's *The Wizard of Oz* is not only a well-worn film classic but also a parable of American life. Young Dorothy, snatched by tornado from her farm home in black-and-white Kansas, awakens in the Technicolor world of Oz, resplendent with the delights and terrors of the imagination. Although Oz is full of wonders, Dorothy longs for home and so begins a pilgrimage to the Emerald City, where, she is told, the great Wizard of Oz can fulfill her longing to return to Kansas. Along the way she meets fellow pilgrims who join her quest to make requests of the wizard: a tin man needing a heart, a lion lacking courage, a scarecrow who longs for a brain. Finally granted an audience with the wizard, the pilgrims are terrified by the awful flashes of light, smoke, and thunderous voice that assail their eyes and ears—until Dorothy's little dog, Toto, pulls aside a veil in one corner of the great hall, revealing a little old man operating buttons and levers, speaking into a microphone, and looking very much like the medicine-show huckster back in Kansas . . . the wonderful Wizard of Oz.

The wizard's terrifying splendor is merely the product of technology and savvy marketing, so he could not deliver the gifts sought by the pilgrims. Then again, he does not need to bestow these gifts, for along the path of their pilgrimage the tin man has revealed his compassion and the scarecrow his ability to think, and even the lion has proved tremulously brave. In other words, through their quest to reach the wizard's court they have already saved themselves, so all that the wizard needs to do is to certify their accomplishments. This is the perfect parable for self-reliant American individualism. It also exhibits a light-hearted cynicism that suspects that nothing in the universe is worth our wonder. People who can fix themselves are not easily impressed by anyone who presents himself as bigger or better than they are. Is anyone or anything intrinsically worthy of awe? Or can we rest in the confidence that what made previous generations marvel and tremble can be explained and therefore rendered ordinary after all?

The loss of awe in the modern world could be attributed to the expansion of scientific understanding, the democratic impulse in world politics, or our growing technological capacity to simulate the miraculous on film, television, and computer screens, where we can create a virtual world in which anything can happen but nothing actually happens. Yet the attempt to replace awe with explanation and artifice fails to convince people who, though they deny or ignore it, are nevertheless created in the image of the God who is awesome in glory. The reduction of human experience to the explicable is a desperate act of faith in our power to create reality ("what we cannot explain cannot exist"), but this faith cannot satisfy. Into the vacuum of transcendence created by naturalism and technolatry, New Age spirituality is rushing, promising the experience of mystery and awe turned inward, without the troubling concept of accountability to the Creator.[1]

The Book of Revelation wages war on the reductionism that chokes awe. Among its most pervasive motifs is that those who see only the surface, who explain human history and experience merely in terms of observable (physical, economic, political, societal) forces, are blind to the pattern that explains why things happen as they do. To see that

1. For a thorough critique of New Age spirituality, see Peter Jones, *Spirit Wars: Pagan Revival in Christian America* (Mukilteo, Wash.: WinePress, 1997).

deep pattern is to experience an awe impervious to cynicism because it is to stand in the presence of the God who is worthy of our fear and wonder. John's vision of the One sitting on the throne and of the Lamb is permeated with their supreme worthiness (Rev. 4:11; 5:9–10, 12; cf. 4:8; 5:13) and therefore by the awe of all who see them.

The Summons (4:1–2)

"After these things"[2] John sees a door opened in heaven, initiating a new series of visions that will reveal "the things that must occur after these things" (Rev. 4:1 dej).[3] John has seen and heard the Son of Man diagnose the "things which are" in his letters to the churches (1:19). Now the focus of attention shifts to the future of the seven churches and the forces that assault them.

The opened door and heavenly call initiate John's summons as prophet to enter the council chamber of the King of kings, to hear his plans and purposes and then to bring his message to his people. "Surely the Lord GOD does nothing unless He reveals His secret counsel to His servants the prophets" (Amos 3:7). The prophetic commissioning of Isaiah (Isa. 6) and Ezekiel (Ezek. 1) entailed their visionary entrance into the Lord's heavenly holy place, the prototype of the earthly temple (Exod. 25:40; Heb. 8:5), to see his glory and receive his word. John's vision blends features from those ancient prophets' visions. Subsequent openings of heaven (Rev. 19:11) and of God's sanctuary in heaven (11:19; 15:5) open new visionary "scenes."[4] The trumpetlike voice that calls John is the one he had heard at first, commanding him to write to the seven churches (1:10–11). It is the voice of the Son of Man (1:13), whose invincible call catches John up into prophetic vision ("in the Spirit"), making visible to him God's throne room in heaven.

2. "After these things I saw" or similar transitions appear also in Rev. 7:1 ("after this"), 9; 15:5; 18:1; 19:1 ("I heard"), marking the beginning of a significant new vision. H. B. Swete, *Commentary on Revelation,* 3d ed. (1911; reprint ed., Grand Rapids: Kregel, 1977), 66; R. H. Charles, *A Critical and Exegetical Commentary on the Revelation of St. John,* 2 vols., ICC (Edinburgh: T & T Clark, 1920), 1:106.

3. The initials dej = author's translation.

4. Michael Wilcock, *I Saw Heaven Opened: The Message of Revelation,* TBST (Downers Grove, Ill.: InterVarsity Press, 1975), 110–15.

The One Who Sits on the Throne (4:2–6)

As in the first vision John first saw lampstands and then, walking among them, "one like a son of man," so now John first sees a throne set in heaven, and then One sitting on it (4:2). This order—the description of the throne, then the disclosure of its occupant—echoes Daniel's vision of the Ancient of Days (Dan. 7:9) and will be repeated in the vision of the martyrs' thousand-year reign (Rev. 20:4). This first glimpse of royal furniture shows that the prophet stands before the Sovereign who has the right and the power to achieve his purposes.

Even in the mode of prophetic vision, which conveys its truth visually, John's description of the appearance of the One on the throne is restrained, offering nothing that could be turned into a forbidden image.[5] Through John's eyes we see no features but only color and texture, conveyed in simile: "like a jasper stone and a sardius in appearance." The name *jasper* was applied to a variety of precious stones in the ancient world, ranging in color from reddish through amber to green, and from opaque to translucent. From the comparison of the radiance of the new Jerusalem to "crystal-clear jasper" (Rev. 21:11, 18–19), we can infer that John's readers would have pictured a stone through which light shines, perhaps the precious green. Sardius, also known as carnelian, is a reddish stone that also appears among the twelve foundation stones of the new Jerusalem (22:20). The emerald-green rainbow surrounding the throne replicates a feature of Ezekiel's opening vision of the Lord on his throne, borne by four living beings (Ezek 1:28). Emanating

5. Moses reminded the Israelites how God limited the visible display of his glory at Sinai: "So watch yourselves carefully, since you did not see any form on the day the LORD spoke to you at Horeb from the midst of the fire, so that you do not act corruptly and make a graven image for yourselves in the form of any figure" (Deut. 4:15–16). Note also Ezekiel's belabored use of the language of resemblance to emphasize that his vision must not be taken literally as a photograph of God: "on that which resembled a throne, high up, was a figure with the appearance of a man. Then I noticed from the appearance of His loins and upward. . . . As the appearance of the rainbow in the clouds on a rainy day, so was the appearance of the surrounding radiance. Such was the appearance of the likeness of the glory of the Lord" (Ezek. 1:26–28).

from the throne, as when the Lord's cloud-veiled court descended to ancient Sinai, were flashes of lightning, voices, and thunders (Rev. 4:4; Exod. 19:16). Before the throne burned seven lamps, the seven Spirits of God, symbolizing the fullness of the Spirit's presence with the Father, and, spreading from its foot, a sea of glass like crystal (Rev. 4:5–6).

This sea, which shows the peaceful purity of God's sanctuary, appeared in various forms to earlier prophets. To Moses, Aaron, Aaron's sons, and Israel's elders, called up to Sinai to dine with God, it appeared as "a pavement of sapphire, as clear as the sky itself" (Exod. 24:10). Ezekiel saw "an expanse, like the awesome gleam of crystal" beneath the Lord's throne (Ezek. 1:22, 26). This sea will reappear as the transparent pavement on which the martyrs stand to celebrate God's victory (Rev. 15:2). This heavenly sea, so tranquil it seems to be glass, contrasts sharply with the earthly sea, a region of chaos and rebellion identified with the abyss, from which the beast emerges to wage war against the saints (11:7; 13:1). That earthly sea, source and symbol of satanic chaos, is destined for destruction with the passing of the first heaven and earth (21:1), but the clarity and purity of the crystalline pavement beneath God's feet will permeate the new Jerusalem (21:11, 18). John's vision of the enthroned One leaves the impression of radiant light and vibrant color, without definition of details.

The Courtiers (4:4, 6–8)

Attending the Lord in his heavenly court are twenty-four elders and four living beings. The twenty-four elders sit on thrones, dressed in white and crowned with gold (Rev. 4:4). Their number, twice twelve, seems to have been symbolically significant to John and the Asian churches, although scholars today disagree as to its import. Perhaps it reflects the twenty-four orders of priests and the twenty-four orders of singers in the Old Testament temple, since they worship in God's heavenly sanctuary (1 Chron. 24:7–19; 25:6–31). Or they may foreshadow the two sets of twelve in the new Jerusalem: twelve gates of pearl, bearing the names of Israel's tribes (21:12, 21), and twelve foundation stones, bearing the names of the Lamb's apostles (21:14, 19–20).[6] Thus the elders are sometimes understood as a portrait of the whole church, under old covenant and new. This identification, however, is problematic. The elders function, as do angels elsewhere, as agents of revelation and explanation to John (5:5; 7:13–14). They speak as third-party observers of the church's redemption, singing together with the four living creatures, "You . . . purchased for God with Your blood men from every tribe and tongue and people and nation. And You have made them to be a kingdom and priests to our God; and they will reign upon the earth" (5:9–10; cf. 7:14–15). Later, the Lamb's army "sang a new song before the throne and before the four living creatures and the elders" (14:3). The elders are therefore the council of the Lord's heavenly servants and advisors rather than a symbolic representation of the church, militant or triumphant.[7]

The four living creatures seen by John (Rev. 4:6–8) share characteristics of the four living creatures (= cherubim, Ezek. 10:20) that Ezekiel saw bearing the throne of God (1:5–14), but they also resemble the seraphim in Isaiah's temple vision of the Lord on his throne, "lofty and exalted" (Isa. 6:2–3). Each of the four living creatures in Ezekiel's vision had four faces (of a man, a lion, a young bull, and an eagle), whereas in John's vision the living creatures have one face each (a lion, a young bull, a man, and an eagle). Although Ezekiel's living creatures had four wings, John's have six, like the seraphim seen by Isaiah; and like the seraphim John's living creatures call ceaselessly, "Holy, Holy, Holy is the Lord." Like the wheels associated with Ezekiel's living creatures, John's living creatures are "full of eyes around and within," reflecting the omniscience of the One whom they worship (Ezek 1:18; Rev. 4:6, 8). Perhaps the most significant difference between Ezekiel and Rev-

6. Jürgen Roloff, *The Revelation of John: A Continental Commentary* (Minneapolis: Fortress, 1993), 70, suggests that the number twenty-four corresponds to the hours in a day, symbolizing the ceaseless praises of the heavenly court.

7. Although the all-wise God needs no advisor (Isa. 40:13; Rom. 11:34), his heavenly court is sometimes presented anthropomorphically, after the pattern of human royalty. See M. G. Kline, *Images of the Spirit* (Grand Rapids: Baker, 1980), 58.

elation is the absence of these wheels in John's vision. Ezekiel's vision assured the exiles in Babylon that, despite the temple's destruction and their deportation, the Lord had not retracted the promise of his presence but would travel with them to the place of their captivity. John's vision opens to the beleaguered church's view, through heaven's door, a glimpse of our God's tranquil sovereignty over earth's turmoil.[8]

We may be confused by the blend of resemblance and variation between John's vision and those of his Old Testament predecessors in prophecy, but the prophetic vocabulary of simile should lead us to expect this fluidity. Prophetic vision is not intended to provide photographic reproduction of what spirits such as cherubim and seraphim look like. Rather, in prophetic vision God adapts to the need of the moment the visual metaphors by which he portrays aspects of truth about himself and his heavenly courtiers.

Although the main activity of the four living creatures in Revelation is worship, they will also implement the judgments ordered by their Lord. In response to the Lamb's breaking of the first four seals on the scroll of God's plan, the living creatures in succession summon the four riders on white, red, black, and ashen horses to "come," bringing afflictions on the earth (Rev. 6:1–8). When the climax of judgment arrives, one of these living creatures will give the seven bowls of God's wrath to the angels who are to pour them on the earth (15:7). Since they resemble the cherubim in Ezekiel's vision, their presence also recalls the cherubim's role as guardians who keep defilement out of God's holy residence, whether it is Eden (Gen. 3:24), the ark of the covenant (Exod. 25:18), or the temple's holiest chamber (1 Kings 6:23–28). Each of these is an earthly replica of the heavenly throne room, in which God sits between the cherubim (Ps. 80:1; 99:1; Isa. 37:16). John could not possibly have entered this divine counsel chamber had not the Son of Man opened the door and summoned him, "Come up here."

---

8. Roloff, *Revelation*, 68: "The dramatic movement, which is characteristic of the Ezekiel vision, has given way here to static rest." More precisely, the enthroned One is at rest, while his retinue of courtiers is engaged in acts of worship: speaking praise, kneeling, presenting crowns at his feet.

The Praises (4:8–11)

The throne scene that spans Revelation 4 and 5 contains five expressions of praise (4:8, 11; 5:9–10, 12, 13). All are poetic in form, although only the central poem, which is the longest, is called a "song" and accompanied by harps (5:8–9). The choir that glorifies the One sitting on the throne and the Lamb expands with each new doxology: first the four living creatures (4:8), then the twenty-four elders praise the One on the throne (4:10). The chorus expands to twenty-eight as the living creatures and the elders together confess the worthiness of the Lamb to take the scroll (5:8), evoking a response from angels numbering in the myriads of myriads and thousands of thousands (5:11). Finally the crescendo reaches its climax as "every created thing which is in heaven and on the earth and under the earth and on the sea, and all things in them" ascribe glory to the One sitting on the throne and to the Lamb together (5:13). Two doxologies extol the enthroned One, two glorify the Lamb, and the final one praises them together.

The first praise, offered by the four living creatures, extols God's perfect holiness (threefold "holy"), omnipotence ("the Almighty") and eternity (Rev. 4:8),[9] ascribing to him "glory and honor and thanks" (4:9). Glory and honor will appear as elements in the following doxologies (4:11; 5:12, 13), but thanksgiving will be given to God only once elsewhere in Revelation, in the response of the heavenly host to the salvation song of the victorious international multitude (7:12). The living creatures' praise is called a thanksgiving, although they speak not of God's deeds but of his attributes. God is to be thanked just for being who he is: the all-holy, Almighty, ever-living One. His eternity is emphasized in the title "him who lives forever and ever" (4:9–10). This title is ascribed to God in Daniel (Dan. 4:34; 6:27; 12:7), but Revelation's hearers would also recall a closer connection: the Son of Man, though once dead, lives forever and ever, sharing divine eternity with the Father (Rev. 1:18).

---

9. In Rev. 4:8 the description of God's eternal life follows the normal chronological order ("who was and who is and who is to come"), unlike the descriptions in 1:4, 8, which begin with the present "who is" to emphasize allusion to the divine name "I Am/He Who Is" in Exod. 3:14.

The elders preface their words of praise with acts of adoration. They prostrate themselves before the Lord and cast their crowns at his feet, acknowledging that all authority derives from him, belongs to him, and returns to him (Rev. 4:10). They then ascribe worthiness to God, the fact that he deserves their awe and adoration as they gladly confess his "glory and honor and power." An unresolved question of worthiness, of deserved authority and rightful claim, will soon plunge John into deep grief amid this celestial joy (5:2–4). It is the crux of the two-movement throne scene that we are considering. Recognition of the supreme worthiness of God evokes a stabbing, sweet sense of awe, to which our modern hearts may be numbed by self-reliance and cynicism. (Before whom would we risk our dignity by flinging ourselves spontaneously facedown on the pavement?) The elders also support their assertion of God's worthiness with a rationale: "for You created all things, and because of Your will they existed, and were created" (4:11). The praises around the throne move from contemplation of who God is in himself, to his work of creation, and then on to the apex of worthiness, the work of redemption accomplished by the Lamb.

The Problem: A Sealed Scroll (5:1–4)

John's attention is now drawn to the right hand of the enthroned One, on which lies a "book"—not a codex with its pages bound along a spine but a scroll written on front and back, rolled and sealed along its outside edge (Rev. 5:1). The scroll is written "on front and back,"[10] like that shown to Ezekiel when he was called as a prophet (Ezek.

10. Ezek. 2:20. LXX: *gegrammena . . . opisthen kai ta emprosthen,* "written on the back and the front." The scroll given to the Lamb in Rev. 5 was introduced similarly: "written inside and on the back" (*gegrammenon esōthen kai opisthen*). The order "inside and on the reverse" in Rev. 5:1 reproduces the Hebrew text of Ezek. 2:10, which is reversed by the LXX. The biblically informed reader and hearers would recognize the allusions to Ezekiel's scroll as a reason to identify the Lamb's scroll of Rev. 5 with the "little scroll" that John will eat in Rev. 10. This allusive link between Ezek. 2 and Rev. 5 and 10 is strengthened by the fact that the processes by which papyrus and vellum (animal skin) pages were produced made the reverse side of the material irregular and hard to inscribe. Papyrus was made by overlaying a row of vertical leaves with a row of leaves in which the fiber lay horizontally, conducive

2:9–3:3). Because Ezekiel's scroll symbolized the message that he was to deliver to God's people, he was commanded to eat the scroll in preparation for his proclamation. There is, however, one great obstacle to John's preaching the contents of the scroll he now sees in God's right hand: the scroll John sees is sealed. In the ancient world documents were sealed with wax impressed with the author's insignia as a token of authenticity (Jer. 32:10–11; 1 Cor. 9:2; cf. John 3:33) but also for security and privacy (Dan. 12:4, 9; Rev. 10:4). A sealed scroll could not be read until the seals were broken (Isa. 29:11); but since the seal symbolized its owner's authority, it could not legitimately be broken without his authorization.[11]

Herein lies the problem that wrings lament from John's heavy heart. A strong angel puts it into words that resound through the universe: "Who is worthy to open the book and to break its seals?" (Rev. 5:2). Who is qualified, deserving by right, and authorized by the scroll's Author to break the scroll's seals and so disclose its message? Among all the splendors of God's majestic retinue in heaven (living creatures, elders, angels) and all creatures on earth and under it, none was found worthy "to open the book or to look into it" (5:3). How wonderful the contents of this book, that none of the heavenly host except the enthroned One has sufficient status to unveil its secrets! What could it contain? At this point John cannot know the specifics; but he has been summoned to heaven to see "what must take place after these things" (4:1). Since the scroll given Ezekiel to eat contained words of lament over judgments to come, we expect that this scroll contains the promises and warnings that are to be the heart of John's message

---

to the printing of straight horizontal lines. On the back, a scribe would have to print across vertical fibers. Vellum scrolls were normally inscribed only on the smooth interior surface of the skin, since it was time-consuming and expensive to scrape the hairy exterior smooth enough to receive writing. For these reasons most ancient scrolls, whether of papyrus or vellum, were written only on the front, which when rolled became the inside face of the sheets. (Thanks to my colleague S. M. Baugh for insight into ancient scroll production.)

11. The sealing of Jesus' tomb by order of the governor was intended to serve notice that no one was permitted to move the stone without authorization of the Roman imperial officials (Matt. 27:66).

for the churches. But what if his mission is aborted for lack of one worthy to unroll the scroll?

If the scroll stays sealed, the consequences are even more serious than the confusion of the churches. The opening of the scroll would be not only an act of revelatory disclosure but also an act of executive authority, carrying its edicts into action. The things written in the scroll "must take place" because they constitute God's plan for history, culminating in the vindication of his servants and the unchallenged establishment of his dominion on earth, as it is in heaven. The strong angel's question is not merely Who is worthy to reveal God's plan? but also Who is worthy to carry out God's plan? Who deserves to receive from the Father's hand all authority in heaven and earth, to make the kingdoms of this world into the kingdom of our Lord and of his Christ (11:15)?

The Lion of Judah (5:5)

The suspense and John's sorrow are broken by the voice of one of the elders, answering the angel's question: "the Lion that is from the tribe of Judah, the Root of David, has overcome so as to open the book and its seven scrolls" (Rev. 5:5). When Israel bestowed a final blessing on his sons, he compared Judah with a lion and foresaw a perpetual royal dynasty from Judah's line (Gen. 49:8–12). God's selection of David as king in place of the Benjamite Saul set the fulfillment of Israel's prophecy in motion. Though the exile would make it seem that David's dynasty had been cut off, like a tree sawn down, leaving only root and stump, Isaiah foresaw a fresh shoot from the stump of David's father Jesse, a fruitful branch springing from a root that seemed lifeless and hopeless (Isa. 11:1, 10).

These promises were finally to reach fulfillment in "Jesus the Anointed (King), Son of David, Son of Abraham" (Matt. 1:1 dej). In view of David's well-known prowess as the warrior-champion of God's people (1 Sam. 16), the elder's announcement that this Lion-King has overcome comes as no surprise. Surely Judah's fierce lion is a victor worthy to open the scroll!

The Lamb Slain (5:6–7)

A surprise awaits, however. In the first vision John had heard a trumpetlike voice and then, turning to "see the voice," had beheld one like a son of man walking among seven lampstands. Here again the disclosure of Jesus' identity begins with what is heard, "Lion of the tribe of Judah," and then turns to what is seen: "a Lamb standing, as if slain, having seven horns and seven eyes, which are the seven Spirits of God, sent out into all the earth" (Rev. 5:6). This is a striking paradox: the conquering lion, warrior-king of Judah's tribe and David's line, champion of the people of God, appears before John's eyes as a lamb slaughtered yet standing. Although the word *lamb* used in Revelation (*arnion*) differs from that in John's Gospel (*amnos,* John 1:29, 36), in the Greek Old Testament both words describe lambs as sacrificial victims. Isaiah compares the suffering Servant with "a lamb (*amnos*) that is led to slaughter" (Isa. 53:7; cf. Acts 8:32; 1 Peter 1:19); and Jeremiah offers a parallel, "I was like a gentle lamb (*arnion*) led to the slaughter" (Jer. 11:19).

In Revelation the Lamb will prove to be a military champion (Rev. 14:1–4), whose wrath his enemies fear and wish to flee (6:16). Yet John's first glimpse of the Lamb stresses not a ram's aggressive strength but a sacrificial victim's passivity.[12] The fact that the Lamb has been slain motivates the longest of the five doxologies in these two chapters: "Worthy are You . . . for You were slain, and purchased for God with Your blood men from every tribe and tongue and people and nation" (5:9). The slaughter suffered by the Lamb is the way he "has overcome" (5:5). His death is the victory that makes him worthy to open the scroll. Therefore the slaughtered sacrifice stands, no longer dead but now alive forevermore (1:18) and ready to open and execute God's plan for the denouement of his mortal combat against the dragon and his forces.

It is almost as if John were saying to us at one point after another: 'Wherever the Old Testament says "Lion", read "Lamb".' Wherever

---

12. *Arnion* can refer to young rams, as the synonymous parallelism in Ps. 114:4, 6 LXX illustrates.

the Old Testament speaks of the victory of the Messiah or the overthrow of the enemies of God, we are to remember that the gospel recognizes no other way of achieving these ends than the way of the Cross.[13]

The Lamb has seven horns and seven eyes. In biblical imagery the horn sometimes symbolizes honor. A psalmist warns those who claim honor vainly, "I said to the boastful, 'Do not boast,' and to the wicked, 'Do not lift up the horn; . . . do not speak with insolent pride'" (Ps. 75:4–5), but another promises the poor that "his horn will be exalted in honor" (112:9). More often, however, the horn is a picture of strength: "The LORD is my rock and my fortress and my deliverer . . . my shield and the horn of my salvation, my stronghold" (18:2).[14] Consequently in the symbolism of the Bible's apocalyptic literature, horns represent powerful kings or nations (Dan. 7:24; Zech. 1:18–21). The Lamb's seven horns show his supreme worthiness to receive the praises that greet his appearance (Rev. 5:9, 12, 13), but they primarily portray his supreme power. They are the visual equivalent of the title *Almighty,* ascribed to the Lord God (1:8; 4:8).

The Lamb's seven eyes show his omniscience as well as the mode of his presence with his embattled churches, for these eyes, like the seven lamps before God's throne, symbolize "the seven Spirits of God, sent out into all the earth" (Rev. 5:6). The prophet Zechariah was shown in vision a lampstand with seven lamps, like that in the tabernacle (Zech. 4:2; Exod. 25:37). These seven lamps were also interpreted as "the eyes of the LORD which range to and fro throughout the earth" (Zech. 4:10). Thus the flexibility of John's symbolism, with two images, lamps and eyes, pointing to one referent, God's Spirit, has prophetic precedent. The Lamb has all power and all knowledge, extending to earth's farthest corner. In omniscience he can say to each church, "I know." In omnipotence he can make a sevenfold guaran-

13. G. B. Caird, *A Commentary on the Revelation of St. John the Divine,* HNTC (New York: Harper & Row, 1966), 75.
14. Further examples: "For You are the glory of their strength, and by Your favor our horn is exalted" (Ps. 89:17); "Blessed be the Lord God of Israel, for He . . . has raised up a horn of salvation for us in the house of David His servant . . . salvation from our enemies, and from the hand of all who hate us" (Luke 1:68–71).

tee of reward to the overcomer. Such is the majesty of the church's champion, who now approaches the enthroned One and receives the vital scroll from his right hand (5:7).

The New Songs of Praise (5:8–14)

The reaction among the celestial audience is immediate: "the four living creatures and the twenty-four elders fell down before the Lamb" and began to sing a new song, accompanying themselves on small harps (Rev. 5:8–9). The supreme worthiness of the Lamb elicits from those who serve constantly in the presence of God expressions of awe, verbal and physical, as they prostrate themselves before this glorious victor.

Besides their harps the living creatures and the elders hold golden bowls full of incense, "which are the prayers of the saints." These incense-prayers will play a crucial role in the judgments that the Lamb will inflict on his enemies, for it is in answer to the martyrs' appeals for justice (Rev. 6:9–11) and the suffering saints' laments from earth (8:3–5) that he will send fiery vengeance on earth, sea, rivers, and sky (8:6–12).

The importance of the "new song," celebrating the Lamb's worthiness to take the scroll and open its seals, is shown not only by its central position and length but also by its content. In the history of salvation new songs were composed to celebrate new events in which the Lord rescued his people. The first such song, celebrating the exodus, was sung by Moses and the Israelites on the east bank of the Red Sea, in which Pharaoh's armies had just been drowned (Exod. 15). Revelation 15 will link that ancient victory anthem with the song of the Lamb sung by those who overcome the beast through their loyalty to the Lamb (15:2–4). In Isaiah 42 God promised a future exodus for his imprisoned people (Isa. 42:7), assuring them that his past faithfulness to his word secures their future hope: "Behold, the former things have come to pass, now I declare new things; before they spring forth I proclaim them to you" (42:9). Their response is a fresh song of praise: "Sing to the LORD a new song, sing His praise from the end of the earth!" (42:10). The international dimension of the new song that will be evoked by the Lord's saving work is the theme of Psalm 96:

Sing to the LORD a new song; sing to the LORD, all the earth. Sing to the LORD, bless His name; proclaim good tidings of his salvation from day to day. Tell of His glory among the nations, His wonderful deeds among all peoples. For great is the LORD and greatly to be praised; He is to be feared above all gods (Ps. 96:1–4).[15]

The new song now sung by living creatures and elders celebrates an exodus that makes previous rescues pale in comparison: "You were slain, and purchased for God with Your blood men from every tribe and tongue and people and nation." Israel's liberation from Egyptian bondage was bound up with the rescue of their firstborn from the plague of death. The application of the blood of the Passover lamb to the Israelites' doorposts signaled that their firstborn sons, like those of their Egyptian oppressors, were liable to the angel's deathblow unless an unblemished substitute died in their place (Exod. 12:2–14). In succeeding generations firstborn animals were to be sacrificed to the Lord in remembrance of that night, but firstborn children were to be redeemed through the presentation of an offering at the sanctuary (Exod. 13:13–16). A later psalmist recalls the exodus in asking God to "remember Your congregation, which You have purchased of old, which You have redeemed to be the tribe of Your inheritance" (Ps. 74:2).[16] Moreover, the Lord lavished on his purchased people extraordinary privilege: "If you will indeed obey My voice and keep My covenant, then you shall be My own possession among all the peoples . . . and you shall be to Me a kingdom of priests and a holy nation" (Exod. 19:5–6). The Lamb's purchase, at the incalculable cost of his lifeblood, likewise

15. The expression "greatly to be praised" (Hebrew: $m^e hullal\ m^e od;$ LXX: *ainetos sphodra*) could also be translated "most worthy of praise" (so NIV), since the Hebrew pual participle $m^e hullal$ and the corresponding Greek adjective *ainetos* mean "praiseworthy" (BDB, 238–39; LS, 37). This expression, which also appears in 2 Sam. 22:4; Ps. 48:2; 145:3, is a close equivalent to Revelation's announcement that God and the Lamb are "worthy" (*axios*) to receive glory, strength, and honor (Rev. 4:11; 5:9, 12, 13). Ps. 96:7 calls the families of the nations to "Ascribe to the LORD glory and strength" (LXX: "glory and honor").

16. Compare Acts 20:28: "the church of God which He purchased with His own blood."

liberated people from enslavement and liability to death, and it made them "a people for God's own possession" (1 Peter 2:9). In this new exodus the multitude purchased by the Lamb comes not from one nation but "from every tribe and tongue and people and nation." Yet to this international assembly the Lamb has given titles that formerly were Israel's: "You have made them to be a kingdom and priests to our God," sharing by grace the Lamb's priestly right to approach the enthroned One and his royal right to rule (Rev. 5:9–10; cf. 1:6, 9; 20:7).

Now joining the praises of the four living creatures and the twenty-four elders is a choir of countless angels ("myriads of myriads, and thousands of thousands"). Since a myriad is ten thousand, these are extremely high multiples of ten: $10,000 \times 10,000 = 100,000,000$; $1,000 \times 1,000 = 1,000,000$. John's expression of the numbers as multiples of immense numbers tends to magnify the amounts in the reader's and hearers' minds. The angels' song, like the praise to the enthroned One for creation and the praise to the Lamb for redemption, begins, "Worthy are . . . to receive" (4:11; 5:9). Thus the three central doxologies of the five in Revelation 4–5 open with the theme of divine worthiness.

The five doxologies are linked in other ways. The first and fifth doxologies mention divine eternity ("who was and is and is to come," 4:8; "forever and ever," 5:13). The first and second doxologies praise the enthroned One, the third and fourth praise the Lamb, and the fifth, both of them together. The second and third are addressed directly to the Object of praise in the second person ("Worthy are You") and give the reason for ascribing worthiness (creation, redemption; 4:11; 5:9–10). The last element of the second doxology ("power") is the first element of the fourth, and the last element of the fourth ("blessing") opens the fifth. "Glory and honor" appear in the three doxologies that list divine excellencies (second, fourth, fifth), as do words expressing strength: "power" (*dynamis,* 4:11; 5:12), "might" (*ischys,* 5:12), and "dominion" (*kratos,* 5:13). The second doxology ascribes three excellencies to God, the fourth song ascribes seven (4 + 3) to the Lamb (see 7:12 for another sevenfold list), and the fifth ascribes four to God and the Lamb. The relations of the doxologies can be viewed in this way:

110

4:8	Holy, holy, holy is the Lord God, the Almighty,	
	who was and is and is to come.	ETERNITY
4:11	Worthy are You, our Lord and our God, to receive	WORTHY + 2ND PERSON
	glory, honor, power.	LIST OF EXCELLENCIES
	for You created. . . .	REASON FOR WORTHINESS
5:9	Worthy are You to receive[17]	WORTHY + 2ND PERSON
	the book. . . .	
	for You were slain, and purchased . . .	REASON FOR WORTHINESS
5:12	Worthy is the Lamb that was slain to receive	WORTHY + 3RD PERSON
	power, riches, wisdom, might,	LIST OF EXCELLENCIES
	honor, glory, blessing.	
5:13	To Him who sits on the throne, and to the Lamb be	
	blessing, honor, glory, dominion	LIST OF EXCELLENCIES
	forever and ever.	ETERNITY

The seven-part rehearsal of the Lamb's excellencies (5:12) may be grouped into a first set of four (power, riches, wisdom, might), describing the resources that qualify him to exercise divine rule over history, and a second set of three (honor, glory, blessing), describing the response to the Lamb's worthiness that is incumbent on all creatures everywhere in his dominion.[18]

When every creature in heaven, on earth, under the earth, and in the sea joins the song, our perspective, which began in adoration of the thrice-holy God from eternity past ("who was and is and is to come," 4:9), is expanded to embrace eternity future: may the enthroned One and the Lamb receive blessing, honor, glory, and do-

17. The Greek verb *lambanō* (here in aorist infinitive form *labein*) can mean either (passively) "receive" or (actively) "take." Since the Lamb's role in the transfer of the scroll seems active in 5:7–8, the NASB continues to translate *labein* as "take" in 5:9, but this obscures for the reader of English the parallelism of wording with 4:11; 5:12.

18. Charles, *Commentary,* 1:149, cites Bousset's view that "the four deal with the power and wisdom that the Lamb assumes; the three with the recognition of the Lamb on the part of mankind." Roloff, *Revelation,* 81, categorizes the first four as "properties of God that are transferred to the Messiah for the execution of his office, while the last three, as in 4:9, describe what happens in the offering of praise."

minion "forever and ever"—literally, "into the ages of the ages" (5:13). Two classic descriptions of the whole created order are blended to emphasize the comprehensiveness of the adoring choir. The whole created universe can be viewed vertically as falling into three regions: heaven, earth, and regions under the earth (Phil. 2:10), but an equally comprehensive description of all that God created is "the heavens and the earth, the sea and all that is in them" (Exod. 20:11; Ps. 146:6).[19] Everything that God has created, he has created because of his will (Rev. 4:11), and his will is that each and every creature, everywhere, should glorify its Creator. Human rebellion has disrupted the paean of praise that the Creator is worthy to receive from all his subjects. Hence it was necessary for the Lamb to be slaughtered in order to transform defiled slaves into pure priests who will lead the rest of the universe in celebrating the worthiness of the God who created and the Lamb who redeemed. The ceaseless praises of the four living creatures (4:8) will be taken up by all creation and will extend indefinitely "into the ages of the ages."

Conclusion

The death of awe in our culture has left us with an oddly credulous cynicism. We are cynical, suspicious of established government, education, technology, and medicine. Yet our cynicism is the recycled remnant of dashed hopes and broken faith, precisely because, having lost sight of the God who is worthy, we have invested such trust in these institutions to save our civilization and us. John's churches lived in a setting where the worship of human power, personified in Rome's emperors who were extolled as lords and saviors, had reached blatant expression, as one city after another vied for the privilege of becoming a temple warden (*neocoros*), maintaining a sanctuary in which the emperor was adored. John will see this pressure to worship human power emerging from the sea as a beast (Rev. 13:3–4) and as a second beast arising from the land to make "the earth and those who dwell in it worship the first beast" (13:12). But the false prophet's miracles,

19. This blending explains the redundant wording "every created thing which is in heaven . . . and all things in them."

like the emerald fireworks and the thunderous voice of the Wizard of Oz, are counterfeit. Government, education, technology, and medicine have roles to play in society; but none can bear the weight of glory, none are worthy of worship. No human institution or individual has created all things or reconciled rebels, making them God's priests and kings. Therefore none is worthy of the adoration that belongs to the enthroned One and to the Lamb.

John would not mislead us into dismissing the threats in this world as illusory. But he points us to a reality more deeply real: the eternal rule of God amid his awesome, adoring courtiers in heaven and the authority of the Lamb to carry out on earth the divine plan for the rescue and restoration of creation to its chief end, the glorification and enjoyment of God.

> This is my Father's world,
> O let me ne'er forget
>   that though the wrong
>   seems oft so strong,
> God is the ruler yet.
> This is my Father's world:
>   the battle is not done;
>   Jesus who died
>   shall be satisfied
> and earth and heav'n be one.[20]

---

20. Maltbie D. Babcock, "This Is My Father's World" (1901), in *Trinity Hymnal,* ed. Lawrence C. Roff, rev. ed. (Philadelphia: Great Commission Publications, 1990), 111.

CHAPTER SIX

Seals:
Instruments, Rationale, and Climax of Judgment
(6:1–8:5)

Asking the Right Question

The experience of Jesus' disciples shows that when we get into the Bible's teaching about things to come, it is easier to ask the wrong question than the right one. We want to ask When? Jesus is more interested in answering Why? and What for?

When his disciples were awed by the architecture of Herod's temple, Jesus brought their wide-eyed wonder down to earth with the prediction: "Truly I say to you, not one stone here will be left upon another, which will not be torn down" (Matt. 24:2). When they arrived at the Mount of Olives, the questions that his statement had started stewing in their hearts bubbled out: "Tell us, when will these things happen, and what will be the sign of Your coming, and of the end of the age?" (Matt. 24:3). His answer must have frustrated their appetite for a clear-cut calendar. He spoke of terrifying trends that were not signs of the end but only symptoms of this fallen world's miserable status quo (vv. 4–14). He gave veiled clues to help them recognize the imminence of the temple's destruction, but then he made a distinction between that divine visitation of judgment, which would occur in A.D. 70, and his personal coming at the end of the age. Regarding his coming Jesus said, "of that day and hour no one knows, not even the angels of heaven, nor the Son, but the Father alone" (v. 36). The disciples' questions "When?" and "What will be the sign of your coming?" are inappropriate attempts to probe off-limits secrets. What Jesus reveals about events to come serves practical purposes: to fortify us to endure (v. 13), to embolden us to evangelize (v. 14), and to awaken us for faithful vigilance (vv. 42–51).

After his resurrection the question When? was still on their lips: "Lord, is it at this time You are restoring the kingdom to Israel?" (Acts 1:6). Again he chastened their date-setting curiosity: "It is not for you to know times or epochs which the Father has fixed by His own authority" (v. 7). Then he redirected their attention to the reason for his resurrection and impending enthronement: their mission to be his witnesses to the ends of the earth and the Spirit's coming to empower them for their mission (v. 8). His words not only rebuked their effort to pry a date from the Father's secret purposes but also challenged their constricted conception of the parameters of the kingdom. Although they sought a restoration merely for Israel, through their witness God would ignite a worldwide expansion of his saving reign, from Jerusalem through Judea and Samaria "to the remotest part of the earth." Jesus' description of his witnesses' destination echoes God's ancient promise to the suffering Servant: "It is too small a thing that You should be My Servant to raise up the tribes of Jacob and to restore the preserved ones of Israel; I will also make You a light of the nations so that My salvation may reach to the end of the earth" (Isa. 49:6; cf. Acts 13:46).[1] Instead of satisfying their curiosity about the when of future events, Jesus focused on the opportunity and responsibility placed before his church by his resurrection and imminent bestowal of the Spirit from his seat at the Father's right hand (cf. Acts 2:32–36).

The sense of anticipation raised by John's vision of the enthroned One and the Lamb who is worthy to open the scroll whets our ap-

1. On Jesus' fulfillment of Isaiah's Servant songs in Luke-Acts, see Dennis E. Johnson, "Jesus Against the Idols: The Use of Isaianic Servant Songs in the Missiology of Acts," *WTJ* 52 (1990): 343–53; and Dennis E. Johnson, *The Message of Acts in the History of Redemption* (Phillipsburg, N.J.: P&R Publishing, 1997), 32–52.

petite (Rev. 4–5). Our brother the prophet has been summoned to heaven to see what is to take place in the future (4:1). We infer that God's secret plan for history lies hidden in the sealed scroll; so when the Lamb takes the scroll from his hand and begins to break its seals, we look through John's eyes for answers to our questions, When? and What? and How long? Instead of answering our questions, the prolonged process of preparing to unroll the scroll presents a series of portraits that answer the question, Why, if the Lion-Lamb has conquered, does the world continue to be a place of evil, violence, and misery?

Seals: Preparing to Disclose the Scroll's Contents

The breaking of a scroll's seals was preparatory to disclosing its contents. The measured pace by which the Lamb breaks the seals in succession, each accompanied by a new vision, builds suspense and anticipation in Revelation's hearers. Not until all seven are broken can the events prescribed in the scroll be disclosed. Yet the visions that accompany the breaking of the seals not only tantalize our curiosity; they also prepare us to understand the visions that John will see when the seventh seal is shattered.

The first four seals belong together, as will the first four trumpets and bowls in later series. Two features link the first four seals with each other. As the Lamb breaks the first four seals, the four living creatures, one after another, issue a thunderous summons, "Come." Responding to the living creatures' summons are four horses with riders. In each case the horse and its color appear first, then its rider and his significance. The colors of the horses (white, red, black, and ashen/pale) roughly correspond to the colors of chariot horses (red, black, white, dappled) in one of Zechariah's visions (Zech. 6:1–8). The chariots that appeared to Zechariah symbolized "the four spirits [or winds] of heaven," sent out from the Lord's presence to the four points of the compass, bringing judgment on the nations that had oppressed Judah. John likewise sees four horses and riders gallop through the earth, summoned by God's attendants to wreak havoc on his enemies. The first four seals show the instruments that the Lamb uses to judge those who oppose his rule and oppress his church.

The breaking of the fifth seal opens a window on the rationale that lies behind the release of these horses of judgment to roam through the earth. Those martyred for the sake of God's word and their testimony about Jesus cry out for justice, echoing the psalmists' lament, "How long?" Although their vindication must await the end of this age of divine forbearance—the age in which the number of martyrs is being filled to completion—their lament has not fallen on deaf ears. Both the restrained expressions of the Lamb's wrath through human aggression in the present (seals 1–4) and the unlimited display of his wrath in the dissolution of the universe at the climax of history (seal 6) show that the martyrs' blood is not forgotten. The fifth seal's vision of martyred souls under the altar anticipates the seventh seal, when John will see the prayers of embattled saints offered with incense upon the heavenly altar (8:1–5).

Seal 1: The Rider on the White Horse (6:1–2)

As the Lamb broke the first seal and one of the living creatures shouted, "Come," John saw a white horse and its rider holding a bow. A crown was given to him, and he went out conquering, and to achieve further conquest. Three of the four riders are given some symbol or form of power. The second rider is given (NASB "granted") the power to take peace from the earth, symbolized in the great sword "given" to him (Rev. 6:4). To the riders on the fourth, pale horse was given authority over one fourth of the earth to kill by means of sword, famine, pestilence, and wild beasts (6:8). The giver of these powers is the Lamb, whose breaking of the seals releases the riders. The four horsemen of the Apocalypse symbolize terrifying desolations sweeping over the earth, as Albrecht Dürer's famous woodcut vividly illustrates. But they do nothing apart from the authorization granted them by God Almighty and the Lamb.

Do this first rider and his white steed bring desolation? In Revelation 19:11 John will see heaven opened and therein a white horse mounted by a rider called Faithful and True, the Word of God, whose flaming eyes, sharp-sword tongue, and dominion over the nations clearly identify him as Jesus, the Son of Man revealed to John in Revelation 1. Is not Jesus, after all, the one who has conquered[2] (5:5)? Many scholars have identified this first rider as the conquering Christ, advancing through the spread of his gospel.[3] There are, however, serious problems with this view. The rider here is armed with a bow and is given one crown (*stephanos*), whereas the Word in Revelation 19 wields a sword and wears many diadems (*diadēmata*). The only visual feature they share is that both ride white horses. The color white, however, is due first to the influence of Zechariah's vision and secondarily to the association of white horses with successful military conquest. Dio Cassius narrates Julius Caesar's victorious return to Rome, after the senate "had voted that sacrifices should be offered for his victory during forty days, and had granted him permission to ride, in the triumph already voted him, in a chariot drawn by white horses."[4]

The clearest indication that the first rider of Revelation 6 is Christ's instrument of judgment but not Christ is this rider's association with the three that follow him, since it is beyond dispute that they symbolize disasters that lead to loss of life: violent warfare, siege and famine, and finally epidemic pestilence and the grave.[5] All four ride forth to afflict the earth in obedience to the cherubim's commands. The rider of the white horse could well be called Conquest. It is appropriate that he lead this terrible cavalry of violence, famine, and death, for the expansionist as-

2. "Conquer" and "overcome" in the NASB represent the same Greek verb, *nikaō*.

3. William Hendriksen, *More Than Conquerors: An Interpretation of the Book of Revelation* (Grand Rapids: Baker, 1939), 113–17, who also cites Bede, Bullinger, Grotius, Irenaeus, Abraham Kuyper, R. C. H. Lenski, and others in support of this view.

4. Dio Cassius *Roman History* 43.14, trans. Earnest Cary, LCL (Cambridge: Harvard University Press, 1987), 233. In Virgil's *Aeneid* the sight of four white horses grazing on a plain is interpreted as an omen portending war (Virgil *Aeneid* 3.537–40, trans. H. R. Fairclough, LCL [Cambridge: Harvard University Press, 1974], 384–85).

5. The majority of Revelation's first recipients experienced its message by hearing it rather than reading the text for themselves (1:3) and would therefore interpret it without the luxury that we enjoy, namely, looking ahead to Rev. 19 or turning back and forth between sections. Admittedly some earlier statements must await clarification later in John's visions (the phenomenon of anticipation noted in chapter 1), but here the immediate context—the other destructive horsemen whom the white horse rider leads—more reliably indicates the meaning of the first horse and its rider than would a leap to John's vision in Rev. 19.

pirations of rulers precipitate military conflict and scarcity of such resources as food and medicine, leading to malnutrition, starvation, epidemic, and death. He is armed with a bow, the weapon of the feared
Parthian mounted archers who threatened the Roman Empire's eastern boundary in the first century—a grim reminder to those who dwelt
in the east (Asia, for instance) that the celebrated *Pax Romana* was not
as inviolable as the Caesars' devotees believed. Yet this portrait of human
avarice for power, galloping greedily through its present domain toward
regions yet to conquer, is nothing more than God's instrument of judgment, sent forth by the Lamb through his breaking of the first seal.[6]

Seal 2: The Rider on the Red Horse (6:3–4)

The second rider, summoned by the second cherub at the breaking of the second seal, rides a horse as red as blood and fire. The great
sword given him portrays the power to remove peace from the earth
as people slaughter one another. Some scholars believe that the rider
of the white horse symbolizes the violence of foreign invasion and
the rider of the red horse the bloodshed of civil war.[7] There is no rea-

6. G. K. Beale initially interprets this and the other three horses with riders as
symbolic of satanic forces waging war against the church specifically: "Therefore,
the first rider represents a satanic force attempting to defeat and oppress believers
spiritually through deception, persecution, or bother" (*The Book of Revelation,*
NIGTC [Grand Rapids: Eerdmans, 1999], 377). Later, though, he acknowledges
with reference to the red horse, "While the woe that this horseman inflicts may be
international strife in general, persecution of Christians is also in mind" (379), and
regarding the famine symbolized by the black horse: "As with the previous two
woes, this plague affects all people, but, again, Christians more specifically may be
in mind." Especially in view of the allusion to Ezek. 14 in "sword, famine, pestilence, wild beasts" (see below), which Beale recognizes, it seems better to view the
primary targets of the destructive forces symbolized by the four horsemen as rebellious, covenant-breaking humanity, "those who dwell on the earth," rather than
the faithful and suffering church.

7. Jürgen Roloff, *The Revelation of John: A Continental Commentary* (Minneapolis:
Fortress, 1993), 86: "He does not stand for external military conquest but rather for
battles and misgivings that divide the citizens of a community among themselves."
Roloff cites Mark 13:8, but Jesus' prediction of "nation raising against nation, and
kingdom against kingdom" seems to speak of international strife (so R. H. Charles,

son, however, to understand the result, "that men would slay one another," as limited to conflict between factions or parties within one political unit. Conquest leads to bloodshed in battle. Both serve the will of the Lamb.

Seal 3: The Rider on the Black Horse (6:5–6)

The rider of the black horse, called forth by the third living creature, carries a pair of balance scales for measuring grain. These are interpreted by "something like a voice in the midst of the four living creatures"—apparently the voice of the Lamb (5:6) or of God on his throne (4:6)—quoting exorbitant grain prices ("a quart of wheat for a denarius, three quarts of barley for a denarius") but also ordering that there be no shortage of oil and wine. Local farming made the province of Asia self-sufficient in two of the three major agricultural products of the Mediterranean, olive oil and wine. Only for grains, the third crop, least expensive but most essential to sustain life, were the cities of Asia dependent on import, especially from Egypt and what is now Ukraine.[8] Since a quart of wheat was considered one day's supply for one soldier and a denarius was one day's wage for an agricultural laborer, the price quoted means that a worker's entire earnings would be consumed on his allotment of bread. The usual price of a quart of wheat seems to have been roughly one-eighth of a denarius, so the price quoted here reflects 800 percent inflation in grain prices.[9] The price is inflated by severely reduced supply, as the mention of "famine" in connection with the fourth horse's riders shows (6:8). Famine can be brought on by natural causes such as drought or infestation (Deut. 28:23–24, 38–42).

A Critical and Exegetical Commentary on the Revelation of St. John the Divine, 2 vols., ICC [Edinburgh: T & T Clark, 1920], 1:158) rather than internal civil conflict.

8. Roloff, *Revelation,* 87.

9. Moses Stuart, *A Commentary on the Apocalypse,* 2 vols. (London: Wiley and Putnam, 1845), 2:155. Charles, *Commentary,* 1:167, calculates on the basis of prices cited in Cicero *In Verrem* 3.81 that "the price in our text was 16 times the lowest price of wheat in Sicily, 10⅔ times the highest, and 8 times the estimate made by the Senate." Roloff estimates that the price is ten times the average (*Revelation,* 87).

But here, in the company of riders symbolizing conquest and warfare, the scarcity of sustenance-level food should be attributed to the conditions of war, disrupting trade and transportation during siege (Deut. 28:49–57; 2 Kings 7).

There is, however, a limit to this judgment, as there is to all God's providential judgments as long as God's patience delays final judgment (2 Peter 3:9; Rom. 2:3–4). Limitations of various kinds distinguish restricted, anticipatory expressions of the wrath of the Lamb throughout history from the unrestrained display of his judgment at the end of history. Here famine affects grains but does not harm oil or wine. The riders of the fourth horse will be able to inflict death over only one-quarter of the earth (Rev. 6:8). [10] At the sounding of the first four trumpets fiery plagues will fall on one-third of the earth, sea, rivers and springs, and sky (8:7–12). This feature of limited judgments is an interpretive key and an encouragement to besieged churches. When we see in John's visions restrained and partial judgment, we are being shown symbols of the course of ordinary history between the comings of Christ. The dangers and disasters that shatter and dismantle arrogant civilizations (in John's day, Rome), which are symbolized in the four horsemen and most of the trumpets, are the Lamb's providential instruments of prewrath wrath and prejudgment justice, foreshadowing the end when God's victory over his enemies will be total. As Christians see societies crumble and collapse, our response should not be terrified alarm, as though our security were bound up with a fragile human network of law and order, but anticipation and confidence: the Lamb is now on the throne, with God's plan for history firmly in hand.

10. Rodney Stark, *The Rise of Christianity: A Sociologist Reconsiders History* (Princeton, N.J.: Princeton University Press, 1996), makes this observation without any reference to Revelation: "In 165, during the reign of Marcus Aurelius, a devastating epidemic swept through the Roman Empire. Some medical historians suspect that it was the first appearance of smallpox in the West. . . . During the fifteen-year duration of the epidemic, from a quarter to a third of the empire's population died from it, including Marcus Aurelius himself, in 180 in Vienna" (73). Stark attributes Christianity's growth in the second and third centuries in part to the hopeful and loving response of Christians in the midst of the widespread suffering and terror that the epidemic evoked in the residents of the empire (74–75).

Seal 4: The Riders of the Ashen Horse (6:7–8)

The color of the fourth horse (NASB: "ashen") differs from its "dappled" counterpart in Zechariah's vision (Zech. 6:3). The horse John sees is literally green, the color of grass and other plants (Rev. 8:7; 9:4; Mark 6:39). As in modern English so in ancient Greek, when applied to people's appearance, "green" signified the pallor of illness or even death.[11] Hence this horse, befitting its riders, exhibits the pale green, ashen color of death.

The name of this horse's rider is "Death," and "Hades," the grave, accompanies him. This pair was linked in the opening vision, for the Son of Man has the keys of death and Hades and thus the authority to liberate their prisoners (Rev. 1:18). This final horse and its riders portray the grisly effects of the preceding three: "authority was given them . . . to kill with sword and with famine and with pestilence and by the wild beasts of the earth" (6:8). The sword[12] represents the second rider, and Famine had just ridden forth on the third, black horse. "Pestilence" (*thanatos* = literally "death," but here in the sense of epidemic disease as often in the Old Testament), like famine, is war's toxic byproduct, spreading death among those who survive the bloodshed. The same collection of deadly afflictions were predicted by Jesus to reassure his followers that their occurrence will not mean that the end is imminent:

> And when you hear of wars and disturbances, do not be terrified; for these things must take place first, but the end does not follow immediately. . . . Nation will rise against nation, and kingdom against king-

11. BAGD, 882, offers the definition *"pale* as the color of a person in sickness as contrasted with his appearance in health," citing as examples texts by Hippocrates, Thucydides, and others. See also LN entry 79.35: "'pale greenish gray' (evidently regarded as typical of a corpse, since the color is used as a symbol of death)."

12. Although different Greek words are represented by the "sword" (*machaira*) given the rider of the red horse (Rev. 6:4) and the "sword" (*romphaia*) wielded by Death and the Grave (6:8), no significant difference in meaning is intended. Every other occurrence of *romphaia* refers to the sword proceeding from the mouth of Christ, symbolizing his word (1:16; 2:12, 16; 19:15, 21). *Romphaia* is used instead of *machaira* in 6:8 to emphasize the allusion to Ezek. 14:21 LXX.

dom, and there will be great earthquakes, and in various places plagues
and famines. (Luke 21:9–11)[13]

Attack by wild beasts completes the quartet of Death's weapons, so
this list echoes God's threat of inescapable judgments in Ezekiel
14:12–21. Not even the presence of righteous Noah, Daniel, and Lot
could protect a treacherous people from God's covenant curses of
famine (vv. 13–14), predatory beasts (vv. 15–16), sword (vv. 17–18),
or plague (vv. 19–20). "How much more when I send My four severe judgments against Jerusalem: sword, famine, wild beasts and plague
(LXX *thanatos*, as in Rev. 6:8) to cut off man and beast from it!" (v. 21).
These four are the Lord's weapons against lands and cities that defy
his authority.

The churches of Asia must realize that through his sovereignty over
all things, from rulers to bacteria, Christ will send all sorts of limited,
providential judgments on the Roman imperial system, exposing the
emptiness of its politico-military confidence and its religious pretensions. One historian summed up the shattering effect of epidemics on
Roman confidence:

> Again and again, the forward march of Roman power and world or-
> ganization was interrupted by the only force against which political ge-
> nius and military valor were utterly helpless—epidemic disease . . . and
> when it came, as though carried by storm clouds, all other things gave
> way, and men crouched in terror, abandoning all their quarrels, un-
> dertakings, and ambitions, until the tempest had blown over.[14]

But Jesus said that despite the world-shaking impact of such disasters,
"the end does not follow immediately." This delay poses the problem
portrayed in the fifth seal.

13. Charles, *Commentary*, 1:158–61, charts the parallels between the records of
Jesus' eschatological teaching in Matthew, Mark, and Luke, and the seal cycle in
Revelation.

14. Hans Zinsser, *Rats, Lice and History* (1934; reprint ed., New York: Bantam,
1960), 99 (cited in Stark, *Rise of Christianity*, 74).

Seal 5: The Souls of the Slain (6:9–11)

When the Lamb opens the fifth seal, the vision shifts from earth (Rev. 6:4, 8) to heaven. The altar, mentioned here for the first time, is an important item of furniture in the sanctuary of God, for approach to God is impossible apart from sacrifice. The Old Testament tabernacle and temple had two altars—one in the courtyard, for the offering of slain sacrificial animals, and then, within the Holy Place, the altar of incense immediately before the veil into the Holiest Place (Exod. 27:1–8; 30:1–10; Heb. 9:3–4). John sees a single altar, "the altar" as he always calls it, which serves the purposes of both altars in the earthly shadow sanctuary (Heb. 8:5; 9:11). From this heavenly altar incense symbolic of the church's prayers rises (Rev. 8:3), but this altar has also witnessed the shedding of blood in the slaughter of Jesus' martyrs (16:6–7).

Here the altar appears as the altar of sacrifice, and John sees "the souls of those who had been slain"[15] for God's word underneath the altar, where the blood of sacrificial animals would be poured out (Exod. 29:12). Although the Greek word translated "soul" (*psyche*) can sometimes refer to the principle of life in animate creatures (Rev. 8:9; 12:11; 16:3), here it refers to human beings' inner, immaterial, conscious identity, which is distinguished from our bodies and continues after the death of the body (see also 18:13, 14; 20:4). John will see the souls of the martyrs in heaven[16] again in his vision of their thousand-year reign (20:4). Whereas the emphasis in Revelation 20 is on the dominion of the martyrs, here in the fifth seal we hear their appeal for vengeance and vindication expressed as a psalm of lament ("How long?"[17]) over God's long-suffering toward his enemies.

The Lord's response to the martyrs' appeal for speedy justice is a gift and a strange word of hope. As the riders of judgment horses were

15. The verb *slain* here, as in the vision of the Lamb (Rev. 5:6), is *sphazō*.

16. The heavenly setting of the martyrs' rule in Rev. 20:4 is shown in the words, "I saw thrones, and they sat upon them, and judgment was given to them," which allude to Daniel's vision of the heavenly court of the Ancient of Days and the Son of Man (Dan. 7:9–10, 13).

17. For example, Ps. 13:1; 89:46.

given a crown, a sword, and authority to kill, so each of these sacrificial victims under the altar is given a white robe, symbolic of victory through faithful purity (Rev. 3:4–5). When we see this multitude of martyrs again in the interlude between seals 6 and 7, their multiethnic character will be evident (7:9), but also their song will have shifted from the minor key of lament to the major chords of celebration for the salvation won by the Lamb (7:10, 13–14).

The word of hope includes the counsel to "rest for a little while longer," anticipating the second of Revelation's seven benedictions, which pronounces "the dead who die in the Lord from now on" blessed because they "rest from their labors, for their deeds follow with them" (14:13). The mixed experience of the church on earth—liberated, consecrated, and crowned by the Lamb but also assailed by enemies—is reflected in the ambivalent status of the martyrs in heaven who are anxiously awaiting justice now delayed but also celebrating Sabbath rest. The strangeness of this word of hope lies in the measure used to mark the duration of the delay: "until the number of their fellow servants and their brethren who were to be killed even as they had been, would be completed also" (6:11). Here is a clear answer to our When? question, but it will only frustrate the date setters. The Lamb will return to avenge his witnesses' blood just as soon as the very last martyr lays down his or her life. More familiar to us and more pleasant is the prerequisite to his parousia that Jesus announced in Mark 13:10 ("The gospel must first be preached to all the nations") and its corollary, that God delays not because he is late but because he is "patient toward you, not wishing for any to perish but for all to come to repentance" (2 Peter 3:9; cf. Rom. 2:4). Accompanying the worldwide spread of God's good news, however, is the prolonged affliction of the church that bears this joyful message. The days on God's calendar are marked off, one by one, in the blood of the martyrs.

Seal 6: The Great Earthquake (6:12–17)

Seal 5 explained the restraint of the judgments of seals 1–4, showing that the end will not come until all martyrs have died. Now seal 6 provides the balancing assurance that the end will come certainly and suddenly. The breaking of this seal precipitates an earthquake of unparalleled magnitude, reaching up into the heavens, blackening the sun, bloodying the moon, shaking the stars loose to fall to earth like figs in the wind, ripping the sky open like rolled papyrus, and then returning to earth to toss mountains and islands from their places.[18]

This symbolic portrayal of the dissolution of "the first heaven and the first earth" (Rev. 21:1) as a massive earthquake-skyquake would have been terrifyingly vivid to Asian Christians who had experienced the two major earthquakes that had crippled the cities of Asia Minor in the first century. Several others elsewhere in the empire, including the eruption of Vesuvius that buried Pompeii in 79, had impressed their horrors on the minds and memories of Rome's subjects.[19]

The theological significance of the earthquake is rooted in Old Testament precedent. In previous biblical narrative and imagery, the earth was set to quaking at the coming of the Lord in his holiness to establish justice. God's descent to Sinai to deliver his law to Moses for the people was accompanied by earthquake (Exod. 19:18).

> Frequently the creation shakes before the coming of God as warrior, leading his hosts to battle against his enemies (Judg 5:4–5; Joel 2:10; Mic 1:4; Ps 78:7–8), before the coming of God to reign over the nations (Pss 97:5; 99:1), before the coming of God to judge the wicked (Isa 13:13; 24:18–20; 34:4; Jer 51:29; Ezek 38:20; Nah 1:5). These aspects are all found together in the apocalyptic descriptions of the great cosmic quake that will accompany the eschatological theophany. . . .[20]

In Revelation the "great earthquake" reappears in the visions of the two witnesses (Rev. 11:13) and of the seventh and final bowl of wrath (16:18). The same dire event is in view when John sees the great white throne and One seated on it "from whose presence earth and heaven

18. This imagery has Old Testament precedent: sun darkened and moon turned to blood (Joel 2:31), stars falling like figs in the wind and sky rolled like a scroll (Isa. 34:4), mountains and islands displaced (Isa. 54:10; Ezek. 38:20).

19. Bauckham, *Climax of Prophecy,* 206–7.

20. Ibid., 199. Bauckham's chapter "The Eschatological Earthquake" is illuminating (199–209).

fled away, and no place was found for them" (20:11). In other words, the sixth seal carries us suddenly to the end of history, when, as the author to the Hebrews interprets Haggai 2:6, God's voice "'will shake not only the earth [as at Sinai], but also the heaven.' This expression, 'Yet once more,' denotes the removing of those things which can be shaken, as of created things, so that those things which cannot be shaken may remain" (Heb. 12:26–27).[21] Everything stained by the dragon's touch and human sin is swept aside before the face of God and the wrath of the Lamb, and rebels from every stratum of society—from king to slave—try in vain to hide from the "great day of their wrath" (Rev. 6:15–17). The terrified sinners ask a desperate, rhetorical question, "Who is able to stand?" assuming that no one can survive the coming cosmic trauma.

The sixth seal carries us beyond the present period of limited, providential judgments on earth (seals 1–4) and martyrs' rest in heaven (seal 5). This destruction falls not on a portion of rebellious humanity or a fraction of the spheres that touch human life but on the whole of the earth and the sky. It falls specifically on those light signs (sun, moon, stars) placed into the firmament at creation's dawn to separate light from dark, day from night, and to mark time's passage as long as the first heavens and earth endure (Gen. 1:14–18). But before the end is revealed, John sees the surprising and positive answer to the rebels' question, "Who is able to stand?"[22]

Delay: Visions of the Victors (7:1–17)

Between the sixth and seventh seals—and specifically in answer to the question that closed the vision of the sixth seal—John receives a double vision of the protected and triumphant followers of Christ. This

21. Note also the contrast between the impermanence of earth and the heavens and the eternity of their Creator in the citation of Ps. 102:25–26 in Heb. 1:10–12. The imagery of the sky rolling like a scroll is derived from Isa. 34:4.

22. See Nahum 1:5–6: "Mountains *quake* because of Him, and the hills dissolve; indeed the *earth* is upheaved by His *presence*, the world and all the inhabitants in it. *Who can stand* before His indignation? Who can endure the burning of His *anger*? His wrath is poured out like fire and the rocks are broken up by Him." (Italicized words represent vocabulary from Nahum 1 reflected in Rev. 6:12–17.) See also Mal. 3:2.

interlude, like the visions that separate the sixth trumpet from the seventh (Rev. 10:1–11:13), serves two purposes. First, the interlude visions reassure the church that the woes inflicted by the wrath of the Lamb on rebellious humanity cannot sever us from his protective care. Second, the interludes dramatize the delay of final judgment, which evoked the martyrs' lament (6:10). Those who hear Revelation read aloud experience delay and suspense in the unfolding of the drama (cf. 7:3; 10:6).[23]

In the first of the twin visions that interrupt the seal cycle, John sees four angels at the earth's four corners (Isa. 11:12; Ezek. 7:2), restraining the four winds from wreaking destruction on earth, sea, and trees, until another angel marks each of God's servants as his property with his seal (*sphragis*) upon their foreheads. The scene takes us back to a time prior to the events of the sixth seal, which showed the destruction of the universe through earthquake and falling stars. No harm will come to earth, sea, or trees until after God's servants are sealed (Rev. 7:3). Note that the order of the visions does not reflect the chronology of the events that they symbolize.

The seal is the name of Christ and of God. This becomes clear when this group of 144,000 reappears, standing with the Lamb on Mount Zion, with "His name and the name of His Father written on their foreheads" (Rev. 14:1). Thus the 144,000 bondservants of God portray the company of the victors, on whom Jesus has promised to write the name of his God, of the new Jerusalem, and Jesus' new name (3:12).

Later we will see a satanic counterfeit of this gracious act, when those who worship the beast are compelled to receive his mark (*charagma*) of ownership on their right hands or foreheads (Rev. 13:16). The difference in terminology is significant, for the word *seal* implies security under the protective authority of God. The beast's "mark" can make no such guarantee. But God's seal on his servants' foreheads does not symbolize a promise that they will be spared physical suffering, for Christ's summons to faithfulness, even to the extremity of martyrdom, pervades Revelation (e.g., 2:10; 12:11). Rather, just as

---

23. Bauckham, *Climax of Prophecy*, 12: "These lengthy interruptions in the sequence of judgments *delay* the final, seventh judgment, and such delay would be particularly felt in oral performance. They serve to incorporate the issue of delay of judgment into the structure of the book."

the binding of God's law on the Israelites' foreheads and hands symbolized his sovereignty over their thoughts and actions (Deut. 6:8), so the Lamb's seal shows that he protects his servants from being deceived by the Serpent and the beasts (Rev. 12:15–17; 13:11–18; 16:13–14). Who can withstand the day of the Lamb's wrath (6:17)? Only those "branded" with the Lamb's seal of ownership.[24] The symbolic character of John's visions shows that we should not expect this seal to appear as a visible mark on believers' physical foreheads. Rather, just as true circumcision is more than skin deep, reaching to the heart (Rom. 2:28–29; 4:11), so also the seal of ownership that marks us as "God's own possession" is the Holy Spirit (Eph. 1:13–14).

Who are the 144,000 who receive God's seal, whose safety from wrath is secured by the name of the Lamb and his Father? Since they are described as belonging to the twelve tribes of the sons of Israel, twelve thousand from each tribe, it is widely believed that this group represents a Jewish remnant, converted to faith in Jesus the Messiah by the rapture of the church prior to the tribulation. According to this view Gentile believers in Jesus will not go through this tribulation, and consequently only these faithful Israelites need God's protective seal. As appealing as this view is to those (myself included) who do not relish suffering for the faith, it faces all sorts of difficulties from the text of Revelation.

In the first place, the list of the twelve tribes corresponds to none of the ways that the twelve tribes were reckoned in the Old Testament. If we think of the twelve sons of Jacob, we are puzzled by the presence of Manasseh, Jacob's grandson, and the absence of Dan. If we think of the twelve tribes who inherited the land, we cannot explain why Joseph appears along with his son Manasseh but not Ephraim and why Levi appears, since this tribe did not receive an apportioned territory—the Lord was Levi's inheritance (Deut. 10:9–10).[25] Second,

24. Similarly Ezekiel was shown in vision a "man clothed in linen at whose loins was a writing case," who was commanded to mark the foreheads of those who lamented the defilement of the temple before God sent his angels of vengeance throughout the city, beginning at the temple, to cut down all those who did not bear his mark (LXX: "sign," sēmeion; Ezek. 9:3–6).

25. Also, if the tribes were listed according to land inheritance, it would be slightly irregular for Joseph to replace his son Ephraim, as seems to be the case in Rev. 7.

the sealing of this 144,000 is identical to the promise that Jesus made to all overcomers from every race in the letter to Philadelphia (Rev. 3:12). Third, in John's later vision of the Lamb's army on Zion the 144,000 are identified as those "purchased" from the earth, as first fruits to God and to the Lamb (14:3–4); and by his blood the Lamb "purchased" for God individuals from every tribe and tongue and people and nation (5:9). This is the ethnic composition of the innumerable multitude that John will see immediately after hearing the census of the tribes of God's sealed servants (7:9). Perhaps their being called the first fruits suggests that these 144,000 are the first installment of a larger harvest, when angels are sent forth to harvest the earth (14:14–20). In that case the 144,000 symbolize not belated believers from a single ethnic group (the Jews) but the faithful martyrs from all the peoples, who through their death are gathered first into God's presence. Fourth, the 144,000 are later portrayed as a holy army composed exclusively of men "who have not been defiled with women" (14:4). This is symbolic of the church's spiritual purity, in no way implying that only single, celibate male servants of God receive his seal of protection.

Christopher Smith has offered a clear and persuasive explanation of the selection and order of the tribes listed in Revelation 7.[26] The disparity of selection between this list and the Old Testament lists of Jacob's sons and Israel's tribes show that the twelve tribes in Revelation are symbolic with respect to the quantity[27] and the ethnicity of the Lamb's army. Smith's explanation of the order in which the tribes are listed shows that its purpose is to symbolize the inclusion of the Gentile nations into this sealed and protected people of God. The start-

26. Christopher R. Smith, "The Portrayal of the Church as the New Israel in the Names and Order of the Tribes in Revelation 7.5–8," *JSNT* 39 (1990): 111–18. See also idem, "The Tribes of Revelation 7 and the Literary Competence of John the Seer," *JETS* 38 (1995): 213–18, in which he answers a critique by Richard Bauckham, "The List of the Tribes in Revelation 7 Again" (*JSNT* 42 [1991]: 99–115).

27. We noted in chap. 1 that the number twelve symbolizes the complete people of God and the council of their leaders (21:12–17), whereas high powers of ten ($1,000 = 10^3$; myriad $= 10,000 = 10^4$) signify great quantities (5:11; 9:16; 20:1–7; 21:16).

ing point is the list of Jacob's twelve sons in Genesis 35:23–26, immediately following the accounts of the birth of the twelfth, Benjamin, and the incest of the first, Reuben—an act that would lead to Reuben's loss of the firstborn son's leadership and inheritance privileges (Gen. 49:3–4; 1 Chron. 5:1–2). The following changes in the order from Genesis 35 explain the order in Revelation 7 in harmony with the theology of Revelation as a whole. Judah is promoted from fourth position to first as the tribe of the Messiah, Jesus. The sons of the concubines (technically slaves of the competing wives Leah and Rachel, pressed by their mistresses into service as surrogate mothers) are promoted from the end of the line to positions three through six, above six of the sons of the wives, Leah and Rachel. The elevation of these descendants of women who were outsiders to the covenant family signifies the inclusion of the Gentiles among "the bond-servants of our God" (Rev. 7:3). Dan, however, is replaced by Joseph's son Manasseh because the tribe of Dan became notorious in Israel's history for leading the northern kingdom into idolatrous apostasy (Judg. 18; 1 Kings 12:29–30) and in intertestamental Jewish literature was associated with the antichrist.[28] Thus the order of the tribes in Revelation 7 symbolizes the reign of Jesus, from the tribe of Judah; the incorporation of outcasts; and the exclusion of idolaters from the covenant community that God shields from his terrible wrath. The rearrangement can be visualized as in the chart on page 133.

This explanation not only makes sense of the selection and ordering of the tribes but also reinforces the unity of the interlude visions in Revelation 7. In the fifth chapter John's lament over the seemingly unanswerable question, "Who is worthy to open the scroll?" is answered first with reassuring words that announce the Lion from Judah's tribe and then with the surprising vision of the Lamb, slain yet standing. Likewise here the seemingly unanswerable question, "Who is able

---

28. Charles, *Commentary,* 1:208–9, cites the church fathers Irenaeus, Hippolytus, and Andreas for the identification of the antichrist with Dan, commenting: "That this tradition of the origin of Antichrist is pre-Christian and Jewish I have shown in the notes on Test[ament of] Dan[iel] v. 6–7, in my edition of the Test[aments of the] XII Patriarchs. . . ." Caird, *Revelation,* 99, also cites the Talmudic tractate *Sanhedrin* 96[a] and the *Jerusalem Targum I,* on Exod. 17:8.

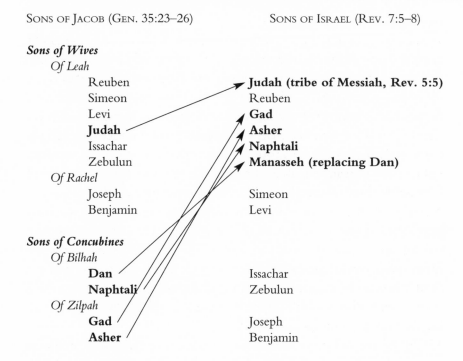

Sons of Jacob (Gen. 35:23–26)   Sons of Israel (Rev. 7:5–8)

Sons of Wives
  Of Leah
      Reuben   **Judah (tribe of Messiah, Rev. 5:5)**
      Simeon   Reuben
      Levi   **Gad**
      Judah   **Asher**
      Issachar   **Naphtali**
      Zebulun   **Manasseh (replacing Dan)**
  Of Rachel
      Joseph   Simeon
      Benjamin   Levi

Sons of Concubines
  Of Bilhah
      Dan   Issachar
      Naphtali   Zebulun
  Of Zilpah
      Gad   Joseph
      Asher   Benjamin

to stand?" (6:17) is answered first with the roster of Israel's twelve tribes and then with the surprising vision of those who have emerged safe from the great tribulation, an uncountable congregation not from a single nation but from "every nation and all tribes and peoples and tongues" (7:9, 14). As Judah's Lion proved to be the slain Lamb, displaying royal power through the weakness of his sacrifice, so the flock he protects sounds like a precisely numbered, exclusively Israelite army braced for battle but looks like a countless, international crowd celebrating a victory already won. The victory was won by the Lamb when he was slain to purchase this multitude from the peoples to become God's treasured kingdom of priests (5:5, 9). The whiteness of the celebrants' robes comes from washing in the Lamb's blood (7:14), for this blood silences our accuser's charges forever (12:11). Their white robes show that these joyful victors are, paradoxically, the martyrs whose souls John saw poured out like sacrificial blood beneath the altar, whose lament was answered by God's consoling counsel and his gift of white robes (6:9–11). The lamenting martyrs, awaiting justice, and the celebrating victors, praising the God who saves, are the same group, viewed from different perspectives. Both perspectives are true: nothing less than Jesus' return, bringing the resurrection of the saints and the destruction of death, the last enemy (1 Cor. 15:23–26), can satisfy our longing for God's justice to prevail. Yet between now and then, those who die in the Lord are blessed in his presence (Rev. 14:13; 2 Cor. 5:6–8). Just as the images of lion and lamb carried distinct and complementary messages about Christ and his victory, so the two images in Revelation 7 enable us to see the church from complementary perspectives: the people of God's covenant, arrayed for battle; and the peoples of the world, redeemed by the Lamb and already celebrating his victory.

The difference between the 144,000 "Israelites" and the countless multiethnic multitude is not in the ethnic composition of the two groups but in their location. The sealed and numbered army of Israel shows the faithful church on earth, shielded from apostasy and from God's wrath by our union with the Lamb (bearing his name, sealed by his Spirit). The innumerable assembly of nations shows the victorious church in heaven, emerging triumphant from tribulation not through a painless rapture but through a faithful death (Rev. 12:11). They have known hunger, thirst, exposure, and tears; but the woes to be released on the world in final judgment on human sin cannot touch those who dwell in God's sanctuary, shepherded by the Lamb to the springs of the water of life (7:15–17).

The international multitude gathers to celebrate a triumphant king. The palm branches in their hands (Rev. 7:9) are props in the ancient world's choreography of praise, as they were when a crowd welcomed Jesus to Jerusalem with the shout, "Hosanna! Blessed is He who comes in the name of the Lord, even the King of Israel" (John 12:13). The white-robed worshipers now lead the heavenly assembly into a new dimension of praise. This is the first time that we hear the church sing to its Sovereign, so it is fitting that this assembly of purchased, purified peoples (Rev. 5:9; 7:9, 14) introduces a new theme to the divine excellencies that were celebrated in Revelation 4–5: "Salvation to our God who sits on the throne, and to the Lamb" (7:10). The church's praise is answered by the chorus of angels, elders, and living creatures in a sevenfold doxology, which virtually replicates the earlier seven-fold praise of the Lamb, with one substitution: in place of "wealth" (5:12), our God now receives "thanksgiving," his creatures' fitting response to his saving grace (7:12).

The elder shows John the safety of this multitude (Rev. 7:15–17) in imagery drawn from Isaiah 49:10: "They will not hunger or thirst, nor will the scorching heat or sun strike them down; for He who has compassion on them will lead them and will guide them to springs of water."[29] In Isaiah's prophecy God is the Shepherd who leads his flock to springs of water (cf. Ps. 23:1–2; Ezek. 34:13). In Revelation the Lamb is "their shepherd" (cf. John 10; 1 Peter 2:25; 5:4). This is fitting, since he is "in the center of the throne" and with the Father receives worship from all creatures everywhere (Rev. 5:13–14).[30] To shelter his flock from sun and heat their Protector "will spread His tabernacle [*skēnoō*] over them" (5:15; cf. Ezek. 37:27), and he "will wipe every tear from their eyes" (Rev. 5:17; cf. Isa. 25:8). These victors already taste the joys of the new Jerusalem, where God will "dwell" (*skēnoō*) among his people, wipe every tear from their eyes, and cause them to drink of the water of life (Rev. 21:3–4; 22:1).

In response to the sixth seal's terrifying preview of final judgment and the desperate question, "Who is able to stand?" these visions assure the Lamb's flock that nothing in the present or the future will be able to separate us from the love of God in Christ. Those marked as God's treasure by the seal of his name are secured and sheltered from his burning wrath to come. They are the people of his covenant, portrayed as twelve complete tribes. But now that the Lamb has con-

29. The detailed echo of the salvation promise of Isa. 49 is noteworthy because the united nations in Rev. 7 are the fulfillment of God's promise to his Servant in that Old Testament context (to which Jesus alluded in Acts 1:8): "It is too small a thing that You should be My Servant to raise up the tribes of Jacob and to restore the preserved ones of Israel; I will also make You a light of the nations so that My salvation may reach to the end of the earth" (Isa. 49:6).

30. R. T. France, "The Worship of Jesus: A Neglected Factor in Christological Debate?" in *Christ the Lord: Essays in Christology Presented to Donald Guthrie,* ed. Harold H. Rowdon (Downers Grove, Ill.: InterVarsity Press, 1982), 17–36, especially 33; also Richard Bauckham, *The Theology of the Book of Revelation* (Cambridge: Cambridge University Press, 1993), 58–65.

quered through his death, God's covenant embraces all nations, tribes, peoples, and tongues. The Israel secured by God's seal is a multiethnic multitude, dressed in robes washed white in the Lamb's blood and praising him for his salvation.

Seal 7: Silence in Heaven (8:1–5)

The sixth seal showed the dismantling of the present earth and heaven through the great earthquake that will shake and shatter earth and sky (Rev. 6:12–14). We might therefore expect that the seventh seal would disclose the new creation that is to come. Instead, when the Lamb breaks the seventh seal, nothing seems to happen: "there was silence in heaven for about half an hour" (8:1). But silence in heaven, even for a short duration, is a surprising and noteworthy development, in view of the glimpses of God's heavenly court that we have received so far. The four living creatures "do not cease to say, 'Holy, holy, holy is the Lord God'" (4:8), and the twenty-four elders constantly confess God's worthiness to receive glory, honor, and power (4:11). When the Lamb receives the scroll, new songs of praise break out in expanding circles of worshipers (5:9–14). The martyrs' lament (6:10) and their song of salvation "day and night" add to the heavenly uproar (7:10, 15). But now . . . silence.

Silence is creation's expectant response to the Lord's impending arrival in judgment. "Be silent, all flesh, before the LORD; for he is aroused from his holy habitation" (Zech. 2:13).

> Be silent before the LORD GOD! For the day of the LORD is near. . . .
> "Then it will come about on the day of the LORD's sacrifice, that I will punish the princes, the king's sons, and all who clothe themselves with foreign garments. . . . On that day," declares the LORD, "there will be the sound of a cry from the Fish Gate, a wail from the Second Quarter, and a loud crash from the hills." (Zeph. 1:7–10)

This silence is the calm before the storm. For God's enemies on earth it is a silence of dread, but for those who dwell in heaven it is the silence of eager expectation.

Now, in the still silence of the seventh seal, another set of voices can be heard. This is the meaning of the incense-burning ritual that John observes in Revelation 8:3–5. In the silence he sees seven angels, ready to sound trumpets that will unleash woes on the earth (8:2), but before they blow their warnings, another angel approaches the altar to offer incense with the prayers of all the saints.[31] God has heard and answered the plea of the martyrs, who now rest safe, awaiting the end (6:9–11). God also hears and answers the appeals of his servants who still live on this strife-torn earth, in the midst of the battle. The content of the saints' prayers is implied in the angel's next act and the trumpet judgments to follow. Having offered the incense that symbolizes the church's prayers, the angel "took the censer and filled it with the fire of the altar, and threw it to the earth" (8:5). Then, as the trumpets begin to sound and the scene shifts to earth, fiery judgments fall from heaven to earth: fire with blood on dry land, a burning mountain into the sea, a star burning like a torch on rivers and springs, a star with a key to open the furnace of the abyss (8:7–8, 10; 9:1–2). In other words, the judgments symbolized in the trumpet cycle come from the altar on which the incense of the saints' prayers has been offered as God's answer to his people's pleas from the midst of the battle. John's first hearers would see Roman society shaken by scandal, split by intrigue, and threatened by external assault, but they were not to be paralyzed in fear. Such traumas were and are merely instruments in the hand of the Lamb, exposing the emptiness of human arrogance and summoning the nations to repentance.

The vision of the angel at the altar, offering the incense/prayers of the saints in heaven's silence, links the seal cycle to the trumpet cycle. The breaking of the seven seals was preparatory to disclosing and executing the scroll's contents. The seal visions profile forces that will be at work in the cycle of trumpet judgments, and they assure us that the most threatening powers must always be subject to the Lamb, to do his will. Thus the riders depicted in the first four seals—insatiable politico-military expansionism, armed conflict, famine, and pestilence, leading

31. Caird, *Commentary*, 108: "According to the Talmud (*Hag.* 12[b]; *'Abodah Z.* 3[b]), the angels sing unceasingly throughout the night, but are silent by day to allow the praises of Israel to be heard in heaven."

to the grave—are the means by which the Lamb who controls providence will thwart the pretensions of his human rivals. Though he seems to delay the justice for which his martyrs long (seal 5) and the deliverance for which his saints pray (seal 7), his patience will not wait forever. When he brings judgment—whether the limited calamities of providence in history (trumpets) or the unrestrained catastrophe at the end (seal 6, bowls)—he does so to rescue and vindicate his suffering church. When he finally and fully reveals his wrath, only those sealed as his property, bearing his name, will greet that day with joy.

CHAPTER SEVEN

Trumpets:
Current and Coming Woes
(8:1–9:21; 11:15–19)

Wars and Rumors of Wars

Jesus fortified his followers for "a long obedience in the same direction"[1] by forewarning them that "wars and rumors of wars," though they are part of God's plan for history, are not in themselves signals that the end is near. International strife, famines, and earthquakes are only the beginning of the birth pangs that will in due time deliver God's kingdom in all its fullness into the world (Matt. 24:6–8). This is the message of the trumpet visions shown to John: wars must happen, but the end is not yet.

The trumpet visions portray limited disasters and distresses in the midst of history, events that are bitter foretastes of the final, unrestrained destruction of all opposition to God's reign at the end of the present world order. The correspondence between the spheres afflicted in the sounding of the first four trumpets and those destroyed

---

1. The title of Eugene Peterson's study of the psalms of ascent, *A Long Obedience in the Same Direction: Discipleship in an Instant Society* (Downers Grove, Ill.: InterVarsity Press, 1980) is taken from Friedrich Nietzsche, *Beyond Good and Evil:* "The essential thing 'in heaven and earth' is . . . that there should be a long obedience in the same direction."

in the pouring of the first four bowls (earth, sea, rivers and streams, sky) shows that God's righteous wrath summons every aspect of our environment to indict human rebellion, both through the flow of history (trumpets) and at its climax (bowls).[2] Unlike the bowl judgments, which will be "the last, because in them the wrath of God is finished" (Rev. 15:1), when the trumpets are sounded the damage affects only one-third of each sphere. The demons released with the fifth trumpet are restrained in other ways: they cannot touch the earth's vegetation or God's sealed servants (9:4), and the duration and severity of the torment they can inflict is limited (9:5, 10). When the sixth trumpet sounds, a vast cavalry of eastern invaders sweeps across the Euphrates, killing one-third of the population (9:18). In each of the first six trumpets God draws the line, dictating that destruction go this far, and no farther. The judgments inflicted with each bowl are universal, pervading their respective spheres. This contrast between trumpets and bowls is consistent with the purposes of trumpets in the Old Testament and the ancient world.

Seven Trumpets

In biblical literature the sound of the trumpet announces the coming of God in splendor and victory. The Lord descended on Mount Sinai to give Moses his law with trumpet blasts of increasing intensity and volume (Exod. 19:16, 19). Two silver trumpets were fashioned to summon Israel to holy assembly before the Lord at his tent of meeting (Num. 10:2–3). Trumpet blasts signaled the good news of release and restoration upon the arrival of the Jubilee year (Lev. 25:9) and the news of a king's coronation (1 Kings 1:34). With a trumpet sound the Lord would assemble nations to inflict his judgment on Babylon (Jer. 51:27). The second coming of Christ will be heralded with the final, resounding trumpet blast (Matt. 24:31; 1 Cor. 15:52; 1 Thess. 4:16).

The seven trumpets used in the siege of Jericho (Josh. 6:2–21) and the trumpet that sounds the alarm before the terrifying day of the Lord

2. In the law of Moses the covenant curses are interpreted as the testimony of heaven and earth against Israel's covenant breaking (Deut. 30:19; 32:1; cf. Isa. 1:2).

in Joel 2 are significant precursors of the trumpets in Revelation. When Joshua led Israel into the land of promise, they immediately confronted the fortified city of Jericho on the Jordan's west bank. God commanded that the Israelite army march around the city wall once a day for six days, with the ark of the covenant and with seven priests sounding trumpets as they marched. On the seventh day the Israelites encircled Jericho seven times; and on the last lap the priests sounded the trumpets, the people shouted, and the walls collapsed. As the priests who blew the trumpets marched before the ark at Jericho, so in Revelation the seventh trumpet brings the ark of God's covenant into view (Rev. 11:19). G. B. Caird suggests that a parallel is being drawn between the ancient Israelites and the afflicted church of the first century: "Like ancient Jericho, which blocked the entry of Israel into the promised land, Babylon the Great must fall before God's people can find their permanent home in the new Jerusalem."[3] The parallel is only approximate, as Caird recognizes, because the sounding of the sixth trumpet destroys only one-tenth of the evil city rather than the whole (11:8, 13), but this is consistent with the restraint of judgment throughout the trumpet cycle.

The purposes of the trumpet cycle are to sound alarms, warning the complacent and calling them to repentance, and to summon the church to holy spiritual warfare. The use of the trumpet to raise alarm before attack is the background of Joel 2:1: "Blow a trumpet in Zion, and sound an alarm on My holy mountain! Let all the inhabitants of the land tremble, for the day of the LORD is coming; surely it is near." The locust army that Joel describes in the following verses supply the imagery in which John will portray demon riders emerging from the abyss when the fifth trumpet sounds (Rev. 9:2–10). The plagues associated with the trumpets proclaim God's supremacy and prefigure coming judgment, but they also leave time to repent. Yet, tragically, even after six trumpets "the rest of mankind, who were not killed by these plagues, did not repent of the works of their hands" (9:20).

3. G. B. Caird, *A Commentary on the Revelation of St. John the Divine*, HNTC (New York: Harper & Row, 1966), 108.

Fire from the Altar

As the angels with the seven trumpets stand waiting in God's presence, another angel approaches the golden altar that is before God's throne. He has a golden censer in which burning coals and incense can be carried, and he is given much incense to offer on the altar with the prayers of the saints. In the tabernacle and the temple the altar of incense was the piece of furniture closest to the ark of the covenant, which symbolized the footstool of God's heavenly throne: "Set the gold altar of incense before the ark of the testimony" (Exod. 40:5). The incense altar stood immediately outside the veil that marked off the inner chamber, the Holiest Place in which the ark rested (Exod. 40:26–27). Its location made it possible for priests to offer incense every morning and evening (Exod. 30:7–8). The smoke of the incense accompanied the prayers of Israel as it ascended before the Lord (Ps. 141:2; Luke 1:10). Although it was located in the outer chamber at the entrance to the Holiest Place, the incense altar belonged to the inner chamber, for on the Day of Atonement the high priest would burn incense until the cloud of smoke engulfed the atonement cover on the ark, shielding him from the consuming purity of the Lord as he entered the Holiest Place with sacrificial blood (Lev. 16:12–13; 1 Kings 6:22). In the heavenly sanctuary that John sees, the incense altar stands directly before the throne. There is no veil.

As the angel offers the incense on the altar, its smoke rises "with the prayers of the saints" in the presence of God (Rev. 8:4). Earlier the incense in bowls held by the cherubim and elders symbolized the prayers of the saints (5:8), and that is its meaning here as well. In the silence imposed by the seventh seal God hears his embattled church's cries, which rise before him as a sweet savor. From the same altar the angel fills the censer with fire, and he throws it to the earth (8:5). The imagery is powerful: Christians' prayers are integral to the downfall of the gospel's enemies. The "flashes of lightning and sounds and peals of thunder" (4:5) and an earthquake that accompany the casting of the fire from the altar echo the terrifying phenomena of the Lord's descent to Sinai to deliver his law to Israel (Exod. 19:16–18).

The fact that the falling fire originates in the heavenly altar before the throne of God alerts us to the symbolic form of the trumpet visions.[4] There are allusions to the physical plagues that fell on Egypt before the exodus, and the forms of falling fire devastate different spheres of the physical order. Yet the purpose of portraying these judgments as the descent of burning objects from the sky is not to equate them with missiles or meteors, atomic fallout, acid rain, or volcanic ash. Rather it is to stress that the destruction that decimates the physical world through warfare, other human evils, or natural disaster is ultimately the outworking of God's sovereign purpose, defending his people and warning his enemies.

Trumpet 1: Hail, Fire, and Blood Cast on Land (8:7)

At the first trumpet John saw hail and fire mixed with blood thrown to the earth, to consume one-third of the earth and its trees and all the green grass, that is, vegetation smaller than trees, including grain crops. In the seventh plague on ancient Egypt hail fell with "fire" (lightning) upon the Egyptians and their animals and crops (Exod. 9:22–26). The judgment in Egypt was limited in two ways: although flax and barley crops were destroyed, the later-ripening wheat and spelt survived (9:31–32); and the region of Goshen, where the Israelites resided, was exempt from the hailstorm (9:26). So also the destructive fire that John sees fall to earth stays within strict boundaries set by its Sovereign.

As the trumpets sound, we begin to see the effects of the riders released with the breaking of the first four seals. The devastation of the earth by burning is an ancient strategy of war. God forbade the Israelites from destroying the fruit trees in the countryside surrounding a city that they were besieging (Deut. 20:19–20), but other ancient armies felt no such compunction. The association of this judgment with warfare is shown by the fact that, mingled with the hail and fire mentioned in Exodus, John sees blood, which is symbolic of violence and reminiscent of the red horse on which War rides (Rev. 6:4). Even when food supplies are not cut off by siege, the burning of crops makes

---

4. The background of this scene is the vision in which Ezekiel sees above the cherubim "something like a sapphire stone, in appearance resembling a throne," and hears the Lord's command to his angel, "fill your hands with coals of fire from between the cherubim and scatter them over the city" (Ezek. 10:1–2).

grain rare, raising prices to the exorbitant levels that were announced as Famine rode forth (6:6). The flames of war will sear the land from which people seek their food, but God in his patience restricts the destruction to a fraction of the earth and its trees.

Trumpet 2: Burning Mountain Cast into the Sea (8:8–9)

When the second trumpet sounded, "something like[5] a great mountain burning with fire was thrown into the sea." Volcanic activity around the Mediterranean basin, especially reports of the eruption of Vesuvius that buried Pompeii and devastated the bay of Naples in A.D. 79, would have magnified the horrifying vividness of this vision in the minds of Revelation's first listeners. But John is not merely giving a poetic description of a volcanic explosion or meteor's fall. The heavenly origin of this fiery judgment is implied. The burning mountain turns one-third of the sea to blood, leading to the death of one-third of the creatures living in the sea and the destruction of one-third of the vessels on it. The order implies that the blood produced by the fiery mountain is not that of the sea creatures, for they die as a result of the transformation of the sea's waters to blood. This scene partially imitates the first plague on Egypt, in which the waters of the Nile were turned to blood, killing the fish in the river (Exod. 7:20–21). It also alludes to God's word of judgment on Babylon, the "destroying mountain" that the Lord will make a "burnt out mountain" and submerge in the waves of the sea (Jer. 51:25, 42).

John sees in symbolic form the disruption of the trade network that kept the Babylon of his day, Rome's sea-centered empire, afloat. Whether through sea battles or natural disasters, the Mediterranean's waters will be bloodied, its fruitfulness as a source of fresh fish fouled, its armadas of merchant ships crippled. When the harlot Babylon's utter destruction is revealed in a later vision, the merchants who had enriched themselves by trade with her lament, "Woe, woe, the great city, in which all who had ships at sea became rich by her wealth, for

---

5. John echoes the prophetic indirection used by Ezekiel to remind readers that his description in words is only a rough approximation of what the prophet perceived in the vision.

in one hour she has been laid waste!" (Rev. 18:19). This great city is
not only a latter-day incarnation of Babylon, the place of Israel's captivity; it was also a new Egypt, the house of Israel's slavery (11:8). The
bloodying of the sea and the death of its creatures parallel the bloodying of the Nile in the time of Moses. The worldly powers that oppress
God's true Israel are to be shaken at the source of their confidence.
Again, however, the judgment on the sea is limited as God's wrath
remains restrained.

Trumpet 3: Burning Star Falls on Rivers and Springs (8:10–11)

The "great star . . . , burning like a torch," which fell from heaven
at the sounding of the third trumpet, was named Wormwood, and it
made one-third of the fresh water sources—rivers and springs—bitter
and poisonous, killing many. Recognizing the confluence of biblical
symbolism will again be our key to understanding this strange picture.
We are not to strain our imaginations to try to picture a single physical star (meteor?) falling on one-third of the fresh water sources that
are scattered around the earth or even across the Roman Empire. Nor
are we to puzzle over the fact that the physical substance wormwood,
while it makes water bitter, does not render it deadly. Biblical symbolism makes wormwood's bitter taste emblematic of lethal consequences.[6] In Jeremiah 9:15, for example, the Lord pronounces judgment on idolatrous Israel: "I will feed them, this people, with
wormwood and give them poisoned water to drink" (cf. 23:15). This
judgment replicates another aspect of the first plague on Egypt, for the
bloodying of the Nile not only killed its fish but also rendered its water
unfit for human consumption (Exod. 8:24).

Today the poisoning of springs and rivers makes us think of acid
rain and industrial pollution of the world's waterways, but John's au-

---

6. Jürgen Roloff, *The Revelation of John: A Continental Commentary* (Minneapolis: Fortress, 1993), 111: "Wormwood, an extremely sharp, bitter vegetal substance,
is by itself not poisonous, but because of its bitterness it frequently appears in the
Old Testament as a symbol for bitter suffering and judgment, which are the conse-
quence of defection from God."

dience would have recognized the ancient strategy of driving a besieged city to desperation by cutting off or defiling its source of drinking water. Hezekiah's tunnel was designed to protect Jerusalem from just this sort of assault by thirst or poisoning (2 Kings 20:20). Through humanity's avarice and violence another basic resource on which life depends, water, is made repugnant and lethal rather than refreshing and life giving. Again, however, the defilement is limited.

Trumpet 4: Sun, Moon, and Stars Darkened (8:12)

The fourth trumpet affects the sky, the source of light. One-third of the sun, moon, and stars is struck, "so that a third of them might be darkened and the day would not shine for a third of it, and the night in the same way." If we had assumed up to this point that the order of John's visions reflects the order of the events to which they refer, we are forced now to recognize John's stylistic device of repetition or recapitulation. At the opening of the sixth seal John saw the sun blackened, the moon turned blood-red, and the stars fallen to earth like figs (Rev. 6:12–13); yet now he sees sun, moon, and stars still shining in the sky and then struck with only a partial dimming. This confirms our conclusion that the sixth seal provided a preview of the final dissolution of the old created order, in preparation for the new heavens and earth. The fourth trumpet judgment, however, symbolizes providential disasters that precede that final cataclysm.

The echo of the ninth Egyptian plague, complete and palpable darkness for three days, is unmistakable (Exod. 10:21–23). John's wording warns us not to envision how this judgment would work physically. Should we picture a 33 percent reduction in the size of the sun and moon and the number of the stars, or in their luminosity, or perhaps in the proportion of hours in the day in which the sun shines and of the nighttime hours in which the moon and stars give their light (the most natural reading of 8:12)? If we try to pin down such details, we misunderstand the visionary genre. If we seek a literal referent for the judgment portrayed in this vision, it may be found in the blackening of the skies by the smoke of burning fields and smoldering cities, sacked and put to the torch by their military conquerors. As the God of the universe brings mighty Rome and all its lesser successors to its knees under the onslaughts of aggressors lurking at its borders, grain and fruit, fish and imports, fresh water, and even light will be in short supply.

The Three Woes (8:13; 9:12; 11:14)

The last three trumpets are set apart from the first four by the warning cry of a heavenly messenger, an eagle flying in midheaven, "Woe, woe, woe" (Rev. 8:13). The last three trumpets are woes to come on "those who dwell on the earth." Whereas the first four affected the spheres surrounding and supporting human life, the last three will target rebellious humanity directly. (In Revelation "those who dwell on the earth" consistently refers to people in rebellion against God and Christ, in contrast to the church, which always belongs to heaven, wherever its members may be living.) This is emphasized in the fifth trumpet, when the locust army from the pit is forbidden from harming vegetation (strange locusts!) and those who bear God's seal (9:4).

The end of the first woe is announced between the fifth and sixth trumpets (Rev. 9:12), and the passing of the second woe is declared before the seventh trumpet sounds (11:14). The seventh trumpet, however, seems to reveal not a woe on earth but a celebration in heaven, responding to the announcement that the kingdom of the world has been "the kingdom of our Lord and of His Christ" (11:15–19). The final woe is the climax of God's wrath on earth, revealed in the outpouring of the bowls containing the seven last plagues, the destruction of Babylon, and the defeat of the beasts, those who follow them, and the dragon.

Trumpet 5: Demons from the Abyss (9:1–11)

A star, fallen from heaven to earth, releases the scourge at the sounding of the fifth trumpet. The evil swarm that emerges from the abyss can do so only by the purpose and permission of the God enthroned in heaven. This fallen star is given the key of the bottomless pit (literally in Greek, "the shaft of the abyss"), indicating his royal authority to command and control its occupants (cf. Rev. 1:18; 3:7). He is therefore called king and "the angel of the abyss" (9:11). He is "the serpent of old who is called the devil and Satan," whom John will later see cast out of heaven and down to the earth (12:7–9). This was the result of Jesus' messianic assault on the kingdom of the evil one, for as his disciples were casting out demons in his name, Jesus saw "Satan fall from heaven like lightning" (Luke 10:18).

When the fallen star opens the abyss, dark smoke as from a great furnace billows up to darken the sun and air, and from the smoke emerges an army of "locusts" whose appearance is "like horses prepared for battle" and whose wings sound like chariots (Rev. 9:3, 7, 9). The eighth plague on Egypt was a swarm of locusts unparalleled in history, which blackened the land and "ate every plant of the land and all the fruit of the trees that the hail had left. Thus nothing green was left on tree or plant of the field through all the land of Egypt" (Exod. 10:14–15). The prophet Joel also foresaw a locust army unparalleled in history, summoned by the trumpet of the day of the Lord (Joel 2:1–2). Fire and the darkening of the sun accompanied this army, and its advance was like the charge of warhorses in appearance and the clatter of chariots in sound (2:3–5, 10). The influence of Joel's vision on the imagery in John's is obvious.[7] Yet the locusts that swarm from the pit in obedience to the angel of the abyss wield their destruction in a sphere very different from the fields and groves of Egypt (Exodus) or Israel (Joel). Though they are presented visually as locusts, the plague they represent is not agricultural but spiritual.

The locust army of the fifth trumpet symbolizes demonic torment inflicted on the minds and souls of "those who dwell on the earth," who lack the seal of God's name on their thoughts and lives. The destructive power of these locusts is great, and yet it is restricted

---

7. A previous locust infestation, apparently the occasion for Joel's prediction of the coming day of the Lord as an attack of a mighty locust army, is described: "A nation has invaded my land, mighty and without number; its teeth are the teeth of a lion, and it has the fangs of a lioness. It has made my vine a waste and my fig tree splinters" (Joel 1:6–7). Lion's teeth are a feature in John's description of the locusts from the pit (Rev. 9:8).

by God. These locusts may not harm the earth's vegetation or trees (Rev. 9:4). They harm only those who do not have the seal of God, so the pain of their sting will not touch the servants of God (cf. 7:3–8; 14:1–5). Therefore the anguish they inflict is not a physical affliction shared by believer and nonbeliever alike. These locusts may not kill their victims but only torment them, and that for a limited period, five months (9:5, 10). Their torture seems to their victims a fate worse than death, but the relief they seek in death eludes them as "death flees from them" (9:6). This vision discloses the tragic double irony of serving Satan. First, as the angel of the abyss, the fallen star releases these demonic hordes not to afflict his enemies, the servants of God (for he cannot touch those shielded by God's seal), but rather to afflict his allies "who dwell on the earth," who receive the beast's mark and worship his blasphemous image (14:14–17). The devil rewards his loyal subjects with cruel torture. Second, the relief that the tortured think they would attain through death is denied them, for the malevolent spirits that poison their minds are forbidden from taking their lives.

Within the parameters permitted them, however, these demons have great power, as their visible characteristics indicate. They appear as locusts, symbolizing their power to destroy, turning an Eden-like land into a barren desert (Joel 2:3). Their king's name is "Destroyer," both in Hebrew (*Abaddon*) and in Greek (*Apollyon;* Rev. 9:11). They sting like scorpions, showing the intensity of unremitting pain they inflict (9:5, 10). Their crowns and human faces signify personal intelligence and authority to carry out their grisly mission (9:7). Though limited in duration and severity, this outbreak of demonic activity among the unbelieving carries the expression of God's wrath in the course of history to a new level, a first woe. The terrors and anxieties during a civilization's dissolution, such as Rome would undergo in the coming centuries, epitomize but do not exhaust the torments of heart and mind symbolized by the army of the fifth trumpet.

Trumpet 6: Invasion from the East (9:13–21)

The sixth trumpet, which is the second woe, is humanity's last warning blast. When it sounds, a voice from the golden altar on which the church's prayers were offered to God commands, "Release the four angels who are bound at the great river Euphrates." This command marks the end of a period of restraint of God's judgment, because it rescinds the earlier command that four angels at the earth's four corners must hold back the four winds until God's servants have been sealed (Rev. 7:1–3). The trumpet judgments have escalated from the one-third destruction of land, sea, rivers (with some human death), and sky, to mental and spiritual torture of unbelievers, and now to the slaughter of one-third of the human population.

The Euphrates River had biblical and contemporary significance. In biblical history the Euphrates connoted a source of oppression and place of exile. Beyond the Euphrates River had stood ancient Nineveh, capital of the Assyrian Empire that conquered the northern kingdom, and Babylon, which had carried Judah into captivity. The Lord had humbled and dismantled Babylon through the rising power of the Medo-Persian Empire and had resettled his people in the land of promise. But prophets of the exile still spoke of foreign powers such as "Gog," who would sweep down from the northeast, from the Euphrates, to afflict God's people (Ezek. 38).

For residents of the Roman Empire at the end of the first century, the Euphrates was the eastern edge of Rome's domain, beyond which were the threatening powers of the East, especially Parthia with its cavalry of mounted archers, always harassing the Roman Empire's eastern outposts. During the 60s, after the conflagration that destroyed large portions of Rome and Nero's disappearance, rumors flew in the capital and the provinces that the megalomaniacal emperor had escaped to the east and was making preparations to reconquer the world at the head of the Parthian cavalry.[8]

In the vision of the sixth trumpet, the imagery of invasion from the East is derived from the Parthian threat, but the horsemen who

8. Richard Bauckham, *The Climax of Prophecy: Studies on the Book of Revelation* (Edinburgh: T & T Clark, 1993), "Nero and the Beast," especially 407–23.

sweep over the Euphrates in John's vision are more terrifying than the Parthians at their worst. John reminds us that we are moving in the symbolic world of prophetic vision with the words, "thus I saw in the vision the horses and those who sat on them" (Rev. 9:17). The reference to the Euphrates must not mislead us into a geographical literalism: what John saw was in a vision, so its symbolic character must be recognized. In this invasion it is not the riders but the horses that are to be feared. The horses' heads are like lions, and from their mouths they spew fire, smoke, and sulfur (brimstone), which are the plagues by which they slay their victims (9:17–18).[9] Their tails are like serpents with heads, showing that their power to wound resembles and is derived from the ancient serpent, the dragon, "who is called the devil and Satan" (12:9; cf. 20:2). This trumpet, like the fifth, portrays visually the release of pent-up demonic venom on earth to torment, and now even slay, vast multitudes of victims. Since demons are immaterial beings, how can they cause the physical death of so many people?[10] They probably do so by the strategy first used by the serpent in the garden: murder by a lie. "He was a murderer from the beginning, and does not stand in the truth because there is no truth in him. Whenever he speaks a lie, he speaks from his own nature; for he is a liar and the father of lies" (John 8:44). In the later bowl cycle, when the sixth bowl is poured out on the Euphrates, John will see three unclean spirits, froglike in appearance, emerge from the mouths of the dragon, the beast, and the false prophet to deceive the kings of the world and gather them for the last battle against God and his church (Rev. 16:12–14). So also these horses of death wield death through the hellish deceit that pours forth from their mouths, hot, smoky, and rancid-smelling as sulfur. Jesus' defeat of demons during his earthly ministry repeatedly showed them to be cruel parasites, in-

9. The red of fire (*pyr*), blue-gray of smoke, and yellow color of sulfur (*theion*) reflect the colors of the riders' breastplates, fiery red (*pyrinos*), bluish jacinth (stone) or hyacinth (flower), and yellow sulfur or brimstone (*theiōdis;* Rev. 9:17).

10. Their authority to "kill a third of mankind" (Rev. 9:15) must be the power to inflict physical death, since the locust demons were permitted to torment but not to kill those who lack the seal of God and are therefore already spiritually dead (9:4–5).

tent on the destruction of the individuals who were their helpless hosts (Mark 5:5, 13; Luke 9:39).

As the sixth seal provided a preview of the traumas that will characterize the dissolution of the first heavens and earth, so the sixth trumpet previews an increase of satanic deception that precipitates growing violence, death, and despair. Such a crumbling of law, order, and safety should shake idolaters' confidence in "the works of their hands" and cure their desire to "worship demons, and the idols of gold and of silver and of brass and of stone and of wood, which can neither see nor hear nor walk" (Rev. 9:20). This wording echoes Daniel's rebuke to Belshazzar (Dan. 5:23). The Old Testament often emphasizes that the idols are senseless (blind, deaf) and immobile (e.g., Ps. 115:4–8; 135:15–18; Isa. 44:12–20; Jer. 10:2–5). Yet, even as demons destroy their own worshipers in despair and violent conflict, the survivors of God's warning blasts of judgment do not repent of their murders, sorceries, immorality, and thefts. These six warning notes, the overture of wrath to come, fall on deaf ears.

The Interlude Visions (10:1–11:14)

Between the sixth and seventh trumpets, as between the sixth and seven seals, an interlude is inserted to dramatize the delay of final judgment and to refocus our attention on God's care for his church in the midst of his providential and escalating judgments on its oppressors. The interlude in the trumpet cycle also reveals the next step in the delivery of the "Revelation of Jesus Christ" to the churches through John (Rev. 10) before the twin visions concerning the protection and suffering of the church (11:1–14). Because of the length and richness of this interlude, our next chapter will be devoted to it.

Trumpet 7: Kingdom Come (11:15–19)

Like the seventh seal, the seventh trumpet shifts the scene from earth to heaven. Unlike the seventh seal, which introduced silence, the seventh trumpet is followed by the joyful shout of great voices, "The kingdom of the world has become the kingdom of our Lord and of

His Christ; and He will reign forever and ever" (Rev. 11:15). As is often true in the New Testament, "kingdom" here refers to the exercise of rule, or dominion, rather than a territory ruled, or domain. So we could paraphrase this announcement: "Dominion over the world, without challenge or rival, has come into the possession of our Lord and his anointed King." From the standpoint of God's eternal and sovereign purpose, he always rules over all his creatures: "He does according to His will in the host of heaven and among the inhabitants of earth; and no one can ward off His hand or say to Him, 'What have You done?'" (Dan. 4:35). But incorporated into his sovereign, secret purpose has been satanic and human rebellion, which contradicts God's revealed, holy will. Consequently Jesus' disciples must pray, "Your kingdom come, Your will be done, on earth as it is in heaven" (Matt. 6:10). The shout of the heavenly voices celebrates the final answer to this prayer. It will reverse the situation described in Psalm 2, when the nations, peoples, kings, and rulers of the earth stood in unified rebellion "against the LORD and against His Anointed" (Ps. 2:1–2). When the last trumpet sounds, such resistance will be a thing of the past, for royal dominion over the earth will belong to the Lord and his anointed King exclusively.

The Lamb has conquered through his atoning death and taken his seat with his Father on the throne of the universe (Rev. 3:21; 5:5–6). In this sense God's kingdom has already come in the power of the Spirit, as Jesus promised: "There are some of those who are standing here who will not taste of death until they see the kingdom of God after it has come with power" (Mark 9:1). On Pentecost Peter points to the Spirit's power as demonstrating that Jesus is enthroned at God's right hand as Lord and Christ (Acts 2:33–36).[11] But the seventh trumpet heralds the future climax of Jesus' present messianic rule. "For He must reign until He has put all His enemies under His feet. The last enemy that will be abolished is death" (1 Cor. 15:25–26). When that

---

11. In Rev. 12:10–12 a heavenly voice announces that "the kingdom of our God and the authority of His Christ have come" because Satan the accuser has been cast down from heaven to earth, evoking joy in heaven and woe on earth. This coming of God's kingdom is that which has occurred through the incarnation, suffering, and exaltation of Christ, the woman's child (12:2–5).

day arrives, the time will have come for the final arrival of God's wrath, quashing the nations' last enraged conspiracy against his reign;[12] the dead to be judged; God's servants to receive their reward; and the earth's destroyers to meet their destruction (11:18).[13] These events are portrayed in the visions of Revelation 19–22: the last battle, the last judgment, the destruction of the destroyers (the beast, the false prophet, and the dragon), and the reward of God's servants in the new Jerusalem.

The vision of the open temple and of the ark of God's covenant within it (Rev. 11:19) brings closure to the series of seal and trumpet visions, which began when John saw a door standing open in heaven and was called up by the trumpetlike voice of the Son of Man (4:1). In that opening vision lightnings, voices, and thunders emanated from God's throne, recalling the terrifying splendors of Sinai (4:4). In the scene of heavenly silence, the bridge from the seal cycle to the trumpet cycle, John saw an additional element: thunders, voices, lightnings, and an earthquake (8:5). Now one more is added: lightnings, voices, thunder, an earthquake, and a great hailstorm. The seven trumpets of God, like those at Jericho, have gone before the ark of his covenant and shattered all resistance to the establishment of his dominion in the earth.

The vision of the opened temple in heaven also prepares us for a new cycle of visions that pierce to the heart of the cosmic conflict of the ages, the battle between Christ the woman's seed and Satan the ancient serpent-dragon. Before we view this war to end all wars, however, we need to return to the threefold vision interlude between trumpets 6 and 7.

---

12. "The nations were enraged" may be John's translation of Ps. 2:1: "Why are the nations in an uproar?" It apparently alludes to the international conspiracy to be brought together "for the war of the great day of God" (Rev. 16:14; cf. 19:19–21; 20:7–10).

13. Although the destructive judgments revealed in the trumpet cycle come from the heavenly altar by the purpose of God, the blame for the earth's destruction falls not on the holy Creator but on those who seduce human beings into resisting him and his Christ, sowing seeds of avarice, suspicion, competition, and hostility that violate the world and its inhabitants.

CHAPTER EIGHT

Scroll Delivered:
The Prophet Eats, Measures, and Testifies
(10:1–11:14)

Can God Protect His Own?

In 1920 Europe was reeling from the Great War, as it was then known, and bolshevism was rising in Russia. Irish Poet William Butler Yeats penned his foreboding sense of his civilization's meltdown in "The Second Coming":

> Things fall apart; the centre cannot hold;
> Mere anarchy is loosed upon the world,
> The blood-dimmed tide is loosed, and everywhere
> The ceremony of innocence is drowned;
> The best lack all conviction, while the worst
> Are full of passionate intensity.[1]

When evil is everywhere and the world is ripe for judgment, can God protect his own? When economies crash, when civil order falters and the social fabric frays, when restraint and respect give way to

---

1. William Butler Yeats, "The Second Coming," in *Modern American and Modern British Poetry,* ed. Louis Untermeyer, rev. ed. (New York: Harcourt, Brace Jovanovich, 1955), 491.

rude aggression and random violence, when greed and animal appetite reign supreme, when consensus and community decompose into culture wars, this question weighs on the hearts of God's people: Can God keep Jesus' little flock safe as they stand, it seems, defenseless in the crossfire? On the one hand, Christian believers will be targeted for attack by people who hate our King, his purity, and even his mercy; on the other, God calls us to stay involved in the broader community, even as it rushes pell-mell toward its rendezvous with God's wrath. Even if our enemies' persecution does not destroy us, might we not be cut down by friendly fire as our champion launches his counterstrike in our defense?

Such misgivings, natural though they may be when the world gives way around us, reveal an underestimation of God's strategic capabilities to focus his judgment on its deserving targets. The history of God's acts of judgment and rescue demonstrates his sharpshooting skill: "For if God . . . did not spare the ancient world, but preserved Noah, a preacher of righteousness . . . , and if he condemned the cities of Sodom and Gomorrah to destruction . . . and . . . rescued righteous Lot, . . . then the Lord knows how to rescue the godly from temptation, and to keep the unrighteous under punishment for the day of judgment" (2 Peter 2:4–9). God has done it before, snatching Noah's family from the floodwaters and Lot's family from the shower of fiery sulfur that consumed the ungodly.[2] He can do so again.

The earlier cycle of seal visions was interrupted to assure John's hearers of this point. When the sixth seal provided a preview of the end, John heard the lament raised by the world's despairing wicked, a rhetorical question to which they expect no answer: "the great day of [the] wrath [of the One seated on the throne and of the Lamb] has come, and who is able to stand?" (Rev. 6:17). God, however, provides his answer in the twin visions interposed between the sixth and seventh seals. God's bondservants, the completed Israel, are sealed with his name, under his protection, before forces are released to destroy earth, sea, and trees (7:1–8; cf. 14:1). And, from another perspective,

2. The trumpet cycle contains echoes of Sodom's destruction: at the first trumpet, hail and fire rained down from heaven onto the earth (Rev. 8:7), and at the sixth, horses breathing fire, smoke, and sulfur appeared (9:17).

these same sealed servants of God appear as the innumerable, international crowd of white-robed worshipers in heaven, sheltered forever from hunger, thirst, sun, and sorrow (7:9–17).

Now between the sixth and seventh trumpets a more complex series of visions is interposed (10:1–11:13). In Revelation 11:1–13 are two closely related scenes, which share with the twin visions of Revelation 7 the theme of God's protection of his people in their suffering. Before these scenes of protection amid suffering, however, John views "another strong angel," who has in his hand an open scroll that John is to eat in preparation for his prophetic ministry (10:1–11). The words and actions of this strong angel complete the chain of transmission that was outlined in Revelation 1:1, for in this scene the Revelation of Jesus Christ is symbolically entrusted to John, completing his commissioning as a spokesman for the risen Lord.

The Angel and His Oath (10:1–7)

John's mention of "another strong angel" alludes to the strong angel who shouted the question that had earlier plunged the prophet into grief, "Who is worthy to open the book and to break its seals?" (Rev. 5:2). This allusion is significant, for this strong angel descends from heaven carrying a book that has been opened, to deliver it to John, God's prophet.

The appearance of the angel replicates the glories of God and of the Son of Man so closely that some readers believe that the angel is Christ (Rev. 10:1).[3] He resembles the radiance by which God led Israel through the wilderness, for he is robed in cloud and his legs are like pillars of fire (Exod. 13:21–22; 14:24). Moreover, it was "with the clouds of heaven" that Daniel saw "one like a Son of Man" approaching the Ancient of Days to receive eternal dominion (Dan.

---

3. G. K. Beale, *The Book of Revelation*, NIGTC (Grand Rapids: Eerdmans, 1999), 522–26, is persuaded by the many resemblances between this "strong angel" and God and Christ that "the angel is the divine Angel of the Lord, as in the O[ld] T[estament], who is to be identified with Christ himself" (525). See also Herman Hoeksema, *Behold, He Cometh* (Grand Rapids: Reformed Free Publishing Association, 1969), 337.

7:13); and the cloud of divine presence enveloped Jesus and his three closest disciples when his glory was unveiled (Matt. 17:5). The rainbow on the angel's head reflects the rainbow surrounding the One seated on the throne (Rev. 4:3). The sunlike luminosity of his face is like that of the Son of Man in John's first vision: "his face was like the sun shining in its strength" (1:16). The angel's voice, resembling a lion's roar (10:3), could well belong to the Lion of Judah (5:5). And in his hand is an opened scroll: who else could he be but the Answer to the first strong angel's question, "Who is worthy to open the scroll?"[4]

Nevertheless we should probably not equate the strong angel with the Lamb whose opened scroll he carries. The radiance of the angel's appearance marks him as one who bears the image of his Master, reflecting the Master's glory as he brings the Master's message. We could compare, on the angelic level, the radiant appearance (lightning, flaming torches, polished bronze) of the angel who appeared to Daniel in the third year of Cyrus's reign (Dan. 10:5). That angel, though his appearance drained Daniel of strength, nevertheless acknowledged that he had been hindered on his mission by "the prince of the kingdom of Persia," until assisted by Michael (Dan. 10:12–14). This hindrance shows that the angel was a finite, creaturely servant of God, though greater in power, mobility, and access to God's sanctuary than we are at present. On the human level, we recall the transformation of Moses' appearance to radiate the brightness of the Lord's presence, on which he had gazed (Exod. 34:29–35; cf. 2 Cor. 3:18). Throughout Revelation angels are superhuman servants of God, doing his bidding and carrying his revelation to the embattled saints on earth. There is no

4. It also could be argued that the "strong angel" is Christ because the speaker of Rev. 11:3 speaks of "my two witnesses," and "witnesses" belong to Jesus (2:13); and because the angel is the last speaker named prior to 11:3 (in 10:9).

However, in 10:11 a plural group of unnamed speakers are heard ("they said to me"), and the wording of 11:1, which introduces the discourse that includes "my witnesses," leaves the singular speaker anonymous—unless, following rigorously the principle of participle-noun agreement in Greek (which Revelation does not always do), the measuring rod itself is the speaker. "There was given me a reed like a rod, as it [the reed] was saying, 'Rise and measure the temple of God' " (dej). Although the speaker of 11:1–13 is probably Jesus, the scene shift between 10:11 and 11:1 and anonymity of the speaker of 11:1–13 prevent us from accepting the second premise as persuasive evidence that the angel of Rev. 10 is the speaker of Rev. 11.

more reason to view this "strong angel" as a divine being than there was to view the first "strong angel" in Revelation 5:2 as the Son of God.[5]

The "little book" that this angel brings to John is the book that the Lamb has opened, seal by seal, in Revelation 6–8. "Little book" in our English versions represents two diminutive forms (*biblidarion* or *biblaridion*) of the word *book* (*biblion*) in Revelation 4–5, but this attention to the smallness of the scroll does not mean that it is a different document from that opened by the Lamb. Early copyists treat the words *book* and *little book* interchangeably in Revelation 10, sometimes using one word and sometimes using another to refer to the same document in the vision. This variety of wording within individual manuscripts shows that copyists saw no great difference in meaning between "book" and "little book." Moreover, some of the earliest manuscripts have "book" (*biblion*) or intermingle "book" and "little book" on the same page.[6] Textual scholars and many modern versions (e.g., NASB, NIV) have concluded that "book" rather than "little book" is probably the original reading in Revelation 10:8. Most later Greek manuscripts contain "little book" four times in Revelation 10 (vv. 2, 8, 9, and 10), but they differ among themselves, some using *biblidarion,* some *biblaridion,* and some a third option yet (*biblarion*).[7] Thus the objection to equating the little scroll brought by the angel

5. Among the scholars who view this "strong angel" as distinct from Christ are Richard Bauckham, *The Climax of Prophecy: Studies on the Book of Revelation* (Edinburgh: T & T Clark, 1993), 253–54; G. B. Caird, *A Commentary on the Revelation of St. John the Divine,* HNTC (New York: Harper & Row, 1966), 125–26; George Eldon Ladd, *A Commentary on the Revelation of John* (Grand Rapids: Eerdmans, 1972), 141; William Hendriksen, *More Than Conquerors: An Interpretation of the Book of Revelation* (Grand Rapids: Baker 1939), 149; H. B. Swete, *Commentary on Revelation,* 3d ed. (1911; reprint ed., Grand Rapids: Kregel, 1977), 126; and Robert W. Wall, *Revelation* (Peabody, Mass.: Hendrickson, 1991), 137.

6. Papyrus 47, probably to be dated in the third century (200–299), has "book" throughout Rev. 10. Codex Sinaiticus (fourth century) has "little book" in the first two verses and "book" in the last two. Codex Alexandrinus (fifth century) has "book" in Rev. 10:8 and "little book" in the other three verses.

7. See Bauckham, *Climax of Prophecy,* 243–57. Beale, *Revelation,* 530–32, finds Bauckham's case for identifying the little book of Rev. 10 and the book of Rev. 5

with the scroll previously opened by the Lamb falls away. This is what we would expect, since Revelation 1:1 prepared us to see a five-link chain of transmission by which God the Father would communicate the Revelation to his servants: God gave it to Jesus Christ, who sent his angel to show John, who bore witness through writing to the churches. In Revelation 4–5 we saw God give the scroll to Jesus Christ the Lamb, and then we observed as the Lamb broke seal after seal, preparing to unroll the scroll and reveal its contents (Rev. 6–8). Now John is confronted by a strong angel holding an open scroll, which John is to eat, in order that he might prophesy. In other words, we see the next two links in the chain (angel to John), with the final link (the churches) implied by John's commission to proclaim. The scroll is that opened by the Lamb, but its carrier is an angel sent by the Lamb from heaven to earth, to deliver "the Revelation of Jesus Christ" to John for the sake of the churches.

This angel descends from the Lamb's throne in heaven to deliver to John on Patmos the scroll that the Lamb has opened. But before he hands over the scroll to the prophet, the angel has a solemn oath to pronounce. The angel takes his stand upon sea and land, laying claim to the environmental spheres afflicted under the first two trumpets (land, 8:7; sea, 8:8–9). With a great voice like a lion's roar he announces the Lord's word of wrath (10:3), which compels John the prophet to speak, as Amos 3:7–8 shows: "Surely the Lord GOD does nothing unless He reveals His secret counsel to His servants the prophets. A lion has roared! Who will not fear? The Lord GOD has spoken! Who can but prophesy?" John is to prophesy "concerning many peoples and nations and tongues and kings" (Rev. 10:11).

The angel's roar first evokes an answer from "seven peals of thunder," but God speaks from heaven, forbidding John's inscription of the seven thunders' message (Rev. 10:3–4). John must "seal up" what

---

plausible but still finds it preferable to interpret the contents of the little book as "on a smaller theological scale than the bigger book of ch. 5" (532). Yet, if Rev. 12–20 express the contents of the "little book," it is hard to characterize the sweeping drama of the conflict between the woman, her Seed, and the dragon, which spans history from the fall into sin until the consummation, as on a "smaller theological scale" than the visions of Rev. 6–11.

the thunders have spoken, keeping its content hidden in the counsel of God. This sudden secrecy seems strange in a book given to reveal to God's servants what must occur. Perhaps this symbolism makes the general point that God's prophets may speak only what God has authorized them to reveal, just as Paul in receiving apostolic revelation "heard inexpressible words, which a man is not permitted to speak" (2 Cor. 12:4). It seems more likely, though, that this unexpected abortion of what could have become another sevenfold vision cycle underscores the angel's oath, "that there will be delay no longer, but in the days of the voice of the seventh angel, when he is about to sound, then the mystery of God is finished" (Rev. 10:6–7). The seal cycle showed that the Lamb's delay of judgment entails a postponement of the martyrs' vindication (6:9–11). The trumpet cycle portrayed the restrained ravages of war, affecting only a third of earth, sea, rivers, and sky: the Lord's long-suffering alarms, summoning earth's inhabitants to repentance (9:21). When the seventh trumpet sounds, however, no cycle of thunder judgments will follow, further delaying the end. The seventh trumpet is the last trumpet (1 Cor. 15:52), and when it sounds no further opportunity for repentance will remain. Unlike the command to Daniel to seal up his prophetic words until a distant time to which they referred (Dan. 12:4, 8–9), John is to seal the thunders' speech forever. God will not allow human rebellion to trace an endless cycle of injustice and misery; in fact, he hastens to his people's relief (Luke 18:7–8).

The strong angel adopts the posture of oath taking, right foot on the sea, left on the earth, and right hand raised to heaven. The raising of the hand invokes God as witness and enforcer of the solemn commitment to be spoken (Dan. 12:7), although often in the Old Testament it is the Lord who lifts his hand to take the oath (Gen. 14:22; Num. 14:30; Deut. 32:40). The linen-dressed "man" who promised Daniel that the affliction of the holy people would come to an end after "a time, two times, and half a time" secured his oath "by Him who lives forever" (Dan. 12:7). But the angel who comes to John invokes a fuller description of the divine Witness: "Him who lives forever and ever, who created heaven and the things in it, and the earth and the things in it, and the sea and the things in it" (Rev. 10:6). As the angel's posture encompasses all the spheres of creation, ascending from the sea's depths to the dry land to the height of heaven, so also the Creator who secures his oath controls all spheres, descending from heaven's heights, to dry land, to the deeps.

The content of the oath, as we have seen, is "that there shall be delay no longer." The sounding of the seventh trumpet (Rev. 11:15) will draw the mystery of God—his secret plan, disclosed by revelation and enacted in history—to its final consummation (10:7). This purpose of God for history's consummation can be viewed from two perspectives, depending on one's relation to the God of history. On the one hand, the end of history is the good news[8] that God preached to his prophets and, through them, to his afflicted saints. Likewise, when the seventh trumpet sounds, we hear celebration in heaven because the world's kingdoms have become the kingdom of the Lord and his Christ—and because the day of judgment has arrived (11:18). On the other hand, to those who persist in rebellion the same final trumpet blast is a death knell, for it precipitates the outpouring of bowls containing the seven last plagues, rapid-fire in succession and comprehensive in extent (15:1; 16). Parallel wording describing the seventh trumpet and the seven bowls shows that they view the same climactic event, though from different angles:

10:7: when [the seventh angel] is about to sound "the mystery of God is finished."

15:1: in [the seven last plagues] "the wrath of God is finished."[9]

The consummation of history brings deliverance to the church and destruction to its enemies. So also the One who sits on the throne will twice utter the climactic, "It is done," first as the final bowl is poured out to destroy Babylon (16:17–19) and then in celebration that death, sorrow, and pain are terminated for the residents of the new Jerusalem

---

8. "He preached" in Rev. 10:7 is *euangelizomai,* "he announced good news."

9. In both texts the Greek verb, *etelesthē,* "is finished," precedes the noun constructions "mystery of God" and "wrath of God," placing emphasis on the finality and completion of God's plan.

162

(21:4–6). The sounding of the seventh trumpet brings us to the end of history (11:15–19). In Revelation 12 a new vision sequence will take us back to history's dawn and lead us to this same end by a different route.

The Prophet Eats the Book (10:8–11)

By divine command ("the voice which I heard from heaven," Rev. 10:8; cf. v. 4) John approaches the angel to receive the opened scroll. As he delivers it to the prophet, the angel commands John to eat it, predicting that it will be sweet in his mouth but bitter in his stomach. The resemblance to Ezekiel's commissioning is unmistakable (Ezek. 2:8–3:3). Like that ancient prophet-priest (see Ezek. 1:3), whom God commanded to eat a scroll written "on front and back"[10] to symbolize the prophet's obligation to "take into your heart all My words which I will speak to you" (3:10), John must internalize the message that he is to deliver to others.

Like Ezekiel's message, the word that John is to deliver is "sweet as honey" in his mouth (Rev. 10:9–10; Ezek. 3:4; cf. Ps. 119:103). Unlike Ezekiel's scroll, the scroll that John must eat turns his stomach sour in indigestion. Yet the context of Ezekiel's ingestion of the word implies that its content too was bitter as well as sweet: "written on it were lamentations, mourning and woe" (Ezek. 2:10); "Son of man, go to the house of Israel and speak My words to them. . . . I have sent you to them who should listen to you; yet the house of Israel will not be willing to listen to you, since they are not willing to listen to Me" (3:4–7). To those who repent in response to the watchman's warning God promises rescue from his coming wrath, but those who fail to heed the prophet's call will die in their sin (3:17–21).

---

10. Ezek. 2:10. LXX: *gegrammena . . . ta opisthen kai ta emprosthen,* "written on the back and the front." The scroll given to the Lamb in Rev. 5 was introduced similarly: "written inside and on the back" (*gegrammenon esōthen kai opisthen*). (The order "inside and on the reverse" in Rev. 5:1 reproduces the Hebrew text of Ezek. 2:10, which is reversed by the LXX.) The biblically informed reader and hearers would recognize this earlier allusion to Ezekiel's scroll as further reason to identify the "little scroll" of Rev. 10 with the Lamb's scroll of Rev. 5.

John's message is bittersweet in two respects. First, it is a double-edged prophecy concerning the nations: "many peoples and nations and tongues and kings" (Rev. 10:11). A chorus of voices ("they said"—presumably the living beings and the elders in the heavenly court) commands John to prophesy "again" concerning this fourfold series, reminding us of earlier passages in which similar lists have appeared. These passages are sweet indeed, for they glorify the Lamb whose blood purchased for God people "from every tribe and tongue and people and nation" (5:9), and they show us this redeemed multitude, secure in God's heavenly tent (7:9–17). But from this point on John's visions of the world's "peoples and tribes and tongues and nations" will concentrate on the bitter motif of humanity's delusion and rebellion under the sway of the beast (11:7–9; 13:7) and the harlot Babylon (17:15). Only once from this point on do we hear good news preached to "every nation and tribe and tongue and people," a summons to fear and worship the God whose judgment has come (14:6–7). Moreover, the bitter theme of God's wrath against the unrepentant is dominant in this commissioning of John, for only here do "kings" replace "tribes" as the fourth element in the quartet. In Revelation "kings" are almost universally arrayed with the dragon, the beasts, and the harlot against the Lord and his Messiah.[11] Although the Lamb's redeemed people are drawn from "every tribe and tongue and people and nation," from this same group are drawn the enemies of the Lamb, destined for destruction. John's prophecy concerning the nations is indeed bittersweet.

Second, John's message to and about the church is a blend of bitterness and sweetness, for he will soon be told of a witness church that is invincible, shielded from God's wrath and protected by God's power from the wrath of its enemies (Rev. 11:5–6) but also vulnerable to the attack of the beast from the abyss, who violently overpowers, conquers, and kills Jesus' faithful witnesses—in the setting in which their Lord was crucified (11:7–8). Neither tribulation nor distress nor per-

11. See Rev. 6:15; 16:12, 14; 17:2, 18; 18:3, 9; 19:18–19. Note also the kings symbolized by the beast's seven heads and ten horns (17:9, 12). The Lamb is the legitimate ruler and king over the earth's kings (1:5; 17:14; 19:16), and the kings will bring their glory as tribute into the new Jerusalem (21:24).

secution nor famine nor nakedness nor peril nor sword can separate Christ's people from his love, but this blessed assurance is precisely for those who are prepared to be "put to death all day long," like sheep to be slaughtered, for Jesus' sake (Rom. 8:35–36). Paradoxically but truly, the witness church's defeat in suffering and death at the blood-stained hands of its enemies is its supreme victory (Rev. 12:11; cf. 2:10: "Be faithful until death, and I will give you the crown of life"). Jesus' call to hopeful courage is blended with rugged realism: "In the world you will have tribulation, but take courage; I have overcome the world" (John 16:33).

The Temple Measured:
The Church Safe While Suffering (11:1–2)

In the two scenes of Revelation 11 John is first given a measuring rod and commanded to measure the temple (11:1–2); then he hears a heavenly voice narrating the prophetic career, assassination, and resurrection of those whom the voice calls "my two witnesses" (11:3–13). This section corresponds to the visions of the 144,000 and the international multitude of Revelation 7 in its placement (between the sixth and seventh of a series), theme (protection of the church amid suffering), and twofold structure. The visions of Revelation 11, however, nuance their portrait of God's protective care with greater complexity. The measuring of the sanctuary (11:1) and the invincibility of the two witnesses until their testifying task is done (11:5) reaffirm the promise of Revelation 7: God will let nothing separate his people from his love. However, the prohibition against measuring the outer court, leaving it vulnerable to trampling by the Gentiles (11:2), and the beast's slaughter of the witnesses (11:7) show that God promises not to spare us from all suffering but to secure our faith fast amid suffering.

As John's consumption of the scroll imitated Ezekiel's prophetic call, so the instruction to John to measure the temple of God echoes Ezekiel's climactic vision, in which he is carried to "a very high mountain" (Ezek. 40:3; cf. Rev. 21:10) to view the final temple, which the Lord will build in the last days (Ezek. 40–48). As Ezekiel looked on, the temple's dimensions were measured off by an angel (Ezek. 40:5),

165

but in John's vision the prophet is given the measuring rod and commanded to mark off the dimensions of "the temple of God and the altar, and those who worship in it" (Rev. 11:1). What immediately follows, however, is not a list of linear measurements like those recorded in Ezekiel 40–48. In Revelation 21 John will hear the perfections of the new Jerusalem portrayed in spatial measurements so extraordinary that their symbolic import is unmistakable (see below). In Revelation 11, however, the symbolic significance of John's charge to measure the temple is shown in other ways.

John must measure not only architectural structures (temple, altar) but also people ("those who worship in it"). The New Testament redefinition of the sanctuary of God as the people of God, expounded by Paul (1 Cor. 3:16–17; Eph. 2:20–22) and Peter (1 Peter 2:4–10; 4:14–17), has already been glimpsed in Revelation. That glimpse occurred in the promise: "He who overcomes, I will make him a pillar in the temple of My God, and he will not go out from it anymore; and I will write upon him the name of My God, and the name of the city of My God, the new Jerusalem, which comes down out of heaven from My God, and My new name" (Rev. 3:12). The identification becomes more explicit when we are told that the beast will blaspheme God's "name and His tabernacle, that is, those who dwell in heaven" (13:6).[12] The new Jerusalem that will appear in Revelation 21 is a wall-to-wall, top-to-bottom temple—its cubic shape marks it as the Holy of Holies—so it needs no other temple than the presence of God and the Lamb (21:22). It is also the bride, the wife of the Lamb (21:2, 9)—a portrait of the church, composed of people from every nation who hold to the word of God and the testimony of Jesus. Thus here John is to measure God's temple, its altar (associated with the suffering church, 6:9; 8:3–4), and the worshipers as a sign of the ultimate invincibility of Christ's church.

The reason that John is forbidden from measuring the court outside the sanctuary building itself is that "it has been given to the na-

---

12. The NASB's addition of the words "that is" to indicate that the phrase "those who dwell in heaven" is in apposition to "his tabernacle," directly equating heaven's residents with God's tent, accurately reflects the implication of the Greek grammar. See Robert H. Gundry, "The New Jerusalem: People as Place, Not Place for People," *NovT* 29 (1987): 254–64.

tions; and they will tread under foot the holy city for forty-two months" (Rev. 11:2). This prohibition shows that what is measured is placed under divine protection, and what is not measured is exposed to assault by the nations. It also implies that the court outside the sanctuary symbolizes the "holy city." The court symbolizes a city, and in Revelation cities symbolize communities of people, not merely collections of buildings and streets. But what is the "holy city" that is left vulnerable to be trod under foot by the Gentiles?

The instructions to John allude to Jesus' prediction of the fall of Jerusalem, which were fulfilled in the year 70: "Jerusalem will be trampled under foot by the Gentiles until the times of the Gentiles be fulfilled" (Luke 21:24, alluding to Dan. 8:13; Zech. 12:3, both of which in the LXX contain verbs related to "trample"). Scholars, however, have drawn two very different conclusions from this parallel. Some, believing Revelation to have been written before 70, see Revelation 11:1–2 as predicting a protection of Jewish Christians in Palestine from the woes of the Roman invasion and siege of Jerusalem under Titus, since they had been warned by Jesus' words to flee the city (Luke 21:20–21).[13] Thus the temple sanctuary symbolizes those first-century Jews who believed in Jesus and were spared the outpouring of God's wrath against those who had rejected and killed the promised Messiah (who are symbolized in the unmeasured outer court, the "holy city"). A variation of this view, less tied to a pre-70 date of composition, is that the measured sanctuary is the whole church, the excluded outer court (= the trampled city) is the Jesus-rejecting Jewish community or "the Jewish polity" as a whole, and the measuring symbolizes that the church has replaced the Jews as the people of God until the restoration of ethnic Israel to faith and faithfulness.[14] Still others hold that the measuring of the sanctuary, interpreted as the Most Holy Place, symbolizes the preservation of the spiritual significance of

13. Moses Stuart, *A Commentary on the Apocalypse,* 2 vols. (London: Wiley and Putnam, 1845), 2:217–18.

14. Swete, *Commentary,* 33. Hoeksema generalizes further, identifying the unmeasured outer court with the false church throughout the ages, which shall be manifest at the end of the age by its persecution of the true church ("the holy city"; *Behold,* 370–73). He rightly recognizes that in Revelation "the holy city" designates

the temple (worship in the presence of God) through the church, while the exclusion of the court points to the destruction of the physical temple and the city of Jerusalem in 70.[15]

The other view contends that the unmeasured outer court and the "holy city" that it represents, trampled under Gentile feet for forty-two months, provide a contrasting perspective on the same true church that is pictured in the measured sanctuary.[16] In the paradoxical way in which Revelation's visions so often describe the church, Christ's holy temple-city is secure and vulnerable: secured from apostasy and divine wrath by the power and grace of the Lamb but vulnerable to attack through persecution by the world's noncovenant peoples. Although elsewhere in the Bible the title "the holy city" refers to the physical metropolis that was the capital of Israel and center of Jewish worship,[17] in the Book of Revelation "the holy city" is the new Jerusalem, the bride of the Lamb (Rev. 21:2; 22:19). Earthly Jerusalem, symbolizing anti-Jesus Judaism, as the site of the Lord's crucifixion, has become identified with "the great city" (11:8), symbolic of human community that stands in the defiant tradition of Sodom, Egypt, and preeminently Babylon (14:8; 16:19; 17:18). Because a Christ-centered redefinition of the people of God has occurred, the name *Jew* no longer belongs to anti-Jesus Jews (2:9; 3:9) and pro-Jesus Gentiles have been redeemed and consecrated as God's kingdom of priests (5:9–10). So

the true community of God, as we shall see, but his refusal to identify the outer court with the holy city is, I believe, incorrect. Hendriksen likewise distinguishes the sanctuary as the true church from the outer court, symbolizing external and nominal Christians, but he sees the Gentile "invasion" of the unmeasured courtyard and city as symbolizing the theological and ethical defilement of this nominal church through the influence of the unbelieving world (*More Than Conquerors,* 153–55).

15. Jay E. Adams, *The Time Is at Hand* (Nutley, N.J.: P&R Publishing, 1977), 68–69; Gentry, "The New Jerusalem," 174.

16. Caird, *Commentary,* 132; Bauckham, *Climax of Prophecy,* 266–73; Wall, *Revelation,* 143.

17. Gentry cites Isa. 48:2; 52:1; Neh. 11:1–18; Matt. 4:5; 27:53, as well as noncanonical Jewish sources, to support his case that "the holy city" refers to the physical, earthly city, Jerusalem (*Before Jerusalem Fell* [Tyler, Tex.: Institute for Christian Economics, 1989],169–70).

also the name "holy city" no longer belongs to earthly Jerusalem, which has become just one more expression of the "great city" that slays the saints (11:7–8; 17:6). The holy city is the bride of the Lamb, who will be revealed in beauty, ready for her wedding, at the end of history.

In the interim, however, the holy city will be trampled by the Gentiles, just as earthly Jerusalem and its temple had been razed and trampled by Roman troops under Titus. The interim here is symbolized as forty-two months, which will be shown in Revelation 12–13 to symbolize the period of the dragon's virulent but frustrated attempts to destroy the church through deception and violent aggression.

Thus the unmeasured courtyard, given to the Gentiles, and the holy city, trampled by the Gentiles, balance the portrait of the church as the measured sanctuary: though protected from apostasy and God's wrath, the church is exposed to physical coercion, social contempt, and violence.

> Like the seal that was set on the foreheads of God's servants, the measuring of the temple betokens an inner security against spiritual dangers. But the angel's orders are to leave the outer court exposed, because God does not offer to the church security from bodily suffering or death. It is his intention that they should remain outwardly vulnerable to the full hostility of their enemies, secure only in their faith in the crucified and risen Lord.[18]

These same paradoxical perspectives on the church, both invincible and vulnerable, are illustrated in more detail in the next vision about Jesus' two witnesses.

The Two Witnesses: Invincible Even in Defeat (11:3–13)

The One who gave John the rod now tacitly identifies himself as Jesus, who gives prophetic authority to "my two witnesses" (Rev.

18. Caird, *Commentary*, 132; cf. Bauckham, *Climax of Prophecy*, 272: "The church will be kept safe in its hidden spiritual reality, while suffering persecution and martyrdom."

11:3). In Revelation, as elsewhere in the New Testament,[19] Christians are Jesus' witnesses (*martys;* 2:13; 17:6), entrusted with the testimony (*martyria*) of Jesus (1:2, 9; 12:17; 19:10; 20:4), for he is *the* faithful witness (1:5). These two witnesses are prophets who bear a message of impending judgment and a call to repentance, as their sackcloth apparel shows (Isa. 37:1–2; Jonah 3:5; Matt. 11:21). They are portrayed as wielding the power to inflict miraculous signs of judgment after the pattern of Moses (water turned to blood and other plagues, Exod. 7–9) and Elijah (shutting up the sky, causing drought, 1 Kings 17:1; and destroying threatening enemies by fire, 2 Kings 1:10–12). They are two in number for two reasons. First, they satisfy the quorum needed to establish reliable evidence in biblical jurisprudence: "on the evidence of two or three witnesses a matter shall be confirmed" (Deut. 19:15; cf. Matt. 18:16; 1 Tim. 5:19). Second, they are portrayed in the imagery of Zechariah's vision of the lampstand supplied with oil by two olive trees in the sanctuary of God (Zech. 4). (Again the imagery of the ancient prophet's vision is modified as its symbolic vocabulary is employed in the revelation to John: Zechariah's one lampstand has become two in Revelation 11:4.)[20] To Zechariah the olive trees are interpreted as "the two anointed ones, who are standing by the Lord of the whole earth" (Zech. 4:14). The context suggests that these are Zerubbabel, the royal figure who is to rebuild God's temple (Zech. 4:6–10), and Joshua, the priest who is to lead worship in that temple (Zech. 3:1–5). Both prefigure the coming Servant of God, the Branch who will unite the royal and priestly offices by building the temple, offering the atoning sacrifice, and ruling on his throne (Zech. 3:8–10; 6:12–13). Thus the two witnesses are explicitly presented as prophets, while the allusion to Zechariah's olive trees implies that they are also kings and priests.

19. Compare Acts 1:8; 5:32; etc., with Isa. 43:10; 44:8. Cf. Dennis E. Johnson, *The Message of Acts in the History of Redemption* (Phillipsburg, N.J.: P&R Publishing, 1997), 34–49.

20. The seven branches that appeared on the lampstand in Zechariah's vision (Zech. 4:2) have appeared in Revelation as seven individual lampstands, symbolizing the churches (Rev. 1:20).

Since we have already seen the church portrayed as priests who reign (Rev. 5:10), we may suspect that these two witnesses symbolize the whole church in its role as witnesses to God's truth and against the world's lies and wickedness. Our suspicion is confirmed by further evidence: The description of the witnesses' death so closely foreshadows a later statement that the two texts must concern the same protagonists:

> 11:7 the beast that comes up out of the abyss will make war with them, and overcome them and kill them.

> 13:7 And it was given to [the beast that comes up out of the sea, 13:1] to make war with the saints and to overcome them.

In both texts the beast "makes war with" God's faithful followers and "overcomes" them. In both contexts note is taken of the fact that people from the world's "peoples and tribes and tongues and nations" support the beast in his aggression against God's representatives (11:9; 13:7). The beast's victory cannot be a spiritual and eternal one, for God soon vindicates the two witnesses. So the only way in which the beast can conquer the witnesses is by killing them, ending their physical life and silencing their indicting testimony; but his triumph is short-lived. Thus the victims of the beast's violence are identified with each other: the "two witnesses" in Revelation 11:7 are "the saints" in 13:7.

The time period in which the two witnesses carry on their prophetic proclamation is symbolized in a way that equates it with the whole span of the dragon's aggressive but frustrated attempts to eradicate the church from the earth. This time span is described in three ways: 42 months (11:2, 13:5); 1,260 days (11:3; 12:6); and "a time and times and half a time" (12:14). The mysterious "a time and times and half a time" is derived from Daniel 7:25, in which it symbolizes one-half of a sabbatical-year cycle: "one year, two years, and half a year" add up to 3½ years. These three designations all measure the same length of time, for in the ancient world a month was calculated as containing 30 days (42 x 30 = 1,260), and a year as containing 360 (3.5 x 360 = 1,260). The statements that contain these temporal markers provide complementary perspectives on the same era of history, as the order of the time designations implies. The era lasts "forty-two months" in the first (Rev. 11:2) and last (13:5) of its descriptions, and in both the focus is on the church's enemies and their aggression against the church. This same era lasts "twelve hundred and sixty days" in Revelation 11:3 and 12:6, and in these descriptions the focus is on the church's witness and protection by God. The one text (12:14) in which the wording from Daniel 7 appears ("a time, times, half a time") is a commentary on the protection of the woman (Rev. 12:6). Thus the texts in which these time markers appear characterize the era that they symbolize in two ways:

1. *Enemies assault the church 42 months:* The "holy city" is trampled by Gentiles (11:1–2).
   2. *The church is protected by God 1,260 days:* The two witnesses prophesy, and their opponents cannot harm them (11:3).
   2' *The church is protected by God 1,260 days:* The mother of the Messiah is nourished in the wilderness, and the dragon cannot destroy her (12:6, cf. the expansion in 12:14–17).
1' *Enemies assault the church 42 months:* The beast wields his authority in blasphemy against God and warfare against his saints (13:5–7).

The common threads that run through these descriptions are opposition and preservation: opposition from the "Gentiles," from the beast, from the "great city" and its international alliance of coconspirators, and from the dragon; but also preservation by God, who will not allow his holy place to be defiled, his witnesses to be silenced, his new Israel to be swept away by the dragon's flood of lies (12:15–16). This mixed situation—this unstable amalgam of deadly danger and divine defense—sounds strangely familiar. It sounds like John's day, and like ours.

The two witnesses cannot be destroyed as long as their prophetic mission remains incomplete. As they preach, God sends judgments of fire and drought, which earlier had been symbolized in the partial plagues of the first four seals and first four trumpets and which are a foreshadowing within history of the lake of fire that will consume all rebels at history's end. When the witness church has completed its mission, however, it will seem as if the beast has had the upper hand, having conquered and killed those who hold to the word of God and the testimony of Jesus. The two witnesses' corpses lie exposed in the street of "the great city," which will be personified in Babylon the harlot in a later vision (Rev. 17–18). But here the great city is called "mystically" (literally, "spiritually," i.e., in symbolism) Sodom, which in biblical tradition was the nadir of human wickedness and object of God's outpoured wrath (Matt. 11:23–24) and Egypt, Israel's slave master and target of God's ten plagues. The "great city" is also identified as the place of Jesus' crucifixion. We noted above that this implies that the earthly Jerusalem and the anti-Jesus Judaism centered there had no claim to the honored title "the holy city." This is not to say, however, that "great city" symbolizes only earthly Jerusalem and Judaism. The great city encompasses all who dwell on the earth, who give allegiance to the beast and rejoice in his ephemeral victory over the witnessing church.

"Those who dwell on the earth," who rejected the two witnesses' call to repentance, will celebrate contemptuously the demise of the church and its testimony to truth (Rev. 11:8–10).[21] But the duration of the beast's apparent triumph will be brief (3½ days) in contrast to the prolonged period (3½ years) of the suffering church's faithful testimony.[22] God intervenes to raise his witnesses from death as "the breath of life from God came into them, and they stood on their feet" like the mighty resurrected army in Ezekiel's vision of the valley of bones (Rev. 11:11; Ezek. 37:10). As their oppressors look on in terror, the witnesses are summoned by God to enter heaven, imitating their Lord's resurrection and ascension in the clouds (Rev. 11:12; cf. Acts 1:9; Dan. 7:13; Matt. 26:64; Rev. 12:5).

Accompanying the resurrection-vindication of the church that has maintained its testimony faithfully, even to death, is a "great earthquake" (Rev. 11:13). This is the first tremor of the cosmic shaking that will re-

21. In the ancient world, refusing burial of a corpse (Rev. 11:9), exposing it to scavenging birds and animals (19:17–21), expressed contempt for the deceased. Sophocles *Antigone;* Deut. 21:23; 1 Sam. 31:9–13; 2 Sam. 21:8–14.

22. A later vision magnifies this symbolic contrast between the long period (one thousand years) in which Satan's desire to destroy the saints is chained and frustrated (Rev. 20:2–3) and the "short time" (20:3) in which he finally assembles an international conspiracy to eradicate "the camp of the saints and the beloved city"—only to have his rebel band consumed by God's lightning bolt (20:7–10).

move the first heavens and earth (cf. 20:11; 21:1), the great quake that
we have seen in the vision of the sixth seal (6:12–17) and will see again
when the seventh bowl is poured out, shattering the "great city" Babylon into three pieces, causing the cities of the Gentiles to fall, and removing islands and mountains (16:17–21). What distinguishes the portrayal of the earthquake that accompanies the witnesses' exaltation from
the later portrayal in connection with the seventh bowl is the limitation
of the damage inflicted here: only one-tenth of the great city is destroyed
and only seven thousand of its inhabitants are killed. (This interlude still
belongs to the sixth trumpet, the second woe, so the final trumpet woe,
which brings full destruction of the old order, is still to come, 11:14.)
In the Old Testament prophets, the fraction one-tenth carries symbolic
association with the faithful remnant who are spared when God inflicts
covenant curses on Israel (Amos 5:3; Isa. 6:13). The same connotation
is attached to the number seven thousand, for, to the self-pitying
prophet's surprise, seven thousand in Israel had not worshiped Baal in
the days of Elijah (1 Kings 19:14–18). In John's vision, however, the
Old Testament imagery is turned upside down, for the tenth of the city
with its seven thousand residents are the first to fall under God's judgment. Those enemies who survive the earthquake, having beheld the
witness church's resurrection (Rev. 11:11) and ascension (v. 12), are
filled with fear, and they give glory to the God of heaven.

Although the narrative line of John's vision is clear and generally
agreed upon, the difficult and more controversial task is to identify the
events or trends to which the vision refers. The questions that confront us include: Does the resurrection–ascension of the two witnesses
point directly to the bodily resurrection–glorification of believers, or
does it symbolize the church's restoration to effective witness within
the course of history, after intense persecution seems to have eradicated it? Does the partial judgment on the great city (one-tenth and
seven thousand) show that this portion of the vision still falls within
the era of divine patience, giving further opportunity for rebels to repent? Do the survivors' fear and glorification of God express eleventh-
hour repentance, leading to salvation,[23] or is it a belated and begrudg-

23. So Caird, *Commentary,* 139–40; Bauckham, *Climax of Prophecy,* 278–83; Wall,
Revelation, 148. Persuasive for these scholars is the fact that elsewhere in Revelation

ing acknowledgment of God's power, compelled from the unrepentant hearts and mouths of the condemned?[24]

An adequate answer to these questions will need to be consistent with the clear teaching of other biblical passages, including and especially those of the Book of Revelation. We begin with Paul's statements that Christ must reign until all his enemies are put under his feet and that the last enemy to be abolished will be death (1 Cor. 15:25–26). The context shows that this abolition of death, the last enemy, occurs at Christ's coming, when those who belong to him enter into the bodily resurrection life that he entered as the first fruits on the third day after his crucifixion (vv. 22–24). John's visions in Revelation likewise portray the general resurrection, last judgment, and destruction of death as the final events that bring "the first things" to a close, making way for the new heaven and new earth (Rev. 20:11–21:5). The sounding of the last trumpet elicits praise in heaven that the time has arrived for the outpouring of God's wrath against his enemies, the judgment of the dead, and the rewarding of God's faithful servants (11:15–18).

In view of these fixed points of biblical revelation about the end of history, we cannot interpret the resurrection of the witnesses as the bodily resurrection of the church and at the same time view the city's partial destruction as symbolizing a postresurrection period in which God offers sinners further opportunity to repent. In view of the parallel that we have observed between the three and a half days of the beast's triumph over the witnesses and the "short time" of the dragon's release to assemble worldwide opposition against the saints (Rev. 20:3, 7–8), the witnesses' resurrection and ascension in full view of their enemies after the three and a half days (11:11) coincides with God's deliverance of the saints and destruction of the devil and his followers after the "short time" (20:9–10)—without any intervening delay to provide further opportunity for the church's enemies to repent.

---

the themes of the fear of God and giving glory to God are expressions of the true worship of the repentant (14:7; 16:9).

24. So Stuart, *Apocalypse*, 2:299–40; Hendriksen, *More Than Conquerors*, 159; Michael Wilcock, *I Saw Heaven Opened: The Message of Revelation*, TBST (Downers Grove, Ill.: InterVarsity Press, 1975), 106.

It seems most consistent, therefore, to see the witnesses' resurrection as portraying the bodily resurrection of all who belong to Christ's true church by faith at his return, accompanied by the great earthquake of judgment that will compel fear-filled praise even from God's enemies (see Phil. 2:9–11). Just as the vision genre sometimes compresses vast historical eons into symbolic images that pass like the twinkling of an eye (see Rev. 12:1–5, which spans redemptive history from Genesis 3 to Acts 1), so also a split-second in time may be expanded in visionary description and simultaneous climactic events presented as successive, in order to help hearers to see different facets of Christ's victory.

Conclusion

The complex of visions between the sixth and seventh trumpets sets the scene for the central drama of the Revelation, which portrays the war of the ages as the conflict between the heavenly woman, her Child, and the living God, on the one hand, and the harlot, the beast, and the dragon on the other. The scroll containing God's plan for history, for the victory of his witness church through suffering, has been opened by the Lamb and delivered to the prophet John to be announced for the comfort and warning of the churches. Despite the rage of its enemies, the church is secure in the presence of its holy champion. Despite its spiritual security as a measured sanctuary, the church is vulnerable to the violent aggression of those who hate its testimony about Jesus and seek to silence its call to repentance. Yet the last word concerning the church's paradox-filled experience in this time between the Lamb's comings is the voice of the seventh trumpet, announcing at history's end: "The kingdom of this world has become the kingdom of our Lord and of His Christ; and He will reign forever and ever" (Rev. 11:15). Once again, however, we need to see this joyful consummation in light of the age-long conflict that has preceded it and the archenemy who provoked that conflict. Therefore John's next cycle of visions returns to the dawn of time, piercing to the deepest level of the war to unmask the antagonist who lurks behind and operates through the church's human enemies: "the great dragon . . . the serpent of old who is called the devil and Satan" (12:9).

CHAPTER NINE

Cosmic Conflict 1:
The Mother, the Dragon, and the Beasts
(12:1–13:18)

The Piercing to the Core of the Conflict

The question Why? can precipitate an almost endless chain of explanations. Why did he die? His brain-wave activity ceased. Why? His brain no longer received the oxygen it needed. Why? His heart stopped beating. Why? A bullet passed through it. Why? It had been propelled toward him at high speed. Why? A pistol hammer had ignited gunpowder in the bullet. Why? His enemy had pulled the pistol's trigger. Why? The enemy carried a grudge. Why? The victim had stabbed the enemy's brother. Why? The brother owed the victim money. Why? A gambling debt. Who knows how many reasons could be traced back from here?

The suffering and tempted church is confronted with a similar set of conundrums as we seek explanations of our experience and of the ways of our God in the world. Why must the martyrs wait for vindication? Why must the church militant endure social ostracism, economic sanctions, and imprisonment? Why do the congregations that are in Jesus' hand exhibit such a mixture of truth and error, purity and compromise, love and indifference? Why do wars, fires, and famine rage, if the Prince of Peace has taken his throne and has taken in hand God's plan of the ages to carry it out until the kingdoms of this world have become the kingdom of our Lord and of his Christ? Explanations that focus on human combatants are true enough at one level, but what lies behind the hostility of human enemies? What about societal structures and systems of thought? And behind human societies, religions, and philosophies: Is there a cause of the cosmic conflict that lies behind the various proximate causes?

Like the peeling of an onion the unfolding of John's visions leads us, layer by layer, deeper into the mystery of God, which is to be completed when the seventh trumpet sounds (Rev. 10:7). In the order of his visionary experience John has heard the final trumpet call (11:15), which sets in motion the earthquake that is to shatter not merely a tenth of the "great city" of man (11:13) but the whole city—the whole structure of life and civilization founded on human autonomy (16:17–21). Yet John does not see immediately the impact of the third woe, the seventh and final trumpet, on earth. Rather, he hears a chorus of celebration and thanksgiving in heaven (11:15–18). He sees a scene that points to even deeper disclosure of the mystery of God: God's sanctuary in heaven opened, bringing the ark of his covenant into view (11:19).

This opening of God's temple reminds us of the vision of the enthroned One and the Lamb, from which the seal visions and the trumpet visions proceeded (Rev. 4–5). In that vision and in this one there is an opening of heaven (4:1), enabling the prophet to see God's throne (4:2; the throne appears as the ark of the covenant in 11:19). In both visions the scene is punctuated by the terrifying lightning, "voices," and thunderclaps that attended the Lord's descent to Sinai to give his law to Moses (4:5; 11:19; cf. Exod. 19:18–20). The scene that meets John's eye when the seventh trumpet sounds is not just a repetition of Revelation 4; it is also a magnification. Added to the lightnings, "voices," and thunderclaps now are an earthquake, as at Sinai, and great hail (Rev. 11:19). And now John sees within heaven a sanctuary (*naos*),[1] a previously veiled chamber implicitly identified as the Most Holy Place by the presence of the ark. This inner sanctum is opened

1. The Greek word *naos* is best translated by "sanctuary," since it typically refers specifically to the building that contains the two chambers, the Holy Place and Most

to introduce a new depth of divine revelation. This deeper level of insight into the core of the conflict is signaled by the appearance of two signs in heaven.

The Woman and the Dragon (12:1–6)

Only three features of John's visions are labeled signs, and two of them appear here, at the center point of the book.[2] A woman appears as a "great sign," and soon afterwards "another sign," a great red dragon, comes into view (12:1, 3). The conflict between the woman and the dragon dominates the drama of Revelation 12, which begins with the dragon waiting to consume the son to whom the woman is giving birth (12:4) and closes with the dragon's frustrated attempts to destroy her and "the rest of her children" (12:17). This chapter consists of two complementary visions, which provide symbolic commentary on the same battle and its sequel. In the first vision the protagonists and preparation for the battle are described in some detail (12:1–4). Then the battle, viewed from an earthly perspective, flashes past in the blink of an eye (12:5), and finally its sequel—the woman's flight to the wilderness for protection for 1,260 days—is stated (12:6). The second vision opens with a heavenly perspective on the battle (12:7–9), followed by a heavenly commentary on its significance (12:10–12); then the same sequel—the woman's flight to the wilderness for protection for three and one-half years (= 1,260 days)—is portrayed in greater detail (12:13–17). Twice we see the dragon's defeat in battle, and twice we see his subsequent frustration in trying to destroy the mother of the Messiah.

The woman is a picture of Messiah's mother, for her child "is to rule all the nations with a rod of iron" (12:5). In Psalm 2 the Lord's

Holy Place (Rev. 11:1–2; 15:5, 8; 16:1). The Greek *hieron* ("temple"), which includes the whole complex including the courtyards (of Israel, of the women, of the Gentiles) and storehouses, is not used in Revelation.

2. The third, "another sign in heaven, great and marvelous," is the seven angels with the seven final plagues (Rev. 15:1). They emerge from the sanctuary of the tabernacle of testimony in heaven when it is opened (15:5–6), reminding us of the opening of the sanctuary in Rev. 11:19.

Anointed (Hebrew *M'shiach* = Messiah, Ps. 2:2) recounts God's decree appointing him universal king: "You are My Son, today I have begotten You. Ask of Me, and I will surely give the nations as Your inheritance. . . . You shall break³ them with a rod of iron" (Ps. 2:7–9). We have just heard a heavenly chorus celebrating the triumph in which "the kingdom of the world has become the kingdom of our Lord and of His Christ" (Rev. 11:15), a striking reversal of the situation with which the second psalm opened, when kings and rulers conspired against the Lord and his Christ (Ps. 2:2).

Before she is portrayed as the mother of the Davidic Messiah, however, the woman is Mother Israel, whose divine Redeemer-Husband will fill her house with children (cf. Isa. 54:1–8). This identification is implied through the symbolism of the light that envelops her, from the twelve-starred crown on her head, to her sun-resplendent robe, to her moon-shod feet. The twelve stars identify her as God's covenant people, who have appeared as Israel's twelve tribes (Rev. 7:4–8) and will appear as the heavenly city-bride founded on the twelve apostles (21:14) and entered through gates bearing the twelve tribes' names (21:12). When Israel's sons first numbered twelve, the people of God appeared in Joseph's dream as sun (Father Jacob), moon (Mother Rachel), and eleven stars (Joseph's brothers), bowing to Joseph, through whose suffering their lives would be spared (Gen. 37:9). So the woman is Israel, the people of God.⁴

But ultimately she is the mother of the promised Seed who would slay the serpent. The conflict between the mother and the dragon is far older than the covenant with Abraham, Isaac, and Israel. The woman's enemy, a red dragon (Rev. 12:3), is then identified as "the

3. The Hebrew word translated "you shall break" is "you shall shepherd" (*r'ah*), as a metaphor for "you shall rule." (Hence the LXX translates it using *poimainō,* "to shepherd," the verb used in Rev. 12:5; cf. 2:27; 19:15.) Since the next line of the psalm describes the nations as "shattered like earthenware," the Messiah's rule focuses on destructive punishment (as in 2:27; 19:15). Thus "break" would be an appropriate translation not only in Ps. 2 but also in Revelation's allusions to it.

4. "She gave birth to a son" (Rev. 12:5) alludes to the promise of Immanuel's birth from a virgin (Isa. 7:14), while the addition of "a male child" evokes the image of Zion/Israel as a pregnant mother bringing her male child to birth (Isa. 66:7 LXX has *arsēn,* as in Rev. 12:5).

serpent of old who is called the devil and Satan, who deceives the whole world" (12:9). When he cannot destroy her royal child, he wages war against "the rest of her children" (*sperma* = "seed") (12:17). The battle began in the garden of God, when the serpent deceived the woman (Gen. 3:13), but God pronounced his curse on the serpent-tempter: "I will put enmity between you and the woman, and between your seed and her seed (LXX: *sperma*); He shall bruise you on the head, and you shall bruise him on the heel" (Gen. 3:15). The mortal combat declared by God against "the serpent of old, the devil and Satan" is seen in the opposition of the two seeds throughout history: Cain against Abel, Ishmael against Isaac, Esau against Jacob, Edom against Israel, Saul against David. From the expulsion from Eden, God's people have been an expectant mother, awaiting the birth of the Seed who would champion their cause against Satan the liar, accuser, and murderer.

The dragon, for his part, is shown in symbols signaling his cunning wisdom (seven heads), great power (ten horns), and authority to influence others (seven diadems; Rev. 12:3). Though his wisdom and power seem to be infinite, rivaling the omniscience and omnipotence of God, they are counterfeit. "His tail swept away a third of the stars of heaven and threw them to the earth" (12:4)—an impressive demonstration of power, to be sure, but hardly comprehensive.[5]

Since the woman is in labor, the dragon takes his stand in front of her, waiting to consume her son when he is born. The strength, intelligence, and ferocity of the dragon seem to make him an overpowering adversary to the woman and her newborn son. Yet the dragon's lethal plot is foiled with split-second speed: "And she gave birth to a son, a male child, who is to rule all the nations with a rod of iron; and her child was caught up to God and to His throne" (Rev. 12:5). This terse statement encapsulates the life, suffering, and exaltation of Jesus: he was born, he was caught up to God, and he shares

---

5. The imagery is drawn from Daniel's vision of a goat with a great horn (Alexander's Hellenistic Empire), shattered into four horns (kingdoms), one of which grows to such dimensions that it throws down some of the stars of heaven to earth (Dan. 8:10). This horn apparently symbolizes the arrogance of Antiochus IV Epiphanes of Syria, who defiled the rebuilt postexilic temple, provoking the Maccabean resistance.

God's throne of infinite authority (cf. 3:21). Neither the serpent's subtle strategies nor his exercise of raw, draconian power could destroy the promised seed of the woman, the Lion/Lamb who gained the victory by being slain (5:5, 9) and who shares his triumph with those who hold fast to his testimony in reliance on his sacrificial blood (12:11).

Since his plot to destroy the Messiah has been thwarted, the dragon turns in rage on Messiah's mother. The dragon's aggressive hostility is implied when we read, "the woman fled into the wilderness where she had a place prepared by God" (Rev. 12:6). As Elijah was fed by many ravens in the wilderness beyond the Jordan (1 Kings 17:2–6), so the woman is nourished by plural providers (the Greek reads, "so that they may feed her"). In Revelation 11–13 the time frame now associated with her desert retreat is measured in three distinct but synonymous ways: 42 months (11:2; 13:5), 1,260 days (11:3; 12:6), or "a time and times and half a time" (3½ years; 12:14). The inverted repetition in which these time measurements appear—42 months, then 1,260 days, then 1,260 days, then 42 months—helps John's hearers to recognize that the same time period is being symbolized throughout these three chapters. The additional "time and times and half a time" makes explicit allusion to the period of the saint's persecution under the fourth beast in Daniel 7:25. As we saw in connection with Revelation 11:2–3, this era is characterized by persecution of the church (holy city, heavenly woman) by its enemies, but also protection of the church by its God (measuring the sanctuary, refuge in the wilderness).[6]

6. See chapter 8. Robert H. Mounce suggests that the length of the three and a half years, derived from Dan. 12:7 (cf. 7:25), originally corresponded directly to "the period of Jewish suffering under the Syrian despot Antiochus Epiphanes in 167–164 BC," but then that it became "a standard symbol for that limited period of time during which evil would be allowed free rein" (*The Book of Revelation*, rev. ed., NICNT [Grand Rapids: Eerdmans, 1998], 215). In Rev. 11–13, however, each reference to this time period emphasizes, along with the powerful exercise of evil, the tight rein that God keeps on those who try to destroy the church. Moses Stuart likewise referred to the period of "desolations caused by Antiochus Epiphanes" as prophesied in Daniel, but also, consistent with his preterist approach, found the fulfillment of John's vision in the Jewish war and siege that climaxed with Jerusalem's destruction in 70 (*A Commentary on the Apocalypse*, 2 vols. [London: Wiley and Putnam, 1845], 2:262).

In other words, the time period symbolized in 1,260 days encompasses the church's ongoing experience of suffering and safety, bold testimony and bitter trial, alienation in the desert but nourishment from God, from the time of Jesus' ascension to heaven until the trauma that precedes his glorious return.

Michael and the Dragon (12:7–12)

Now a complementary vision shows the same conflict and sequel but from a different perspective. Now the birth on earth of the woman's seed (the virgin's son, Zion's male child) and his exaltation to the throne of God is seen as the turning point of war in heaven. In the Book of Daniel, Michael is a "great prince" in the unseen spiritual realm who assists God's angelic messengers in their mission and stands guard over God's people (Dan. 10:13, 21; 12:1).[7] Michael's power and holiness make him the fitting captain for the hosts of God's loyal angels as they join battle with the dragon and his angels.

Again the conflict seems brief: the dragon had no strength, a place was no longer found in heaven for him and his forces, and consequently they were cast down to earth (Rev. 12:8–9). As a great voice in heaven makes clear, the battle symbolizes the truth that Satan has been disbarred from his status as prosecutor in the court of divine justice: "the accuser of our brethren has been thrown down, he who accuses them before our God day and night" (12:10)—but now no longer! In the background are those Old Testament glimpses of God's tribunal in heaven, in which Satan stood among the "sons of God" to bring indictment against God's people. Satan's allegation that Job was no more than a hireling, whose fair-weather friendship with God would wither unless watered by a steady stream of bribes, was disproved (Job 1:6–12; 2:1–6). The accuser's charges against the postexilic high priest Joshua were apparently justified, however, for in Zechariah's vision Joshua

7. Jude 9 describes Michael as "the archangel" who did not presume to curse Satan in his own authority but instead appealed to God's judgment: "The Lord rebuke you." In Zech. 3:2, to which Jude alludes, the angel of the Lord utters these words, "The LORD rebuke you, Satan!" as he defends the defiled high priest from Satan's accusations.

was defiled, his filthy garments exposing his guilty heart (Zech. 3:1–3). Yet the Lord rebukes Satan and commands that Joshua's stained clothing be replaced by spotless festal robes (vv. 4–5), for Joshua is a preview of deep cleansing to come, when God's servant the Branch arrives (vv. 8). The accuser's banishment from heaven shows that the Branch has now arrived. He is the woman's son. No longer can Satan lodge accusation against those for whom the Lamb has shed his blood: "our brethren . . . overcame him because of the blood of the Lamb and because of the word of their testimony, and they did not love their life even when faced with death" (Rev. 12:10–11).

Thus the battle that issues in the dragon's expulsion from heaven is not the primeval conflict before Adam's fall, when Satan and other angels who had been created good inexplicably turned against their Creator. Rather, the war in heaven that John sees in symbol was fought on earth, when Jesus suffered and died on a cross outside Jerusalem and then rose from the dead. The dragon's banishment from heaven to earth marks the coming of God's kingdom and of his Christ's authority (Rev. 12:10).[8] At the seventh and last trumpet heavenly voices celebrated the final coming of God's kingdom, when all opposition to Christ's rule will be eradicated from the earth (cf. 11:17–18). The coming of God's kingdom celebrated in Revelation 12:10–12, however, precedes that final victory; for it speaks of the devil, now deprived of authority to indict believers and aware that his days are numbered, venting his frustration by wreaking havoc on earth. This is the kingdom's coming promised by Jesus and fulfilled in his disciples' lifetime through his death and resurrection, his heavenly enthronement and pouring out of the Spirit in power (Mark 1:15; 9:1; Acts 2:30–33). From heaven's perspective, it is the coming of the kingdom that produces unmitigated joy, for the accuser's authority to prosecute "our brethren" has been nullified by the shed blood of the Lamb. To earth, however, the

8. The coming of God's kingdom was exhibited in the authority that Jesus gave his disciples to expel demons, an authority rooted in the decisive battle that he would win over the prince of demons in his death and resurrection. Therefore when the seventy disciples returned from the kingdom-advancing mission on which Jesus had sent them and marveled at the demons' subjection to them in Jesus' name, he responded, "I was watching Satan fall from heaven like lightning" (Luke 10:18).

dragon's defeat now brings increased trauma and woe (Rev. 12:12), though the sequel shows that his rage to destroy God's people through deceit and violence is thwarted by the church's divine Protector.

The Woman and the Dragon—Reprise (12:13–17)

The battle's sequel shown briefly in Revelation 12:6 is now magnified so that we can see more detail. We see that the woman flees to the desert because the dragon is pursuing her, seeking to destroy her (v. 13). She flies on the great eagle's wings, a symbol that portrays her escape in the imagery God had used to recall the exodus: "You yourselves have seen what I did to the Egyptians, and how I bore you on eagles' wings, and brought you to Myself" (Exod. 19:4). In the wilderness she is fed, as Israel and Elijah were (Exod. 16; 1 Kings 19:4–8), by God's special care and provision.

God has placed his people, Messiah's mother, beyond the reach of her great enemy, "[away] from the presence of the serpent." So Satan launches a new but actually very old strategy of destruction: "the serpent poured water like a river out of his mouth after the woman, so that he might cause her to be swept away with the flood" (Rev. 12:15). In Revelation what proceeds from the mouth symbolizes words and their power. Thus John sees a sharp sword proceeding from the mouth of the Son of Man (1:16), whose sovereign pronouncement of judgment on false teachers will bring destruction unless they repent (2:12, 16). This same Son of Man, armed with the same sword proceeding from his mouth, is the faithful and true captain of heaven's cavalry, the Word of God (19:11, 13, 15, 21). The word of Jesus' two prophetic witnesses is so strong that "if any one wants to harm them, fire flows out of their mouth and devours their enemies" (11:5). John will see emerging from the mouths of the dragon, the beast, and the false prophet deceiving demonic spirits in the form of frogs, sent out to gather the world's kings to wage war against God (16:13–14).

Here the floodwaters from the dragon's mouth symbolize deceptive teaching that would, if believed, drown the church's faith, destroying its life. Such threats are present in the churches of Asia in the form of the Nicolaitans' lies and Jezebel's promise of deep knowledge into secret things (Rev. 2:2, 6, 14–15, 20–24). In his first epistle John called the church to exercise discernment in testing prophetic spirits, since many false prophets, controlled by the spirit of the antichrist and denying the incarnation, had gone out into the world (1 John 4:1–6). Isaiah rebuked Israel for thinking that they could find their own place of refuge to keep them safe when the floodwaters of disaster burst from the gates of the grave (Isa. 28:14–15). Such self-reliant hope was futile, for "hail will sweep away the refuge of lies and the waters will overflow the secret place. Your covenant with death will be canceled, and your pact with Sheol will not stand; when the overwhelming scourge passes through" (28:17–18). The only safe place to stand is the tested cornerstone laid by the Lord in Zion (28:16). Because the heavenly woman finds her refuge in the place prepared by God, he makes good his promise to her: "When you pass through the waters, I will be with you; and through the rivers, they will not overflow you" (Isa. 43:2). As in the wilderness in Moses' days the ground swallowed up the priestly pretenders Korah, Dathan, and Abiram (Num. 16:31–33), so now the earth swallows the dragon's pretentious lies, protecting the people of God.

Twice thwarted—unable to consume the Son or drown his mother in a river of lies—the dragon turns to wage war against "the rest of her children, who keep the commandments of God and hold to the testimony of Jesus" (Rev. 12:17). He will do so through the beast, who is about to arise from the sea to receive the dragon's power to wage war on the saints (13:2, 7). The mention of "the rest of her seed" (dej) reminds us of the early promise of Genesis 3:15, fulfilled in the dragon's great defeat, when the woman's male child ascended to share God's throne, as the dragon was cast down (12:5, 7–9). The woman's other children share her son's victory as they testify their trust in Jesus the Lamb (see 12:11), showing their faith to be genuine. Because the woman seems to be distinguished from "the rest of her children," some commentators have identified the woman with a Jewish remnant who believe in Jesus and "the rest of her children" with Gentile Christians.[9]

9. Cf. Jesus' "other sheep" in John 10:16 and the comment that Jesus would die "not for the nation only, but that He might also gather together into one the children of God who are scattered abroad" (11:51–52).

In John's visions, however, distinct symbols often point not to different referents but to differing perspectives on the same referent.[10] So here the protection of the mother promises that "the church shall never perish," and the dragon's war against her offspring reminds us that God shields the church's members not from physical violence but from spiritual destruction.

The Beast from the Sea (12:18–13:10)

The dragon takes his stand "on the sand of the seashore," for from the sea will emerge the monster to whom he will give his great power and through whom he will wage war against the church. A subtler symbolic significance may also be suggested. Although "the sand of the seashore" is an established biblical metaphor for a countless multitude (e.g., in God's great promise of seed to Abraham, Gen. 22:17), it appears only once elsewhere in Revelation: at the end of the thousand years the dragon is loosed to gather the nations at earth's ends, "Gog and Magog," for the last battle. This evil army's numerical strength is "like the sand of the seashore" (Rev. 20:8). Thus the dragon's stand on the sea's sand, like the harlot's seat on the sea's waters in a later vision, shows his sway over "peoples and multitudes and nations and tongues" (17:1, 15). This international authority he bestows on the beast who bears his image (13:2, 7).

The sea is the chaotic region from which threat and rebellion arise, an apt portrait of the abyss, the proper home of all uncleanness and hostility toward God. When that legion of unclean spirits who tormented the demoniac of Gerasa met their match in Jesus, they pled for a delay of their banishment to the abyss, asking instead to be sent into swine (Luke 8:31). They received their request, only to be carried by the swine into the sea, where they belong—small reprieve! The beast that now comes up from the sea is the beast that, in John's earlier vision, came up from the abyss to wage war on Jesus' witnesses (Rev. 11:7).

10. The seven lamps before the throne and the seven eyes of the Lamb provide complementary perspectives on the one Spirit of God (Rev. 4:5; 5:6), and the measured sanctuary and the unmeasured courtyard show us the eternal security and the external vulnerability of the same church (11:1–2).

The beast reflects the dragon who invests it with malevolent power. As the dragon has "seven heads and ten horns" (Rev. 12:3), so also the beast is its mirror image, with "ten horns and seven heads" (13:1). But the replication is not exact: the dragon has seven diadems on its seven heads, whereas the beast's ten horns bear ten diadems.

Daniel's vision of the Ancient of Days who invests the Son of Man with eternal dominion (Dan. 7) began with "four great beasts . . . coming up from the sea," symbolizing four successive Gentile kingdoms that would wield power over the people of God (7:3, 17, 23).[11] In Daniel's vision Chaldea (Neo-Babylonia) appeared as a lion with eagle's wings; the Medes and Persians who conquered Chaldea as a bear raised up on one side; and Alexander's Hellenistic regime, followed after his early death by its fourfold subdivision, as a leopard with four wings and four heads (7:4–6). The fourth beast, Rome, was not compared with any of the predatory animals in nature, for it was to be far worse than its predecessors in destructive power (iron teeth, ten horns), crushing, devouring, and trampling its victims (7:7–8, 19–21). The beast that John now sees combines them all: "having ten horns . . . the beast. . . was like a leopard, and his feet were like those of a bear, and his mouth like the mouth of a lion" (Rev. 13:1–2).

In one sense, this monster is Daniel's fourth beast, as is evident from the fact that both speak arrogant boasts and blasphemies (Dan. 7:8, 11, 20; Rev. 13:5–6) and wage war against the saints (Dan. 7:21; Rev. 13:7). Rome was the expression of the beast that would threaten the churches of Asia Minor and throughout the Mediterranean world in the decades and generations after John received his visions. In another sense, though, the monster that John now sees is bigger than Rome,

11. This vision, shown to Daniel in the first year of Belshazzar's reign, parallels in content, though it differs in imagery, the earlier dream that troubled Belshazzar's ancestor Nebuchadnezzar (Dan. 2). Nebuchadnezzar saw a statue in four parts: head of gold, chest of silver, midsection of bronze, legs of iron with feet of iron mixed with clay. The statue symbolized four successive empires of progressively declining splendor: Nebuchadnezzar's Chaldea, the Medo-Persian kingdom that would conquer it, the Hellenistic empire of Alexander and his successors, and finally Rome. During Rome's rule God would establish his eschatological kingdom, which would never be replaced (symbolized in a stone carved out without human hands, growing into a vast mountain).

as the merging of imagery from all four of Daniel's beasts shows. The beast is given "authority to act for forty-two months" (13:5). We have seen that this period (42 months = 1,260 days = 3½ years) symbolizes the whole span of time from Christ's resurrection until the outbreak of intense evil just before his second coming. During this period the church will be persecuted and protected, witnessing invincibly and yet trampled underfoot, conquered but not destroyed. Therefore this beast and its persecuting power would outlast the fall of Rome in the fifth century. It continues to find various expressions, some more overt and potent than others, down to our day.

Often in popular prophetic teaching the beast of Revelation 13 is assumed to be the antichrist. The title *antichrist* is not used in Revelation; it appears only five times in the Bible, all in 1 and 2 John. Applying "antichrist" language to Revelation's beast may be appropriate, as long as we see clearly the reality that it describes in John's epistles. As he writes to first-century Christians, John affirms, "Children, it is the last hour; and just as you heard that antichrist is coming, even now many antichrists have appeared; from this we know that it is the last hour" (1 John 2:18). Because "the last hour" is identifiable by the appearance of antichrist, the activities of "many antichrists" in John's day mark that time period in which first-century Christians lived and in which we still live as "the last hour." How can we recognize "antichrist"? John's epistles trace his/their profile: The antichrist is anyone "who denies that Jesus is the Christ," for in so doing he denies the Father and the Son (1 John 2:22). Every spirit that refuses to confess that Jesus is Christ come in the flesh is the spirit of the antichrist (1 John 4:3; 2 John 7). Although John's readers have heard that a specific and personal expression of Satan's rebellion against Jesus Christ is to come at some future point, John wants them to recognize the satanic deceptions that surround them today, to see that "this is the last hour" (already in the first century), and therefore to be on guard.

Paul's discussion of the "man of lawlessness" in 2 Thessalonians 2 has the same perspective, though the problem he addresses in Thessalonica seems the opposite of that answered by John. If the recipients of 1 John were not sensitive enough to how eschatologically charged their own days were, the Thessalonians were eschatologically supercharged, troubled by rumors that the "day of the Lord" had already arrived, leaving them behind. In order to calm their last-days fever, Paul flatly asserts that the day of the Lord will not come before the appearance of the man of lawlessness, who will be destroyed by the splendor of Jesus' presence and the breath of his mouth when he returns in final victory (2 Thess. 2:3, 8). That lawless one will be the personal epitome of Satan's attempts to usurp God's authority and worship (2:4). Yet those evil trends that will reach climactic expression in the man of lawlessness are operative even now, though under restraint: "For the mystery of lawlessness is already at work; only he who now restrains will do so until he is taken out of the way. Then that lawless one will be revealed" (2:7–8). The New Testament portrait of the present and the future is consistent, wherever we turn. The dragon's violent hostility against Christ and his church is a constant that characterizes the whole era between Christ's resurrection and his return. John's first-century hearers and his twenty-first century readers are both living in "the last hour." The dragon's expression of his hatred, which is restrained by God's sovereign control for the present, at the end will reach unparalleled ferocity in a form[12] that will take the evil one's divine pretensions and persecuting aggression to new depths.

Returning to John's vision in Revelation 13, we see that the beast is not only an image bearer of the dragon but also an imitation of the Lamb. One of the beast's heads is "as if it had been slain," yet its "fatal wound" was healed (v. 3). The parallel between John's vision of the Lamb standing "as if slain" (*hōs esphagmenon*, 5:6) and the beast's head, which appeared "as if slain" (*hōs esphagmenēn*) is unmistakable. Jesus was slain yet "came to life" (*ezēsen*, 2:8); now the beast is proclaimed

---

12. Will this "form" be a single human individual such as Antiochus Epiphanes, the Hellenistic-Syrian tyrant whose profanation of the temple in the time of the Maccabees became the archetype ("the abomination of desolation," Dan. 12:11; Mark 13:14) of pagan oppression of the people of God? Paul does speak of "the man of lawlessness, the son of destruction" (2 Thess. 2:3). Yet the beast symbolism derived from Daniel 7 suggests that John's vision in Rev. 13 focuses on institutional expressions of politico-military power such as Babylon or Rome. Then again, in the Johannine epistles the antichrist phenomenon, whether present or future, seems to appear in theological-spiritual terms as a denial of the incarnation and a dissemination of false teaching, without individual or institutional politico-military associations.

as having received a fatal blow, yet it "came to life" (*ezēsen*, 13:14).[13] The counterfeit resurrection of the beast's horn evokes amazement and worship from all who dwell on the earth (13:3–4), whose names were not inscribed before the world's foundation in the book of life that belongs to the slain Lamb (13:8).[14] This wound, paradoxically lethal and yet healed, is associated by many commentators with rumors that circulated throughout the Roman Empire in the social and political turmoil that followed the mysterious disappearance (suicide)[15] of the emperor Nero in 68: "Nero was not really dead; he had gone into hiding in Parthia, and would return at the head of a vast Parthian army to take revenge on Rome."[16] Nero's return from Parthia (beyond the empire's northeastern border—that is, east of Asia Minor) was dreaded in some circles but hoped for in others. Though despised in Rome as a cruel "beast" who murdered his mother in his grasp for power,[17] Nero had

13. G. R. Beasley-Murray, *The Book of Revelation*, NCB (Grand Rapids: Eerdmans, 1981), 210: "The Christ of God has risen, but the world declared it a lie . . . or madness. The 'Christ' of the Devil comes from death—and the world worships him!"

14. The perfect passive participle, "slain" (*esphagmenou*), is picked up from Rev. 5:6 and repeated in 13:8 to stress the parallel between the Lamb and the beast's "resurrected" head. Note also that the NASB is correct in attaching "from the foundation of the world" to the writing of names in the book of life, not to the slaying of the Lamb. This is evident from 17:8, where the writing of names in the book "before the foundation of the world" is again mentioned, but the slain Lamb to whom the book belongs is not.

15. Suetonius *Nero* (Lives of the Caesars, book 6), 49, describes Nero's death at a villa outside Rome. Upon receiving written notice of the senate's condemnation of him as a public enemy and hearing the armed guard approaching on horseback to take him into custody, Nero plunged a dagger into his throat with the help of his secretary. *Suetonius*, vol. 2, trans. J. C. Rolfe, LCL (Cambridge: Harvard University Press, 1970).

16. G. B. Caird, *A Commentary on the Revelation of St. John the Divine*, HNTC (New York: Harper & Row, 1966), 164.

17. Philostratus *Life of Apollonius* 4.38, describes Nero: "I have seen many, many wild beasts of Arabia and India; but this beast (*thērion*), that is commonly called a tyrant, I know not how many heads it has, nor if it be crooked of claw, and armed with horrible fangs." Cited in Richard Bauckham, *The Climax of Prophecy: Studies on the Book of Revelation* (Edinburgh: T & T Clark, 1993), 410. As Suetonius's *Nero* (n. 15 above) shows, finally the Roman senate pronounced the emperor an enemy of the people and empire of Rome.

been popular among the cities of Asia. Dio Chrysostom, writing probably during Domitian's reign, says of Nero:

> so far as the rest of his subjects were concerned [other than his immediate retinue], there was nothing to prevent his continuing to be Emperor for all time, seeing that even now everybody wishes he were still alive. And the great majority do believe that he is, although in a certain sense he has died not once but often along with those who had been firmly convinced that he was still alive.[18]

The association of the beast with Nero finds support in Revelation 13:17–18, where John speaks of the number of the beast's name and then invites the intelligent person to "calculate the number of the beast," which is the number of a man, namely 666. In calling the beast's number the "number of its name" and inviting the reader to "calculate" it, John signaled to first-century readers the presence of a kind of ancient code called gematria. Since the letters of ancient alphabets also carried different numerical values, names or words could be encoded by being represented as the mathematical sum of the values of the letters they contained. To make the code harder to crack, especially in mystical or apocalyptic writings, the key name was first transliterated into a foreign alphabet, then its total computed in terms of the values of those foreign characters. In the Greek Apocalypse of Baruch (3 Baruch 4:3–7), for instance, a dragon drinks from a sea fed by 360 rivers—360 being the numerical value of the letters in "dragon," when the Greek word *drakōn* is transliterated into Hebrew characters.[19] Likewise, when the Greek word *thērion* ("beast") is put into Hebrew letters, their total is 666—so in gematria, this figure is literally the number of "beast." But it is also "the number . . . of a man" (Rev. 13:18). That man is the emperor Nero, whom some Greek-speakers called

18. Dio Chrysostom *Discourses (xii—xxx),* trans. J. W. Cohoon, LCL (Cambridge: Harvard University Press, 1939), 281 (discourse 12.10).

19. Bauckham, *Climax of Prophecy,* 389. Bauckham also reports that a few sentences later (3 Baruch 4:10) this apocalypse states that 409,000 giants perished in the flood of Noah's time, a total probably derived from fact that when the Greek word *kataklysmos* ("flood") is transliterated into Hebrew, the sum of the values of its Hebrew letters is 409.

Nerōn Kaisar, a name that, spelled in equivalent Hebrew letters, "is calculated" to equal 666.[20] (The second-century Sibylline Oracles use an abbreviated form of gematria in referring to Nero as "a sovereign who has the letter of fifty, a direful serpent causing grievous war," murdering his family members, disappearing and then returning.[21] The "letter of fifty" is N, the initial of Nero.)

The lethal wound on one of the beast's seven heads, which seemed to kill the beast (Rev. 13:12, 14), was the decomposition of Nero's rule, climaxing with his flight from Rome and suicide at the age of thirty in the year 68. In the next year civil war brought three men (Galba, Otho, Vitellius) to imperial power for a few months each. In 69 Vespasian, general of Roman armies charged to put down an uprising inflamed by Zealots in Judea, left his son Titus to continue the siege of Jerusalem and to complete it with the razing of city and temple the following year. Vespasian returned to Rome to restore order to the city and the far-flung empire and to establish himself as emperor. Through his decade-long rule and the tenure of his sons Titus (ruled 79–81) and Domitian (81–96) it seemed that the glory and power of Rome, dealt a virtual death blow in the upheaval surrounding Nero, had come back from the dead. Thus strands of recent Roman history are woven as symbols into John's portrait of a beast that is bigger than Rome. In the same way Jesus used Daniel's expression "abomination of desolation," which originally referred to the Syrian Antiochus Epiphanes' defiling of the temple in 167 B.C. (Dan. 11:31), to prophesy the temple's complete destruction at Roman hands in A.D. 70 (Matt. 24:15).

The sobering announcement that from an earthly perspective the beast will conquer the saints (Rev. 13:7; cf. 11:7) evokes an exhortation to the listening church to endure suffering with perseverance: "If

---

20. Although this solution to the puzzle of the "number of the beast's name" did not appear in the history of New Testament study until 1831, many commentators have found it persuasive, especially in view of the use of gematria in other writings contemporary with the New Testament. A thorough and persuasive case for this interpretation is offered by Bauckham in *Climax of Prophecy,* "Nero and the Beast," 384–452.

21. Sybilline Oracles 3:28ff., cited Beasley-Murray, *Book of Revelation,* 211.

anyone is to go into captivity, into captivity he goes; if anyone is to be killed with the sword, with the sword he will be killed. Here is the saints' endurance and faith" (13:10 dej).[22] Introducing these words is a formula, "If anyone has an ear, let him hear," which echoes the refrain in the letters to the churches: "He who has an ear, let him hear what the Spirit says to the churches" (e.g., 2:7, 11, 17). This dire prediction that captivity and death are unavoidable by those for whom these woes have been ordained is likewise the Spirit's word to the churches. The beast will wage ongoing war against the saints, and, as far as the world can see, it will overcome them by killing them. Imprisonment and martyrdom are part of God's plan for his church in this age. Because suffering is the church's inevitable path to glory, the saints must demonstrate enduring faith. The "here is" formula in Revelation identifies the response that is called for by the truth that precedes it, as if John were saying, "What is needed in this situation is . . ."[23] The church participates in God's kingdom, but since our pilgrimage to kingdom joy passes through the desert of affliction, our present responsibility is endurance (1:9). Persistence in the word of our testimony to the Lamb is the means of our victory over the dragon who empowers and authorizes the beast (12:11).

The Beast from the Earth (13:11–18)

The second beast, which arises out of the land rather than the sea, has no precedent in Daniel's vision of the four beasts and the Son of

22. The abundance of textual variants complicates the task of establishing the original reading and meaning of this verse. The NASB follows a different group of manuscripts, reading, "if any one kills with the sword, with the sword he must be killed." Although the external evidence for the NASB reading is much stronger in terms of number of textual witnesses, that reading seems to be dependent on Matt. 26:52 and not to fit the purpose of Rev. 13:10 in context, which is to reassure Christians that if they are to die by the sword, even such a martyrdom is within God's plan. (If the NASB reading is original, presumably its thrust is "If you are arrested, submit peacefully rather than taking up the sword in self-defense.")

23. See Rev. 13:18 ("Needed here is wisdom" to calculate the number and name of the beast); 14:12 ("Needed here is the endurance of the saints," for their enemies' [Babylon, beasts] days are numbered); 17:9 ("Needed here is a mind possessing wisdom" to decipher the symbolism of the beast that carried the harlot).

194

Man. It is "like a lamb" in appearance, with two horns, but its speech is like "a dragon." Later this beast will be called the false prophet (Rev. 16:13; 19:20). This is fitting, for the contradiction between appearance and reality, reflected in the content of its speech, is its distinguishing characteristic. Whereas the power of the first beast in its boastful pride is overt and coercive, the influence of the second is covert and deceiving. It is a counterfeit John the Baptist, simulating but not sharing the spirit and power of Elijah (cf. Luke 1:17; Matt. 11:14; Mal. 4:5–6). Like Elijah at Carmel, this false prophet calls fire to fall from heaven (Rev. 13:13; 1 Kings 18:38); but he uses this wonder to promote worship of the beast rather than calling the peoples to worship the true God, as Elijah did. In Revelation 11:5–6 the church, portrayed as Jesus' two witnesses, exercised the judging authority of Elijah to shut the skies in drought and to consume its enemies with fire (1 Kings 17:1; 2 Kings 1:10, 12). This false prophet, like the Egyptian magicians who managed to simulate a few of the mighty attesting signs God gave to Moses, presents imitation wonders to lead earth's peoples astray after the beast.

The beast from the earth commands the world's peoples to construct an image of the beast and manages by his magic arts to impart "spirit" (NASB "breath") to the image, so that it becomes the medium by which the beast utters its blasphemous boastful claims to divinity (Rev. 13:14–15). This seeming prophetic inspiration of the beast's image alludes to claims made for various idols in ancient paganism: namely, that the physical statue, though not equated with the deity it represented, was a medium of revelation from the god.[24] This climactic expression of idolatry creates an illusion that seems to refute the Old Testament's exposé of idolatry's emptiness: "They have mouths, but they cannot speak. . . . They cannot make a sound with their throat" (Ps. 115:5, 7). The earth beast's wonders, whether achieved through occult collusion with the demonic world or through arts of

---

24. The second-century Christian apologist Athenagorus claimed that pagan polemicists who portray idols as means of communication with the immaterial gods "bring in proof of the operations performed by certain statues." Athenagorus *Embassy for the Christians,* section 18, trans. J. H. Crehan, Ancient Christian Writers 23 (New York: Newman, 1955), 49.

illusion, are directed toward satanic ends: to delude the world's people into receiving the beast's mark of ownership and to destroy those it cannot deceive (Rev. 13:15–16).

The beast's mark, like the seal of God applied to the church (Rev. 7:1–3), is no outward tattoo or insignia on the body but rather a symbol of the beast's ownership and control of his followers' thoughts (forehead) and deeds (right hands). Immediately after this discussion of the beast's mark, the sealed army of God reappears in the company of the Lamb, their champion; and the seal they received is interpreted as "having His name and the name of His Father written on their foreheads" (14:1). Ancient Israelites were to tie the law of God on their foreheads and hands in order to signify that their thoughts and actions were in submission to the Word of the Lord (Deut. 6:8). Now the beast, assisted by its false prophet, blasphemously demands the world's universal allegiance.

The beast from the earth is the sea beast's religiously oriented accomplice. This false prophet's lying wonders support the sea beast's arrogant boasts and slanders against God, luring those who dwell on the earth into worshiping the beast. What does this earth beast/false prophet symbolize? Just as the beast from the sea is Rome and yet is much bigger than Rome, so the beast from the earth is the imperial cult indigenous to Asia Minor but also a larger phenomenon that continues in our day. As we saw in the background to the letters to the seven churches, several of those ancient Christian congregations found themselves in cities that competed vigorously for the honor of building a temple or shrine to the ruling Roman emperor and/or to the empire's patron goddess, Roma. A city that bore the honored designation "temple warden" (*neocoros*) had enhanced its social prestige and its political and economic status. In the decades following John's reception of the Apocalypse, religious devotion in the form of burning incense to the emperor would be made the test of political loyalty to Rome and its ruler. The worship of rulers as gods, descendants of the gods, or gods in the making (after death—*apotheosis*) is less overt in Western culture today than it was in the ancient world. Even in so-called secular states, however, governments can arrogate to themselves quasi-divine powers and issue quasi-divine promises of salvation to their loyal and believing subjects. Such states have no qualms about exploiting religious establishments in the interests of civic loyalty and cultural conformity. But people who, in allegiance to "another king, Jesus," resist the state's claim to ownership over forehead and hand, mind and deed, are seen as threats to good order and the common weal—and must be eliminated.

Conclusion

At the center point of the book John sees visions that disclose the core of the conflict that manifests itself in various visible symptoms and struggles in the seven Asian churches and our churches today. Why do those churches face opposition from "those who say they are Jews" but are a synagogue of Satan? Why the social pressure from the cult of the emperor "where Satan's throne is"? Why are they threatened internally by the seduction of the Nicolaitans' and the prophetess Jezebel's deceptive teaching or the lethal complacency that afflicted the Laodiceans? Why does the church today in Sudan, China, India, Indonesia, and elsewhere suffer persecution? Why does the church in Europe, North America, and elsewhere languish in spiritual ennui in the midst of economic prosperity? Because we are engaged in spiritual warfare, locked in mortal combat against a foe whose strength and cunning are intimidating: a dragon with seven heads and ten horns. Yet our foe has been defeated decisively by the One who came in weakness, the son of the woman, the Lamb whose blood overcame the dragon on behalf of all those who hold the testimony of Jesus.

But the dragon, though thwarted, defeated, hemmed in, prevented from devouring the child or drowning his mother in lethal lies, is not dead. His time is short, and in this short time—a mere time, two times, half a time between the child's ascent to God's throne and his descent as the conquering captain of heaven's cavalry (Rev. 19:11–21)—the dragon unleashes his emissaries against the rest of the woman's seed. Therefore the church is called to endure in faith and hope until the end. The messianic pretensions of Rome, its predecessors and its successors, are expressed in its coercion, threat, and violence against the church. Institutional religion too often plays into the hands of the state, supporting its pseudo-messianic claims and justifying its persecuting aggression against those who will not confess, "We have no king but Caesar."

Through John's central vision we have glimpsed the deep spiritual struggle that lies behind history's surface events, the combat between the woman's son and the dragon, between Christ and Satan. We have seen that the dragon's present aggression, expressed in the beast's violent force and false prophet's lies, is no more than a frustrated reaction to his decisive defeat and rapidly approaching destruction. With these God-given insights into the core of the cosmic conflict, believers in Jesus the Lamb can meet the dragon's worst with endurance and faith—as victors through the blood of the Lamb.

CHAPTER TEN

Harvest:
Celebration
(14:1–15:8)

Victory Songs

When the enemy is vanquished, songs celebrate the triumph. Of course some conflicts yield no clear-cut victory but only dissipate into a state of exhaustion in which wearied combatants lack the stamina to go on bludgeoning each other. When decisive victory is won, however, the conqueror sings the joy of successful struggle and anticipated peace; his people, delivered from danger and death, extol their champion's prowess.

Down through biblical history, when Israel's divine Warrior won the victory, his triumph was celebrated in song. When the Lord led Israel out of slavery and drowned their Egyptian oppressors, Moses led the song of celebration, "I will sing to the LORD, for He is highly exalted; the horse and its rider He has hurled into the sea," while Miriam and the women offered antiphonal response, with tambourines and dance (Exod. 15:1–21). King David also sang Psalm 18 on a day of victory, as the psalm's title, echoing 2 Samuel 22:1, shows:

David . . . spoke the words of this song in the day that the LORD delivered him from the hand of all his enemies and from the hand of Saul. And he said,

"I love You, O LORD, my strength."
The LORD is my rock and my fortress and my deliverer,
My God, my rock in whom I take refuge. . . .
I call upon the LORD, who is worthy to be praised,
And I am saved from my enemies. . . .
He gives great deliverance to His king,
And shows lovingkindness to His anointed,
To David and his descendants forever. (Ps. 18:1–3, 50)

The visions of Revelation 14–15 set the stage for the book's fourth and final cycle of seven: the seven bowls that contain "seven plagues, which are the last, because in them the wrath of God is finished" (Rev. 15:1). Whereas the woes symbolized in the seal and trumpet cycles were limited in scope, when the bowls are poured out, all-inclusive destruction devastates everything and everyone infected by the futile rebellion of the dragon, the beast, and the false prophet (16).

As each previous cycle was introduced by a vision that gave a glimpse of heaven and its King, who rules history,[1] so now, as we reach the cycle that consummates God's wrath against rebels, John sees two complementary visions of heaven. There the choir of the redeemed, whom the Lamb has led to victory, celebrate their triumphant champion (14:1–5; 15:1–4). In the first vision the Lamb's choir sings "a new song," which they alone may learn (14:3). In the second, their song blends old and new victory anthems, "the song of Moses, the bondservant of God, and the song of the Lamb" (15:3).

Between these scenes of the heavenly choir are two brief vision cycles: proclamation by three angels, followed by a heavenly benediction (Rev. 14:6–13), and two harvests, first of the earth's grains and then of the earth's grapes (14:14–20). The angelic announcements summon all earth's peoples to fear God (14:6–7), since Babylon, bar-

---

1. A vision of the radiant Son of Man among his churches introduced the seven letters, in which he displayed his knowledge of their past and present and his lordship over their future (Rev. 1:9–20). A summons to enter heaven's door, to see the enthroned One and the Lamb, preceded the breaking of the scroll's seven seals (4:1–5:14). The seven trumpets were introduced with the offering of saints' prayers as incense on the heavenly altar, from which fire then fell to earth with each trumpet blast (8:1–6).

200 ✑

maid to the world, is ruined (14:8) and people drunk on her adulteries will drain God's goblet of wrath (14:9–11). The harvest visions show history's end, when the final sweeps of God's scythe will gather Jesus' followers as grain into the storehouse (14:14–16) and Babylon's drunken followers as grapes to be crushed in God's winepress of holy wrath (14:17–20; cf. 19:15).

The Lamb's Holy Soldiers Sing a New Song (14:1–5)

The site of the Lamb's victory celebration is heaven. John sees the Lamb "standing on Mount Zion," in keeping with the Lord's pronouncement in Psalm 2:6: "But as for Me, I have installed My King upon Zion, My holy mountain."[2] The details of the vision make clear that this Mount Zion is not on earth but in heaven. The 144,000 choristers who accompany the Lamb sing "before the throne and before the four living creatures and the elders" (Rev. 14:3; see 4:2–8). John hears a voice from heaven, like the sound of waterfalls, thunder, and harps (14:2). This is the song of the Lamb's redeemed choir-army. When these singers reappear, they are "standing on the sea of glass" (15:2), the same transparent pavement that John had seen extending before God's throne in heaven (4:6).

The 144,000 are the same loyal disciples who earlier were marked with God's seal on their foreheads, securing their protection from the coming wrath of God and the Lamb (Rev. 7:3; cf. 6:16–17). Now we see that the seal is the name of the Lamb and his Father. They are branded as God's property, under his protection; and they are imprinted with his identity, to share his holiness. Every overcomer has been promised a permanent place in God's presence as a temple pillar, inscribed with the name of God, of his city, and of Jesus (3:12). In the new Jerusalem all God's servants will bear his name on their foreheads (22:4).

This scene of the Lamb and his sealed army contrasts sharply with what immediately precedes it. The beast's deluded devotees are

2. The New Testament regularly identifies the coronation/enthronement spoken of in Ps. 2, in which the Messiah begins his invincible rule as God's Son, with the resurrection and ascension of Jesus (see Rev. 12:5; Acts 13:33–34).

branded with the beast's "mark" (*charagma*) on right hand or forehead (Rev. 13:16). That mark was associated with the "name of the beast or the number of his name" (13:17), as the divine seal is the name of God and of the Lamb. Both symbolize ownership and control of those who are thus branded. But the beast's mark does not deserve to be called a "seal" (*sphragis*). Seals signify not only ownership but also security, protection under the authority of the One whose name we bear. But the beast's mere "mark" brings those who bear it no shelter from the coming wrath of God. Thus in these back-to-back visions John sees all humanity divided into two camps, bearing two different brands. Either people bear the name of the Lamb and his Father, finding safety in their ownership; or people are claimed by the world system that opposes the Lord and his Christ, a system that is destined to be shattered like pottery when the Son appears.[3]

The Lamb's company is further described in images portraying its purity: virgin soldiers who have abstained from sexual relations, a holy first fruits offering, guileless servants of the Lord, and a blameless (unblemished) sacrifice (Rev. 14:4–5).

They have not been defiled with women, for they are celibate (*parthenoi* = "virgins"). Recognizing the symbolic form of the vision will keep us from inferring that only unmarried, celibate males can be followers of the Lamb, although that is the way that the vision presents them. The Mosaic law had instructed Israel's warriors to maintain rigorous ceremonial purity when waging the Lord's holy war against pagan enemies (Deut. 23:9–11).[4] The ceremonial symbolized the spiritual, and here the appearance of the whole church—men and

---

3. Note Rev. 13:8: All those not enrolled in the book of life—"all who dwell on the earth"—will worship the beast.

4. Abstinence from ordinary marital relations was demanded also when Israel awaited God's descent to Mount Sinai to impart the covenant to Moses. This prohibition was a ceremonial symbol of the purity that the awesome holiness of God demands as he comes among his people (Exod. 19:15). While David was being pursued by King Saul, he rigorously imposed the same ceremonial purity on his band (1 Sam. 21:5). Later, however, to cover his own adultery, David tried to influence the loyal Uriah to violate God's expectation of militant celibacy by sleeping with his wife while the Lord's armies were in the field. Uriah resisted the suggestion with shocked protestation (2 Sam. 11:8–13).

women, single and married—under the image of an army of celibate soldiers portrays the single-minded loyalty that we all owe to our captain. The same spiritual monogamy will be symbolized later when the whole church—women and men, married and single—appears as a virgin bride adorned for her Husband (19:7; 21:2), the antithesis of Babylon the shameless prostitute. So here the church appears with the Lamb as a pure army victorious in holy war, the antithesis of the beast's defiled and deluded troops (13:7–8, 14–17).

The Lamb's army has been "purchased" from the whole human family as "first fruits" (Rev. 14:3– 4). The term *purchase* recalls the earlier doxology to the worthy Lamb, whose blood "purchased" for God persons from every tribe, tongue, people and nation, to become a royal priesthood (5:9–10). Here, however, John sees assembled in heaven just the first fruits of a much larger harvest, the foretaste in miniature and in promise of a full harvest to come. At the Feast of Weeks, seven weeks after Passover, Israel was to offer the first fruits of their grain, to express thanks to the Lord for the wheat harvest about to be gathered (Exod. 23:16; Lev. 23:15–22; Num. 28:26–31; Deut. 16:9–12). In biblical imagery "first fruits" symbolizes a preliminary installment that portends the fullness of blessing to come.[5] So here John sees the believers who have held their faith fast to the death (Rev. 12:11) as the first installment that guarantees the ingathering of all God's people from all the peoples. John will soon see that final sweep of the sickle, which will bring every Jesus-trusting seed of the woman safely into God's granary (14:14–16).

The symbolic celibacy of the Lamb's army is further interpreted when they are described as guileless ("no lie was found in their mouth") and "blameless," as a spotless sacrifice pleasing to God (Rev. 14:5). As those who speak only truth, they bear the image of the Lord's Servant, who was led like a lamb to slaughter although there was no "deceit in his mouth" (Isa. 53:9). The word *blameless* (*amōmos*) has moral

---

5. Because Christ is the first fruits of those who sleep in death, his resurrection secures the future harvesting of his own from the grave (1 Cor. 15:20, 23). The Spirit's presence with believers is the "first fruits," the tantalizing foretaste of our full adoption, the final resurrection-redemption of our bodies from death (Rom. 8:23). Epaenetus was the first fruits of a larger harvest from Paul's ministry in Asia (Rom. 16:5), as was Stephanus's household in Achaia (1 Cor. 16:15).

and ceremonial overtones, since it is used in the Greek Old Testament
to describe the absence of physical defect or blemish required of sacrificial animals (e.g., Lev. 1:3, 10; 3:1 LXX). We have seen the martyrs "underneath the altar," where the blood of sacrificial animals would
flow (Rev. 6:9). Here again this ceremonial-sacrificial imagery is picked
up to affirm that this martyr church is spiritually pure and morally flawless, purged in the blood of the Lamb (7:14). Those who are spiritually and morally compromised are excluded from God's presence and
his holy city-bride (21:8; 22:15).

The voice that John hears in heaven is like the sound of many waters and loud thunder (Rev. 14:2), similes used by Ezekiel to describe
the voice of the Almighty (Ezek. 1:24). Yet this voice also resembles
the trills of harpists strumming harps. The voice has overpowering
strength but also heartbreaking sweetness. It is the united voice of the
Lamb's army-choir, accompanying their new song on harps. When
they appear again, they will be holding the harps of God (Rev. 15:2).[6]
A new song, accompanied on the harp, is the time-honored tribute
that God's people offer him when he has come to their rescue: "I will
sing a new song to You, O God; upon a harp of ten strings I will sing
praises to You, who gives salvation to kings, who rescues David His
servant from the evil sword" (Ps. 144:9–10; cf. 96:1; 98:1). The lyrics
of these celebrants' song are secret, known only to them. The purpose of this secrecy is not to keep God's glory veiled but to symbolize the astonishing truth that sinful people redeemed by the Lamb are
qualified by that experience of salvation to extol him in a way that
even the purest, highest angel cannot. Into the mystery of our salvation even angels long to look (1 Peter 1:12).

Three Angelic Announcements and a Blessing (14:6–13)

The spotlight turns from heaven to earth with the proclamations of
the three angels. Each bears words of dire warning to those in league

6. The double reference to harps confirms that these visions (14:1–5; 15:1–4) are
two windows on the same heavenly choral concert. Besides Rev. 14:2 and 15:2
"harp" (*kithara*) appears only once elsewhere in Revelation, in the hands of the
twenty-four elders (5:8).

with the dragon, the beasts, and the harlot Babylon, the sea beast's villainous queen consort.

The first angel (Rev. 14:6–7) brings "an eternal gospel" to "those who live on the earth"—that is, to those from every nation, tribe, tongue, and people who have allied themselves with the dragon and worshiped the beast and its image (13:7, 12–14). Although he proclaims that the hour of God's judgment has come, his announcement is still good news ("gospel," *euangelion*) because he also summons earth's rebels to "fear God" and to worship the Creator of "the heaven and the earth and sea and springs of waters."[7] His summons to fear and worship means that it is almost but not quite too late to heed the warnings of the restrained trumpet judgments that have fallen as fire on earth, sea, springs, and sky (8:7–12).[8]

The second angel announces as a fait accompli the fall of "Babylon the great" (Rev. 14:8)—a surprising declaration, since John has not yet so much as mentioned Babylon's name. Such foreshadowing is not uncommon in Revelation, however. The "holy city" is first mentioned, almost incidentally, as trampled by the Gentiles for forty-two months (11:2), long before this holy city is seen as the beautiful bride descending from heaven, ready for her wedding (21:2). The beast from the abyss is mentioned first as it wars against and conquers the witness church (11:7), and only later is it seen coming up out of the sea to receive power from the dragon to war against the saints (13:1, 7). So here when we hear of Babylon's fall—so certain to occur that it is announced as already accomplished—we expect eventually to see a vision of the height from which she has fallen (17–18). Although her identity will be disclosed in that later vision, the well-known role of Nebuchadnezzar's Babylon in the exile of ancient Judah would signal to first-century Christians that "Babylon" is code

7. This fourfold description of the Creator's handiwork—heaven, earth, sea, springs—reflects the four spheres affected by judgments in the first four trumpets (Rev. 8:7–12) and the first four bowls (16:2–9).

8. This angel's message is linked to the first four trumpets not only by the same fourfold description of the created order (see n. 7) but also by his flight path, which runs "in midheaven," like that of the eagle that John saw after the fourth trumpet sounded (Rev. 8:13).

for the pagan power now oppressing them, Rome and the world system it embodies (cf. 1 Peter 5:13).

The reason for Babylon's fall is her seduction of the nations, intoxicating them with her mixed brew of rage[9] and sexual license. God will soon reciprocate her wrath against his saints by making her to drink to the dregs the wine of his wrath (Rev. 18:6; 19:2; cf. 16:4–6). Those who imbibe now with Babylon in her self-indulgence and violence will also drink her cup of divine wrath then, in that soon-coming day of judgment (14:10, 19).

The third angel's announcement distributes the consequences of corporate Babylon's fall to the individuals who have cast their lot with Babylon, the beasts, and the dragon (14:9–11). Virtually identical descriptions of their crime against the Creator open verse 9 and close verse 11, enveloping the announcement of their fate: "if anyone worships the beast and its image and receives a mark on his forehead or on his hand . . . those who worship the beast and its image and if anyone receives the mark of its name" (dej). Those who succumb in mindset and action to the myth that Rome or any world system deserves ultimate allegiance and trust are alienated from the Lamb and excluded from his book of life (13:8). Apart from the protective seal of his name and blood, nothing can shield people from the fiery torment of God's righteous wrath. The presence of the Lamb, which brings pure joy and comfort to his redeemed people (14:1), will bring unmitigated anguish to those who stake their lives on the dragon's lies (14:10). In Revelation wine symbolizes God's wrath in two ways. When grapes are crushed, their red juice flows from the winepress, like the blood of God's enemies when he treads them down (14:19–20; cf. 19:13, 15; Isa. 63:3); and when the wine is fermented, its mind-numbing strength symbolizes the confused stupor of those who will drink God's cup of wrath (14:10;

9. Although *thumos* can sometimes be translated "passion" (as in NASB), elsewhere in Revelation it consistently refers not to sexual lust but to the passion of rage, anger, or wrath (12:12; 14:10, 19; 15:1, 7; 16:1; 19:15). The two occurrences of "the wine of the *thumos* of her sexual immorality" (14:8; 18:3) should still be understood as indicating the harlot's rage against the saints, which does appear in combination with her illicit sexuality. The wine in her cup is the blood of the saints (17:6).

18:6). The angel here uses this second association of wine with divine
wrath, alluding to Old Testament passages such as Psalm 75:7–8: "God
is the Judge. . . . For a cup is in the hand of the LORD, and the wine
foams; it is well mixed, and He pours out of this; surely all the wicked
of the earth must drain and drink down its dregs."

The eternal torment with "fire and brimstone" will, it seems, include endless physical pain. The sea and the grave will give up their
dead to face sentencing at the last judgment (Rev. 20:13–15). For unbelievers as well as for believers, body and soul will be reunited to receive the verdict of the Judge who sits on the great white throne. But
the physical torment is also symptomatic of a relentless restlessness,
which permeates the whole person: "they have no rest day and night"
(14:11). The second of Revelation's seven benedictions is about to be
pronounced on those who die in the Lord, promising "rest from their
labors" (14:13), entrance into the final Sabbath celebration that includes
relief from suffering and release from struggle.[10] Not so the wicked!

In response to these three announcements—the hour of judgment
has come, Babylon has fallen, the beast's followers face torment—
John, in the Spirit, interjects a word of direct application to his hearers: "Here is the perseverance of the saints who keep the commandments of God and their faith in Jesus" (Rev. 14:12). This is the third
of four sayings of similar structure. In each saying the introductory
"Here" implies "Here is the appropriate response." Twice this formula alerts listeners to challenging symbolism that demands extra reflection to be understood: "Here is wisdom (needed)" to interpret the
number and name of the beast (13:18); and "Here is the mind having
wisdom (needed)" to crack the code of the beast's heads (17:9). The
first of the four sayings is a summons to enduring trust in the face of
the graphic portrayal of the beast's war against the saints: "Here is the

10. The only other instance of the verb *rest* (*anapauō*) in Revelation is in the counsel to the martyrs' souls to "rest for a little while longer" (6:11). The only other instance of the noun *rest* (*anapausis*) besides 14:11 describes the constant and tireless
praises of the living creatures before God's throne, who have no rest "day and night"
as they say, "Holy, holy, holy" (4:8). A sharper contrast could hardly be imagined
between the cherubim's joyful "restlessness" in worshiping God and damned humans' tortured restlessness in the lake of fire, the outcome of their worshiping the
beast and its image.

perseverance and faith of the saints" (13:10). In other words: "Though the beast seems so strong, do not be intimidated, but keep on believing that your champion is stronger." Again in Revelation 14:12 the saints are summoned to persevere in trusting Jesus and keeping God's commands, but here we are called to endure not despite our enemies' present power but because of their future destruction.

A voice from heaven commands John to inscribe a blessing on those who endure in faith even to the death (Rev. 14:13)—the second of seven benedictions (1:3; 16:15; 19:9; 20:6; 22:7, 14). "The dead who die in the Lord" include the martyrs, but there is no reason to limit this blessing to those who have been slain for their testimony to Jesus.[11] The focus is on their life of steadfast obedience, not the circumstances of their death, as we see in the reasons given for their blessedness: "they may rest from their labors [*kopos*]" and "their deeds follow with them." Endurance is important not only because external threats from state or synagogue may intimidate believers but also because the demands of servanthood may make us become "weary" and "lose heart in doing good" (Gal. 6:9).[12] Thus the first blessing of those who die in union with Jesus is rest from the wearying labors. Even as they await final vindication through resurrection (Rev. 6:9–11), deceased saints have already entered the eternal Sabbath of undistracted enjoyment and glorification of God. Yet the labors of this life are not forgotten. The second reason for their blessedness is that their deeds accompany them into God's rest. The biblical hope of bodily resurrection entails the expectation that "deeds in the body" for the love of Jesus mean something eternally (2 Cor. 5:10). Though our deeds have been done in a body defiled by sin and disabled by the curse, a body destined to be planted in the earth as a dead seed (1 Cor. 15:42–43), nevertheless the grace and power of the risen Lord transforms them into thank offerings pleasing to the Father. The encouragement that concludes Paul's rich resurrec-

11. When the martyrs are specifically in view, their description makes this explicit: "the souls of those slain because of the word of God, and because of the testimony they had maintained" (Rev. 6:9) or "the souls of those who had been beheaded because of the testimony of Jesus and because of the word of God" (20:4).

12. Jesus had commended the Ephesian Christians for their work and labor (*kopos*), which had not worn them out (*kopiaō;* Rev. 2:2–3).

tion chapter flows directly from the resurrection hope he has expounded throughout: "Therefore, my beloved brethren, be steadfast, immovable, always abounding in the work of the Lord, knowing that your toil [*kopos*] is not in vain in the Lord" (1 Cor. 15:58). Even before that final resurrection, as saints' souls now rest in the presence of their Master, their comfort and joy are sustained by his "well done" (Matt. 25:21).

The Harvest of Earth's Grain (14:14–16)

Having heard three angelic announcements of the end, John sees a twofold vision of history's end, the harvesting of the earth. Ancient prophets portrayed the future coming of the Lord as a last harvest:

> Let the nations be aroused
> And come up to the valley of Jehoshaphat,[13]
> For there I will sit to judge
> All the surrounding nations.
> Put in the sickle, for the harvest is ripe.
> Come, tread, for the wine press is full;
> The vats overflow, for their wickedness is great.
> (Joel 3:12–13 [Hebrew 4:12–13])

The common expectation was that the Messiah would immediately execute this harvest judgment when he appeared, but Jesus' parables (the sower, the tares among the wheat) taught that he came to inaugurate the long-awaited kingdom of God not as a grim reaper but as a patient planter (Matt. 13:1–30, 36–43).[14] Through sowing the word as seed, apparently so vulnerable to the world's hostile environment, Jesus would launch a harvest of grace in his first coming and continue it through the church's gospel witness (John 4:35–38). In the story of the tares Jesus made clear that the final harvest foretold through the prophets, when weeds are separated from wheat, would come only at "the end of the age" (Matt. 13:40). John now sees this final separation in his vision.

13. "Jehoshaphat" means "the Lord judges."
14. Herman Ridderbos, *The Coming of the Kingdom* (1962; Nutley, N.J.: P&R Publishing, 1975), 129–39.

The harvest is implemented by two heavenly beings in response to two angelic commands. First "one like a son of man" appears on a white cloud, and an angel from the temple tells him to harvest the earth with his sickle (Rev. 14:14–16). This is a harvest of grain, for the "ripeness" of earth's harvest consists in its having dried (NASB "ripe" translates a passive form of the Greek verb *xērainō,* "dry"), yellowed stalks bearing heads of mature seed (14:15). Then another angel emerges from the heavenly temple to harvest the grapes from earth's vine, to be trampled in the winepress of God's wrath (14:17–20).

Two questions emerge regarding these visions of grain and grape harvesting. Who is the "one like a son of man" who harvests the grain? Do the grain and grapes symbolize the same people or different groups for whom the harvest will have different outcomes?[15]

The "one like a son of man" is seated on a white cloud and crowned with a golden crown (14:14, 16). The allusion to Daniel's vision of "one like a son of man," coming with clouds to the Ancient of Days in his heavenly court (Dan. 7:13–14), is unmistakable, as it was in John's opening vision (Rev. 1:13). In Revelation 1:7 the promise, "He is coming with the clouds," refers to Christ's second coming in judgment, so John and his hearers have good reason to identify the harvester in Revelation 14:14 with Jesus, for whose promised coming we await. Yet some object to this identification, considering it beneath Christ's dignity to receive God's command through an angelic intermediary and citing the mention of "another angel" as evidence that the "one like a son of man" is also a created angel.[16] And did not Jesus say in the parable of the tares among wheat, "The reapers are angels" (Matt. 13:39)? Yet this picture shows his submission to the Father's timing, of which Jesus spoke while on earth (Mark 13:32; Acts 1:7; cf. 3:20–21). The three "other angels" in the harvest visions do not imply that the son of man is the same sort of messenger as they are. Rather, they are "other" in relation to the three angels who just announced the end (Rev. 14:6, 8, 9). Centered between these two

15. See David E. Aune, *Revelation 6–16,* WBC (Waco: Word, 1998), 800–803, for an analysis of these questions, though my answers to both differ from Aune's.

16. Aune, ibid., 800–801, offers these and other arguments to support the view that the "one like a son of man" is an angel.

triads of angels and set apart from them by his crown, his cloudy throne, and his title "one like a son of man," is Jesus the Messiah and final judge, the Son of Man whom John saw at the beginning of his visions.

The harder question is whether the grain harvested by the Son of Man and the grapes harvested by the angel are the same people or different groups. Four views have been proposed:

(1) The grain and grapes symbolize the same group, both harvest scenes showing the judgment of the wicked.[17]
(2) The grain and grapes symbolize the same group, both scenes showing the salvation of the church through martyrdom.[18]
(3) The harvest of the earth gathers the church and rebellious unbelievers, whereas the gathering and crushing of the grapes in God's winepress of wrath portrays the judgment of the wicked.[19]
(4) The harvest of the grain symbolizes the gathering of the church for salvation, and the grape harvest portrays the gathering of the wicked for destruction.[20]

The fourth view is the most persuasive. Against the second view is the fact that John's vision picks up the imagery of Joel 3:13: "Put in the sickle,

17. Moses Stuart, *A Commentary on the Apocalypse,* 2 vols. (London: Wiley and Putnam, 1845), 2:291, 301–3; R. H. Charles, *A Critical and Exegetical Commentary on the Revelation of St. John,* 2 vols., ICC (Edinburgh: T & T Clark, 1920), 2:18–26; Aune, *Revelation,* 801–3; G. K. Beale, *The Book of Revelation,* NIGTC (Grand Rapids: Eerdmans, 1999), 770–78.

18. G. B. Caird, *A Commentary on the Revelation of St. John the Divine,* HNTC (New York: Harper & Row, 1966), 191–94.

19. Isbon T. Beckwith, *The Apocalypse of John: Studies in Introduction, with a Critical and Exegetical Commentary* (1919; reprint ed., Grand Rapids: Baker, 1979), 662–65; G. R. Beasley-Murray, *The Book of Revelation,* NCB (Grand Rapids: Eerdmans, 1981), 228–29.

20. H. B. Swete, *Commentary on Revelation,* 3d ed. (1911; reprint ed., Grand Rapids: Kregel, 1977), 190; William Hendriksen, *More Than Conquerors: An Interpretation of the Book of Revelation* (Grand Rapids: Baker, 1939), 187–88; George Eldon Ladd, *A Commentary on the Revelation of John* (Grand Rapids: Eerdmans, 1972), 198–202; Michael Wilcock, *I Saw Heaven Opened: The Message of Revelation,* TBST (Downers Grove, Ill.: InterVarsity Press, 1975), 136.

for the harvest is ripe. Come, tread, for the wine press is full; the vats overflow, for their wickedness is great." The treading of grapes in the winepress thus pictures retribution to sinners for their wickedness. The harvesting and treading of grapes has the same connotation in Revelation, where wine and the winepress are associated with God's wrath against evil (Rev. 14:10; cf. 19:15).

Against the first and third views is the fact that although Joel spoke of one harvest, John sees two, one of grain and the other of grapes. The respective harvesters are distinct, with greater prominence given to the Son of Man who harvests the earth than to the angel who gathers the grapes. The "harvest of the earth" consists in grain that has ripened by drying (*xērainō*) in the ear, whereas earth's vine yields ripened (*akmazō*, only here in the New Testament) grapes, full of juice. The harvesting of earth is completed in a single act, whereas the harvesting of the vine involves two actions, first gathering and then treading the grapes in the winepress. The third view, which interprets the grape harvest as a subset of the general harvest performed by the Son of Man, minimizes these distinctions, as does the first view, which sees both harvests as symbolizing the destruction of the wicked.

A further obstacle to the first view is that the Lamb's victorious armychoir has been described as "first fruits to God and to the Lamb" (Rev. 14:4). This first fruits imagery, recalling the Old Testament Feast of Weeks at the start of the wheat harvest (Exod. 23:16) leads us to anticipate the full and final harvest of the Lamb's "wheat" into his barns (Matt. 3:12; 13:30). If martyrs and other believers who have died in persevering faith constitute the first fruits, already gathered on Mount Zion to praise God and the Lamb, the rest of the grain to be gathered by the Son of Man is the complete harvest of his saints. The end of history, therefore, will bring not only a great grain harvest, as the saving sweep of Christ's sickle gathers his faithful followers, but also a great grape harvest, as Christ's enemies are gathered to be crushed in the winepress of God's wrath.

The Harvest of Earth's Grapevine (14:17–20)

The command to harvest the earth's grapevine is issued through "another angel, the one who has power over fire" and who comes out

from the altar (Rev. 14:18). In the sacrificial rituals of the Israelite sanctuaries, both tabernacle and temple, the altar is associated both with
the blood of slain animals and the fire that consumed their carcasses.
Thus John has seen the souls of martyrs under the heavenly altar, where
the blood of sacrificial victims would flow (6:9); he has seen an angel
draw fire from the altar, from which the church's prayers ascend as incense, to fling that fire in judgment on rebellious earth dwellers (8:3–5).
This angel, who has "power" or authority (*exousia*) over the fires of
judgment, brings God's command to gather rebellious humanity, to
be crushed in God's press until their blood—the blood of those who
have shed the martyrs' blood—flows like a flood of red wine. This
heavenly altar will attest God's justice in giving bloodthirsty persecutors, who murdered the martyrs, blood as their beverage (16:4–7).

The harvest of grapes from earth's vine is accomplished by the second of the three angels mentioned in the harvest visions. As the vision of the Lamb's army as first fruits in heaven anticipated the grain
harvest, so the angelic pronouncement that rebels will drink the wine
of God's wrath (14:10) foreshadowed the grape harvest and the crushing of the wicked in "the great wine press of the wrath of God" (14:19).

The great winepress belongs to God, for he will trample the grapes
cast into it, as Isaiah foretold:

> Who is this who comes from Edom,
> With garments of glowing colors from Bozrah,
> This One who is majestic in His apparel,
> Marching in the greatness of His strength?
> "It is I who speak in righteousness, mighty to save."
> Why is Your apparel red,
> And Your garments like the one who treads in the wine press?
> "I have trodden the wine trough alone,
> And from the peoples there was no man with Me.
> I also trod them in My anger
> And trampled them in My wrath;
> And their lifeblood is sprinkled on My garments,
> And I stained all My raiment. . . .
> I trod down the peoples in My anger
> And made them drunk in My wrath,
> And I poured out their lifeblood on the earth." (Isa. 63:1–3, 6)

213

In Isaiah wine symbolizes God's judgment in two ways. God's enemies are trodden as grapes, and their blood is the wine that flows from his winepress. Wine is also the beverage with which God intoxicates his enemies and renders them senseless. In Revelation 14 wine pictures judgment in the same two ways: God's enemies will drink the cup of his wrath (14:10), but they are also the grapes cast into his press, from which their blood flows as high as the bridles of war horses,[21] flooding the land to its borders (14:20).[22] In Revelation 19 John will see the Word of God riding forth on his white horse, his robe stained with blood as in Isaiah 63, ready to strike the nations with his sword and to tread "the wine press of the fierce wrath of God, the Almighty" (19:13–15).

When the sweep of God's sickles brings final harvest to the earth, separating grain from grapes, the present system of power and prestige will be reversed. The pagan persecutors who now tread the holy city underfoot (Rev. 11:2) will be trodden underfoot by the church's mighty avenger (14:20). Their defiling blood pours from a winepress "outside the city," for those who belong to earth's so-called "great city," which wages war on God's church (11:8; 17:18), have no share in God's holy, heavenly city. No one unclean shall ever enter the holy city, the new Jerusalem, "but only those whose names are written in the Lamb's book of life" (21:27).

The Victors Sing the Song of Moses and the Lamb (15:1–4)

The scene shifts again, from earth to heaven, from which a final judgment cycle is about to be revealed. John sees "another sign in heaven, great and marvelous," seven angels entrusted with the last plagues (Rev. 15:1). By calling it "another" great sign John connects it with the vision of the heavenly woman and the dragon who wars against her and her child (12:1, 3). The world-shaking signif-

---

21. Richard Bauckham, *The Climax of Prophecy: Studies on the Book of Revelation* (Edinburgh: T & T Clark, 1993), 40–48, cites Jewish apocalyptic texts to show the widespread use of horses' stature (chest, nostrils) to measure the depth of blood that signifies the complete slaughter of an army in battle.

22. Charles, *Commentary*, 2:26, suggests that sixteen hundred stadia (NASB: "two hundred miles") may represent the length of the land of promise, north to south.

icance of these seven angels is clear from the fact that they carry the plagues which are "the last, because in them the wrath of God is finished." The outpouring of the bowls will reveal the end of history, the termination of the "first heaven and earth" (21:1), from seven perspectives. The bowls cycle in Revelation 16 therefore brings us a deeper and more detailed portrait of the cosmic conflagration that we glimpsed in the sixth seal (6:12–17: destruction of earth and sky) and the seventh trumpet (11:15–18: celebration in heaven). Further perspectives on this completion of God's wrath at the climax of history will come into view in Revelation 19:19–21 and 20:9–11. (The order of John's visions is not necessarily the chronological order in which the events that they symbolize occur in history.) Visions that follow the bowl cycle—the disclosure and dismantling of the harlot Babylon (17–18) and the defeat of beasts and dragon (19–20)—provide varying camera angles on the same history-consummating battle, in which our God and his Christ will triumph.

As with the trumpets,[23] John glimpses the seven angels who will inflict the last plagues (Rev. 15:1) and then views heavenly worship (15:2–8) before the angels inflict God's judgments on the earth (16). The intervening scene of worship in heaven is a second appearance of the Lamb's holy army on Mount Zion (cf. 14:1–5).

The heavenly singers are "those who had been victorious over the beast" (Rev. 15:2). When this group was called "first fruits" in the earlier vision (14:4), that title identified them as those who persevered in faith even in the face of persecution unto death (14:12–13). They are the foretaste of the whole harvest of all God's people. Now their description as victors (participle of *nikaō,* often translated "overcome" [2:11; 11:7; etc.]) shows that appearances on earth are a negative image of reality as it is rightly perceived from heaven. From an earthly perspective, the beast overcame God's witnesses, the saints (11:7; 13:7). But the reality is that they overcame their enemies by the blood of the Lamb, holding fast to their testimony (12:11). Now we see them in

---

23. The angels receive their trumpets in Rev. 8:2 but do not prepare to sound them until 8:6, after the saints' prayers have been offered as incense on the heavenly altar.

heaven, standing on "something like"[24] a sea of glass mixed with fire, radiating holy glory. This sea is the crystalline pavement proceeding from God's throne (4:6), the firmament that earlier prophets had seen as heaven's floor and earth's ceiling (Exod. 24:10; Ezek. 1:22). They stand before God's throne to sing their victory song (cf. Rev. 14:3).

Their song is "the song of Moses, the bond-servant of God, and the song of the Lamb" (Rev. 15:3). It is Moses' song because God's victory in liberating his people and destroying their enemies stands in continuity with the ancient exodus, which Moses and the Israelites celebrated in song as they watched the Red Sea close over Pharaoh's pursuing forces (Exod. 15:1–18). But it is also the Lamb's song, a "new song" (Rev. 14:3) for the triumph of the Lamb in his sacrificial death, resurrection life, and coming judgment is the last and great exodus, the ultimate salvation that was foreshadowed when the Israelites left Egypt in Moses' day. God's new acts of redemption call forth new songs of praise from his people: "O sing to the LORD a new song, for He has done wonderful things, His right hand and His holy arm have gained the victory for Him. The LORD has made known His salvation; He has revealed His righteousness in the sight of the nations" (Ps. 98:1–2).

The wording of the victors' new song is a blend of Old Testament praises for God's perfections, revealed through his mighty and righteous interventions on his people's behalf, judging their enemies. The most direct allusions are "great and marvelous" (Deut. 28:59 LXX [NASB: "honored and awesome"]); "righteous and true are Your ways" (Deut. 32:4); "King of the nations" and "Who will not fear . . . and glorify Your name?" (Jer. 10:7); "You alone are holy," and "All the nations will come and worship before You" (Ps. 86:9); and "Your righteous acts have been revealed" (Ps. 98:2).

In the confession, "Great and marvelous are your works," which opens the song, the works of God are specifically his deeds of judgment, punishing his enemies and vindicating his people. The same combination, "great and marvelous," described the plagues that God inflicted on Egypt in preparation for the exodus (Deut. 28:59 LXX)

---

24. Prophets describe their visions in such cautious and ambiguous similes in order to keep readers from a wooden literalism, lest we forget the limited capacity of human experience and language to convey heavenly reality. See Ezek. 1:26–28.

and the sign in heaven that consists in the seven angels who have the seven last plagues (Rev. 15:1). God's justice is the prominent theme of the song, extolled at the beginning ("Righteous and true are your ways") and the conclusion ("Your righteous acts have been revealed"). The martyrs' earlier aggrieved lament, appealing for just vindication (6:10), is now transposed into a song of celebration because the completion of God's wrath is imminent.[25] Justice has come! When the third bowl is poured out, turning rivers and springs into blood, the angel of the waters will praise God's justice in giving blood to those who have been bloodthirsty for the saints' blood: "Righteous are You . . . O Holy One" (16:5–6). The heavenly altar, witness to the saints' martyrdom (6:9), will respond with an echo of the victors' song: "True and righteous are Your judgments" (16:7).[26]

The appropriate response to this climactic display of God's justice is holy fear expressed in glorifying God's name (Rev. 15:4). Since God is "King of the nations" (v. 3), all nations will come to worship him. The beleaguered church on earth, so seemingly weak and outnumbered, must never forget the mystery of God's kingdom growing powerfully through our frailty. The innumerable international host whom John has seen gathered before God's throne ("every nation and all tribes and peoples and tongues," 7:9) provide a preview of the new Jerusalem, in which the nations walk in the light of the Lamb (21:23–24), bring their glory and honor to lay at his feet (21:26), and find healing of all woes in the leaves of his tree of life (22:2–3).

Seven Angels Receive Bowls of Wrath (15:5–8)

The angels introduced in Revelation 15:1 as having the seven last plagues are now introduced with more elaborate protocol. As at the start of the seal cycle (4:1), the trumpet cycle (8:1–5), and the drama

25. In the fifth seal vision (Rev. 6:10) the martyrs' souls confess God to be "holy (*hagios*) and true (*alēthinos*)" and ask how long he will refrain from "avenging (*ekdikeō*) our blood." The victors' choir now confess God's ways to be "righteous (*dikaios*) and true (*alēthinos*)," since his "righteous acts (*dikaiōmata*) have been revealed" (15:3–4).

26. Again we see the inversion of adjectives linking passages that are somewhat distant from each other: "Righteous and true" (Rev. 15:3), "True and righteous" (16:7).

of the woman and the dragon (11:19), the bowl cycle begins with an opening of heaven: "the sanctuary of the tent of testimony was opened" (dej). Commissioned in the intimate presence of God in the holiest chamber of the heavenly tabernacle, the angels emerge to receive their golden bowls, each brimming with the righteous rage of God against those who dwell on the earth, who torment his people and destroy his good creation. Like the mighty angelic messenger whose appearance so overpowered Daniel (Dan. 10:5), they are clothed in luminous linen and girded with golden sashes (see Rev. 1:13).

God's overpowering glory is suddenly displayed in a cloud of smoke that fills the temple and prevents anyone from entering it "until the seven plagues of the seven angels were finished" (Rev. 15:8). This cloud of unapproachable holiness had filled the tabernacle at its consecration in the days of Moses (Exod. 40:34) and the temple when it was completed by Solomon (1 Kings 8:10–11; cf. Isa. 6:1). In both instances the effect was so intimidating that the priests could not enter the sanctuary to perform their ministry. In John's vision the unapproachability of the cloud of God's glory not only conveys his utter holiness but also draws our attention to the terminus of his creatures' exile from his holy presence: "until the seven plagues . . . were finished." The term *finished* is repeated from Revelation 15:1, where we heard that in these seven plagues "the wrath of God is finished."[27] Trumpet calls of warning have all been sounded. God's patient delay of judgment has drawn to an end (10:6). Plagues will pour from the bowls without interruption, wielding desolation on everything infected by the curse on man's sin. The end has come.

Conclusion

Twin scenes of God's redeemed people, singing a new song to celebrate the Lamb's triumph and the song of Moses and the Lamb to celebrate the final revelation of God's justice, mark the boundaries of this section of Revelation (14:1–5; 15:1–4). Between these scenes of celestial song John hears three angels, who announce the coming judg-

---

27. Rev. 15:1: *etelesthē,* aorist passive indicate of *teleō;* 15:8: *telesthōsin,* aorist passive subjunctive of *teleō.*

ment (14:6–13), and then he sees the Son of Man and three angels, who reap the earth's inhabitants—harvesting believers as precious grain into God's storehouses and gathering unbelievers as grapes to be cast into the winepress of God's wrath (14:14–20).

The announcing angels introduce Babylon, the last character to come on stage in the cosmic drama that began with Revelation's first "great sign," the heavenly mother of the Messiah (12:1). They predict not only Babylon's catastrophic fall but also the eternal torment of fire and brimstone that awaits those who have sold themselves to serve the beast, whether Rome or any other incarnation of concentrated human political-military-economic-cultural power that cherishes pretensions to divinity. The heavenly harvesters remind us that the martyrs are first fruits of a vast crop of the faithful, not one of whom will be lost; but also that the destiny of the faithless, who have plunged themselves into a senseless stupor with the world's intoxicants, is to drain to the dregs the cup of God's righteous rage. "God is not mocked; for whatever a man sows, this he will also reap" (Gal. 6:7). Seven angels sent out from God's heavenly sanctuary stand ready to pour out bowls full of plagues, bringing utter destruction to the old, sin-stained, curse-infected earth, and to all who think themselves at home there.

CHAPTER ELEVEN

Bowls:
The Last Woes
(16:1–21)

Closing the Gap between Threat and Reality

Iain Duguid has summed up the life of Abraham as "living in the gap between promise and reality."[1] The description fits Abraham and us, his spiritual children all down through history. God's promises are sure, but by their nature as promises they point our faith forward to wait in hope for fulfillment yet to come. Abraham shows us what it means to "live by faith" (Rom. 1:17). Realities that he would not see before dying—a seed who would bring blessing to all nations, a homeland secure from all enemies—became the lodestar by which Abraham navigated his life.

Scripture offers another perspective on Abraham's waiting in the gap for promises to be fulfilled. As believers wait for God to turn his promises into the joyful reality of blessing, so God waits to turn his threats against unbelievers into the grave reality of judgment. Abraham will not take possession of Canaan in his day; but his descendants, after four centuries of slavery, will return to receive the land of promise. The delay—the gap—is not only because God calls Abraham and

1. Iain M. Duguid, *Living in the Gap between Promise and Reality: The Gospel according to Abraham* (Phillipsburg, N.J.: P&R Publishing, 1999).

his children to live by faith, not sight. It is also because the land's current occupants have not "filled to the brim" their quota of wrath-deserving wickedness. God promises Abraham, "Then in the fourth generation [your descendants] will return here, for the iniquity of the Amorite is not yet complete" (Gen. 15:16). God has, as it were, a vessel of justice into which the Amorites are pouring their evil, idolatry, and violence, until the foul brew reaches the bowl's brim and overflows in a flood of divine wrath. Jesus uses the same analogy in addressing his Jewish contemporaries, who hypocritically distance themselves from earlier generations' murder of the prophets while conspiring to destroy the Messiah of whom the prophets spoke: "Fill up, then, the measure of the guilt of your fathers" (Matt. 23:32).[2]

These two time gaps are concurrent: Abraham must wait for God to close the gap between the promise and the reality of blessing because God will wait to close the gap between the threat and the reality of condemnation. God will fill believers' cup of blessing to overflowing only when the wicked have filled their bowl of cursing to overflowing. The vision of the fifth seal unveiled this divinely planned coincidence: the martyrs' lament, "How long until you avenge our blood?" receives the surprising answer, "Not until the number of martyrs is filled up" (Rev. 6:11 paraphrased dej).[3] The vindication and relief of the suffering church will coincide with the completion of its enemies' violent aggression in the slaughter of the last martyr. When the cup of the martyrs' blood is full, God's patience will wait no more. The outpouring of seven bowls, brimful of the wrath of the ever-living God (15:7), will bring the seven last plagues on people who are at home in this sin-cursed earth. These plagues are last because in them God's wrath is completed (15:1), his unrivaled reign is revealed (11:15–18), and his oppressed people are avenged (see 16:5 below).

2. "Fill up" translates the Greek verb *plēroō*, which often in the New Testament refers to the "fulfilling" of prophecy. For another use of this verb in the Greek Bible in a semimetaphorical sense, conveying completeness under the image of the filling of a vessel, see Dan. 8:23 LXX, a prophecy concerning the Hellenistic Empire, which describes "the end of their kingdom" as the time when "their sins are filled up."

3. The Greek verb here paraphrased "is filled up" (NASB: "would be completed") is *plēroō*, as in Matt. 23:32; Dan. 8:23 LXX.

We have noticed the correspondence in spheres and the difference in scope between the first four trumpets and the first four bowls. In both cycles the spheres and their sequence are the same: earth, sea, rivers and springs, and sky (affecting the heavenly lights). In the trumpet judgments, however, devastation is limited to one-third of each sphere, whereas destruction is comprehensive when the bowls are poured out. The similarity between trumpets and bowls shows that providential disasters, whether natural catastrophes or those caused by human evil, are not random events but restrained expressions of God's righteous wrath and previews of coming, comprehensive judgment. The escalation in the scope of destruction reveals that the bowl cycle portrays history's end, when God's patience will wait no longer and his common grace will be withdrawn from all who persist in unrepentant rebellion.

In Leviticus 26 God threatened the same kind of escalation in imposing covenant curses if Israel proved rebellious against his commandments. A first cycle of covenant curses would include disease of body, futility in farming, and defeat in warfare (Lev. 26:14–20). "If then, you act with hostility against Me and are unwilling to obey Me, I will increase the plague on you seven times according to your sins" (26:21). Sevenfold increase of wasting judgments should turn Israel to the Lord (26:23), but if they fail, desolation and eventual banishment from the land will ensue (26:33). In the same way when the bowls full of the seven last plagues are poured out, not only the rebels but also the "first heaven and earth," defiled and destroyed by their idolatry (cf. Rev. 16:20 with 20:11), will be destroyed.[4] The revelation of God's

4. G. K. Beale, *The Book of Revelation,* NIGTC (Grand Rapids: Eerdmans, 1999), 803, calls attention to Lev. 26 as the source of the terminology "seven plagues" to describe the bowl's contents (Rev. 15:6). He nevertheless believes that the first five bowls recapitulate the trumpets' visions of woes characteristic of the entire period between Christ's comings (808–12): "Generally speaking, the first six trumpets and the first five bowls cover the time between Christ's resurrection and his final Parousia, while the last trumpet and the last two bowls narrate the last judgment" (810). This insistence on direct recapitulation between the trumpet and bowl cycles ignores the escalation motif in Lev. 26 and the announcements that the bowls, "which are the last," bring God's wrath to its consummation (Rev. 15:1). We should rather see the seven bowls as contained within and elaborating on the seventh trumpet and the sixth seal.

wrath at the last trumpet marks the arrival of the time "to destroy those who destroy the earth" (11:18)—who are admiring devotees of "the great city" (16:19), "the great harlot who was destroying the earth with her harlotry" (19:2 dej).[5]

The judgments symbolized in the bowl visions echo the physical plagues inflicted on Egypt, leading to the Israelites' exodus under Moses. The "great city," which represents the pagan world system in opposition to Christ and his church, has already been identified as Sodom and Egypt and indicted not only for the crucifixion of Jesus but also for the murder of his faithful witnesses (Rev. 11:8). Though the imagery is derived from physical plagues inflicted on the Egyptians' bodies, property, and environment, the referents to which the bowl visions point should not be taken so literally. All interpreters recognize that the "outpouring" of each bowl is not a physical action but a symbol of world-devastating judgment that is purposed by God's sovereign will and executed by his almighty power. The divine source of this history-ending complex of catastrophes is signified by the fact that the angels of the plagues have come out of God's heavenly sanctuary (15:6) to receive the golden bowls of God's wrath and the fact that "a loud voice from the temple" commands the angels to pour them out (16:1). As the bowls belong to the symbolic dialect in which John's visions bring their message, so also the effects of the outpoured bowls are conveyed in symbolic impressions, not photographic reproductions.

First Bowl on the Earth: Sore on the Beast's Worshipers (16:2)

The first bowl is poured out on earth, where people live and work. Unlike the fire that fell with the first trumpet (Rev. 8:7), however, this judgment targets not trees and grass but those people who are in league with the beast, "who had the mark of the beast and who worshiped his image." In John's earlier vision this mark, which branded them as the beast's willing property, was applied to idolaters' bodies,

---

5. In Rev. 11:18 and 19:2 the same verb, *phtheirō* ("destroy"), appears in the construction "destroy the earth" (though NASB translates it "was corrupting" in 19:2).

on right hand or forehead (13:16). It symbolizes the world system's control of their minds and therefore of their actions. So now God inflicts on those who bear the beast's mark "a loathsome and malignant sore," a visual reflection of the despairing, death-seeking anguish symbolized in the demon locusts' stings under the fifth trumpet (= the first woe; 9:5–6).[6]

The sixth plague by which God humbled the Egyptians and prepared for Israel's liberation was sores or boils on man and beast (Exod. 9:8–12). The grotesque vividness of these festering wounds still stood as a stark warning to a new generation forty years later, at the end of Israel's wilderness wanderings. In a passage parallel to Leviticus 26, Moses rehearsed on the plains of Moab the sanctions that should motivate Israel to covenantal fidelity: blessings for obedience (Deut. 28:1–14) and curses for disobedience (28:15–68). Specifically, if Israel breaks covenant with its God,

> The LORD will smite you with the boils of Egypt and with tumors and with the scab and with the itch, from which you cannot be healed. . . . The LORD will strike you on the knees and legs with sore boils, from which you cannot be healed, from the sole of your foot to the crown of your head. (Deut. 28:27, 35)

Even such head-to-toe physical torment, however, pales in comparison with the hopelessness of heart that God inflicts on those who have trusted the beast as their savior and protector. The beast's mark is useless to shield its servants from coming divine wrath.

Second Bowl on the Sea: Blood and Death (16:3)

The second bowl turns all the sea to blood "like that of a dead man" and kills all the creatures that had filled the sea. The corresponding trumpet had shown limited bloodying of the sea and destruction of its animal life and the ships that sail it (Rev. 8:8–9). The ships that tra-

---

6. Those "locusts" did not inflict physical harm on earth's vegetation but brought spiritual and mental torment to those who lacked the seal of God, who persisted in foolish unrepentance (Rev. 9:4, 20).

versed the Mediterranean Sea turned it into Rome's worldwide web
of trade and transportation. As a portrait of God's providential judgment, that trumpet vision symbolized the disastrous consequences of
sea battles, disrupting shipping routes and hindering the attempts of
fishermen to draw food from the waters. But again, such limited traumas are only a faint foreshadowing of the coming wrath.

The turning of water to blood reflects the first plague on Egypt,
when the Nile's waters turned bloody and "the fish that were in the
Nile died. . . . And the blood was through all the land of Egypt" (Exod.
7:21). The effect of the third bowl on the fresh water sources, rivers
and springs, also echoes that first Egyptian plague.

The destruction of the ships is not mentioned here as it was in the
second trumpet, but a lament for fallen Babylon will soon be on the
lips of every shipmaster, sailor, and nautical traveler (Rev. 18:17–19).
Perhaps ships are not mentioned in connection with the second bowl
because in this final judgment cycle "the sea" portrays not so much
the Mediterranean Sea, which was the heart of Rome's far-flung empire, but the satanic spiritual realm from which opposition to God's
reign arises in the form of the beast (13:1). In the new heaven and
earth the sea, from which the beast emerged, is no more (21:1). The
bloodying of the sea "like the blood of a dead man" may symbolize
the destruction of the tumultuous peoples that have served the beast
and lusted after his whore. The harlot Babylon will soon be seen to
be enthroned on "many waters," which are interpreted as "peoples
and multitudes and nations and tongues" (17:1, 15).

Third Bowl on the Rivers and Springs:
Blood as Beverage (16:4–7)

When the third angel pours his bowl into the rivers and springs of
water, they too turn to blood, becoming undrinkable like the Nile
long ago (Exod. 7:21). In the third trumpet the fouling of these fresh
water sources had been portrayed with an emphasis on the resulting
bitter taste (wormwood) and toxic outcome (Rev. 8:11). Now the
turning of all the rivers and springs into blood, though not literally

rendering the water lethal, signals again an escalation in the intensity of the judgment.

Two outbursts of praise to God reinforce the appropriateness and justice of the form of this plague. The angel who has authority over the waters extols God for the perfect retributive equity of this plague, in view of its victims' crime (Rev. 16:5–6). "Righteous are You" echoes Moses' song of witness in Moab, just prior to Joshua's conquest of Canaan (Deut. 32:4). Earlier in Revelation God was identified as the one "who is and who was and who is to come" (Rev. 1:4, 8; 4:8), a title derived from his self-designation at the burning bush (Exod. 3:13–15). Now, however, the future-oriented member ("who is to come") of this threefold confession is deleted. When the bowls are poured out, the coming One will have come in holy justice. The holy One[7] is answering at last the lament of his martyrs, whose shed blood cried out for justice even as their souls cried out from under the altar, "How long?" (Rev. 6:10).

To those who poured out the blood of saints and prophets God has poured out a bowl, thereby giving them blood to drink.[8] The gruesome implication is that the persecutors will drink their own blood, as the allusion to Isaiah 49:26 shows: "I will feed your oppressors with their own flesh, and they will become drunk with their own blood as with sweet wine; and all flesh will know that I, the LORD, am your Savior and your Redeemer, the Mighty One of Jacob." John has heard an angel declare that God's enemies will drink the wine of God's rage from the cup of his wrath (Rev. 14:10), and he has seen the blood of those enemies flowing from God's winepress to defile the earth (14:20). In Isaiah 49 those two images of wine as symbolizing judgment are

7. The Greek substantive adjective here is not *ho hagios* but *ho hosios* (see also Rev. 15:4: "You alone are holy"), a term that underscores God's fidelity to those with whom he is bound in covenant (see also Ps. 16:10; Isa. 55:3 LXX—brought together in Acts 13:34–35).

8. Compare Ps. 79, a lament over the Gentiles' destruction of Jerusalem and slaughter of its inhabitants: "they have poured out their blood like water round about Jerusalem. . . . Let there be known among the nations in our sight, vengeance for the blood of Your servants which has been shed. . . . And return to our neighbors sevenfold into their bosom the reproach with which they have reproached You, O Lord" (Ps. 79:3, 10, 12).

linked. John will soon see the Roman economic system and the whole pagan culture that sustains it as the harlot Babylon "drunk with the blood of the saints, and with the blood of the witnesses of Jesus" (17:6). But the cup of divine wrath that she is to drink will be the exact duplicate of the cup of affliction that she had mixed for others (18:6–8).[9]

The heavenly altar affirms the angel's acclamation of divine justice: "Yes, O Lord God, the Almighty, true and righteous are Your judgments" (Rev. 16:7). This heavenly altar has witnessed the suffering of saints, for under it the martyrs' souls await their vindication (6:9) and upon it the prayers of suffering saints have been offered as incense (8:3–4). From this altar, fire has fallen in limited judgments on earth's rebels (8:5) and the angel of the fire emerged to authorize the gathering of the wicked like grapes, to be crushed by God's righteous wrath (14:18–19). The altar's response echoes with variation the song of the victors, "Righteous and true are Your ways" (15:3), and it will be picked up again in the shout of a great heavenly multitude, celebrating Babylon's destruction, by which God has avenged the blood of his servants (19:2).

Fourth Bowl on the Sun: Burning Heat (16:8–9)

When the fourth bowl is poured on the sun, the result is not a dimming or darkening, as in the fourth trumpet.[10] Rather, the sun's intensity increases, with the result that earth's rebellious inhabitants are "scorched with fierce heat" (Rev. 16:9). This plague has no counterpart in the ancient plagues on Egypt. The fiery hostility of the created order against people who are hostile to the Creator makes the sun's light and warmth, in themselves necessary and delightful, instruments of torture when taken to extreme.

John has seen the saints in heaven, from every nation and tongue, clothed in white robes. And he has heard an elder affirm that, shaded by God's tabernacle, they are forever safe from the curse unleashed throughout the world by human sin: "They will hunger no longer,

9. Likewise, the irony of Haman's end brings satisfaction and hope to victims of injustice: "So they hanged Haman on the gallows which he had prepared for Mordecai, and the king's anger subsided" (Esther 7:10).

10. Darkness will fall with the fifth bowl.

228

nor thirst anymore; nor will the sun beat down on them, nor any heat" (Rev. 7:16). By contrast, John will see the world system Babylon betrayed by her accomplices and the horns (kings) on which she once rode high turned to gore her: "And the ten horns which you saw, and the beast, these will hate the harlot and will make her desolate and naked, and will eat her flesh, and will burn her up with fire" (17:16; cf. 18:8). Scorching sunlight without shade spells certain death, and so it provides an apt picture of life bereft of the relief that God previously provided even the wicked in his common grace (Gen. 8:22; Matt. 5:45; Acts 14:17). In the end he will withdraw even this expression of his undeserved kindness.

The end of the age of God's longsuffering and common grace is also signaled by the reaction of the people on whom the plague of scorching sunlight falls: "they blasphemed the name of God who has the power over these plagues, and they did not repent so as to give Him glory" (Rev. 16:9). Their refusal to repent is the same stubborn and foolhardy response as that of the survivors of the plagues revealed in the sixth trumpet (the second woe, 9:20–21). Their refusal to give God glory disobeys the eternal gospel proclaimed by the angel who announced the arrival of the hour of God's judgment (14:7). The clearest symptom of their hardness of heart, however, is their blasphemy of the name of God who has the authority to impose these plagues on wrath-deserving sinners. In this blasphemy they show the horrifying effect of bearing the beast's mark, for they now imitate their owner and the object of their worship. The beast's heads bear blasphemous names, and from the beast's mouth proceed blasphemies against God's name and sanctuary (13:1, 5–6). Now his followers do likewise, even though their anguish only confirms the futility of looking to the beast for refuge from the Lamb's coming wrath. They react with the same arrogant blasphemies to the plagues of the fifth and seventh bowls (16:11, 21).

Fifth Bowl on the Beast's Throne: Palpable Darkness (16:10–11)

The darkening of the beast's kingdom when the fifth bowl is poured on its throne reproduces the ninth plague on ancient Egypt (Exod.

229

10:21–23). The beast's reign has always been shrouded in spiritual darkness, for its foundation is the lie that the beast is incomparable (Rev. 13:4), which directly contradicts the truth affirmed by Moses' song: "Who is like You among the gods, O LORD . . . majestic in holiness, awesome in praises, working wonders?" (Exod. 15:11). The next bowl will show that the dragon, the beast, and the false prophet continue to spit out lies, deluding their gullible followers even to the end (Rev. 16:13–14; cf. 13:14; 19:20; 20:8). This palpable darkness thus exposes the beast's rule for what it is, a domain of delusion and confusion. John has noted elsewhere that guilty people love darkness for the cover it offers for their evil deeds (John 3:19–20; cf. Eph. 5:11–13). Yet the beast's followers find no comfort in the darkness of his domain, but only a disorienting anguish that makes them chew their tongues in despair. The new Jerusalem, by contrast, is a community where truth prevails, flooded with light and radiating its light to the world: "And the city has no need of the sun or of the moon to shine on it, for the glory of God has illumined it, and its lamp is the Lamb. The nations will walk by its light" (Rev. 21:23–24; cf. vv. 10–11).[11]

The mention of the beast's "throne" recalls "Satan's throne" located in Pergamum and overshadowing the life of the church there (Rev. 2:13). The presence of Satan's throne in that city seems to have been the cause of the murder of Antipas, Jesus' faithful witness. The presence of several prominent pagan temples, including one to the divine Augustus and Roma, divine patroness of the empire, was probably the reason that Jesus designated Pergamum as the city in which Satan's throne is located. The world system's center of power, the beast's Oval Office, cannot be insulated from the wrath of God, who will expose the devil's darkness for all to see.

Yet again, as in the sixth trumpet and the fourth bowl, men react with blasphemy and a refusal to repent (Rev. 16:11). As distressing as the confusion and alienation of darkness are, hardened rebels still prefer their pain to the humbling exposure of stepping into God's light. They follow blindly in the steps of the ancient Pharaoh, whose hard

---

11. During the Egyptian plague of darkness "all the sons of Israel had light in their dwellings" (Exod. 10:23).

heart almost wavered but in the end ignored even the penultimate plague, darkness, refusing to release Israel and banishing Moses from his presence (Exod. 10:27–28). The object of people's blasphemy is "the God of heaven." This title appears in Daniel 2:18–19 to underscore the supremacy of the Lord, the God of Israel, as the Sovereign over all history and the Revealer of all mysteries. Hard hearts, defiant toward the God before whom they should fall down in contrition and adoration, instead stagger in darkness toward destruction.

Sixth Bowl on the River Euphrates: Gathering for the Battle (16:12–16)

The sixth bowl reveals preparations for the last battle, the final showdown between God and his enemies. The route is prepared for the invaders by the drying up of "the great river, the Euphrates" (Rev. 16:12), and then the invading armies are gathered by the lies of the dragon, the beast, and the false prophet (16:13–14, 16). In the midst of these preparations for war is embedded the third of Revelation's seven blessings, summoning the church to vigilance and purity, in view of the unpredictable timing of Jesus' coming (16:15).

The Euphrates first appeared in John's visions in connection with the sixth trumpet. There it was a restraining boundary holding back impending judgment. At the command of a voice from the golden altar "the four angels who are bound at the great river Euphrates" were released from their bondage, and a cavalry two hundred million strong swept across the river to kill a third of mankind (Rev. 9:13–15). In biblical history[12] the Euphrates is identified with regions to the north and east, from which Israel's and Judah's captors, Assyria and Babylonia, had come:

> Now therefore, behold, the Lord is about to bring on them the strong and abundant waters of the Euphrates, even the king of Assyria and all his glory; and it will rise up over all its channels and go over all its banks.

12. Residents of the Roman Empire would associate the Euphrates with the empire's eastern boundary, beyond which the much-feared forces of Parthia menaced (see p. 150).

> Then it will sweep on into Judah, it will overflow and pass through, it
> will reach even to the neck; and the spread of its wings will fill the
> breadth of your land, O Immanuel. (Isa. 8:7–8)

The prophets predict that God will dry up the Euphrates, exposing
Babylon to attack from forces even further east. Cyrus will lead his
Persian armies from the east (Isa. 41:2) and the north (v. 25) as "a bird
of prey from the east" (46:11). When he comes upon Babylon, his
way will have been cleared by the Lord: "It is I who says to the depth
of the sea, 'Be dried up!' and I will make your rivers dry. It is I who
says of Cyrus, 'He is My shepherd! And he will perform all My desire'" (44:27–28). Through Jeremiah also God pronounces his judgments on Babylon in terms of the drying of the River (Jer. 50:38;
51:36). Just as the drying of the Red Sea cleared the path for Israel's
liberation from Egypt (Exod. 14:21–25) and the drying of the Jordan
River opened the way for conquest of the land, exposing the peoples
of Canaan before the advancing armies of God (Josh. 3), so the drying of the Euphrates that John now sees signals the coming relief and
release for the church and defeat for its enemies.

The enemies' defeat, however, will take them unawares. The drying of the river removes an impediment that had hindered their assault
on the church, so "the kings from the east," who stand for "the kings
of the whole world" (Rev. 16:14), gleefully gather for the kill. Surely,
now that this barrier no longer restrains their violence and separates
them from their prey, their victory is imminent! But they are sadly mis-
taken. In fact, they are assembling to meet their own destruction.

The world's rulers gather for the war only because the dragon, the
beast, and the false prophet have deceived them. From those three villains' mouths spring three demonic spirits in the form of frogs. An invasion of frogs was the second plague on Egypt (Exod. 8:2–11), but
these three "frogs" are unclean spirits who serve the dragon's deceptive and destructive agenda. Like the false prophet (Rev. 13:13) and
the magicians of Egypt (Exod. 7:11, 22), these demons deceive their
dupes by performing miraculous signs. Their purpose is to gather the
world's kings and their forces for "the war of the great day of God,
the Almighty" (Rev. 16:14). John will see twin visions of this last battle, the first showing the outcome for the beast, the false prophet and

their followers (19:17–21) and the second showing the outcome for the dragon (20:7–10). In both of these visions the enemy forces are gathered against Christ and his church for "the war," and the reference is back to the single, climactic conflict for which preparation is made here.[13] These frog demons, then, are visual representations of the subtle demonic process by which the dragon, released at last from the restraint that kept him from deceiving the nations, will "come out to deceive the nations which are in the four corners of the earth, Gog and Magog, to gather them together for the war" (20:8). Yet when they gather to besiege "the camp of the saints and the beloved city," expecting to overwhelm the church, the enemies have assembled to facilitate their own destruction (20:9).

At this point, before a final comment identifying the site at which the beast's followers will gather for the last war, Jesus interjects a promise, which also carries an implied warning (Rev. 16:15). He speaks in the first person, "Behold, I am coming like a thief," using the image he had used during his ministry on earth (Luke 12:39–40) and in his wake-up call to the church at Sardis (Rev. 3:3; cf. 1 Thess. 5:4). His return will be sudden and unpredictable. In light of the gathering conspiracy portrayed in the preceding verses, we may say that his return will occur when matters seem most bleak for his church on earth, as its enemies close in to snuff out its life (cf. Rev. 11:7–13). In view of this unpredictability, Jesus' beatitude promises divine favor to the soldier who stays on watch, fully clothed "so that he will not walk about naked and men will not see his shame." Jesus had counseled the church

13. Few English versions accurately reflect the presence of the definite article before "war" (*ho polemos*) in Rev. 19:19 (NASB: "assembled to make war") and 20:8 (NASB [correctly here]: "to gather them together for the war"). Nevertheless the presence of the definite article signals that a specific war or battle, the war first introduced in 16:14 with the fuller title, "the war of the great day of God, the Almighty," is in view in both passages—there is one last battle, not two. The presence of the article in 19:19 and 20:8 is noteworthy, since Revelation often uses *polemos* ("war") without the article when referring to warfare generically (9:7, 9; 11:7; 12:7, 17; 13:7). See R. Fowler White, "Reexamining the Evidence for Recapitulation in Rev 20:1–10," *WTJ* 51 (1989): 319–44, especially 328–30. In chapter 13 we will examine further parallels that demonstrate that the same war is described in 19:17–21 and 20:7–10.

at Laodicea to receive the white garments that he alone can give, so that "the shame of your nakedness will not be revealed" (3:18). So this beatitude promises blessing to the overcomer who avoids the weaknesses of the two weakest Asian churches, the drowsiness of Sardis and the illusory self-sufficiency of Laodicea. Soon the harlot Babylon's lovers, the rulers and merchants and the beast itself, which once shared her lusts and luxury, will strip her naked, exposing her shame (17:16; cf. Ezek. 16:36–39). This is no time to get in bed with the "great city's" fast-fading beauty. This is no time for Jesus' followers to be lulled to sleep by the promise of pleasure and prosperity offered by a culture that rests on arrogance toward God and ruthless violence toward his church.

The final detail in the gathering of the nations for the last war is to designate their place of assembly: "And they gathered them together to the place which in Hebrew is called Har-Magedon" (Rev. 16:16). Har-Magedon (often rendered "Armageddon" in English) in Hebrew means "mount of Megiddo," and clearly John intends his readers to note its Hebrew meaning. This place name is problematic for several reasons. The topographical feature in Palestine that bears the name Megiddo is a broad plain with which nothing high enough to be called a "mountain" is associated. Megiddo was the site of several significant battles (Judg. 5:19; 2 Kings 23:29), so it is not surprising to find this plain, located roughly two days' walk northeast of Jerusalem, used in Revelation as a symbol of the eschatological battlefield.[14] The cognitive dissonance evoked in hearers by identifying the Megiddo plain with a mountain is a further reminder that John's visions speak the language of symbols, not that of photographic reproduction. Old Testament prophecy pictured the final gathering of pagan nations for war against the Lord and his people as occurring not on the plain of Megiddo but at Jerusalem and its environs:

> It will come about in that day that I will make Jerusalem a heavy stone for all the peoples; all who lift it will be severely injured. And all the nations of the earth will be gathered against it. (Zech. 12:3)

> For I will gather all the nations against Jerusalem to battle, and the city will be captured, the houses plundered, the women ravished and half

14. Beale, *Revelation,* 838–41.

of the city exiled, but the rest of the people will not be cut off from the city. Then the LORD will go forth and fight against those nations, as when He fights on a day of battle. (Zech. 14:2–3)[15]

John's vision would jar against the eschatological imagery of the ancient prophets, if its purpose were to identify the physical site of the last battle at so great a distance from Jerusalem. At the other point in Revelation in which he gives a name in Hebrew, John also provides its Greek equivalent: the angel of the abyss is called Abaddon in Hebrew and Apollyon in Greek (9:11). Both names mean "destroyer." Here, however, Greek-speaking hearers are given no clue to the meaning of the Hebrew place name.

M. G. Kline, developing an earlier proposal of C. C. Torrey, argues that *Har-Magedon* represents an alternative Greek transliteration of the Hebrew expression "Mount of Assembly (Gathering)," which would be transliterated into English as *Har Mōʿed*.[16] If Kline's view is correct, the context of the name in Revelation 16:16 does provide its interpretation in Greek, after all: "they gathered them together (*synēgagon*) to the place which is called . . . Mount of Gathering" (dej). In the Old Testament the mount of assembly is heaven (Isa. 14:13), but it is also Mount Zion, heaven's earthly reflection (Ps. 48:1–2, linked to Isa. 14:13 by the shared phrase rendered "in the recesses of the north" or "in the far north"). Thus the deceivers are gathering the world's rebel forces to lay siege to the church as the earthly expression of the heavenly Mount Zion, where the Lamb has gathered his select and holy soldiers.[17] This foolhardy siege against

15. Zech. 12:11 compares a future day of great mourning in Jerusalem to "the mourning of Hadadrimmon in the plain of Megiddo" (Hebrew spelling here: *Megiddon*).

16. M. G. Kline, "Har Magedon: The End of the Millennium," *JETS* 39 (1996): 207–22. The Hebrew consonant *ʿayin*, represented by ʿ in the English transliteration, is a hard glottal stop less pronounced than *gimmel* (= Greek *gamma*, hard English *g*), but Kline argues that *ʿayin* was sometimes replaced by *gamma* in Greek transliteration.

17. Kline believes that the "Mount of Gathering" represented by Har-Magedon in Rev. 16:16 is not Zion in God's holy city but a demonic, antichrist counterfeit mountain, a lying rival to the true heights from which the true King reigns (ibid., 213–18).

"the camp of the saints and the beloved city" will end suddenly with the besiegers' sudden defeat and destruction (Rev. 19:19–21; 20:9–10).[18]

Seventh Bowl on the Air:
Earthquake Shattering the Great City (16:17–21)

The seventh bowl gives us a final camera angle on the completion of God's wrath in judgment on rebellious humans and the created order that they have defiled.[19] The finality of this perspective and of the bowls cycle as symbolizing God's climactic judgments at history's end is affirmed by the voice from God's heavenly temple as the bowl is poured: "It is done." Though this is a different Greek verb from that rendered "is finished" in Revelation 15:1, 8, its import is the same.[20] "It is done" will again punctuate God's announcement that he is renewing all things, creating a new heaven and earth, for then the first heaven and earth will have passed away (21:5–6, cf. v. 1).

The bowl is poured out on "the air" perhaps because biblical cosmology sometimes identifies "the air" as the realm of Satan's evil dominion (Eph. 2:2; cf. 6:12). It effects cosmic cataclysm in the skies overhead and the earth below. In the skies are the phenomena of divine theophany, a terrible invasion by the Lord of hosts on the storm clouds: "flashes of lightning and sounds and peals of thunder" (Rev.

---

18. Beale (*Revelation,* 839–40) and G. K. Beasley-Murray (*The Book of Revelation,* NCB [Grand Rapids: Eerdmans, 1981], 245) discuss the Torrey-Kline argument that "Har-Magedon" should be understood as "Mount of Gathering," but they conclude that the proposed transliteration equivalencies are farfetched. David E. Aune (*Revelation 6–16,* WBC [Waco: Word, 1998], 898–99) mentions this view among others to illustrate his conclusion that the name "has never been satisfactorily explained."

19. This camera angle is the final scene in the bowl sequence, although in a sense we can view the following visions (the harlot Babylon and her demise, the last battle at the end of the thousand years, the last judgment, presentation of the new Jerusalem as Bride) as contained within the bowls cycle, as we see from the role of bowls angels in revealing the Harlot and the Bride (17:1; 21:9).

20. "It is done" in Rev. 16:17 translates *gegonen,* a perfect (completed) aspect form of *ginomai.* The verb in Rev. 15:1, 8 is *teleō.*

16:18).[21] From the skies fall huge hailstones, of lethal weight (16:21). This shaking of the sky had its precursor in the seventh plague on Egypt, in which death-inflicting hailstones fell on man and beast exposed in the field, accompanied by thunder and lightning (Exod. 9:18–35).

On earth "a great earthquake" splits the great city Babylon into three parts, causing the cities of the nations to fall in ruins as well, and making islands flee and mountains disappear (Rev. 16:18–20). Just as the ancient hailstorm was unparalleled in previous Egyptian history ("such as has not been seen in Egypt from the day it was founded until now," Exod. 9:18), so this quake that shatters the earth will be unparalleled in all human history ("such as there had not been since man came to be upon the earth," Rev. 16:18).[22] Seal 6 gave us a preview of this great quake, which not only set earth shuddering, so that "every mountain and island were moved out of their places," but also shook the stars from the sky like figs "shaken by a great wind" and split the sky itself like a scroll (6:12–14). The repetition of terms—"great earthquake," "every mountain and island" (order reversed in 16:20)—shows that the seventh bowl gives us a second glimpse of the climactic event portrayed in the sixth seal.

Zechariah had prophesied that the day of the Lord's battle against the nations, when he comes to defend his people, will be marked by a terrifying earthquake that splits the Mount of Olives (Zech. 14:3–5). The fulfillment that appears before John's eyes shows this earthquake to be worldwide, even universe-wide in scope. This is the final shakedown prophesied in Haggai 2:6, as Hebrews shows us: "Yet once more I will shake not only the earth, but also the heaven"—not only the earth, as at Sinai, but also the created heavens as well, "the removing of those things that can be shaken, as of created things, so that those things which

21. The Lord descended on Mount Sinai to deliver his law to Moses in the midst of a storm cloud, full of flashing lightning and the roar of thunder (Exod. 19:16). Of course, lightning, thunder, and other awe-producing sounds have accompanied John's visions of God in his heavenly court throughout Revelation (4:5; 8:5; 11:19).

22. Daniel also foresaw "a time of distress such as never occurred since there was a nation until that time," marking the time of rescue for God's people and the resurrection of the dead (Dan. 12:1–2).

cannot be shaken may remain" (Heb. 12:26–27). The flight of islands and disappearance of mountains epitomizes the flight of the first earth and heaven, stained by human sin and its toxic waste, from the coming of the Lord; "and no place was found for them" (20:11). This removal of the first heaven and earth makes way for the new heavens and earth (Rev. 21:1; cf. Isa. 65:17), the home of righteousness (2 Peter 3:10–13).

The "great city" Babylon is the bull's eye in the target of this world-shattering strike by divine wrath, dead center in God's cross hairs (Rev. 16:19). We have seen the great city as the site of our Lord's crucifixion and his witnesses' violent death (11:8). We have heard Babylon's fall announced and her malevolent role in seducing and intoxicating the nations identified (14:8). Now we catch a glimpse of her demise, a sneak preview that will be expanded in the next two chapters of Revelation. Split into three parts, she pulls down with her the cities of the nations. In one sense, like ancient Babylon, she is a physical city, one situated on seven hills—unmistakably Rome, for John's first readers (17:9). In another sense, however, like the beast from the sea, this Babylon is more than a single city or even civilization. The power grid of fallen human culture (political, economic, military, religious, social) is so tightly interlocking that when its heart is shattered, the whole edifice crumbles. With Babylon's fall, all the world's cities fall.

This scene of the city's destruction reassures the church that "Babylon the great was remembered before God, to give her the cup of the wine of His fierce wrath" (Rev. 16:19). Babylon has made the nations drunk with the wine of her immorality (14:8; 17:2), and John will soon see her cup brimming not only with abominations but also with the blood of the saints, the witnesses of Jesus (17:4, 6). She not only seduces those who are ensnared by her luxury and sensuality but also employs the vicious beast on which she sits to assault and murder believers who resist her wiles. She seems to have the upper hand and boasts of her freedom to sin with impunity, with none to call her to account (18:7). But her smug sense of security is sheer delusion. God has record books and will judge both individuals and societies according to their deeds (20:11–15). "God has remembered her iniquities" (18:5), and he will repay her in kind for her arrogant assault on his honor and his people (cf. Gal. 6:7–8).

Still human hearts are hard. Even as the fragile falsehoods in which they have trusted shatter around them, still "men blasphemed God because of the plague of hail," their petrified hearts incapable of repentance (Rev. 16:21). Neither the backwash of sin's bitter aftertaste nor the first fruits of its lethal harvest can soften hearts of stone. Only God's Spirit, applying the gospel of grace, can turn stony hearts into hearts of tender flesh, but the bowls show us a moment in time when the Spirit's gentle and irresistible wooing is complete, the Son's sheep have been gathered, and the Father's patience has waited long enough.

Conclusion

That day is coming, but it is not yet. The followers of Jesus still live in the gap between promise and reality, and that means that we endure affliction with longing for justice long delayed, or so it often seems to us. But the existence of the gap, despite the pain it prolongs for us, is good news. It means that "the iniquity of the Amorite is not yet complete," that the evil and insult that unbelievers now pour into God's bowls of wrath has not yet reached the rim.

God's common grace still shields even the rankest, most arrogant rebel from the despair and destruction that are rebellion's inevitable consequences. He sends his rain on just and unjust, bearing witness to his majesty and generosity by giving fruitful harvests even to those who give thanks for those harvests to the fantasies of their own minds (Matt. 5:45; Acts 14:15–17). His kindness is intended to draw his chosen ones out of their idolatries and into repentance (Rom. 2:4). This very purpose—to bring his own to repentance—explains his patient forbearance, though many mistake it for tardiness or, worse, a complete failure of his promise (2 Peter 3:4–9). God will close the gap between promise and reality for Abraham's faith children precisely when he closes the gap between threat and reality for Satan's offspring, duped by the serpent's lie and destined to share his destruction. While this gap stays open, before the last bowls are poured out on an unrepentant world, the church is called to hold fast and hold forth the testimony of Jesus, who drained the cup of wrath and suffering for all who turn and trust in him.

239

CHAPTER TWELVE

Harlot:
Babylon's Luxury, Violence, and Destruction
(17:1–19:10)

Beauty and the Beast

"Appearances can be deceiving." "People are not always what they seem." "Don't judge a book by its cover." These familiar phrases convey the same lesson, too often learned only through painful experience. Fairy tales know and teach this truth. An arrogant but insecure queen repeatedly invites her truth-telling magic mirror to praise her as the fairest in the land. Then one day, to her shock and outrage, the mirror praises the peasant girl Snow White as more beautiful than the queen. All along the queen's beauty has been only skin deep, belying the ugly, self-absorbed heart within. Only when the queen disguises herself as a hag to poison her rival does her outward appearance finally reflect her repulsive inner reality. The Beast whom Beauty grows to love, despite its repugnant appearance and gruff manner, was once a human prince, handsome on the outside but twisted by selfish arrogance within. The enchantment that turned him into a beast had translated the ugliness hidden in his heart into an abomination for all to see. Then there is naïve Pinocchio—duped, exploited, and even enslaved by one false friend after another, as he explores the so-called freedom of being a real boy. Anyone who has been abandoned by a friend or lover, lied to by an advertiser, or disappointed by a parent or leader knows that these stories ring true: People are not always what they seem to be. Although we know this is true intellectually, we may still be easy prey for the flashy image, the manipulative hype, the convincing come-on that had its origins in the garden, when the serpent persuaded the woman that it, not God, had her best interests at heart.[1]

Jesus knows that his churches can be gullible. The church at Thyatira can tolerate a Jezebel who seduces its members into spiritual adultery against our lawful and loving Husband. Laodicea can congratulate itself on its affluence and self-sufficiency, oblivious to its real poverty and blind to its blindness. Others have stained themselves and traded away their integrity through compromise with the culture. If churches like these are wowed by the attractiveness of the empire's luxuriant economy, no one will be surprised. But Jesus will be displeased.

The vision that opens before John's eyes first paints the harlot Babylon's superficial attractiveness, which explains how she can be alluring not only to pagans but also to Christians. Then John will see the ugliness under the cosmetics and accessories; and finally he will see Babylon's shameful decomposition at the hands of her paramours. Through this dramatic, detailed unpacking of the brief description of Babylon's fall in the seventh bowl, Jesus challenges his people to look past appearances and perceive the horrendous spiritual reality at the rotten core of Rome's impressive culture. First-century Christians might have wondered, "How can Rome be so bad when she looks so good?" or, "How could Rome ever fall when she looks so strong?" Twenty-first-century Christians living in cultures confident in their affluence and technology may have the same questions. Jesus' answer is the vision of the harlot Babylon, her beauty, and her demise.

1. G. B. Caird, *A Commentary on the Revelation of St. John the Divine,* HNTC (New York: Harper & Row, 1966), 214, alludes to another fairy-tale motif to convey how this vision distinguishes appearance from reality: "The magic is broken; the fairy godmother, who has put her spell on the whole world through the brilliance of her appearance and the munificence of her presents, is revealed as the old witch, old in sorcery before ever Rome grew to be her latest and most powerful incarnation."

Debut of the Harlot Babylon (17:1–6)

The angel's "Come here, I will show you" (Rev. 17:1) marks the vision of the harlot as parallel to—really the negative image of—the vision of the bride, the wife of the Lamb (21:9). The beast's woman and the Lamb's woman are opposites, each with her own sort of splendor (gold, precious stones, pearls, and fine linen). But the attractiveness of the harlot is both hollow and short-lived, to be turned to ashes "in one hour" (18:10, 17, 19), whereas the beauty of the bride is genuine and eternal. The harlot Babylon whom John is about to see "sits on many waters," just as the ancient Babylon rested in smug confidence on the Euphrates River (Jer. 51:13). The harlot's seat "on many waters" is symbolic of her dominion over "peoples and multitudes and nations and tongues" (Rev. 17:15), for this scarlet woman is a picture of "the great city, which reigns over the kings of the earth" (17:18).

From the beginning of the vision Babylon's reign over earth's kings and residents is portrayed as seduction to sexual immorality (Rev. 17:2), but this is a pervasive prophetic metaphor for spiritual infidelity, that is, idolatry (e.g., Ezek. 16:15–34). The description of the harlot's wealth, her making the nations drunk, her boastful self-confidence, and her collapse are derived from ancient prophecies against pagan nations that idolized their own politico-military power (Nineveh, Nahum 3:4; Babylon, Jer. 50–51) and against Tyre, which boasted in its affluence through trade (Isa. 23; Ezek. 27–28).[2] We have seen that the beast portrays Rome from the perspective of its physical threat to the church through violence but that it also transcends Rome, being a composite of all four beasts/kingdoms in Daniel 7. So also the harlot Babylon shows us Rome from the perspective of the spiritual threat of compromise through economic seduction, yet she also transcends Rome and encompasses every expression of the idolatry that worships

---

2. From the Phoenician region dominated by Tyre and Sidon came Jezebel, princess of Sidon, wife of Israel's King Ahab, and archenemy of God's prophet Elijah. Through Jezebel Baalism reinfected the northern Israelite tribes. The false prophetess at Thyatira is a Jezebel, luring others into spiritual adultery with her promise of insight into the "deep things of Satan" (Rev. 2:20, 22, 34).

economic prosperity and cultural achievement, whether in Nineveh, Chaldean Babylon, Tyre, Rome, or later entrepreneurial empires.[3]

The angel carries John to a wilderness to view the harlot's judgment (Rev. 17:3), as John will later be taken to a high mountain to view the bride's presentation at her wedding (21:10). The wilderness vantage point from which John views Babylon's fall corresponds to Isaiah's oracle concerning "the wilderness of the sea" (Isa. 21:1), in which the prophet saw horsemen, one of whom declared, "Fallen, fallen is Babylon; and all the images of her gods are shattered on the ground" (21:9). Earlier in Revelation the wilderness was the region in which the heavenly woman found protection from the pursuing dragon, where she could not be drowned by the flood of lies from the dragon's mouth (Rev. 12:6, 13–16). Thus the angel carries John to the wilderness to place him out of reach of the allure of the harlot's deceptive appearance, so that he can see accurately and testify truthfully against her immorality and violence.[4] In the end Babylon will be turned from majestic city back into uninhabited wilderness, "a dwelling place of demons . . . and a prison of every unclean and hateful bird" (18:2).[5] In fact, the beast on which she rides will "make her desolate" (*erēmoō*, the cognate verb to *erēmos*, "wilderness"; 17:16). From this perspective the harlot city in the wilderness contrasts sharply with the great mountain from which John views the bride-city descending from heaven. For John and the church the wilderness combines physical suffering and spiritual safety; for Babylon, it is her destiny of desolation.[6]

---

3. Thus Caird rightly describes the harlot as far older than Rome, and Rome as "her latest and most powerful incarnation" (n. 1 above).

4. Caird, *Commentary*, 213: "Only from that place of security and detachment was it possible for him to see the seducer in her true colours. . . . Only there could he be safe from the lies of the dragon, the threats of the monster, and the seductions of the whore." See also Michael Wilcock, *I Saw Heaven Opened: The Message of Revelation*, TBST (Downers Grove, Ill.: InterVarsity Press, 1975), 160.

5. Isa. 13:19–22 predicts that Babylon, "the beauty of kingdoms," will be turned into a wasteland, inhabited only by desert creatures. The Hebrew word rendered "shaggy goats" (v. 21 NASB; margin: "goat demons") is translated "demons" in the LXX.

6. G. K. Beale, *The Book of Revelation*, NIGTC (Grand Rapids: Eerdmans, 1999), 852: "As in 12:6 and 12:13ff., the 'desert' has both positive and negative connota-

The woman sits on a scarlet beast, full of blasphemous names, with seven heads and ten horns (Rev. 17:3)—clearly the beast that John had seen earlier emerging from the sea (13:1), which spoke arrogant blasphemies against God and his heavenly court (13:5–6). The beast's color is now given: scarlet (*kokkinos*), a shade of red. Its color, as well as its seven heads and ten horns, shows that it is the image of the "great red [*purros*] dragon" (12:3). Scarlet also identifies the beast with the woman who rides him, for she is "clothed in purple and scarlet [*kokkinos*]" (17:4).

Babylon's clothing and accessories are indeed sumptuous (Rev. 17:4). Purple and scarlet[7] fabric (to which "fine linen" is added in 18:16) make up the raiment of royalty, so Roman soldiers threw a scarlet robe on Jesus' bleeding shoulders to mock his messianic claims (Matt. 27:28).[8] The fabrics and the gold, precious stones, and pearls that make up the harlot's ensemble provide a preview of the precious imports by which Rome enriches the merchants of the ancient world (Rev. 18:12). Her appetite for the finer things of life is voracious, so her fall will plunge the world's entrepreneurs into mourning for a once-thriving and insatiable consumer economy, now crashing all around them (18:11–17). Yet the harlot is also a counterfeit of the true wife of the Lamb, for John will also see the bride's beauty portrayed in the imagery of gold (21:21), precious stones (21:18–20), pearls (21:21), and fine linen (19:8, "bright and clean"—not scarlet or purple, but dazzlingly white, symbolizing her purity [3:4; 6:11; 7:13–14]).

The harlot's golden goblet is "full of abominations and of the unclean things of her immorality" (Rev. 17:4). "Abominations" expresses God's view of her idolatries, by which she makes the nations and their kings drunk (14:8; 17:2). The term has emotive impact because of its use in the construction "abomination of desolation," which first described the Syrian tyrant Antiochus IV's desecration of the Jerusalem

---

tions." He cites as a precedent Ezek. 20, which recalls the wilderness as the site of God's protection of Israel but also of Israel's rebellion.

7. Scarlet dresses, golden jewelry, and heavy eye shadow are also the tools of the ancient prostitute's trade to try to make herself attractive, according to Jer. 4:30.

8. Mark (15:17) and John (19:1–2) describe the robe as purple, the other royal color worn by the harlot.

temple in 168 B.C. (Dan. 9:27; 11:31) and then was used by Jesus when he prophesied the temple's destruction by Roman armies (Matt. 24:15).

The woman is labeled "Mystery: Babylon the Great, the mother of prostitutes and of the earth's abominations" (Rev. 17:5 dej). "Mystery" signifies that the woman is a visionary symbol that requires explicit interpretation, like the seven stars in the hand of the Son of Man (1:20). The angel will provide this interpretation, explaining the mystery to John (17:7). This woman represents fallen human culture in all the apparent glory of its achievement and the true repugnance of its arrogance. In John's day, seven-hilled Rome was her contemporary expression, but long before Rome arose and after Rome fell, the harlot Babylon was giving illegitimate birth to daughters like herself, seductive in appearance and repulsive in reality.[9]

The woman offers her disgusting cocktail to the kings and residents of the world, while she herself is "drunk with the blood of the saints . . . the witnesses of Jesus" (Rev. 17:6). Her seductive affluence and the beast's coercive violence are symbiotic; the nations bow to Rome not simply because its legions suppress insurrection (beast) but also because Rome's far-flung administrative efficiency maintains societal stability and economic prosperity (harlot). The threat of force and the allure of affluence work perfectly together, so of course Babylon celebrates the slaughter of Jesus' people, since they refuse to buy into her economic internet. Christians will not submit their thoughts and actions to the beast's sovereignty, symbolized in the mark on forehead or hand that is required of those who wish to profit in the world's system of financial exchange (13:16–17). Therefore the harlot delights in their martyrdom.

Babylon and the Beast Interpreted (17:7–18)

The sight of the harlot overwhelms John with amazement: "When I saw her, I marveled a great marvel" (Rev. 17:6 dej). Because the verb *marvel* (*thaumazō*, NASB "wonder") also describes unbelievers'

9. See Prov. 7:6–27; 9:13–18: Folly, the adulteress dressed as a brazen harlot, lures the naïve young man, promising love and feasting, but she draws him to his death, "as an ox goes to slaughter" (7:22). Her house is the gate of the grave (7:27).

adoring amazement at the beast (13:3; 17:8), some commentators infer that even in the desert, insulated from Satan's lies, John feels the appeal of the harlot's visual allure and luxury.[10] Although John's amazement elicits the rebuke expressed in the angel's question, "Why do you wonder?" (17:7), it is not likely that John would be attracted by this woman who is drunk on saints' blood, however stylish her wardrobe. His wonder is rather a blend of confusion and fear: What ominous enemy does this woman represent, and how can Christ's church endure her assault when all the world is in love with her, and when the beast on which she rides seems all-powerful? The same language of wonder (in the sense of horrified astonishment) describes Daniel's response to the impending judgment symbolized in King Nebuchadnezzar's dream of the great tree, cut down by God's command (Dan. 4:19 LXX).[11] The angel dispels John's perplexity and calms his anxiety by unlocking the mystery of the woman and the beast that carries her.

The symbiosis between woman and beast is so close that the revelation of the mysterious identity of the woman tells more about the beast and its impending defeat at the hands of the Lamb (Rev. 17:8–14) than it does about the woman and her impending destruction at the hands of the beast (17:15–18). The beast "was, and is not, and is about to come up out of the abyss and go to destruction" (17:8; cf. 17:11).[12] It is a negative image, a counterfeit of the true and living God, "who is and who was and who is to come" (1:4), and especially of the Son of Man, who is "the living One," once dead but now "alive forever-

10. Caird, *Commentary,* 213; Wilcock, *I Saw Heaven Opened,* 160. Beale, *Revelation,* 861–63, grants that admiration is probably a component of John's awestruck wonder at the harlot, though fear and perplexity are the dominant motifs.

11. Daniel was similarly alarmed and troubled by the vision of the four beasts and the Son of Man (Dan. 7:15), until his perplexity was relieved by an angel's interpretation.

12. In Rev. 13:3 John saw one of the beast's heads "as if it had been slain, and his fatal wound was healed"—possibly a reference to the seemingly fatal blow that had been dealt to Rome by Nero's disappearance and suicide, and the ensuing rivalries among military leaders, in the mid-60s. Again, though, John's main point seems to be that the beast offers its worshipers a fake, nonsaving alternative to the Lamb, who was indeed slain and now lives forever (Rev. 5:6).

more" (1:18). Scholars have interpreted the comment that the beast "is not, and is about to come up out of the abyss" and the later reference to seven kings, the sixth of whom is presently ruling (17:10), as signals pinpointing the specific date of composition.[13] We shall see, however, that this information does not lead to an unambiguous conclusion about the date of John's visions and writing.

One temporal indication is nevertheless clear. As John receives and writes his visions, the beast has not yet emerged from the abyss to wage war against Jesus' witnesses (Rev. 11:7). Although Rome already threatens the church with coercion and persecution, its oppressing power is still restrained in contrast to the coming day when the beast will come out of the pit with power not only to attack but also to "overcome" the saints (13:7). John has seen that day of climactic conflict as the gathering of earth's kings for the battle at Har-Magedon (16:13–16), and he will see it again as the day when the dragon is released for a short time to deceive the nations to gather them for the battle (20:7–8). The beast's ascent from the abyss and the dragon's release from the abyss will lead not to their victory but to their destruction.

As wisdom was required to crack the code of the beast's number and name (Rev. 13:18), so now "the mind which has wisdom" is needed interpret the beast's seven heads and ten horns (17:9).[14] In the flexibility of visionary symbolism, the seven heads stand for seven mountains and for seven kings. The seven mountains refer to the well-known geography of Rome's site.[15] But in prophetic imagery mountains are associated with great power or rule (Dan. 2:35, 44–45; cf. Rev. 14:1), and God had called ancient Babylon a "destroying mountain": "Behold, I am against you, O destroying mountain, who de-

---

13. See, for example, Moses Stuart, *A Commentary on the Apocalypse,* 2 vols. (London: Wiley and Putnam, 1845), 2:434–52, "Excursus III."

14. The beast's seven heads and ten horns make it resemble the dragon (Rev. 12:3; 13:1). Its ten horns are a detail derived from Daniel's description of the fourth beast (Rome) in his vision of the four beasts and the Son of Man (Dan. 7:7–8, 19–26). Beale also mentions that the total number of heads among the four beasts is seven, since the third beast has four heads (*Revelation,* 868).

15. R. H. Charles, *A Critical and Exegetical Commentary on the Revelation of St. John,* 2 vols., ICC (Edinburgh: T & T Clark, 1920), 2:69, cites references to Rome as "the city of seven hills" in Horace, Virgil, Martial, Cicero, and Propertius.

stroys the whole earth. . . . I will make you a burnt out mountain" (Jer. 51:24–25). So both mountains and kings symbolize the world-wide (sevenfold = comprehensive) authority given to the beast to rule "every tribe and people and tongue and nation" (Rev. 13:7).

Of the seven kings, "five have fallen, one is, the other has not yet come; and when he comes, he must remain a little while longer" (Rev. 17:10). The details of the description sound so specific that it seems to invite attempts to draw a one-to-one correlation with a series of particular kings (emperors) or kingdoms, since the four beasts in Daniel's vision are interpreted as four kings, though they plainly symbolize four kingdoms (Dan. 7:17).[16]

Various proposals have been offered on the supposition that the seven kings stand for seven Roman emperors, the sixth of whom is presumably on the throne as John writes. If the information supplied in Revelation 17:10 were intended to identify the reigning emperor, he could be anyone from Nero on into the early second century. This would depend on whether one begins with Julius Caesar, who was technically pre-imperial but founded the dynasty from which early emperors descended, or with Augustus, the first official emperor. It also depends on whether one includes all emperors or only those honored by the senate with posthumous deification and whether one omits or includes the three rivals who struggled for power in the year after Nero's death. Admittedly "a mind of wisdom" is needed to crack the code, but with so many variables yielding so many plausible alternatives, there is reason to question whether the purpose of the symbolism is to comment on political history, much less to locate John's visions within the chronology of first-century imperial succession.[17] Doubts about the political history interpretation increase when we

16. The Aramaic *malkin* ("kings") is translated *basileiai* ("kingdoms") in the LXX. In Dan. 7:23 the fourth beast is interpreted as a "kingdom" (*malku*) in the Aramaic original as well as the Greek of the LXX.

17. Various commentators list the emperors in order, with potential identifications of the five who have fallen, the one who is, and the seventh whose brief reign is yet future, depending on the variables mentioned above. Their general consensus is that, tempting though this history-of-emperors approach may be, in the end it is not sustainable. See, for example, G. R. Beasley-Murray, *The Book of Revelation*, NCB (Grand Rapids: Eerdmans, 1981), 257: "this whole procedure should be

meet the complications of Revelation 17:11, where we are told that the beast is both "one of the seven" (or "descended from the seven")[18] and an eighth king who will succeed the seventh, short-lived ruler.

The proposal that the seven (eight) "kings" are world kingdoms, particularly those that have conquered or will conquer the people of God, seems more promising at first. The sixth kingdom, which "is" as John writes, must be Rome, so five must precede it. Three of these must be those symbolized by the first three beasts of Daniel 7: Chaldeans, with ancient Babylon as their capital; the Medes and Persians; and the Greeks, including their Seleucid successors. The other two would perhaps include Egypt, which enslaved the Israelites before the exodus and is one of the symbolic names given the "great city" in Revelation 11:8. Sodom is the other name given the great city; yet Sodom, though notorious for immorality, was not a persecutor of God's people. Assyria, conqueror of the northern kingdom, would be a plausible nominee, since God indicts its capital, Nineveh, as a harlot and spreader of harlotry (Nahum 3:4). The kingdom interpretation falters, however, when we try to identify the seventh kingdom that will follow Rome and remain briefly, thereafter to be replaced by the beast. Which kingdom comes after Rome? Barbarian invaders from the north? Centuries later, Islam expanding from the southeast? Many centuries later, Nazism or communism? Or has this approach to the symbolism led us into another blind alley?

The solution to the puzzle may be simpler, if understanding the message of the seven or eight kings is not dependent on historiographic expertise: Seven symbolizes completeness, so it shows that the beast's

---

viewed as misguided. The symbolism of the beast's seven heads was not created by John to suit the Roman historical situation, but was an eschatological dogma with roots reaching into past millennia." Caird, *Commentary*, 218: "Since our problems [in identifying emperors] is not due to any lack of historical information, there is no reason to think that John's first-century readers would have been in any better case than we are. It is probable, therefore, that we have been looking for the wrong sort of solution. After all, John did not arrive at the number seven by counting emperors." See also Beale, *Revelation*, 870–76.

18. Beale, *Revelation*, 876, argues that the expression "of/from the seven" (*ek tōn hepta*) means that the beast is an offspring of the seven and thus shares their evil nature (cf. Rom. 9:10 for the same grammatical construction in this sense).

reign apparently holds sway over the whole history of fallen humanity. Yet from the perspective of God's plan to establish his kingdom
under the scepter of the Lamb, the beast's time is drawing short—five
out of seven already "have fallen." To be sure, John's readers are not
yet at the very end of the conflict of the ages. The one king who "has
not yet come" and must "remain a little while" shows that, though
the dragon has been decisively defeated by the blood of the Lamb and
therefore "has only a short time" (Rev. 12:11–12), nevertheless the
church must be prepared to endure further suffering.

The church must persevere not only under the pressure of present
levels of suffering (the seventh king) but also under the coming, crushing conspiracy of its enemies at the end (the beast to arise as an eighth
king). This final assault against the church by the dragon, the beast,
the false prophet, and their allies is pictured in various ways throughout Revelation: the emergence of the beast from the abyss to wage
war against the witnesses and overcome and kill them (11:7); the emergence of the beast from the sea to wage war against the saints and overcome them—killing those who refuse its mark (13:1, 7, 15); the gathering of the kings to wage the war of the great day of God, the
Almighty (16:13–16); the gathering of the beast with earth's kings and
residents to wage the war against the Word of God, who rides the
white horse, and his army (19:19); the dragon's "short time" of release from the abyss, when he will gather the nations for the war against
the camp of the saints and the beloved city (20:7–10, cf. vv. 1–3). In
our present text, this last battle is pictured in the future coming of the
beast out of the abyss as an eighth king, who belongs to the seven, at
least as the climactic expression of their arrogance toward God and
hostility toward his people. At its root every pagan world empire is
another incarnation of the same satanic spirit that will reach full intensity just before it shatters before the glory of the Lamb and "goes
to destruction" (17:8, 11). The final conspiracy is also symbolized in
the ten kings (ten horns) who receive authority with the beast "for
one hour,"[19] for the sole purpose of putting that authority at the beast's

19. "One hour" will recur in the laments over Babylon to emphasize the rapid-
ity of her plummet from queenly glory and supremacy to ruin and shame (Rev.
18:10, 16, 19).

251

disposal as it launches its last desperate assault on the Lamb and his "called and chosen and faithful" followers (17:12–14). The camera angles on this last battle vary as we move from Revelation 12 to Revelation 20, but the story line they tell is consistent. Jesus' followers must be prepared for a period of unparalleled, intense persecution at the end, when evil forces now restrained will be released to work their worst against the church. Yet that time of trauma will be brief, and our enemies' final conspiracy will end not in the downfall of the church, as they expect, but in their destruction.

What will become of the harlot Babylon, whose judgment John was to see (Rev. 17:1)? Now she "sits" enthroned over the world's peoples, multitudes, nations, and tongues. She controls them in her arrogant confidence, through the heart-stealing seduction of her promises of prosperity and through the brute force of the beast's military might (17:15).[20] But when the dragon's worldwide web of wickedness starts to unravel, the harlot will be the first casualty: the beast and its military allies "will hate the harlot and make her desolate and naked, and will eat her flesh and will burn her up with fire" (17:16). This gruesome end includes elements of covenant curse that God declared would come to his wife, Israel, because she had played the harlot:

> I will gather all your lovers with whom you took pleasure. . . . I will gather them against you from every direction and expose your nakedness to them. . . . I will also give you into the hands of your lovers, and they will tear down your shrines, demolish your high places, strip you of your clothing, take away your jewels, and will leave you naked and bare. . . . They will stone you and cut you to pieces with their swords. They will burn your houses with fire and execute judgments on you. (Ezek. 16:37–41)

So "the great city, which reigns over the kings of the earth" (Rev. 17:18), will be plundered, helpless, exposed to the shame of nakedness, dismantled and consumed by the paramours whom she seduced

---

20. In Rev. 13:7 John saw that the beast was given authority over "every tribe and people and tongue and nation." "Tribe" (*phylē*) is replaced by "multitudes" (*ochloi*) in 17:15, but the allusion to the beast's domain is unmistakable.

and intoxicated in her prime. Satan's kingdom will be divided against itself and will not stand. Forces of violence and bloodshed, on which Roman culture and all man-centered cultures rely for the stability that makes commerce (18:11–16), transportation (18:17–19), music and the arts (18:22), and everyday domestic life possible (18:23), will turn on the civilization they have sustained and attack it. Like the beast it is, the beast will turn on the harlot and tear her limb from limb.

The irony of Babylon's fall magnifies the incomparable power and wisdom of God. The beast and its allies, raging in hostility toward the Lamb and his bride, will be the weapons that God uses to bring down the harlot, who was once the beast's royal consort. "For God has put it in their hearts to execute His purpose by having a common purpose, and by giving their kingdom to the beast, until the words of God will be fulfilled" (17:17). If there is one thing in all the world that the rebels do not want to do, it is the purpose of God. But they are helpless to keep that sovereign purpose out of their hearts, to protect their minds from invasion by the Lord God Almighty. In doing what they want to do, hating the harlot and ripping her to pieces, they are doing precisely what God wants. And in gathering to wage their war against the Messiah, they are merely assembling for their own execution.

The Glorious Angel:
Babylon's Fall Celebrated in Heaven (18:1–3)

Revelation 18 is dominated by two angels and "another voice from heaven," who interpret the significance of Babylon's catastrophic fall. The first angel, who descends from heaven with great authority and a brilliant glory that lights up the earth (18:1), repeats and expands the earlier angelic proclamation of Babylon's fall (18:2–3; cf. 14:8). The voice from heaven affirms the justice of God in destroying Babylon, quoting the laments of kings and merchants to demonstrate her lethal seductiveness (18:4–19) and calling God's people to separate themselves from Babylon's pollution and to celebrate her fall, which is their vindication (18:4, 20). The second angel illustrates Babylon's downfall by hurling a millstone into the sea, declaring that when God's covenant curse falls on "the great city," all that makes the city emblematic of human culture and achievement—music, craftsmanship, food preparation, domestic life, and commerce—will cease (18:21–24).

The angel whose glory illuminates the earth repeats the death-knell refrain first declared by the second of three herald angels in Revelation 14:8: "Fallen, fallen is Babylon the great." As we have seen, the wording comes directly from Isaiah's oracle concerning the wilderness of the sea, against ancient Babylon (Isa. 21:9). The great city's fall will make her an uninhabitable ruin, no longer a metropolis full of human life and culture but a ghost town where only demons, unclean spirits, and unclean birds live (Rev. 18:2). Through ancient prophets God had declared that his judgments would turn proud pagan cities into wastelands, occupied only by desert beasts, birds, and demons (Isa. 13:21–22; 34:11–15). The focus of this angel's proclamation of doom is on Babylon's destiny as a prison of demons and unclean spirits. Of course, even in her heyday of popularity, pleasure, and power, Babylon has been a culture permeated with demons. The "wine of the passion (or wrath) of her immorality," by which she seduces world rulers (Rev. 18:3), is another perspective on the work of the false prophet, who deceives earth dwellers into worshiping the beast (13:14), and the mission of the frog demons, which gather the kings for destruction (16:13–14). Today Babylon looks to John's readers like a confident and beautiful queen, a city teeming with energetic activity and overflowing with the good things of life. In reality, however, Babylon is even now a hag, a hollow husk, and the haunt of demons, defilement, and death. That inward reality will become outwardly visible at Babylon's fall, when her mask is torn away.

The Other Voice:
Babylon's Fall Lamented on Earth (18:4–20)

Further divine commentary on Babylon's fall comes from "another voice in heaven," which calls God's people to stay separate from Babylon's sins in view of her impending judgment (Rev. 18:4). Looking back to the exodus from Egypt, Isaiah foresaw a future exodus from exile and showed Israel that God's promise of deliverance entails his summons to separate from all that defiles:

> Depart, depart, go out from there,
> Touch nothing unclean;
> Go out of the midst of her, purify yourselves,
> You who carry the vessels of the LORD.
>   (Isa. 52:11, cf. 52:4; 2 Cor. 6:17)

Three times in the doom oracle against Babylon in Jeremiah 51 God calls his people out: "Flee from the midst of Babylon, and each of you save his life!" (51:6); "Forsake her and let us each go to his own country" (51:9); and, "Come forth from her midst, My people, and each of you save yourselves from the fierce anger of the LORD" (51: 45). Dalliance with Babylon's sins will bring affliction with her plagues, for God's justice cannot be mocked.

The voice particularly extols the justice of God in rendering equitable retribution to Babylon, punishment that balances and befits the magnitude of her offenses. The sky-high compost pillar of her sins has not escaped God's notice, for he "has remembered her iniquities" (Rev. 18:5; cf. 16:19). The new covenant promise that God will "remember no more" the sins of his people assures us of both forgiveness and release from punishment (Jer. 31:34). By contrast, the assurance that God "remembers" Babylon's sins means that he holds her fully accountable, so that her punishment is inescapable.

Babylon will be repaid in kind and quantity for her contempt for God, her seduction of the nations, and her violence against the church: "Pay her back even as she has paid. . . . To the degree that she glorified herself and lived sensuously, to the same degree give her torment and mourning" (18:6–7). This principle of strict *lex talionis*, eye-for-eye equity is reinforced in Revelation 18:6b, which should be translated, "Give back to her a duplicate of her deeds; in the cup which she has mixed, mix an *equivalent* for her to drink" (dej). The Greek words (*diploō, diplous*) usually translated "a double portion" or "twice as much" (NIV, NASB) do not mean that Babylon will receive twice the judgment that she deserves in the light of her deeds but that her judgment will be the duplicate that exactly corresponds to the severity of her offenses.[21] This is precisely what Revelation 18:6a, 7a assert: that the same measure used by Babylon to torment others will be used to mete out her torment, and the height of her haughty arrogance will be equaled by the depth of her descent into shame. Her cup was full of martyrs' blood (17:6), and with her fall "God has avenged the blood of His bond-servants on her" (19:2).

She smugly boasts of her security, "I sit as a queen and I am not a widow" (Rev. 18:7). In this boast she echoes ancient Babylon, "queen of kingdoms" (Isa. 47:5), who boasted, "I will be a queen forever. . . . I am, and there is no one besides me. I will not sit as a widow, nor know loss of children" (47:7–8). Sadly, the church at Laodicea exhibits the same blind self-satisfaction (Rev. 3:17). The Creator, who alone is self-sufficient, will not let such empty boasts by mere creatures and their institutions stand unchallenged. Just as "in one day" he brought ancient Babylon to the desolation of childless widowhood (Isa. 47:9), so "in one day" he will bring plagues of lethal epidemic, mourning, famine,[22] and fire on the world system that expressed itself in the ancient Chaldean empire, and in Rome in John's day, and in various other forms since then (Rev. 18:8).

The drama of Babylon's freefall, from a beauty admired by all into a horror repugnant to all, is now underscored by a chorus of laments from kings (Rev. 18:9–10), merchants (18:11–17a), and seamen (18:17b–19). Kings had been seduced by Babylon's strength ("Babylon, the strong city!" 18:10), and entrepreneurs had profited from her voracious consumer appetite ("no one buys their cargoes any more," 18:11; "all who had ships at sea became rich by her wealth," 18:19). Now her destruction spells their ruin as well.

The extensive list of imports that will no longer flow into Babylon (Rev. 18:12–13; cf. 18:16) throws the spotlight on Rome's voracious materialistic consumerism. This list is reminiscent of the catalogue in

21. M. G. Kline, "Double Trouble," *JETS* 32 (1989): 171–79, demonstrates that the Hebrew terms standing behind the LXX's *diplous* in Isa. 40:2; Jer. 16:18, when interpreted in context, refer to equivalent retribution, not double punishment.

22. In Rev. 6:8 the riders on the ashen horse, Death and Hades, had power to kill people with sword, famine, "pestilence" (as in 18:8, *thanatos* ["death"] here refers to epidemic disease, probably specifically the bubonic plague), and wild beasts.

Ezekiel 27, which names nations and cities that do business with the Phoenician merchant navy controlled by Tyre, identifying each customer with categories of goods bought or sold: metals, slaves, beasts of burden and warfare, ivory and ebony, precious stones and fine fabrics, foods and spices, sheep and goats, garments and carpets (Ezek. 27:12–25). Although trade in slaves occurs early in Ezekiel (27:13), in Revelation commerce in human flesh is the last of Babylon's imports, the culmination of a decadent culture's ruthless pursuit of pleasure, whatever the cost to others (18:13).[23] The heavenly voice concludes the catalogue of imports with a commentary addressed to Babylon directly: "The fruit of your soul's desire left you, and all things luxurious and luminous[24] disappeared from you, and they will find them no more" (18:14 dej). Babylon's appetite for the world's rich resources will go unsatisfied, so the merchants who have supplied her wants and fed her whims will stand apart from her, viewing in fear and mourning as the super consumer is consumed in flames (18:15). Their lament recalls the sumptuous clothing and jewelry in which she had first appeared to John's view (18:16; 17:4), expressing shock at how rapidly ("in one hour") the rich city had been reduced to poverty (18:17a), just as earth's kings had lamented that the strong city had fallen before her divine Judge "in one hour" (18:10; cf. 18:8).

Representatives of the transportation industry—pilots, passengers, sailors, dockworkers, ship owners—join the lament as the smoke of Babylon rises over her ruins (Rev. 18:17b-19). They too have lost livelihoods and the hope of profit through Babylon's sudden fall. They echo the rhetorical question earlier uttered by the beast's adoring worshipers: "Who is like the beast?" (13:4). That question was a pre-

23. "Slaves and human lives" (NASB) reflects Greek that would be translated more literally "bodies" and "souls of men." In the Greek syntax, "bodies" is grouped with "horses and chariots" (all three in the genitive case), reinforcing the dehumanizing view and treatment of human slaves as mere means of production, "thinking tools" or "speaking tools," as some ancients called them.

24. "Luxurious and luminous" seems to capture both the meaning and the alliterative flow of the Greek adjectives that are joined here, *lipara* and *lampra*. The second adjective, *lampros* (NASB "splendid"), refers to visual brightness elsewhere in Revelation (15:6; 19:8; 22:1, especially 22:16) and the New Testament (Luke 23:11; Acts 10:30).

sumptuous parody of Moses' affirmation that the Lord, who sets his people free, is truly incomparable: "Who is like You, . . . majestic in holiness, awesome in praises, working wonders?" (Exod. 15:11). Now the praises of the beast's and the harlot's adherents have turned sour in shocked disillusionment. "Who is like the great city?"[25] (Rev. 18:18) is no longer a proud declaration of human self-confidence but a cry of shocked perplexity, for the megalopolis has been turned into wasteland, into wilderness.[26]

The lament of earth dwellers, whose hopes—fixed on nothing more than human power and culture—are dashed, evokes rejoicing in heaven (Rev. 18:20). Saints and apostles and prophets may celebrate Babylon's fall, "because God has pronounced judgment for you against her." The difficult Greek syntax behind this clause probably means, "God has inflicted on her the judgment you received from her."[27] The martyrs' blood is vindicated as Babylon receives a duplicate of violence that she unjustly inflicted on Jesus' holy and faithful witnesses.

The Strong Angel: Babylon's Fall Enacted (18:21–24)

The strong angel's act of throwing a great millstone into the sea shows that Babylon's fall is permanent and irremediable (Rev. 18:21). Jeremiah had been instructed to write on a scroll the calamities that were to come on Babylon and then to tie the scroll to a stone and throw it into the Euphrates, the river in which Babylon prided herself, declaring, "Just so shall Babylon sink down and not rise again be-

25. NASB: "What [city] is like the great city?" is semantically accurate but obscures the syntactic parallelism between the questions of Rev. 13:4 and 18:18: *tis homoios tō thēriō* (13:4); *tis homoia tē polei* (18:18). Note also the Old Testament background in Ezek. 27:32: "In their wailing they will take up a lamentation for you and lament over you: 'Who is like Tyre, like her who is silent in the midst of the sea?'"

26. The verb translated "laid waste" (NASB) in Rev. 18:17, 19 is a passive voice form of *erēmoō*, cognate to the noun *erēmos* "wilderness" (see comments on 17:1; 18:2 above).

27. Caird, *Commentary*, 228, cites Old Testament laws demanding life for life not only in the case of murder (Gen. 9:5–6) but also in the case of a malicious witness who falsely accuses another of a capital crime (Deut. 19:16–19). He proposes as a translation of our text: "God has imposed on her the sentence she passed on you."

258

cause of the calamity that I am going to bring upon her" (Jer. 51:60–64). In John's vision the weight of the millstone, a massive boulder turned slowly by oxen to grind grain, underscores the impossibility of Babylon's rising from the depths of the sea of judgment in which she is submerged, never to be found again (cf. Ezek. 26:21).[28]

The strong angel further comments that Babylon's fall will remove not only her economic and religious hegemony over the nations but also the sounds and sights associated with everyday life, wherever human beings live in community. The melodies and harmonies of musical instruments will not be heard in Babylon. Their silence is a sign of covenant curse (Isa. 24:8; cf. Ezek. 26:13). Craftsmen no longer ply their trades. G. K. Beale suggests plausibly that the absence of craftsmen, a detail apparently not derived from an Old Testament prophecy, is in retribution for the ostracism of Christians from the trade guilds, the backbone of manufacturing in the Roman Empire.[29] The sound of the mill grinding grain will no longer be heard, nor will the voice of groom and bride, and the light of a lamp will not shine (Rev. 18:22–23). These details are all drawn from Jeremiah's prophecy of ancient Babylon's destruction: "I will take from them the voice of joy and the voice of gladness, the voice of the bridegroom and the voice of the bride, the sound of the millstones and the light of the lamp" (Jer. 25:10; cf. 7:34; 16:9). The silence of the mill (*mulos*) corresponds with the casting of the millstone (*mulinos*) into the sea, but it also speaks of Babylon's devastation, leaving neither grain to be ground nor a miller to grind it.

The strong angel, like the glorious angel and the voice from heaven before him, emphasizes the strict justice of God in casting Babylon from its height of affluence and culture down to the depths. The reasons for the great city's fall are clear: she misled the nations and slaughtered prophets and saints. The harlot's cup, brimming with the wine of immorality by which she intoxicated earth's kings and peoples (Rev. 17:2, 4), is now interpreted as the sorcery by which she deceived the nations.

---

28. When Jesus states that one who causes a child to "stumble" can expect worse punishment than being tied to a millstone and tossed into the sea's depths, his assumption is that there is no escape from the millstone in the sea—much less will there be for anyone who leads a believing child into sin! (Matt. 18:6).

29. Beale, *Revelation*, 919–20. See chapter 4, especially the letter to Thyatira.

It is as if the harlot Babylon is a worldwide magnification of the Jezebel in Thyatira, who lured the naïve into immorality and idolatry, into the deep things of Satan (2:20, 24). To say it another way, the Thyatiran prophetess is a concrete local expression of the worldwide, history-long threat symbolized in the harlot, the subtle pressure to cultural conformity and the seductive rewards it brings in financial and social security.

Again, however, the harlot's seduction of willing admirers is not the great city's worst offense. She deserves what she will receive from the wrathful hand of God because "in her was found the blood of the prophets and of saints and of all who have been slain on the earth" (Rev. 18:24). When John first heard of "the great city which mystically is called Sodom and Egypt," the corpses of Jesus' faithful witnesses lay in her streets, slain by the beast from the abyss (11:8). When John first saw her, she was drunk with the blood of the saints, the witnesses of Jesus (17:6). Her promise of influence to those who wish to be "the great men of the earth" (18:23) and her promise of wealth to those who sell themselves to her values and play her game make her outwardly appealing. But all she is and has rests on the bloodthirsty ruthlessness of the beast, and the gifts she promises to her lovers are purchased with the blood of God's faithful prophets and witnesses, and "of all who have been slain on the earth"—every helpless victim who stood in the way of her insatiable cravings and was therefore eliminated.

The Great Multitude:
God's Justice and Reign Celebrated in Heaven (19:1–10)

Suddenly John hears the response of heaven's residents to the invitation in Revelation 18:20: "Rejoice over her, O heaven, and you saints and apostles and prophets." Peal after peal of praises breaks out in celebration of the display of God's justice in the destruction of the harlot. A great multitude in heaven shouts, "Hallelujah!" extolling God for demonstrating that "his judgments are true and righteous" by avenging, at last, the blood of his servants (19:1–2). Both their description as "a great multitude" and the salvation theme that opens their praise imply that this choir is the international assembly of victors who had emerged from the great affliction into their heavenly refuge in Revelation 7:11–17.[30] They sing, "Hallelujah"—Praise the Lord! This Hebrew imperative appears in each of the Hallel Psalms (Ps. 113–18) and elsewhere in the Psalter (note especially Ps. 104:35), but in the New Testament it occurs in Greek transliteration only in its fourfold use in this text (Rev. 19:1, 3, 4, 6).

The reason for the multitude's praises to God is the establishment of his justice in the overthrow of the harlot, for now "He has avenged the blood of his bond-servants on her" (Rev. 19:2). No longer must the souls of those slain for the word of God cry out, "How long, O Lord, . . . will you refrain from avenging our blood?" (6:10).[31] With the pouring of the third bowl, the altar that bore witness to their suffering affirmed that God's judgments are "true and righteous" (16:7), and the detailed commentary on Babylon's fall in Revelation 17–18, expanding on the brief description in 16:17–21, has demonstrated the truth of the altar's confession.

The multitude's second "Hallelujah" celebrates the perpetual rising of Babylon's smoke (Rev. 19:3). This occasion for rejoicing may strike our postmodern ears as especially vindictive, as if the saints' eternal joy is enhanced by eternally witnessing Babylon's punishment. We should note, however, that this reference to Babylon's smoke rising "forever and ever" is yet another Old Testament allusion (Isa. 34:10). In the context of the preceding verse (Rev. 19:2), Babylon's smoke serves as an ongoing testimony to God's zeal for justice on behalf of his persecuted church. The assertion that the smoke "rises up forever and ever" carries the same message as the millstone cast into the sea (18:21): When the day of judgment comes, judgment will be irreversible. The implication that Babylon's smoke ascends eternally ("forever and ever") is prophetic hyperbole, as later statements in Revelation make clear. Ultimately God promises a complete removal of the

---

30. "Multitude" (*ochlos*) appears in the singular in Revelation only in 7:9; 19:1, 6 (once in the plural in 17:15). Both multitudes joyfully affirm that "salvation . . . belongs to our God."

31. The verb *avenge* (*ekdikeō*) appears in Revelation only in 6:10 and 19:2, linking these passages closely to each other. Of course, the concept that God will repay with violence those who have done violence to his saints occurs often (16:5–7; 18:4–8, 20, 24). The wording of 19:2 especially is reminiscent of the invitation to celebration at the end of Moses' song of covenant witness (Deut. 32:43).

"first heaven and earth" (20:11; 21:1), and with them God's curse against human sin, with all its adverse effects (21:4; 22:3). Babylon, the man-centered substructure of civilization, grounded in brute force and intoxicated by idolatrous adoration of pleasure and possessions, belongs to this old cosmic order for which "no place is found" when the new heavens and earth appear.

In response the members of God's heavenly court—the twenty-four elders and four living creatures who worship before the throne (Rev. 4:8–11; cf. 7:11; 11:16–18)—now add their "Hallelujah!" to those of God's redeemed and vindicated people (19:4). A voice from the throne summons all God's servants, small and great, to worship their triumphant champion (19:5).

Another voice, deafening in its resonance, celebrates the arrival of the kingdom and the marriage of the Lamb (Rev. 19:6–8). The majesty of this voice is reinforced by a threefold simile: "like the voice [*phōnē*] of a great multitude," "like the voice [*phōnē*] of many waters," "like the voice [*phōnē*] of strong thunders" (dej). Through these comparisons the voice is identified with the "great multitude" of redeemed saints (7:9; 19:1), with the voice of the Son of Man (1:15)—which is the voice of the Almighty, as the allusion to Ezekiel's "the sound of many waters" shows (Ezek. 1:24; 43:2)—and with the thunderous theophany at Mount Sinai (Rev. 4:5; 8:5; 11:19; Exod. 19:16). Yet this mighty speaker is neither God nor the Lamb but merely John's fellow servant, unworthy of the worship that belongs to God alone (Rev. 19:10). The voice's "Hallelujah!" celebrates the fact that "the Lord our God, the Almighty has begun his royal rule" (Rev. 19:6 dej). The verbal form translated "reigns" by NASB (*ebasileusen*) is not in the present/progressive tense/aspect, as though it were simply affirming the eternal truth of God's sovereignty. The aorist tense of this verb signals the initiation of God's rule, the establishment of his redemptive and eschatological kingdom in its full and final phase, with the subjection of all his enemies and rivals.[32] Thus this announcement re-

---

32. Especially in the case of stative verbs, which refer to an ongoing condition or activity, the selection of the aorist tense rather than a progressive tense (present or imperfect) often indicates the commencement of the ongoing state (inceptive aorist). *Basileuō* ("to rule or reign") is such a stative verb.

capitulates the heavenly praises that break forth when the seventh trumpet is sounded: "The kingdom of the world has become the kingdom of our Lord and of His Christ. . . . You have taken Your great power and have begun to reign" (11:15, 17).[33] God has always been the almighty Creator whose will cannot be thwarted (4:11), even by evil forces hostile to his authority (17:17). That truth, however, has not always been evident throughout history as the nations have raged in tumult against the Creator and his Messiah (Ps. 2:1–2; Rev. 11:18). At history's end this mighty voice declares that all will see that God's rule without rival has arrived.

With the kingdom comes the wedding. With the destruction of the harlot comes the presentation of the bride (19:7–9). John's vision of the bride will not occur until Revelation 21:9; but, as the harlot was first mentioned in 14:8 and then revealed in 17:1, so the bride is announced before her entrance. The heavenly celebration is not primarily backward looking, exulting over fallen enemies; it is forward looking, anticipating the consummation of love between God's people and the Lamb, their bridegroom. The bride's identification as symbolic of God's faithful followers is seen from the start in the "fine linen, bright and clean" that is given her as her wedding dress. This pure linen is reminiscent of the white robes given the martyrs as they await their vindication (6:11) and celebrate their salvation (7:9, 13–14). It pictures "the righteous acts of the saints," accomplished through faith in the Lamb, in faithfulness to the Lamb (19:8). Such "righteous acts," if referring to the believers' obedient actions and pursuit of spiritual purity,[34] are not our personal achievement. This fine linen wedding garment is given to the bride by her Groom, as the background in Isaiah 61:10 makes clear:

33. NASB correctly reflects the inceptive implication of the aorist form, *ebasileusas*, in Rev. 11:17: "you . . . have begun to reign." The aorist form of the same verb in 19:6 conveys the same inceptive force and should be similarly translated.

34. Beale, *Revelation*, 934–38, points out that *ta dikaiōmata tōn hagiōn*, traditionally understood as "righteous deeds performed by the saints," could also be interpreted as "[God's] righteous actions on behalf of the saints," that is, vindicating the saints.

I will rejoice greatly in the LORD,
My soul will exult in my God;
For He has clothed me with garments of salvation,
He has wrapped me with a robe of righteousness,
As a bridegroom decks himself with a garland,
And as a bride adorns herself with her jewels.

The voice now instructs John to inscribe the fourth of Revelation's seven benedictions: "Blessed are those who are invited to the marriage supper of the Lamb" (19:9). The culmination of God's redemptive plan is often pictured in Scripture as a feast overflowing with joy and rich food and drink (Isa. 25:6–9; see Luke 14:15–24). Through the prophets God promised another wedding day in which he would clasp his bride to himself with joy and passion, despite Israel's past infidelities (Isa. 62:4–5). Weddings and feasting belong together (Matt. 22:1–14), and the blessed guests who are invited to the Lamb's wedding feast are themselves included in the bride who is so honored by her Husband's love.

John is so thunderstruck by the mighty voice and the message of indescribable joy that he falls down to worship the messenger—and is soundly rebuked (Rev. 19:10)! This is the second rebuke that John has received in the section concerning Babylon's fall.[35] He is not to marvel at Babylon's apparent wealth and power (17:7), nor is he now to worship God's messenger as though he were God. As divine as his voice sounds ("the sound of many waters" = the voice of the Almighty), the angel will not let John respond to him on the basis of appearances but will confront John with the truth. The angel is a mere fellow servant of John and of all who cling to the testimony of Jesus. Unlike the beast, the false prophet, the harlot, and the dragon who backs them all, this faithful servant of God will not tolerate any worshiping of himself, a creature, instead of the Creator. God alone is to be worshiped, and the prophecy that this messenger has delivered to

35. A similar interchange occurs at the conclusion of the vision of the bride, the wife of the Lamb. John attempts to worship the angel who has shown him the holy city, new Jerusalem, and has pronounced the sixth benediction; and again the angel rebukes him, identifying himself as John's fellow servant and commanding, "Worship God" (Rev. 22:7–9).

John by the Spirit[36] is a testimony that comes ultimately from Jesus, the faithful and true Witness (3:14) and the true Word of God (19:13; cf. 19:19).

Conclusion

The beauty that turns people's heads is often no more than skin-deep. Through John's prophetic eye we have seen that this is true not only of people but also of civilizations and cultural institutions. In John's day Rome seemed unchallengeable in military and political dominance and unsurpassable in economic vitality. Before Rome, Egypt, Assyria, Babylon, Persia, Greece, and other empires had had their day in the sun. After Rome, other world powers would rise to wield influence through conquest, diplomacy, trade, or intellectual achievement. Then they too disappear. Finally the harlot Babylon, in all her institutional reincarnations down through history, will be shaken to ruins by God's final earthquake and put to the torch by the same violent forces that once sustained her affluent lifestyle. Jesus' churches need to see clearly through the appearances, to discover that the world system that promises pleasure and prosperity now in exchange for our allegiance and integrity is more beast than beauty, intent on our destruction, not our fulfillment.

Which is the dragon's more dangerous weapon as he assaults the church in our time and place: Is it the beast, symbolic of the state's power to intimidate through violent persecution and even martyrdom? Or the beauty, the harlot, portrait of the culture's power to seduce through the intoxicating idolatry of prosperity and the alluring invitation to adulterous compromise? Through John's vision of the harlot's pseudo-glory and her devastating fall, the church should be forearmed against her wiles and stirred with longing for God's ulti-

---

36. Although most versions and many commentators take "spirit" in "the spirit of prophecy" as impersonal, rather than a direct reference to the Holy Spirit, in Revelation the role of the Spirit in initiating prophetic vision and authorizing the prophet's commission makes the personal interpretation, "the Spirit who brings prophecy," more probable (see 1:10; 4:2; 17:3; 21:10; and the discussion of these texts in chapter 2).

mate justice and the consummation of his courtship with the true beauty, the bride of the Lamb. This bride is the church that we now see embattled on the earth, in which we live each day. On that great wedding day she—we—will be clothed with radiant linen, a robe of righteousness, the gift of our divine Groom and Protector, whose victory over the harlot's allies—beast, false prophet, and dragon—John is about to see.

CHAPTER THIRTEEN

Cosmic Conflict 2:
The Thousand Years and the Last Battle
(19:11–20:15)

Exeunt Villains

Those who have read through a play by Shakespeare may vaguely recognize the archaic term *Exeunt*. It is a stage direction, signaling that multiple characters are to leave the stage at that point in the script. If one actor leaves the scene, he or she exits. If more than one, they exeunt. We have reached the scenes in the grand drama of Revelation in which the villains leave the stage, for God has written the harlot, the beasts, and the dragon out of the script. John is shown that climax in the plot when their power to afflict the church comes to an end, and they have no future in the new heavens and earth that God has promised to his faithful witnesses.

The conflict that leads to the complete establishment of God's kingdom began with the pregnancy of the heavenly woman and the menace of the first and primal enemy: a great red dragon waiting to devour her child (Rev. 12:1–2). The woman and her newborn son seem defenseless before so strong and fierce a foe, yet that vision shows that God keeps his promise to Eve, Israel, and David: the dragon, the ancient serpent, meets his match in the woman's male child, who ascends to God's throne to commence his rule of the nations with a rod of iron (12:5). From that opening scene other villains, coconspirators with the dragon-serpent, were introduced: a beast emerging from the sea, encompassing in itself the terrifying power and ruthlessness of the oppressive pagan empires of the past (13:1–10). Then a second beast appears out of the land, a false prophet who deceives the world's peoples into worshiping the first beast and submitting to his dominion (13:11–18). Finally, the harlot Babylon is unveiled, and her attractive affluence wins the world's devotion (17:1–7). As the villains spring onto the stage of "the drama of history,"[1] they seem poised to overpower the struggling church in the world. The dragon, though prevented from destroying the Child or the heavenly woman, wages war on the rest of her children (12:17). The sea beast not only has authority over all the world's peoples but also attacks the saints and overcomes them (13:7). The earth beast "causes all, the small and the great, and the rich and the poor, and the free men and the slaves," to receive the mark that signifies their submission to the sea beast in thought and in deed (13:16). The harlot sits on the waters, symbolizing her influence over "peoples and multitudes and nations and tongues" (17:15). Who could withstand, much less conquer, this devilish quartet?

With the vision of Babylon and her destruction, however, the tide of the war on earth begins to turn. These four villains, the dragon and the puppet powers by which he tries to intimidate, deceive, and beguile the church, are disposed of one by one. They exeunt the stage in reverse order from their entrances. The dragon appeared first, then the beasts, then the harlot. Now the harlot has already met her end (Rev. 17:16–19:6).[2] John will receive two visions of the last battle: the

1. Michael Wilcock, *I Saw Heaven Opened: The Message of Revelation,* TBST (Downers Grove, Ill.: InterVarsity Press, 1975), 110, sums up the theme of Rev. 11:19–15:4 with this title. He helpfully approaches the book as a whole under a theatrical metaphor, suggesting that the "openings" of heaven mark the major "scene changes" in the script of John's visions.

2. Here especially it is crucial to keep in mind the distinction between the literary order of the visions and the historical-chronological order of the events to which the visions refer. The series of visions given in Rev. 17:1–20:15 all provide different camera angles or perspectives on the completion of the wrath of God against his enemies, symbolized in the seven bowls of Rev. 16. The meltdown of civilization,

first focusing on the fate of the beasts when they gather earth's forces for the final war against the Lamb's army (19:11–21), and the second as a video replay, as it were, of that conflict, with the camera focused on the defeat of the dragon (20:7–10).[3]

What has produced this surprising plot turn, with God's enemies falling from power and influence into destruction and Jesus' witnesses rising from hopeless defeat into glorious victory? We have seen that Babylon's comrades in crime, the beast and the world's kings, will be the weapons used to dismantle the great city, as they turn on her in poetic justice, stripping her naked, eating her flesh, burning her with fire (Rev. 17:16–17). But how will the beast be brought to justice? And what of the ultimately demonic power behind the institutional expressions of human hostility against God and idolatrous devotion to false gods? Who is strong enough to destroy the dragon? The heavenly woman's son, whose ascent to heaven at the turning point in history's cosmic conflict effected Satan's expulsion from heaven and descent to earth (12:5, 7–9), will reappear from heaven at the consummation of the conflict. Then he will appear not as a vulnerable infant but as the divine Warrior and anointed King, mounted on a white war horse and ready to rule the nations with a rod of iron (19:11, 15).

The Champion: Faithful and True, Word of God, Lord of Lords (19:11–16)

As at earlier points in Revelation, a new vision cycle begins as John sees heaven opened. When John was called to enter the door opened

---

commerce, and arts symbolized in Babylon's fall will essentially coincide (historically-chronologically) with the last battle in which the beasts and the dragon meet their doom.

3. The chiastic or mirror-image ordering of the characters' introductions and destinies in the drama of Rev. 12–20 is shown in Vern S. Poythress, *The Returning King: A Guide to the Book of Revelation* (Phillipsburg, N.J.: P&R Publishing, 2000), 64–65. This feature of John's visions of the cosmic conflict, in which characters are introduced into the drama in one order and then dismissed in the opposite order, corresponds to the literary devices of chiasm or inverted verbal parallelism that appear on a smaller scale throughout Revelation. See, for example, chapter 2, notes 25 and 27.

in heaven to view the enthroned One and the Lamb (4:1–2), he glimpsed God's purposes at work in providential control of the traumas and forces of history (seals, trumpets). When the temple of God in heaven was opened (11:19), it was the prelude to visions exposing the deep, cosmic conflict that lies behind the changing tides of political and social trends and events (heavenly woman and child, dragon, beasts). When the sanctuary of the tent of testimony in heaven was opened (15:5), the completion of God's wrath destroyed earth's deluded and defiant residents (bowls, harlot). Now in the opened heaven John sees the victorious champion of the church: Jesus the Son of Man, the faithful and true Witness, the Word of God, the messianic King, the Lamb, the Lord of lords and King of kings.

Jesus' appearance, names, and companions call believers to rest our hope confidently and completely in his almighty power to vindicate his saints and eradicate his enemies. The presentation of his appearance begins with the white horse on which he is mounted (19:11). As we saw in the victory parade granted to Julius Caesar upon his return from a successful campaign and the first rider, Conquest, in Revelation 6, white horses symbolize triumphant military achievement.[4] Even before John's eyes are lifted from the mount to its rider, we are assured that this Warrior will win. "His eyes are a flame of fire" (19:12), as they were when he appeared as "one like a son of man" (1:14). None can hide from his heart–piercing gaze (2:18). On his head are "many diadems" (19:12), conveying visually his infinite authority and dominion, as does his name, "King of kings, and Lord of lords" (19:16). The dragon appeared with seven diadems, pretending to universal rule (12:3), and the beast to which the dragon gave his power, throne, and authority had ten diadems (13:1). Both numbers symbolize comprehensive authority, but this rider far excels them with his many diadems.

"He is clothed with a robe dipped in blood" (Rev. 19:13). This is the blood of God's enemies, a preview of the defeat of the beast and the false prophet, with the slaughter of earth's kings and armies (19:21). His robes are soaked blood red because he "treads the wine press of the fierce wrath of God, the Almighty" (19:15), from which his enemies' blood flows deep and wide (14:20). The imagery of this vision

4. See chapter 6, note 4.

270

is drawn from Isaiah 63:1–6, quoted above (chap. 10) in the exposition of Revelation 14:17–20. Such a presentation of a divine Warrior, full of wrath and vengeance against those who disregard his authority, is offensive to many today. How can such an image be made winsome to people attracted more by tolerant love than by strict justice? Scripture, however, paints a realistic picture of the moral structure of the universe. Despite the preferences of naïve wishful thinkers, at the cosmic level there can be no true mercy, no genuine redemption, apart from justice. "Day of vengeance" and "year of redemption" are closely associated by the parallelism in Isaiah 63:4:

> For the day of vengeance was in My heart,
> And My year of redemption has come.

Redemption for those who are God's friends by grace entails vengeance on those who stubbornly persist as God's enemies.

Miroslav Volf, reflecting on his Croatian people's suffering at the hands of Serbian aggressors, concludes that only the biblical confidence that God will bring the unjust to justice at history's end can enable victims to respond to their attackers with nonviolent grace in the present. "The presupposition of God's just judgment at the end of history is the presupposition for the renunciation of violence in the middle of it."[5] He anticipates, "My thesis that the practice of nonviolence requires a belief in divine vengeance will be unpopular with many Christians, especially theologians in the West." To his objectors he proposes that they imagine themselves lecturing on the thesis "we should not retaliate since God is perfect noncoercive love" to people living in a war zone, whose villages have been plundered and burned, whose daughters and sisters have been raped, and whose fathers and brothers have been murdered. "Soon you will discover that it takes the quiet of a suburban home for the birth of the thesis that human nonviolence corresponds to God's refusal to judge. In a scorched land, soaked in the blood of the innocent, it will invariably die."[6]

5. Miroslav Volf, *Exclusion and Embrace: A Theological Exploration of Identity, Otherness, and Reconciliation* (Nashville: Abingdon, 1996), 302.

6. Ibid., 304.

John's visions are for Christians who have experienced or will soon experience the atrocities of which human evil and injustice are capable. The vision of the righteous Judge who will not spare the wicked is precisely what they and we need to sustain their persistent and nonviolent response to their oppressors. The sharp sword proceeding from Christ's mouth (19:15), another feature drawn from the opening vision of the Son of Man (1:16), is the implement of righteous vengeance by which he will strike down the nations (cf. Isa. 11:4). It is drawn together with the "iron rod" with which the Messiah (Ps. 2:9), who is the woman's child (Rev. 12:5), will rule or shatter the nations (see the fuller allusion to Ps. 2 in Rev. 2:27). When Christians are victimized by injustice and cannot fight back, they must not despair. The strong and righteous Judge is coming. When they can fight back, they need not and should not retaliate, repaying evil with evil, for their strong Judge assures them, "Vengeance is Mine, I will repay" (Rom. 12:17–19).

Four names reveal the warrior-king's qualifications to enter into battle on behalf of God's saints. He "is called Faithful and True" (Rev. 19:11), attributes earlier identified with his role as witness on behalf of God's truth (1:5) and against complacent compromisers within his church (3:14). The divine message that distinguishes the church from the world is "the testimony of Jesus" (19:10; 1:9). Martyrs have died for this testimony concerning Jesus and from Jesus, staking their very lives on his faithfulness and truth (6:9; 12:11). It is their hope and comfort to know that the faithful and true witness is also the righteous judge: "in righteousness He judges and wages war" (19:11). Closely related to Jesus' twin attributes of faithfulness and truth is a second name, "The Word of God" (19:13). Elsewhere in Revelation the expression "the word of God" has been linked to "the testimony of Jesus" as alternative descriptions of the message revealed in Scripture and proclaimed by the apostles and the church (1:2, 9; 20:4; cf. 6:9). Its use as a personal name here is reminiscent of John 1:1–14, and it underscores the point that fidelity to the gospel's message is not mere intellectual concurrence but personal allegiance to the Son who uniquely reveals the Father, having been with the Father from the beginning and having become flesh that we might see the Father's glory through him.

The warrior's other two names emphasize his sovereignty. "He has a name written on Him which no one knows except Himself" (Rev. 19:12). This is a puzzling comment in view of the fact that three other names are openly attributed to him. This unrevealed name is usually explained as symbolizing "the mystery of his person . . . that finite minds will never fully grasp."[7] The secrecy of Christ's name here somehow corresponds to the name he promises to bestow on the overcomer, a name known only to the donor and the recipient (2:17). Christ's secret name is closely associated with (perhaps inscribed on?) his diadems, just as the beast's heads bore its blasphemous names (13:1) and Babylon's name was written on her forehead (17:5).[8] It is also noteworthy that in the ancient world the knowledge of a name was an implement of power. Jacob's request to learn the name of his mysterious wrestling opponent at Peniel receives a mild rebuke, "Why is it that you ask my name?" (Gen. 32:29). Although God (the mysterious opponent) blesses Jacob, Jacob will not be entrusted with the divine name if his intent is to use it to gain leverage over the Lord.[9] The hiddenness of this war-

7. Robert H. Mounce, *The Book of Revelation,* rev. ed., NICNT (Grand Rapids: Eerdmans, 1998), 353. Cf. G. K. Beasley-Murray, *The Book of Revelation,* NCB (Grand Rapids: Eerdmans, 1981), 280: "his nature, his relationships to the Father, and even his relationship to humanity, transcend all human understanding." George Eldon Ladd, *A Commentary on the Revelation of John* (Grand Rapids: Eerdmans, 1972), 254: "the human mind cannot grasp the depth of his being." G. B. Caird, *A Commentary on the Revelation of St. John the Divine,* HNTC (New York: Harper & Row, 1966), 242: "there are depths of his being which pass even [the glorified saints'] comprehension. . . . When they have joined all the glorious names that adoring wonder can ascribe to him, he still confronts them with an ultimate mystery." R. H. Charles, *A Critical and Exegetical Commentary on the Revelation of St. John,* 2 vols., ICC (Edinburgh: T & T Clark, 1920), 2:32, dismisses the clause as a later interpolation and declines to interpret it.

8. Moses Stuart, *A Commentary on the Apocalypse,* 2 vols. (London: Wiley and Putnam, 1845), 2:346, calls attention to the inscription of the secret name on Christ's "imperial diadem," suggesting its implication of royal power. But he also suggests a connection with the inscription of God's covenant name (regarded by the Jews of John's day as too holy to be pronounced), on the crown of the high priest's turban (cf. Exod. 28:36–37; 39:30).

9. Isbon T. Beckwith, *The Apocalypse of John: Studies in Introduction, with a Critical and Exegetical Commentary* (1919; reprint ed., Grand Rapids: Baker, 1979), 732–33,

rior's name means not only that no creature can understand him exhaustively but also, more importantly in this context, no opponent can get a handhold to overthrow him or slow his advance.[10]

Finally, he is "King of kings and Lord of lords" (19:16). The title "Lord of lords and King of kings" was attributed to the Lamb in Revelation 17:14 to explain why he would overcome the beast and the "ten kings" allied with it as they wage war against the Lamb and his company, "the called and chosen and faithful." It now reappears in reverse order as the inscription on the rider's garment and thigh in order to identify the rider as the Lamb and his cavalry as those called and chosen by God. This title shows his supremacy over all other rulers, in earth or heaven (cf. Eph. 1:20–22; Phil. 2:9–11); and it signals that the final war predicted in Revelation 17:11–14 is about to occur.

The companions of the victorious, faithful, and true Word of God, who is Lord of lords, are "the armies which are in heaven" (Rev. 19:14). Elsewhere in the New Testament we learn that at his second coming Christ will be accompanied by an army of his angels to gather his people and bring deserved retribution to the disobedient (Matt. 16:27; 24:30–31; 25:31; 2 Thess. 1:7). Here, however, the clothing of "fine linen, white and clean" identify this cavalry, mounted, like their captain, on the white steeds of victory, as the saints—particularly those who have won the victory by persevering faith, whether through martyrdom or other confessing death. As we have seen, white robes of purity and triumph clothe the souls of the martyrs under the altar and the international throng before God's throne in heaven (6:11; 7:9), and a few sentences before this text John was told that the bride's wedding dress is made of "fine linen, bright and clean" (19:8). Through-

---

citing Enoch 69 and the Ascension of Isaiah 9, refers to "the current belief in the marvelous power of a secret name. . . . In this hidden name, though not in this alone, the Messiah possesses a power to subdue his enemies miraculously."

10. G. K. Beale, *The Book of Revelation*, NIGTC (Grand Rapids: Eerdmans, 1999), 955–56, views the concealment of this name as only temporary, for in his coming his character is to be experienced by humans, either in redemption or in judgment. "In the O[ld] T[estament] to know a name means to have control over the one named. Therefore, the confidential nature of the name here has nothing to do with concealing a name on the cognitive level but alludes to Christ's being absolutely sovereign over humanity's experiential access to his character."

out Revelation we have been forewarned that the cosmic conflict is not only between Satan and his beast and God and his Christ. Rather, each stands in the midst of a community, and the destiny of each community rests with the success or failure of its champions. When the dragon cannot get at the woman's child, he goes after "the rest of her children" (12:17). When the beast and its allies gather for the war to end all wars, their intended victims are the Lamb and his comrades in arms, the called, chosen, and faithful ones who are his army, "the camp of the saints, the beloved city" (17:14; 19:19; 20:9). Yet just as Christ's white horse promises his certain victory, so the white horses of the riders who follow him assure the church that his triumph will be ours as well.[11]

The Last Battle: Take 1 (19:17–21)

Our confidence of victory is reaffirmed by a macabre dinner invitation that an angel now issues to the carrion-eating birds that fly through the sky (Rev. 19:17–18). An angel standing in the sun issues the summons in a loud voice, "Come, assemble for the great supper of God," to eat the flesh of kings, commanders, mighty men, horses and riders, freemen and slaves, small and great. The sun's blinding light makes this angel resemble the angel whose glory illumined the earth (18:1). Both angels cry in a strong voice. The first angel announced Babylon's fall, making the once-glorious city into a wilderness inhabited by demons and unclean birds; the second invites those birds to dine on the corpses of the Lamb's enemies, exposed and unburied on the field of battle. The invitation and the list of categories represented among the slain show that this war will mark the fulfillment of the eschatological battle prophesied in Ezekiel 38–39. In that prophecy Gog of the land of Magog is an archetypal pagan power, plotting to invade, overrun, and devastate helpless Israel. But the Lord promises to come to his people's defense, taunting Gog: "You will fall on the mountains of Israel, you and all your troops and the peoples who are with

11. The Lamb has already appeared in victory on the heavenly Mount Zion, surrounded by his complete army—144,000 strong—soldiers of unblemished purity, "who follow the Lamb wherever He goes" (Rev. 14:1–5).

you; I will give you as food to every kind of predatory bird and beast of the field" (Ezek. 39:4). The Lord commands Ezekiel to issue the supper invitation:

> Speak to every kind of bird and to every beast of the field, "Assemble and come, gather from every side to My sacrifice which I am going to sacrifice for you . . . on the mountains of Israel, that you may eat flesh and drink blood. You will eat the flesh of mighty men and drink the blood of the princes of the earth. . . . You will be glutted at My table with horses and charioteers, with mighty men and all the men of war." (Ezek. 39:17–20)

We are about to witness the Lord's last-days battle against the pagan aggressors called Gog and Magog in Ezekiel's prophecy and the battle's grisly aftermath, as "the birds were filled with their flesh" (Rev. 19:21). In the recapitulation or replay, the pagan peoples deceived and gathered by the dragon to assault God's holy community are named "Gog and Magog" (20:8), confirming that Revelation 19:17–21 and 20:7–10 contain complementary visions of the same last battle.[12]

We also need to notice the universal extent of the fallen army whose corpses the birds consume. Earlier summaries that anticipated the gathering of the beast's evil army explicitly mentioned "kings," who would be deceived by demons and cede their power to the beast (Rev. 16:14; 17:12–14). Now, however, we hear that it is not only the world's rulers but also all sorts of people—all who, deceived, have received the beast's mark (19:20). The beast's fallen followers will include not only those normally associated with armed conflict—kings, commanders, warriors, horses and riders—but also "the flesh of all men, both free men and slaves, and small and great" (19:18). When the beast and false prophet are cast into the lake of fire, and "the rest" are killed by the judging sword of the Word and their flesh consumed by the birds (19:21), there will be no human survivors except for the faithful army of saints who follow the Lamb.

12. R. Fowler White, "Reexamining the Evidence for Recapitulation in Rev 20:1–10," *WTJ* 51 (1989): 326–28.

In the drama of John's visions the clash at history's turning point, the dragon's attempt to "devour" the Messiah, seemed to pass its crisis point in an instant: the woman's son caught up to God's throne and the dragon expelled from the heavenly court, disbarred from his authority as accuser (Rev. 12:4–5, 7–9). So also the battle that ends history is resolved in the blink of an eye. One moment John sees the beast, the kings allied with it, and their armies gathered[13] to make "the war" (dej) against Christ and his armies (19:19).[14] The next, the beast and false prophet are seized and cast, still living, into the lake of fire which burns with brimstone (19:20)—another fulfillment of the prophecy of judgment on Gog and Magog (Ezek. 38:22) and another connection between this vision and the reprise of the last battle in Revelation 20:7–10. "The rest," their human accomplices and followers, are slain by the sharp sword from the mouth of the captain of the Lord's cavalry (19:21), just as the Lord had announced that he would slay Gog's invading army with a sword (Ezek. 38:21). The birds enjoy their gruesome feast, the fallen bodies of the Lord's enemies. The almost instantaneous brevity of the battle underscores a theme woven throughout Revelation: Satan's attack on the church, especially through persecution, will escalate greatly in intensity immediately before the end, in contrast to the present restraints that frustrate

---

13. NASB has "assembled" rather than "gathered," but the verb (*synagō*) is the same as that used in Rev. 16:14 and 20:8 and provides another strand in the cord that ties these three texts together.

14. The definite article, present in Greek but omitted at this point by NASB, is significant. This scene marks the realization of the purpose for which the dragon, the beast, and the false prophet sent out the frog demons during the sixth bowl: "to gather [the kings of the whole world] for the war of the great day of God, the Almighty" (Rev. 16:14). Consequently the definite article points the reader back to that reference. The gathering has been accomplished, and *the* war—that war previously announced as "the war of the great day of God"—is about to break out. John uses the Greek noun translated "war" or "battle" (*polemos*) without the article when he intends a general reference to military action (9:7, 9; 11:7; 12:7, 17; 13:7), so the use of *polemos* with the article is significant and designates "the [specific] war/battle mentioned earlier." Note that in 20:8, the third reference to this same war, NASB correctly includes "the," reflecting the presence of the Greek definite article. For further development of this grammatical point see White, "Reexamining the Evidence," 328–30.

him (Rev. 12:13–17; 20:1–3, 7–8).[15] Nevertheless this final period of hyperintense persecution will be brief—only "three and a half days" (11:11), "one hour" (17:12), or "a short time" (20:3). The fact that the beast and false prophet are thrown alive into the fiery lake, whereas their followers are slain by the sword, confirms that the beast and false prophet, like the harlot Babylon, symbolize not particular human individuals (for example, "the antichrist" understood as a single, eschatological world ruler) but rather institutional structures by which human civilizations and cultures oppose God, his truth, and his church. If the beast and the false prophet portrayed mere human beings, there would be no reason for Christ to spare them the first death (physical death) before casting them into the second death, the lake of fire (20:14). Their followers will experience both.

The last battle is over, and the Lamb has triumphed. The seventh bowl is empty, poured out on God's enemies, so "the wrath of God is finished" (Rev. 15:1).

The Thousand Years (20:1–6)

We have reached what are probably the most controversial six verses in Revelation. For this reason this chapter needs to be longer than others, and its discussion more detailed. John sees an angel descending from heaven, seizing, chaining, and locking the dragon into the abyss for a thousand years—in Latin, a millennium—to keep the dragon from continuing to deceive the nations for that extended period (Rev. 20:1–3). Then he sees thrones, and the souls of martyrs beheaded for their testimony, who come to life in "the first resurrection" and reign with Christ for the same period of time, one thousand years (20:4–6). Over these two visions—what they mean, and where they fall in God's

---

15. Two careful studies within a premillennialist context establish that the New Testament writers consistently prepare Christians to endure not only routine sufferings and opposition but also a period of radically intensified persecution—the tribulation—immediately before Jesus' return. See Robert H. Gundry, *The Church and the Tribulation* (Grand Rapids: Zondervan, 1973); idem, *First the Antichrist: A Book for Lay Christians Approaching the Third Millennium and Inquiring Whether Jesus Will Come to Take the Church out of the World before the Tribulation* (Grand Rapids: Baker, 1997).

agenda for history—interpreters of Scripture have debated for not quite two millennia.[16]

Premillennialism holds that Jesus' physical return to earth will occur before ("pre") the thousand years. In relation to how we should read this section of Revelation, that means that premillennialists are convinced that in Revelation 19–20, at least, the order in which John received the visions is intended to convey the order of the events to which the visions refer. Because John sees the return of Christ from heaven and his Har-Magedon battle against the beast in Revelation 19:11–21, before he sees the binding of Satan for a thousand years (20:1–3), premillennialists believe that the second coming and Har-Magedon must occur in history before the thousand years. Some premillennialists take the time designation "thousand years" literally, indicating a period of 365,000 twenty-four-hour days; others, recognizing the symbolic use of numbers in Revelation, interpret "a thousand years" as signifying a very long time, the exact duration of which Revelation does not intend to specify. Since they believe that Jesus will have returned in his resurrection body before the thousand years, premillennialists typically view the millennium as a period in which Christ reigns on earth (according to their interpretation of texts elsewhere in Scripture, from Jerusalem in Israel). Believers, who will have received their new sin-free and curse-free bodies, will have returned with Christ to earth and will rule with him. Because of Christ's rule on the present earth during that time much, though not all,[17] of the curse against human sin—injustice, violence, disease, sorrow, death—will be radically suppressed. Human beings who were not clothed with the immortality of the resurrection body at the start of the millennium when Jesus returned will still die, but only at a ripe old age (cf. Isa. 65:20–25).[18] At the end of the millennium, however,

16. For a thorough, thoughtful, and respectful presentation of each view, with interaction among the proponents, see Darrell L. Bock, ed., *Three Views on the Millennium and Beyond* (Grand Rapids: Zondervan, 1999).

17. Only in the new heaven and earth "there will no longer be any curse" (Rev. 22:3).

18. Craig A. Blaising, "Premillennialism," in Bock, *Three Views,* 202–3.

Satan will be released and will be able to gather a vast army of fallen humans to rebel against Christ's reign and besiege Jerusalem, precipitating a second great battle like that in which the beast and false prophet had been defeated a thousand years before. Only after this second battle is the last enemy, Satan the dragon, seized and thrown into the lake of fire. At this point also the first heaven and earth, and the sin-caused sorrows and curses that had clung to them even through the millennium's golden years, are removed; a new heaven and earth, free of sin and the curse, appear (Rev. 21:1–4; 22:3).

Postmillennialism (with amillennialism) believes that Jesus' physical second coming will be after ("post") the age symbolized by the thousand years. Some postmillennialists believe that the war between the rider on the white horse and the beasts (Rev. 19:11–21) symbolizes a historical event or trend that precedes the thousand years. This is not Christ's bodily return to destroy all his enemies but his coming in providential judgment on unbelieving Judaism through the Roman army's destruction of Jerusalem (70). Or he comes in providential judgment on Rome the pagan persecutor in the fourth century; or even, interpreting the sword proceeding from Christ's mouth in a gracious sense, he comes in the Spirit and conquers the nations through the gospel. Others, however, recognize recapitulation in this portion of Revelation and identify 19:11–21 with 20:7–10 as twin portraits of the second coming and triumph over the beasts and the dragon, which will occur "when the thousand years are completed" (20:7). What is distinctive about postmillennialists' reading of Revelation is their interpretation of the two elements in John's vision that are explicitly attributed to the thousand years: the dragon is bound, preventing him from deceiving the nations; and martyrs come to life and reign with Christ. Postmillennialism sees these two features in combination as symbolizing not only the worldwide spread of the gospel among the nations but also the overwhelming fruitfulness of this evangelistic advance in the salvation of individuals and in the transformation of cultures, countries, and world civilization as a whole[19]—all before the

19. Kenneth L. Gentry Jr., "Postmillennialism," in Bock, *Three Views,* makes the exegetical case for his expectation of worldwide evangelization, conversion, and ref-

physical return of Christ. As a vast majority of the world's population become Christians, families, societies, and nations are transformed by disciples of Jesus who honor his lordship over every dimension of life, public as well as private. The "first resurrection" is the regeneration experienced by Christians, and both martyrs and living confessors participate in Christ's reign through discipleship and dominion in their spheres of influence.[20] Increasing justice, compassion, peace, economic stability, flourishing and wholesome fine arts, and even physical health and longevity will provide irrefutable evidence within history[21] that Jesus is King and his Word provides the only wise basis for living for individuals, families, governments, and cultures. Toward the end of this extended age, in which God's kingdom expands through the church's gospel proclamation and through Christians' reformation of culture, there will be a period of intense rebellion against God's Word and persecution against his church throughout the world. Then Christ will return in the glory of his resurrection body, to raise and judge the dead and to effect the sin-free, curse-free new heaven and earth.

Amillennialism shares with postmillennialism the belief that Christ's bodily second coming will occur after the time period symbolized by the thousand years in John's vision. The prefix *a-* negates what follows, so it would be natural to conclude that amillennialists believe that there is "no millennium."[22] That conclusion would be valid in

---

ormation from such biblical texts as Ps. 2; Isa. 2:2–4; Matt. 13; John 12:31–32; Matt. 28:18–20; and 1 Cor. 15:20–28 (a total of eighteen pages). He devotes five pages to the interpretation of Rev. 20:1–10.

20. Ibid., 53–54.

21. Postmillennialists find unsatisfying the amillennialist conviction that one climactic, end-of-history event—the bodily return of Jesus, effecting the resurrection of the dead, the last judgment, and the new heavens and earth—is God's decisive vindication of his Son, his gospel, and his church. To say that until Christ's return, Christians are called to overcome the dragon and the beast by holding faith fast as they are slain in martyrdom does not sound like real victory—the kind of victory that impresses unbelievers that we, not they, are on the winning side—in postmillennial ears.

22. Those who hold the view commonly called amillennialism do believe that John's vision of the thousand years is meaningful and true, so they affirm the Jo-

only one respect: amillennialists do not believe that Revelation 20 or any other Scripture promises a millennium in the sense in which pre-millennialists or even postmillennialists define it, either before or after the return of Jesus. Thus, while amillennialism agrees with postmillennialism that Christ's second coming will occur after the thousand years, it demurs from postmillennialism's and premillenialism's shared belief that Christians can expect a semi-curse-free, semi-suffering-free era within the context of the "first heaven and earth," prior to the consummation of the new creation with the new heaven and earth, the home of righteousness. Amillennialists believe that this new heaven and earth will appear at Christ's bodily return, not a thousand years later. Thus they eagerly hope for the second coming as "the grand finale of redemptive history,"[23] immediately defeating the last enemy, death, by raising believers' bodies to life and restoring unbelievers to bodily existence to endure the second death; executing the last judgment; consuming the first heaven and earth, thereby eradicating every impurity introduced by human sin; and introducing the new heaven and earth.[24] Amillennialists, like many postmillennialists, see the thousand years as symbolizing the age from the exaltation of Jesus until just before his second coming. The binding of the dragon means that throughout this period, until just before the end, Satan cannot hold the nations in darkness, blinded to the gospel; specifically, he cannot assemble an organized, worldwide conspiracy to attack the church through violent persecution. The "resurrection" and reigning of the souls of the martyrs from heavenly thrones dramatizes the reality that Christ's faithful witnesses, though apparently conquered and killed by their persecutors on earth, are those who have conquered and who

---

hannine sense of "millennium," insisting that it be rightly interpreted. Because of the mixed signals potentially sent or received by the term *amillennialism,* some amillennialists prefer a more descriptive title. Beale, *Revelation,* 972, for example, prefers "inaugurated millennialism"; but even this term, which is clearer, does not set this view apart from postmillennialism.

23. Robert B. Strimple, "Amillennialism" in Bock, *Three Views,* 100.

24. Compare Strimple's interpretation (ibid., 101–12) of John 5:28–29; 2 Thess. 1:5–10; Rom. 8:17–23; 2 Peter 3:3–14; 1 Cor. 15:20–26. His interpretation of Rev. 20:1–10 is ten pages long and is similar to that presented below.

live with God in heaven. We will develop this perspective in relation to the details of Revelation 20:1–10 below.

Essentially these three views differ from each other in their answers to two questions. (1) What is the historical-chronological relationship between the physical second coming of Christ and the age designated the thousand years in John's vision? Will Jesus return in person before or after this long period of time? (2) What general conditions on earth should be expected to characterize the thousand years? The first question can be answered by a careful reading of Revelation 20:1–10 in the context of Revelation as a whole. To answer the second, all three schools look outside Revelation to other biblical texts for greater light and detail than are provided in these ten verses. This is an appropriate hermeneutical strategy (we have seen its fruitfulness repeatedly in exploring Revelation's Old Testament roots), as long as the connections we draw are warranted by a careful analysis of what Revelation 20 says about the state of affairs during the thousand years. What does it say?

John sees an angel descending from heaven, clearly with authorization from God (Rev. 20:1). The angel holds the key to the abyss, like the star that John saw fall from heaven to earth when the fifth trumpet sounded (9:1). The unfolding of that earlier vision, however, showed that "star" to be "the angel of the abyss," whose names mean "destroyer" (9:11). In other words, that fallen star was Satan, authorized by God to release his demons on earth to torment unbelieving people (9:4). The angel that John now sees, however, is one of God's obedient servants and has come to seize, bind, and imprison Satan. The multiplication of visual features—key, chain, hand, dragon, throwing, locking,[25] and sealing—underscores the symbolic genre of the entire vision, since John's audience knows well that Satan is not a literal dragon who can be bound with a physical chain or locked away in a physical pit.[26]

---

25. NASB "shut" (also translating the same verb in Rev. 3:7) is weaker than the Greek verb (*kleiō*) which, used in proximity to its cognate noun *key* (*kleis*), must refer not merely to closing what was open but securing its closure through locking. The "sealing" (*sphragizō*) then adds God's legal sanction to the physical lock (cf. 5:1–3), reinforcing the impossibility of the prisoner's escape (cf. Matt. 27:66).

26. Beale, *Revelation*, 974.

The fourfold identification of the prisoner—dragon, serpent of old, devil, Satan (Rev. 20:2)—interprets the symbolism and reminds John's hearers of how dangerous this villain is: he is the serpent who deceived Eve long ago, and the "Satan" (accuser) who prosecutes the guilty before God's tribunal (12:10; Zech. 3:1). Equally important is the fact that the fourfold identification reproduces the wording of Revelation 12:9,[27] signaling a close connection between this vision of the thousand years and that vision of Satan's expulsion from heaven to earth and his frustrated efforts to destroy the heavenly woman through the deception he pours from his mouth (12:15). How closely these visions are tied, we are about to see.

The dragon is bound, locked, and sealed in the abyss for a particular purpose: "so that he would not deceive the nations any longer, until the thousand years were completed" (Rev. 20:3). In the context of the drama of Revelation, this purpose statement makes clear that the historical-chronological referent of "the thousand years" in which the dragon is "bound" must precede the battle that John just saw, in which the rider vanquished the beast, the false prophet, and all their followers (19:11–21). The millennium must occur before the second coming and the last battle for several reasons.

(1) Although it is true throughout history that Satan, the ancient serpent, "deceives the whole world" (Rev. 12:9), in this vision a specific deception to obtain a specific objective is in view. We see this objective when, at the end of the thousand years, the dragon is released and comes out "to deceive the nations which are in the four corners of the earth, Gog and Magog, to gather them together for the war" (20:8). "The war,"[28] as we have seen, is a reference to "the war of the great day of God, the Almighty," for which the world's kings were gathered by three unclean spirits that proceed from the mouths of the dragon, the beast, and the false prophet

27. For Greek speakers the echo of Rev. 12:9 in 20:2 would be all the more noticeable because of a grammatical solecism in the latter text: although "dragon" appears in the Greek accusative case as the object of the verb "he laid hold of," the second title, "the serpent of old," appears in the nominative case (as it does in 12:9) instead of the accusative, as ordinary Greek grammar would lead us to expect.

28. On the significance of the definite article in "the war," see note 14.

(16:13–16).[29] Their role is to deceive the kings in order to gather them, as is shown by the demons' origin in the mouths of the archvillains and the signs they perform, as the false prophet deceives those who dwell on the earth through his signs (13:14). In light of this explanation of the aim behind the dragon's deception (20:8), his binding during the thousand years prevents Satan from gathering the nations in a worldwide conspiracy to blot out the church.

(2) As R. Fowler White points out, the precaution of binding Satan to keep him from "deceiving the nations" would be superfluous if it followed the battle of Revelation 19:11–21 in historical-chronological sequence.[30] The beast's troops, who were slaughtered in that battle, included not only kings and military personnel (commanders, mighty men, cavalry riders) but also "all men, both free men and slaves, and small and great" (19:18).[31] These same terms express the universal scope of those deceived into receiving the mark of the beast. The earth beast, later identified as the false prophet, "causes all, the small and the great, and the rich and the poor, and the free men and the slaves, to be given a mark" (13:16).

29. Note that the frog demons proceed from all three—dragon, beast, and false prophet—to gather the kings for one war, not two. The role of the beast and false prophet in this war of the gathered kings and troops is shown in Rev. 19:11–21, where the dragon is not mentioned. The role of the dragon in the gathering of the nations and the war is the subject of the recapitulation of the vision in 20:7–10.

30. White, "Reexamining the Evidence," 321–25, summarizes the point before responding to postmillennial and premillennial counterexplanations: "In other words, the discrepancy consists in this: it makes no sense to speak of protecting the nations from deception by Satan in 20:1–3 after they have just been both deceived by Satan (16:13–16, cf. 19:19–20) and destroyed by Christ at his return in 19:11–21 (cf. 16:15a, 19)" (321).

31. Note also the implication in the description of the false prophet (Rev. 19:20) that those deceived and gathered for the war included not only kings and their armies but also all people who bear the beast's mark rather than the seal of the Lamb. These elements in the text of Rev. 19 are overlooked by Blaising, "Premillennialism," 220, in his critique of White's argument (n. 29): "The gathering of the nations for this battle is not a gathering of all their inhabitants but of their armies. This point is made explicit in 19:19: 'I saw the beast and the kings of the earth and their armies gathered together to make war against the rider on the horse [Christ] and his army.' When 19:21 says, 'the rest of them were killed . . . ,' it refers to the destruction of these armies, not all the inhabitants or even all the wicked inhabitants of the na-

The echo of this verse in the description of those on whose corpses the birds will feast (19:18) is unmistakable and shows how universally John understands the composition of the beast's army. Committed to the premise that the order of John's visions (first the Har-Magedon battle, then the binding of Satan) represents the chronological order of the events and ages symbolized, premillennialists respond to this incongruity by qualifying the universal scope of the slaughter. But these efforts are unconvincing in explaining away the comprehensiveness of the language in Revelation 19:18 and its background in 13:16.[32]

(3) We have noted the verbal connection between this vision and twin visions of Revelation 12, especially in the fourfold identification of the dragon (12:9). There too the dragon was "thrown" out of heaven into the earth, and the flood of deceit from his mouth, by which he tried to destroy the heavenly woman, met with frustration, enraging the dragon even further (12:16–17). Yet the woman was safe in the wilderness, sustained by God and protected "from the presence of the serpent" for a time, two times, and half a time (= 3½ years, 12:14)—or 1,260 days, as the same period had been measured in Revelation 12:6. These 1,260 days also marked the span of time in which the two witnesses bore their testimony and in which no one could harm them (11:3, 5). Only at the conclusion of that period could the beast from the abyss attack, overcome, and kill them (11:7). So we have three vi-

---

tions, as White apparently thinks." In this extended note Blaising makes no mention of 19:18, which indicates the composition of the beast's army (including "all, free and slave, small and great") or of its background in the description of those deceived by the false prophets into receiving the beast's mark (13:16).

32. Mounce, *Revelation,* 359, comments on Rev. 19:21: "Punishment has been meted out to all who accepted the mark of the beast and pledged to him their allegiance. Their destruction is complete. There now remains but one who must still meet a like fate—Satan himself." Yet in trying to reconcile this picture of total destruction with the puzzle that "now in chapter 20 the nations are pictured as still in existence," he first appeals to apocalyptic "overlapping of scenes and repetition of figures" (flirting, it seems, with recapitulation) and finally offers as a harmonization: "If consistency is called for, it is probably best to understand the nations of 20:3 as the remnant from the nations who opposed the Messiah rather than select nations here and there who never entered the final battle" (363). So it seems that in Mounce's view there were survivors, the wording of Rev. 19:18 notwithstanding.

sions—the two witnesses (11), the heavenly woman and the dragon (12), and the binding of the dragon (20)—which together affirm the divinely imposed restraint that hinders the dragon from fulfilling his desire to destroy the church. The visionary imagery is different, admittedly. In Revelation 11 fire proceeds from the witnesses' mouths to consume anyone who presumes to assault them before the completion of their mission. In Revelation 12 the ground swallows up the torrent from the dragon's mouth, so Messiah's mother cannot be destroyed during her 3½-year sojourn in the wilderness. And in Revelation 20 the dragon is bound and imprisoned so that, until the thousand years are completed, his mouth cannot utter the lies that will gather the nations to besiege the camp of the saints. Yet these are three windows on the same stage in the conflict—the age in which the faithful church is both suffering and spiritually safe, which began with the sacrifice and exaltation of Christ the seed of the woman and which will conclude just before his return.

If the time period that the thousand years symbolize historically precedes the deception, gathering, and battle envisioned in Revelation 19:11–21, two further questions remain.

First, what is the purpose of the dragon's binding that he might "not deceive the nations any longer"—looking back to a previous time in which he was free to deceive them? Should we not expect the text to say, "so that he would not yet deceive the nations"—looking ahead to a future time when he will be free to do so? Revelation 20:3 sounds as if the chain and the abyss have stopped the dragon from doing what he had already been doing, rather than preventing him from starting. The answer is that the old serpent has always been a deceiver (12:9), especially of the Gentile nations. In their spiritual darkness the Gentiles, with rare exceptions, did not bless or receive blessing through Abraham's seed during the ages of promise (Eph. 2:1–2, 11–12). Rather, the benighted Gentile powers (Egypt, Philistia, Assyria, Babylonia, Medo-Persia, Hellenistic Syria, Rome) oppressed the people of God, often violently. Jesus' exorcisms were one indication that Satan, the "strong man," had been bound by the arrival of God's kingdom in the person of the Messiah (Matt. 12:29).[33] Another indication, which the

33. The verb for binding is *deō,* as in Rev. 20:2.

apostles make explicit after Jesus' death and resurrection, is that the light of the kingdom now breaks forth on the nations that had been enslaved in satanic darkness (Matt. 4:14–16; Luke 2:32; 4:18). In his sermons to Gentile audiences at Lystra (Acts 14:15–17) and Athens (17:30–31), Paul characterizes the dire spiritual status of the Gentile nations before Christ's coming: "In the generations gone by [God] permitted all the nations to go their own ways" (14:16), but no longer.

> Therefore having overlooked the times of ignorance, God is now declaring to men that all people everywhere should repent, because He has fixed a day in which He will judge the world in righteousness through a Man whom He has appointed, having furnished proof to all men by raising Him from the dead. (Acts 17:30–31)

The resurrection of Christ is the great spiritual watershed for the nations. Satan no longer has free rein to deceive the nations, and this is good news to the Gentiles (Acts 13:47; Rev. 7:9–10). But it is also good news to the church: not until the "short time" at the end, determined by God in his sovereign plan of the ages, can there be a world power or coalition with the potential to erase the people of God from the earth, as Egypt, and Babylonia, Persia, Hellenistic Syria under Antiochus, and Rome could have done.

The second question is Why does John receive and record this vision here, following the last battle in Revelation 19? The answer lies in the great length of time symbolized in the imagery of the thousand years. Jesus is reminding his churches that despite their experience of persecution and the traumas that had shaken the Roman Empire in the first century, such seemingly world-shaking troubles do not necessarily mean that "the last battle" is imminent. In his Olivet Discourse Jesus told his disciples:

> When you hear of wars and rumors of wars, do not be frightened; those things must take place; but that is not yet the end. For nation will rise up against nation, and kingdom against kingdom; there will be earthquakes in various places; there will also be famines. These things are merely the beginning of birth pangs. (Mark 13:7–8)

Much of what John sees "must soon take place" (Rev. 1:1, 3), but that does not mean that the first-century Asian churches are to be living in a state of eschatological hysteria. Their present persecutions are painful, but they are "light" when compared with the intensity of the tribulation to come at the end. Now the dragon is chained and locked away, prevented from pulling together a worldwide conspiracy to obliterate the church. However severe their present or imminent persecutions may be, Christ's followers could take courage from this assurance. "Though the wrong seems oft so strong, God is the ruler yet." At the end, when the dragon is released to pull together his evil conspiracy, it will seem as if all is lost—the witnesses slain and the godless world celebrating (11:7–9), the camp of the saints surrounded by a countless army that fills the breadth of the earth (20:8–9). But even in that dire moment, the church's divine Protector will defend and vindicate his own.

Moreover, the end is not necessarily as near as their present pain may lead them to hope. The complementary visions of Revelation 12 and Revelation 20 strike the same balance that we see often in the New Testament's expectation regarding Jesus' second coming. On the one hand, God does not needlessly delay (2 Peter 3:8–9) but rather hastens to the relief of his saints (Luke 18:7; Mark 13:20). On the other, suffering saints were not to assume that "the kingdom of God was going to appear immediately" (Luke 19:11), but rather they must endure patiently and alertly, even if their Master seems to delay (Luke 12:35–40). In the language of John's visions, the age bracketed by Jesus' two comings is brief—only three and a half years, half of a sabbatical sequence. Yet the same age is very long—one thousand years. Paradoxically, the time until the second coming will prove to be shorter than it now seems and longer than we may have expected—prolonging the martyrs' wait for vindication (Rev. 6:10) but also long enough for the gathering of God's children from all the world's nations, cultures, and tongues (7:9).

John sees a second vision concerning the thousand years (Rev. 20:4–6), and this vision gives a new perspective on the condition of the martyrs, whose "How long?" lament is being answered. John first sees thrones and then gradually the identity of the rulers occupying

289

the thrones is revealed (20:4). This parallels his opening glimpse of God in heaven (4:2) but even more explicitly echoes Daniel's vision of the Ancient of Days and the Son of Man: "I kept looking until thrones were set up, and the Ancient of Days took His seat. . . . The court sat, and the books were opened. . . . The Ancient of Days came and judgment was passed in favor of the saints of the Highest One, and the time arrived when the saints took possession of the kingdom" (Dan. 7:9–10, 22). As in Daniel, so in Revelation the thrones appear before their royal occupants: "I saw thrones, and they sat on them, and judgment was given to them" (Rev. 20:4). The wording of the last clause ("judgment was given to them") so closely resembles Daniel 7:22 LXX that we should probably translate it, as in Daniel, "judgment was given on their behalf"—the verdict of the heavenly court came down in their favor and against their persecutor (see Rev. 18:20).[34] The allusion to Revelation 4 and Daniel 7 signals to John's hearers that these thrones are located in heaven. The identification of the enthroned rulers as "the souls of those who had been beheaded because of their testimony of Jesus and because of the word of God" confirms this heavenly locale. These souls had earlier appeared as sacrificial blood poured out under the altar (Rev. 6:9); now they appear as risen and ruling overcomers, for indeed they overcame the dragon because of the blood of the Lamb and the word of their testimony, which they maintained even to the death (12:11). Yet these victors are not limited to those slain for their faith in a particular way (beheading), or necessarily to martyrs only. All faithful followers of the Lamb who have died are included, for these rulers are also described as those who did not worship the beast or its image and who refused its mark on forehead and hand. This fidelity, not the circumstances or method of their death, distinguishes them as qualified to share the Lamb's rule (cf. 3:21).

The vision lays emphasis on these heavenly rulers' resurrection in three ways: the verb "they came to life" (*ezēsan*); the comment that the rest of the dead did not "come to life" (*ezēsan*) during the thousand years (20:5); and the identification of this coming to life as "the first resurrection," with the accompanying benediction (Revelation's

---

34. Beale, *Revelation,* 997.

fifth) on those who share in this first resurrection (20:5–6). Premillennialists interpret this resurrection as the physical resurrection of believers at the beginning of the millennium, separated by the thousand years from the resurrection of unbelievers before the last judgment. This interpretation pretty much requires them to locate the thrones not in heaven but on earth. This conclusion agrees with their general conception of the millennium as an extended period of reign by Jesus and his risen saints in world that, though not freed from the cancers of sin and the curse, is expected to be in remission. There are several problems, however, with equating the resurrection of souls that John sees in this vision with the resurrection of physical bodies in history.

(1) As we have seen, the introduction of the scene with the thrones that John saw places what follows in a heavenly, not an earthly, locale in the minds of readers familiar with the visions of Daniel 7, a key piece of Old Testament background throughout Revelation.

(2) The adjective *first* in this section of Revelation is used to designate elements that belong in one way or another to the present, sin-cursed creation order, in contrast to the new heaven and new earth. The new heaven and earth will appear before John's view when "the first heaven and the first earth passed away" (21:1; cf. 20:11), and with them "the first things," namely, tears, death, mourning, crying, and pain (21:4).[35] Scripture consistently teaches that the bodies that believers will receive in their resurrection belong to the new creation order and participate in its imperishability and immortality (1 Cor. 15:42–44, 50–54).[36] John will see one bodily resurrection of all the dead in Revelation 20:13, even as Jesus had spoken of the coming hour "in which all who are in the tombs will hear His voice, and will come forth; those who did the good deeds to a resurrection of life, those who committed the evil deeds to a resurrection of judgment" (John 5:28–29). The "first resurrection" granted to deceased saints in Revelation 20:4–6, since it belongs to the present, preconsummation order, is not their reception of the bodies

35. Note that the "first resurrection" is set in contrast to the "second death," which is the final destiny of God's enemies, the locale of eternal damnation even as the new heaven and earth are the locale of eternal blessing.

36. M. G. Kline, "The First Resurrection," *WTJ* 37 (1975): 366–75.

made like Christ's glorious body, fitted for immortal residence in the curse-free new earth (Phil. 3:21).

(3) The previous point is confirmed when we consider Paul's striking statement in 1 Corinthians 15:25–26: "For He must reign until He has put all His enemies under His feet. The last enemy that will be demolished is death." Later in his discussion Paul will quote Isaiah 25:8, "Death is swallowed up in victory," as reaching its fulfillment in the bodily resurrection of believers "at the last trumpet" (1 Cor. 15:52–55), and earlier he states that this resurrection will occur at Christ's coming (15:23).[37] When John sees the souls of martyrs "come to life" to reign with Christ a thousand years, the historical referent of his vision cannot be the last trumpet, last-enemy-destroying return of Christ to raise believers' bodies. Interpreters of all schools agree that Revelation 20:7–10 teaches that at the end of the thousand years, there will be other enemies to be conquered and destroyed by Christ. If death is, as Paul says it is, the last enemy, the return of Christ and the resurrection of the dead in him must occur at the end of the thousand years, when the rebel nations are destroyed (20:8–9) and the devil, along with the beast and false prophet and with death and Hades, is thrown into the lake of fire (20:10, 14).

(4) These difficulties with the view that the "first resurrection" refers to believers' bodily resurrection at the beginning of the millennium arise from an inability to distinguish the visionary, referential, and symbolic levels of meaning from each other.[38] Consider a noncontroversial piece of prophetic symbolism in Revelation. Interpreters of all schools recognize that when we read that John "saw a great red dragon" (visionary level), we must draw a distinction between the dragon that John saw and the referent (the devil) symbolized by the dragon. We also recognize that aspects of the vision convey commentary about the vision's referent (symbolic meaning): the dragon's red color symbolizes bloodthirsty violence; seven heads symbolize great intelligence and cunning; and ten horns symbolize great power. Since the Old Testament background leads us to expect a heavenly scene in Revelation 20:4–6, and since interpreting the martyrs' "first resurrection"

37. Strimple, "Amillennialism," in Bock, *Three Views,* 110–12.
38. Vern S. Poythress, "Genre and Hermeneutics in Rev 20:1–6," *JETS* 36 (1993): 41–45.

as bodily would bring this passage into conflict with 1 Corinthians 15, we need to apply the same distinctions to meanings of this resurrection that we do to the dragon. At the visionary level, John sees a resurrection, a coming to life. At the referential level, his vision must refer to something other than the resurrection of saints' bodies at Christ's return, destroying the last enemy, death. At the symbolic level, the event to which John's vision refers ushers those who experience it into the privileges of priests who worship in God's presence and kings who share in Christ's rule (Rev. 20:6).

What, then, is the referent of John's vision of the "first resurrection," in which departed saints' souls "come alive"? As alternatives to the premillennial identification of the referent as the physical resurrection of the saints, cases have been made for interpreting "the first resurrection" as regeneration, which brings people out of spiritual death and into eternal life (John 5:25–29; Eph. 2:5–6),[39] and Christ's resurrection as the first fruits, in which believers share by union with him (1 Cor. 15:20).[40] Neither of these approaches, however, gives due weight to the heavenly locale of the thrones on which the resurrected rulers sit or to the fact that these rulers are described as the "souls" of the martyrs and other believers who resisted idolatry. These details lead to the conclusion that the referent of the "first resurrection" is, paradoxically, the physical death of believers.[41] Paradox is no stranger to those familiar with John's visions. The lion who has conquered is the lamb who has been slain. The carefully counted Israelite army of 144,000 celibate males is an innumerable multitude from every nation and people. The church is safe from destruction, yet exposed to persecution, even to the death. The beast overcomes Jesus's witnesses and kills them, yet in so doing the beast inadvertently forfeits to them the real victory, for in their fidelity to the death they overcome the dragon-accuser who animates the beast (Rev. 12:11). From one perspective the martyrs in heaven can be viewed as sacrificial victims,

39. Norman Shepherd, "The Resurrections of Revelation 20," *WTJ* 36 (1974–75): 34–43.

40. Philip E. Hughes, "The First Resurrection: Another Interpretation," *WTJ* 39 (1976–77): 315–18.

41. Kline, "First Resurrection," 370–74.

awaiting just vindication; but from another—even now, while the "first things" (death, mourning, pain) still exist—they have experienced a "first resurrection," the deliverance of their souls from all that threatened them on earth (cf. 7:15–17). They enjoy the rest from enemies promised to those blessed by God, with the assurance that their deeds of faith and faithfulness accompany them (14:13). But their first resurrection also includes the priestly privilege of worship in God's presence (7:9–17) and the assurance that even now, as they await final vindication through the resurrection of their bodies and judgment of their enemies, they participate in the Lamb's reign through the ongoing fruit of their testimony in their words, their life, and their death.[42]

The Last Battle: Take 2 (20:7–10)

The completion of the thousand years brings with it the release of the dragon from his prison, and he emerges to deceive the nations throughout the world, now explicitly called Gog and Magog, "to gather them together for the war" (Rev. 20:7–8). John's vision of the thousand years carried his hearers back to Satan's defeat at the cross of Christ and the devil's resultant inability to hold the Gentile nations in darkness and use their power as a weapon to destroy the church. Now, as the thousand years draw to a close, John's vision has again reached that point in history immediately before the coming of the Lamb to complete God's wrath against his enemies, when the dragon's demonic deception will have gathered a worldwide conspiracy against the Lord and his church.[43]

Both descriptions of the last battle (Rev. 19:11–21; 20:7–10) connect it with the Lord's war against the aggressor Gog, of Magog, proph-

---

42. For a more extensive presentation of this interpretation of Rev. 20:4–6, with answers to objections, see Beale, *Revelation*, 995–1017.

43. As we have seen, the vision of the sixth bowl—deceiving demons going out from dragon, beast, and false prophet to gather the kings for "the war" (Rev. 16:13–16)—and the vision of the rider on the white horse and his defeat of the beast and its followers, who had been gathered for "the war" (Rev. 19:11–21), portray the same history-ending battle. Three strands—deception, gather, the war—bind these three texts together, showing the hearers that each symbolizes the same final combat.

esied in Ezekiel 38–39. In Revelation 19 echoes of Ezekiel are heard in the slaying of God's enemies by the sword and the consumption of their corpses by birds of prey, summoned by God to this gruesome feast. Now the enemies are explicitly called "Gog and Magog," and their destruction by fire (Rev. 20:9) likewise fulfills Ezekiel's prophecy: "And I will send fire on Magog and those who inhabit the coastlands in safety; and they will know that I am the LORD" (Ezek. 39:6). "I will rain on him and on his troops, and on the many peoples who are with him, a torrential rain, with hailstones, fire and brimstone" (Ezek. 38:22). Both scenes of the last battle pick up the combination "fire and brimstone" from Ezekiel's prophecy to characterize the lake of perpetual destruction into which God's enemies—beast and false prophet (Rev. 19:20), dragon (20:10), and all their followers (20:15) will be cast.

Both versions of the battle stress that all who are not in covenant with the Lamb are in league with the devil, the beast, and the false prophet and included in their assault forces attacking the church. In Revelation 19 the universal extent of God's judgment was expressed in the invitation to the birds to eat "the flesh of all men, both free men and slaves, and small and great" (19:18). Now this universal extent of the final rebellion is expressed both geographically—"the nations which are in the four corners of the earth" (20:8), "upon the broad plain of the earth" (20:9)—and numerically—"the number of them is like the sand of the seashore" (20:8). Sand on the seashore is an ancient biblical metaphor for a countless multitude (cf. Gen. 22:17), but in Revelation it receives added significance. It was on the sand of the seashore that the dragon stood, and from that sea the beast emerged to receive the dragon's power and wage the dragon's war against the saints (Rev. 13:1). As the harlot's seat on the waters symbolized her economic influence over the world's peoples, so the dragon's standing on the sand shows his spiritual dominion over the rebellious nations, which now follow his lead against the church—to their own destruction.

As in Revelation 19, in this reprise of the last battle the conflict ends almost before it starts (20:9). The besieging forces gathered on the breadth of the earth surround "the camp of the saints." Like ancient Israel, the church on earth is a wilderness community, camping but not at home in the earth. The church does, however, have a lasting identity despite its present temporary status as sojourners, so John adds a second description, "the beloved city."[44] John has seen the church as God's "holy city," trodden underfoot by the nations throughout the span between Christ's exaltation and his return (forty-two months, Rev. 11:2). He has heard the church described as the bride of the Lamb (19:7) and will soon see her revealed in radiant beauty (21:9–22:9). He has also heard Jesus reassure the harassed church at Philadelphia, "I will make [your persecutors] come and bow down at your feet, and make them know that I have loved you" (3:9). Jesus will consume with fire those who attack his bride not only to demonstrate the justice of his wrath but also to express his passionate love for his own.

The devil is cast into the lake of fire and brimstone, where John saw the beast and false prophet cast in his earlier vision, to be tormented constantly ("day and night") and everlastingly (Rev. 20:10). The torment signified by the "lake" and its "fire and brimstone" is not merely physical, since the devil is a spirit and the beast and false prophet represent not individual human beings but institutional forces (politico-military and religious). But for the wicked who are returned to bodily existence (Revelation refuses to label this "resurrection") for the purpose of standing before God's white throne of judgment (20:12–13), the lake of fire will mean unremitting anguish of body as well as of soul. The last of the three message-bearing angels in Revelation 14 described the intense anguish of the lake of fire as restlessness without relief: "If anyone worships the beast . . . he will be tormented with fire and brimstone in the presence of the holy angels and of the Lamb. And the smoke of their torment goes up forever and ever; they have no rest day and night" (14:9–11).

The Last Judgment (20:11–15)

This scene paints in more detail the final triumph of God's justice and grace, which was announced with thanksgiving by the twenty-four elders at the sounding of the seventh and last trumpet: "the time

44. Ps. 87:2–3: "The LORD loves the gates of Zion. . . . Glorious things are spoken of you, O city of God." The psalm goes on to rehearse the nationalities of Gentiles who are to be registered as citizens of Zion in the last days.

came for the dead to be judged, and the time to reward Your bond-servants the prophets and the saints and those who fear Your name, the small and the great, and to destroy those who destroy the earth" (Rev. 11:18). The elders' song anticipated the dual outcome of this final moment of justice: God's prophets and saints will be rewarded, and those who destroy the earth by their evil will be destroyed. Revelation 20:11–15 resumes and elaborates on this sobering theme.

As he did when first summoned to enter heaven "in the Spirit" (in prophetic vision), so now again John sees the divine throne "and Him who sat upon it" (Rev. 20:11; cf. 4:2). The throne is white, a color that elsewhere in Revelation symbolizes purity (3:4) and vindication or victory (6:11; 19:11).[45] In this courtroom context, with its echoes of Daniel 7, the whiteness of the throne perhaps reflects the white vesture and hair of the Ancient of Days, the presiding judge (Dan. 7:9; cf. Rev. 1:14). If so, it symbolizes his infinite wisdom to render judgment with utter equity (cf. 1 Kings 3:9, 16–28).

From this awesome judge "earth and heaven fled away, and no place was found for them" (Rev. 20:11). This sums up the full extent of the trauma to the created order portrayed earlier in the sixth seal (6:12–17), the resurrection-vindication of the two witnesses (11:11–13), and the seventh bowl (16:17–21). Earlier visions portrayed this cosmic shake-down and meltdown (cf. 2 Peter 3:7, 10) in terms of concrete particulars: a great earthquake, unparalleled in previous history (Rev. 6:12; 16:18), throwing mountains and islands out of place (6:14; 16:20) and shattering the great city (11:13; 16:19); the darkening of sun and moon, and plunging of stars to earth (6:12–13; cf. great hailstones, 16:21); and the splitting of the sky itself "like a scroll when it is rolled up" (6:14). The "first" heaven and earth, as they are characterized in 21:1, are partially personified, and their flight from the presence of the holy Judge signifies their having been defiled by the taint of human sin. In the first vision of this cosmic quake, sinful humans tried to hide "from the presence of Him who sits on the throne, and from the wrath of the Lamb" (6:15–16). Now the whole created order flees, and with it disappears the "first things" introduced by the sin and rebellion of the dragon and those deceived by him: death, mourning, crying, pain

---

45. Beale, *Revelation,* 1032.

(21:4). "No place was found for them" echoes an alternate Greek translation (Theodotian) of Daniel 2:35, describing the disappearance of the rubble from the large statue in Nebuchadnezzar's dream—symbolizing the destruction of world kingdoms that presume to rival God's coming kingdom. The certainty that this day would come, in which God's unshakable kingdom alone stands forever (Heb. 12:28), was secured when the dragon and his angels were defeated by Christ's sacrifice and resurrection, "and there was no longer a place found for them in heaven" (Rev. 12:8).

The defendants standing before the last judgment tribunal represent all of humanity, "the great and the small" (20:12). This pair (always in the opposite order, "small and great") earlier in Revelation encompasses all of God's faithful servants (11:18; 19:5) or all of the beast's deceived slaves (13:16; 19:18). That believers and unbelievers are included is also shown by the fact that this last judgment takes account of two sets of books: the books that record each person's deeds, and the "other book," the book of life. Their "standing" implies that they are no longer dead but that a general resurrection has occurred,[46] as Revelation 20:13 makes explicit: "And the sea gave up the dead which were in it, and death and Hades gave up the dead which were in them; and they were judged, every one of them according to their deeds."

"Books were opened" is a direct allusion to the courtroom scene in Daniel 7. After the thrones were set up and the Ancient of Days took the throne of honor as chief justice "the court sat, and the books were opened" (Dan. 7:10). The opened books contain records of each person's actions, for "the dead were judged from the things which were written in the books, according to their deeds" (Rev. 20:12). Throughout Scripture God's justice is shown in his repaying his creatures according to what they have done, whether good or evil (e.g., Ps. 62:13; Prov. 24:12; Matt. 16:27; Rom. 2:6; 2 Cor. 5:10). In Revelation we have seen this principle at work in God's giving blood as beverage to those who thirsted for his saints' blood (16:4–7) and in his

46. Compare the resurrection of the two witnesses, "the breath of life from God came into them, and they stood on their feet" (Rev. 11:11), which draws its wording from Ezekiel's vision of the valley of dry bones and the "resurrection" of Israel (Ezek. 37:10).

repaying the harlot Babylon a judgment that duplicates her iniquities (18:5–8). Yet the key distinguishing factor in this judgment is "another book," the book of life. Written in this book are not deeds but names (20:15; cf. 3:5). When this book appeared earlier in Revelation we were told that these names were inscribed "from the foundation of the world" (17:8), and that the book belongs to the Lamb that was slain (13:8).[47] It is the registry of those from every nation whom he "purchased for God" with his blood (5:9), and it is the one book in all the universe that spells the difference between eternal life and unending death. While people are justly judged according to their deeds, only those inscribed in the Lamb's book of life will escape the lake of fire (20:15). They have been judged already according to Jesus' deeds—his obedience as the faithful witness and his sacrifice as the Lamb—and consequently their vindication is sure.

John sees death and Hades cast last into the lake of fire (20:14), so his vision accords perfectly with Paul's affirmation: "The last enemy that will be abolished is death" (1 Cor. 15:26). Now the lake of fire is identified as "the second death"—that punishment that cannot threaten the overcomers, who participate in the first resurrection, who die faithful to the testimony of Jesus (Rev. 2:11; 20:14). This death is called "second" because it is not the cessation of physical life that permeates the first earth and its "first things" as a result of human sin. Rather, it is the eternal and irreversible destiny of those who worship the creature instead of the Creator, who bear the beast's brand rather than the Lamb's seal.

Conclusion

Twice in these chapters we have seen God's victory over the vicious and violent enemies of his church. At history's end the deceivers (dragon, beast, false prophet) will dupe the world's kings and nations, gathering them to wage the war against Jesus and his people. In this visionary form John sees a coming period of intense and worldwide persecution against the church, an attack so vicious that it cannot be

---

47. For Old Testament background of God's registry of saints, see above on Rev. 3:5 (chap. 4).

compared with anything that the people of God have experienced since the resurrection of Christ. Revelation does not minimize the suffering that the Asian churches had already experienced and the afflictions that the worldwide church would experience down through history. But the visions of the thousand years, standing between the two windows on the last battle, put our present sufferings into perspective: the dragon is still bound, unable to gather his global conspiracy against God's beloved. Persecution is bad now, but it will get worse then, just before the end. Yet even when Satan is unleashed to work his worst, it only will be for "a short time," and the outcome of the conflict is certain to be the defeat and destruction of dragon, beast, false prophet, and all who worship and obey them. John has seen history's ugly end; now he will see eternity's beautiful beginning.

CHAPTER FOURTEEN

Bride:
New Jerusalem, Wife of the Lamb
(21:1–22:21)

The Wedding Day at Last

In the past two years I have had a privilege that few parents can enjoy: I have officiated for the weddings of two of our four children and preached in the weddings of the other two. Weddings are always emotionally moving for the parents of the bride and groom, sometimes more so than for the happy couple themselves. The heart-rending joy is all the more intense, however, for the father who walks his daughter, radiant in white, down the aisle, presents her to her beaming groom, and then calls the couple to vow lifelong love and loyalty to each other. The experience is every bit as powerful when a dad looks at the young man who just yesterday (or so it seems) was building with Legos and learning to kick a soccer ball, as he witnesses this son's covenant to be a loving, protective, gentle, faithful husband to his lovely bride. It doesn't get much better than this—at least, not this side of the wedding between the Lamb and his bride, new Jerusalem, the church, which John is about to witness.

Weddings not only bring parents great joy (perhaps a little sadness, too). There is also a profound sense of relief that months of planning and preparation have reached their goal. Maybe now (except for the bills) life can get back to something closer to normal. These years have taught me in a new way that meaningful weddings, whether large or small, are major productions requiring astute strategizing and hours of work. It is a labor of love, but there is no denying that it is labor. So on the wedding day, besides sharing the bride's and groom's joy, their families share a collective sigh of relief. Yet, just as our weddings now are only the faintest reflections of the glory and joy of the coming wedding, so the price of our preparations in time and effort and money are a pittance when compared with the Lord's elaborate preparation for that celebration that begins a whole new world. My sons-in-law overcame other suitors' efforts to win my daughters' hearts and hands, but even their most strenuous pursuit did not have to come to blood-shed—happily, no pistol duels or fistfights were called for to gain the women of their dreams. But Revelation has shown us the history-long combat in which Jesus the Lamb has been engaged in order to win and beautify his bride.

The consummation of this romance is what Revelation has been about from the start. The blood and fire, locusts and smoke, falling stars and trembling earth, the dragon, the monsters, the scarlet woman—the whole terrifying conflict has been about the divine Husband's jealous love for his bride, a love so jealous that he will fight all comers in order to have her all to himself, a love so sacrificial that he lays down his life to protect her from every threat and enemy. John has seen this "holy city" as the temple's outer court, left "unmeasured" and exposed to trampling under the nations' feet, persecuted and de-spised by the unbelieving world (Rev. 11:2). Now he will see the holy city, beautified for her Husband and radiating the light of his glory (21:2, 11). Now the city is measured top to bottom (21:15–17), so se-cure from enemies that no longer exist that it never needs to shut its gates against invaders (21:25). He has seen this "beloved city" sur-rounded by the nations as a great besieging army, countless in num-ber (20:9). Now he sees the nations walking in the city's light and kings bringing their glory into it (21:24). The new Jerusalem, the bride, the wife of the Lamb (21:9–10) is an almost blinding, imagination-overloading image of the people whom God loves passionately. John's concluding visions reveal the new home that the Groom has prepared for his bride and the presentation of the bride—the church—in the beauty of holiness.

Preparing a New Home for the Bride (21:1–8)

This section is linked to the one before it by the mention of the disappearance of the first heaven and earth at the beginning (Rev. 21:1; cf. 20:11) and the mention of the lake of fire and brimstone at the end (21:8; cf. 20:14–15). It also looks ahead to the following revelation of the bride, the holy city, new Jerusalem (21:2; cf. 21:9–10). This section shows us the outcome of the last judgment for those whose names are written in the Lamb's book of life, with one further reminder that the faithless have no claim on the astonishing joy awaiting overcomers (21:8). But its primary purpose is to prepare us to view the bride by giving us a glimpse of the home that her Husband has prepared for her.

John sees "a new heaven and a new earth" taking the place of the "first" heaven and earth, which had fled from the presence of God in the eschatological "shaking" of heaven and earth (Rev. 21:1; 20:11). The description echoes God's promise through Isaiah: "For behold, I create new heavens and a new earth; and the former things will not be remembered or come to mind" (Isa. 65:17; cf. 66:22). The "former things" are the woes that Israel has endured under God's covenant curse for their sins, as the following verses show by portraying the reversal of the curse: no weeping or crying, premature death, no frustration in home building or farming, "no evil or harm in all My holy mountain" (Isa. 65:25).[1] Likewise in the new heaven and earth which God creates as a home for his bride, the "first things have passed away," and these first things are the woes that infected the first created order through human sin: death, mourning, crying, and pain (Rev. 21:4). The "sea" that no longer exists symbolizes that realm from which chaos and rebellion have emerged to ravage the first earth. Daniel saw four hostile beasts, representing pagan powers that would arise in history

---

1. In another commentary on Isaiah's prophecy about the "new heavens and earth," Peter notes that in this new created order, which emerges from the fiery purging of the present heavens and earth, righteousness will dwell (2 Peter 3:13).

to oppress God's people, come up out of the sea (Dan. 7:3); and it was from the sea that John saw the beast emerge to receive the dragon's devilish power and wage his devilish war against the saints (Rev. 13:1). The sea in heaven is calm and clear as glass (15:2), but the earthly sea that gave rise to the beast stormed with restless, threatening rebellion. Its absence in the new earth further dramatizes the eradication of enemy forces that would have threatened the new home's peace and purity.

Every element of John's first glimpse of the new Jerusalem (Rev. 21:2) will be repeated, with far greater detail, when one of the angels with the bowls takes him to the mountain to see "the bride, the wife of the Lamb" (21:9). The bride is mentioned here to raise hearers' anticipation for the vision to come. This is a frequent literary strategy in Revelation: John sees the angels with trumpets before the saints' prayers are offered as incense, after which the trumpets are blown (8:1, 6–7). He sees angels bearing seven bowls before hearing the heavenly praises of the victorious church, after which the bowls are poured on the earth (15:1, 7–8; 16:1). He first hears the beast named (11:7) long before he sees the beast's ugliness (13:1–8); and he hears of Babylon's fall (14:8) long before he sees her (17:1–7). The announcement of the bride before her entrance also emphasizes that this radical and cosmic renovation—creating for the first time in all history the perfect home—is for her sake.

A loud voice from heaven now offers commentary on what John has seen (Rev. 21:3–4), followed by a series of announcements and instruction from the enthroned One, God (21:5–8). The voice proclaims the final fulfillment of the Immanuel (God with us) theme that runs throughout redemptive history: "Behold, the tabernacle of God is among men, and He will dwell among them" (21:3). The intimacy with God that made Eden truly paradise, the garden of God, was lost through human sin. The tabernacle of God in the midst of Israel's wilderness camp picked up motifs from that lost home, in the fruit-tree patterns of its curtains and the towering cherubim guarding its inmost sanctuary. Yet both tabernacle and temple in Old Testament times were faint previews of the eventual, eternal dwelling of God among his people. God's presence marks the consummation of an intimate covenant commitment, often expressed in the Old Testament in words such as, "My dwelling place also will be with them; and I will be their God, and they will be My people" (Ezek. 37:27; cf. Lev. 26:12), which are echoed here.[2]

The wicked tried to hide from the presence of God (Rev. 6:16–17), and the first heaven and earth had fled from him (20:11). But for those who are his people, redeemed by the blood of the Lamb, the nearness of God will be infinite comfort: "He will wipe away every tear from their eyes" (21:4), removing the mourning veil that covered the peoples and swallowing up death for ever, as he had promised through Isaiah (Isa. 25:8, also echoed in Rev. 7:17). This vivid image of our Lord's personal comfort to each grieving heart shows that it is his presence among us (21:3) that will do away with the "first things" that now threaten our joy and peace. Because God himself dwells with his peoples, "there will no longer be any death . . . mourning, or crying, or pain" (21:4; cf. Isa. 65:19–20).

God himself now speaks from his throne: "Behold, I am making all things new" (Rev. 21:5). Through Isaiah the Lord had announced his purpose to do "new things" to redeem his people, saving acts that would cause "former things" to be forgotten (Isa. 43:18–19; 42:9). Now John foresees the comprehensive, cosmic renewal that will flow from the completion of God's redemptive agenda. He commands John to write and reinforces this instruction and his renewal promise with the solemn declaration, "These words are faithful and true" (Rev. 21:5). Embattled churches of the first and twenty-first centuries, whether intimidated by oppression or beguiled by societal seduction, need to realize that this promise of God is more certain than all that their eyes can see. As Revelation closes, three persons guarantee the reliability of its message: God, the divine author (22:6); Jesus, the divine revealer, who is the faithful and true Witness (22:16; cf. 3:14); and John, the faithful recorder (22:8).

2. A significant group of early manuscripts reads the plural, "his peoples" (so NRSV), instead of the singular, "his people." This unexpected reading could well be original; a copyist would not intentionally change so familiar an expression. If it is, the plural may call attention to the fact that while God's people are unified and can be pictured as a single city, they are also gathered from all the world's peoples (Rev. 5:9; 7:9). Cf. Robert H. Gundry, "The New Jerusalem: People as Place, Not Place for People," *NovT* 29 (1987): 257.

God's pronouncement, "It is done" (Rev. 21:6), echoes the word[3] uttered by a great voice from the throne, when the last bowl was poured out (16:17). There the word looked back to the completion of judgment on God's enemies, for the bowls signify the full and final expression of God's wrath (15:1, 8). Here the word looks forward to the fulfillment of God's favor to his servants, as the following promises of refreshment to the thirsty and inheritance to the overcomer show (21:6–7). God repeats his titles "Alpha and Omega" (interpreted as "the beginning and the end," since Alpha begins the Greek alphabet and Omega ends it) from Revelation 1:8 to remind us of his lordship over all of history and the eternity beyond history in both directions, past and future. Yet the repetition of these titles is more than a reminder. These words of God on the throne anticipate the joyful self-identification of the groom, the divine Son: "Behold, I am coming quickly. . . . I am the Alpha and the Omega, the first and the last, the beginning and the end" (22:12–13). Here we glimpse the mystery of the Trinity. The Father is the beginning and the end, the Creator who stands at history's opening and the Consummator who stands at history's close; and the Son is the beginning and end. They are distinct divine persons, yet one God, who promises his people refreshment and an eternal home.

These two promises not only highlight different dimensions of the bliss that God bestows but also view the recipients of God's favor from different angles. "To the one who thirsts I will give from the spring of the water of life—free of charge"[4] (Rev. 21:6 dej); the one "who overcomes will inherit these things, and I will be to him God and he will be to me son" (21:7 dej). The first promise views us from the standpoint of our need, the thirst of our hearts. The Laodicean church's sense of self-sufficiency is sheer self-delusion, and only those aware of

3. "It is done" translates a single Greek word, *gegonan,* a perfect form of *ginomai* ("it occurs, happens"), which in the perfect tense or aspect means "its occurrence is completed."

4. The adverb *dōrean,* which I have translated "free of charge," highlights the fact that God's grace is given to us freely, though we do not deserve or earn it, in such passages as Rom. 3:24: "being justified as a gift by His grace through the redemption which is in Christ Jesus." Cf. Matt. 10:8; 2 Cor 11:7.

their deep thirst, which God alone can quench by grace, will taste the water of life. John has seen the victorious saints secured in heaven from earth's trials: "They will hunger no longer, nor thirst anymore . . . for the Lamb . . . will guide them to springs of the water of life" (7:16–17). Soon he shall see the river of the water of life, flowing from the throne of God and of the Lamb (22:1). The throne is the spring from which life flows like refreshing water.[5] Because the Lamb has overcome through his sacrifice and sits on the throne, it is the throne of grace (Heb. 4:16).

The second promise views its recipient from the standpoint of the spiritual conflict in which we are called to contend and overcome, drawing on the life and refreshment that are God's free gifts (Rev. 21:7). Each of the seven letters to the churches closed with a promise to "the one who overcomes," and the promises looked ahead to these closing visions of the new heaven and earth and the new Jerusalem. This promise sums up them all in two related blessings of adoption as God's sons: inheritance and authority. Though Christians may be as impoverished as the church at Smyrna was (2:9), even dispossessed and homeless (cf. Heb. 11:37–38), all who overcome the dragon, the beasts, and the harlot through humble, persevering faith are heirs of everything. The homestead that they inherit is not the first heaven and earth, sin-stained and curse-infected, but the new heaven and earth in which every impurity, pain, and sorrow has ceased to be. Along with inheritance the son receives authority. "And I shall be to him God and he shall be to me son" (dej) blends the familiar covenantal promise ("I shall be your God and you shall be my people") with the messianic promise made to David: "I will be a father to him and he will be a son to Me" (2 Sam. 7:14). In the original context of this promise, as well as its elaboration in Psalm 2 (oft alluded to in Revelation), sonship entails participation in God's royal authority over the nations (Rev. 12:6; 11:15, 18). Though Christians may seem as socially impotent as the church at Philadelphia was (3:8), they will administer the Father's rule along with the Lamb, their shepherd (2:26–27).

5. See below for discussion of the background in Ezekiel's vision of the temple (Ezek. 47:1–12; see also Zech. 14:8).

The glories of God's promises to faithful overcomers shine all the more brightly when contrasted with the dire consequences of the last judgment for those who have been captivated by Satan's appealing lies, as the warning of Revelation 21:8 shows. Robert H. Gundry plausibly suggests that this warning targets not the pagan oppressors outside the church (who, in John's visions, were already destroyed), but the hypocrites and traitors within. The list of sinners—cowards, unbelievers, the spiritually repulsive, murderers, the sexually immoral, sorcerers, idolaters, liars—may describe those who, under the pressure of persecution, denied the faith, "murderously betrayed their fellow Christians to the persecuting authorities and practiced the sexual immorality and magic that went along with idolatry."[6] Their inheritance is not in the pain-free new earth, but their "part"[7] is in the lake of fire and brimstone.

Presentation of the Bride (21:9–22:9)

John now sees the genuine bride, of whom the harlot Babylon was a shoddy counterfeit.[8] As we have seen, parallel wording at the opening and closing of the visions of the harlot and the bride reinforces the contrasting parallel between these two women.[9] Both are introduced by one of the angels with the bowls, who summons John with the words, "Come here, I will show you" (Rev. 17:1; 21:9) and carries John away in the Spirit to a lookout point (17:3; 21:10; cf. Ezek. 8:3). At the conclusion of both visions the angel affirms the truthfulness of the divine words he has brought (Rev. 19:9; 22:6), whereupon John kneels to worship the angel and is rebuked (19:10; 22:8–9). The similarities simply magnify the radical difference between the beast's whore and the Lamb's pure bride.

6. Gundry, "New Jerusalem," 258.
7. "Part" here translates *meros,* which sometimes refers to a portion of property allotted through inheritance (Luke 15:12).
8. See Vern S. Poythress, *The Returning King: A Guide to the Book of Revelation* (Phillipsburg, N.J.: P&R Publishing, 2000), 17–22, on the theme of satanic counterfeiting: the dragon counterfeits God; the beast counterfeits the Lamb; the false prophet is a sham "Holy Spirit"; and the harlot is a fake church.
9. See chapter 2.

308

Whereas John was carried to a wilderness to see the harlot, he is taken to "a great and high mountain" to view the bride (Rev. 21:10). The Old Testament background is Ezekiel 40, in which, immediately after the visions concerning the defeat of Gog and Magog (Ezek. 38–39), the prophet is brought to "a very high mountain" to view the measurement of a new temple (Ezek. 40:2–3). The bride appears as "the holy city, Jerusalem, coming down out of heaven from God." Yet the details of its description—its massive dimensions, its building materials, and the names on its gates and foundations—show that the city symbolizes something else, as its title "the bride, the wife of the Lamb" has led us to expect. The bride-city symbolizes the saints, the church in its eschatological beauty.[10] The luminous wedding gown given to the bride by her Groom has already been interpreted as "the righteous acts of the saints" (or "God's just acts vindicating the saints"),[11] and all the details of the city's appearance illustrate aspects of the church's loveliness in the eyes of God.

Dazzling light is the first impression that imprints itself on John's consciousness, for the city has the glory of God and shines with the brilliance of a costly, crystal-clear jasper (Rev. 21:11). Semiprecious jasper, as it appears in nature, may have a mustard or gold color, but it is opaque, not "crystal-clear." John is straining the limits of his hearers' experience to try to communicate a beauty that lies beyond the capacity of the "first earth." Light will pervade his description (21:23–26; 22:5), as will the loveliness of jasper and other precious stones (21:18–21) and the transparency of crystal (21:18, 21). In other words, the radiance that John once saw emanating from the throne of God, whose glory appeared like jasper and sardius (4:3), now permeates the city.[12] The Lord of glory indwells his people and floods his new community with the beauty of his holiness.

10. Gundry, "New Jerusalem," offers ample exegetical evidence to establish this case.

11. See chapter 12, note 34.

12. Cf. Zech. 14:20–21: "In that day there will be inscribed on the bells of the horses, 'HOLY TO THE LORD.' And the cooking pots in the LORD's house will be like the bowls before the altar. Every cooking pot in Jerusalem and in Judah will be holy to the LORD of hosts." When every vessel in Jerusalem is as holy as the temple vessels, the whole city will have become the Holy of Holies, filled with God's

John next notices the city's "great and high wall," and its twelve gates, three on each of its four sides (Rev. 21:12–14). At each gate stands an angel, a reminder of the cherubim with the flaming sword who guarded the gate of Eden (Gen. 3:24) and a symbol of the city's complete security. Never again will this "holy city," God's church, be trodden underfoot by the Gentiles for forty-two months (Rev. 11:2), as it was when John wrote and is as we read his words. As the vision proceeds, other symbols of the city's security will be multiplied—the gates never close, night never falls (21:25)—so the presence of twelve guardian angels may seem superfluous. But every aspect of this portrait is larger than life, as God goes overboard to assure his people that nothing can thwart his plan to transform his people into his royal palace.

Inscribed on the gates are the names of "the twelve tribes of the sons of Israel," and on the wall's foundations are the names of the twelve apostles of the Lamb (Rev. 21:12, 14). The names of the twelve tribes, though not given here, must be those listed in the registry of the 144,000 (7:4–8). Therefore their significance is the same as in Revelation 7. Like that army, sealed with the name of God and the Lamb (14:1), so also this city embraces the covenant people of God, led by the Messiah (Judah promoted to first place) and encompassing believers from all the Gentile nations (sons of the concubines promoted from the end to positions 3–6). This city symbolizes the whole Israel of God, redeemed by the Lion/Lamb of Judah from every tribe and tongue and people and nation to become God's kingdom of priests (5:9–10; cf. Exod. 19:6).

The names of the apostles on the city's twelve foundation stones emphasize the authority of "the word of God and the testimony of Jesus" to define and establish the church. The word *apostle* appears only twice elsewhere in Revelation: the Ephesian church is commended for testing and exposing false apostles (2:2); and the apostles are invited, with the saints and the prophets, to celebrate Babylon's

---

presence. Cf. Edmund P. Clowney, "The Final Temple," *WTJ* 35 (1972–73): 156–89: "So holy will the city become that the inscription of the high priest's tiara will be on the bells of the horses and the wash pots will be as temple vessels (Zech. 14:20)" (164).

fall (18:20). Nevertheless, behind the significant combination "the word of God and the testimony of Jesus" (1:2, 9; 20:4; cf. 6:9; 12:11) stands the testifying role of Jesus' apostles, called and authorized to be witnesses of his resurrection (Acts 1:21; 13:30) and of his whole redemptive mission (1:8). Using the temple metaphor, Paul identifies the apostles and prophets in the early church as the foundation, of which Jesus is the chief cornerstone (Eph. 2:20). They serve as the temple's foundation specifically by receiving and relaying to the church "the mystery" that God kept hidden in past ages but has now revealed in the gospel (Eph. 3:3–6). So also John sees these twelve servants of the Word as foundational for the city—which, as it turns out, is a temple that is filled with God's glory, wall to wall, top to bottom.

Having sketched the general outline of the city, with its wall, gates, and foundations, John now adds dimension and color to the portrait (Rev. 21:15–21). The angel, he now sees, has a gold measuring rod for the purpose of measuring the city, its gates, and its wall (21:15). The imagery is derived from Ezekiel's vision of a temple, to follow Israel's return from exile, which is measured by an angel (a man whose appearance was like bronze) as the prophet watched intently (Ezek. 40:3–5). In Ezekiel 40–42 the precise measurement of each and every feature of this vast, visionary temple (extending for ninety-one verses) dramatizes God's promise to the Jewish exiles in Babylon that the promise of his presence and love will yet see a new and unimaginable fulfillment. That fulfillment focuses on the incarnation of the Son of God, "tabernacling" among us (John 1:14; 2:19–21) and reaches its consummation in the new Jerusalem, which needs no separate building to function as its sanctuary, "for the Lord God Almighty and the Lamb are its temple" (Rev. 21:22).[13] The dimensions that John is about to report dwarf those of Ezekiel's temple, showing not only the symbolic nature of the vision but also, more importantly, the breathtaking majesty and magnitude of Christ's church.

As we saw in the brief vision of Revelation 11:1–2, the activity of measuring a sanctuary area symbolizes its protection from unwelcome and defiling intruders. Then John had been told not to measure the

13. Clowney, "Final Temple," 164–89.

outer court but to leave it exposed to nations that would tread it under foot. This prohibition signified that the holy city, the church that is to appear in all its splendor (21), would suffer outward persecution throughout the present age, even though the church's true and inward identity (the measured sanctuary) remains secure, hidden with Christ in God (cf. Col. 3:3). Here the entire city is measured as another token of its complete safety from every enemy that formerly threatened its holiness and happiness. The dimensions of the city and its walls reinforce the theme of security (21:16–17). The city's overall dimensions are 12,000 stadia by 12,000 stadia by 12,000 stadia—"its length and width and height are equal." Calculated in physical terms, this would make the city approximately 1,365 miles wide and long and high— almost ten times the distance from Dan, Israel's northern border town, to Beersheba in the south. As for height, the top of a city wall standing 1,365 miles above the earth would extend into the orbit path of some manmade satellites. These measurements, however, are not to be understood as physical data but as enhancing the vision's imagery concerning the church's immensity and security. The number 12,000[14] recalls the number from each of Israel's twelve tribes who were to be sealed before the winds of final judgment would be released (7:1–8). We have been reminded of that vision in the mention of "the twelve tribes of the sons of Israel" (21:12). Gundry makes the intriguing proposal that John's vision of "the city foursquare" likewise contains twelve sets of 12,000, since its cubic shape has twelve edges—the base of the wall on each of four sides, the top of the wall on each side, and the four corners.[15] Perhaps more significantly, the city's cubic shape, with dimensions equal in length, width, and height, reproduces the proportions of the Holiest Place that housed the ark of the covenant in the tabernacle and the temple (Exod. 26:15–25; 1 Kings 6:20; cf.

---

14. Unfortunately, NASB, which usually follows a translation philosophy that enables readers to discern the structure of the underlying Greek text, transposes the measurements from 12,000 stadia into an American equivalent, "fifteen hundred miles," moving the symbolically significant figure 12,000 from the text into a marginal note. NIV, more accurately, retains "12,000 stadia," placing modern equivalents in a marginal note.

15. Gundry, "New Jerusalem," 260.

Ezek. 41:4). [16] The city needs no separate sanctuary structure, for God's presence fills the whole city, making it all sanctuary (Rev. 21:22).

Likewise the size[17] of the wall is conveyed in a multiple of twelve, 144 cubits (roughly 216 feet), to reinforce the "people of God" significance that twelve typically carries throughout Revelation and the rest of the New Testament (e.g., Matt. 19:28; James 1:1). By contrast, the wall surrounding Ezekiel's temple was only about 10½ feet thick, according to the formula given in Ezekiel 40:5. "The city-wall is so thick and high that no invading army could penetrate or scale it if they were able to gain a foothold on the mountain (21:12a). . . . John is not describing an eternally secure place. He is describing eternally secure peoples."[18]

Description of the gorgeous materials of which the city is constructed adds to the theme of impregnable strength the additional quality of irresistible attractiveness (Rev. 21:18–21). The wall, like the city (21:11) and God (4:3), appears as jasper; and the city is composed, as its street will be (21:21), of pure gold, transparent as pure glass. The gold that John's hearers and we are familiar with is lovely and can be highly reflective, but it in no way resembles the transparency of glass. The vision stretches and even breaks the paradigm of our experience in order to convey the precious value and purity that distinguishes the bride-church's beauty in the eyes of her Husband.

John lists the twelve foundation stones one by one (Rev. 21:19–20). Since he did not here list names of the twelve tribes or the twelve apostles, this list—jasper, sapphire, chalcedony, emerald, sardonyx,

16. Ibid., 261; Vern S. Poythress, *The Shadow of Christ in the Law of Moses* (Brentwood, Tenn.: Wolgemuth and Hyatt, 1991; reprint ed., Phillipsburg, N.J.: P&R Publishing, 1995), 15–18.

17. Gundry, ibid., takes the 144 cubits as a measurement of thickness, since so short a wall would hardly fit so tall a city (216 feet vs. 7.2 million feet). G. K. Beale, *The Book of Revelation,* NIGTC (Grand Rapids: Eerdmans, 1999), 1076–77, considers 144 cubits a measurement of the wall's height on the basis of the background in Ezek. 40:5; 42:20 and the ancient practice of evaluating a city's security by the height of its walls (e.g., Deut. 3:5; 28:52). They nevertheless agree that this dimension, like those of the city, demonstrates the figurative nature of John's vision and symbolizes the complete security of Christ's church.

18. Gundry, "New Jerusalem," 260.

sardius, chrysolite, beryl, topaz, chrysoprase, jacinth, and amethyst—
carries its own important message. Three Old Testament backgrounds
open up this message.

At least eight[19] of the twelve stones are identical to gems that adorned
the high priest's breastplate at the building of the tabernacle (Exod.
28:17–20 LXX). It is possible that even the other four[20] are John's
translation equivalents (differing from the Septuagint) for the remaining four stones on that breastplate.[21] Since each of the stones on the
high priest's breastplate bore the name of one of Israel's twelve tribes,
the gems' role was to symbolize the amazing truth that the high priest
represented all Israel when he entered the Holiest Place on the Day
of Atonement.[22] In John's vision, however, the Old Testament shadow
has been transformed by its New Testament fulfillment, for, as we
have seen, the names written on the foundation stones of this new
Jerusalem are not those of Israel's sons but those of the Lamb's apostles. The city shows us the complete people of God, and not one tribe
or elect individual is missing. However, God's people are defined not
by descent from Israel but by fidelity to the gospel attested founda-
tionally by the apostles—and with them, prophets, martyrs, and other
faithful confessors. Because the colors of the stones reflect the spec-
trum of the rainbow, from deep red and orange through golden yellow and green to blue, their beauty reflected the radiant glory of the
faithful and holy God whom the high priest was approaching. In Revelation 4:3 sardius (transparent red), jasper (opaque red, yellow, or

19. Jasper, sapphire, emerald, sardius, chrysolite, beryl, topaz, and amethyst.

20. Chalcedony, sardonyx, chrysoprase, and jacinth. Exod. 28:17–20 LXX includes ruby/carbuncle, *ligurion* [LS does not attempt an English translation], agate,
and onyx. NASB translations of the Hebrew names of these stones vary from the
LXX at points, confirming the observation of Caird in the following note.

21. G. B. Caird, *A Commentary on the Revelation of St. John the Divine*, HNTC
(New York: Harper & Row, 1966), 275: "Most ancient writers were somewhat
vague in their identification of precious stones, so that a single Hebrew stone could
easily be equated with more than one Greek one."

22. God had already made this symbolism explicit in his instruction that the names
of Israel's sons were to be engraved on the two onyx stones to be mounted on the
high priest's shoulder pieces: "Aaron shall bear their names before the LORD on his
two shoulders for a memorial" (Exod. 28:12).

green), and emerald (transparent green) are mentioned to paint the beauty of the Lord, his throne, and the rainbow around him.[23]

Second, the stones reappear in a lament over the king of Tyre, which paints in cosmic, Edenic terms the privileged position from which he would fall through arrogance (Ezek. 28:12–19):

> You were in Eden, the garden of God;
> Every precious stone was your covering:
> The ruby, the topaz and the diamond;
> The beryl, the onyx and the jasper;
> The lapis lazuli, the turquoise and the emerald;[24]
> And the gold, the workmanship of your settings and sockets,
> Was in you.
> On the day that you were created
> They were prepared.
> You were the anointed cherub who covers,
> And I placed you there.
> You were on the holy mountain of God;
> You walked in the midst of the stones of fire. (Ezek. 28:13–14)

Proud Tyre's adornment with precious stones and gold, which reflected creation's pristine beauty in the garden of God, was an antecedent to the harlot Babylon's adornment in gold, precious stones, and pearls

23. R. H. Charles, *A Critical and Exegetical Commentary on the Revelation of St. John,* 2 vols., ICC (Edinburgh: T & T Clark, 1920), 2:165–68, and Caird, *Commentary,* 275–77, discuss at length the variation of order between the stones on Aaron's breastplate and the foundation stones of the new Jerusalem. Charles's solution, adopted by Caird, is that the order in Rev. 21 is an exact reversal of the signs of the zodiac, with which the twelve stones on the breastplate are identified in Philo and Josephus and apparently on Egyptian and Arabian monuments. Thus Caird summarizes the meaning of the order: "[John] must have derived his list not directly from Exodus, but from his knowledge of astrology; and he then deliberately reversed it to indicate his total disavowal of astrological interest." This explanation of the order of the stones is more plausible than others, but it does require of John's hearers a complex process to decipher the meaning of the symbolism. Perhaps the order of the stones does not carry a distinct symbolic import in John's vision.

24. Although the Hebrew text, reflected here in the NASB, lists nine stones plus gold, the LXX lists twelve stones in the same order as those on the high priest's breastplate, along with silver and gold.

(Rev. 17:4; 18:12, 16). Therefore in Ezekiel 28 the beauty of the stones underscores the arrogant king's culpability for responding to God's lavish gifts with self-congratulating ingratitude and violence.

The stones' value and loveliness are reminiscent of the goodness of Eden before the fall (cf. the gold, bedellium, and onyx of Eden, Gen. 2:12). As these stones now beautify the foundations of the new Jerusalem, they mark it as Paradise Restored, in which John will soon see the tree of life, no longer barred from our access but now bearing fruit that feeds and leaves that heal the nations (Rev. 22:2).

Finally, precious stones appear as the foundations of Jerusalem in a prophecy of comfort given to suffering Israel:

> O afflicted one, storm-tossed, and not comforted,
> Behold, I will set your stones in antimony,
> And your foundations I will lay in sapphires.
> Moreover, I will make your battlements of rubies,
> And your gates of crystal,
> And your entire wall of precious stones. (Isa. 54:11–12)

Isaiah's imagery of precious stones as foundations associated with city walls is the closest biblical antecedent to John's vision. It reminds us that John received these visions in order to bring comfort and courage to embattled churches ("afflicted . . . stormed tossed, and not comforted"), just as Isaiah's prophecy comforted ancient Israel. Though now scorned and harassed by world powers that seem to dwarf Jesus' church, believers can take heart. The church's priceless value and eternal safety are secured by the God who founds and surrounds his city with precious stones.[25]

The twelve gates, bearing the names of the Israelite tribes, are each composed of a single pearl, its luminous white enhancing the glory and purity of the city (Rev. 21:21). The city's street, like the city (cf. 21:18) is pure gold, of infinite value, and transparent as glass, of infinite purity and radiant with glory. Again we remember that the vision speaks in visionary symbolism not of the physical components of

25. See Beale's extended discussion of the Old Testament and Jewish background of the gems (*Revelation*, 1080–88).

a coming metropolis but of the spiritual qualities of the people of God, the true identity of the bride, which is to be revealed from heaven at Christ's return. Perhaps our attention is drawn to the street to emphasize the pervasive glory of the city, extending even to the avenue on which people's feet will tread. As Zechariah foresaw a Jerusalem in which every cooking pot in every household would be as holy as the temple vessels (Zech. 14:20–21), so John sees a city in which even the humble pavement underfoot is gilded with transparent gold.

John now sees signs that positive but provisional elements of the first earth, and not only its negative features (death, crying, mourning, pain, Rev. 21:4), will disappear when the church's enemies are destroyed and our identity as the bride of the Lamb is fully revealed (21:22–27). He sees no temple sanctuary in the city, "for the Lord God Almighty and the Lamb are its temple" (21:22). Israel's physical sanctuaries, the tabernacle and later the temple, served the dual function of providing intimacy with God and insulation from his consuming holiness. God dwelt in the midst of his people, but not every one of his people could demand a face-to-face audience with this holy King of kings, as the Israelites observed with horror in the destruction of Korah, Dathan, and Abiram (Num. 16–17). Weak Israel needed the Lord's presence in their midst to protect them from foes and, more importantly, to define their identity as a people (Exod. 33:15–16). But sinful Israel needed the walls and curtains of the sanctuary to protect them from the Lord, to provide a buffer and heat shield between them and this consuming Fire (Exod. 33:5; Deut. 4:24). Now, however, John sees an image of the new Jerusalem that speaks of a people so purified, washed so clean objectively (justification) and subjectively (sanctification) through the blood of the Lamb that they need not fear direct contact with their Lord and Redeemer.

From God and the Lamb radiates bright and constant light, making the luminaries of the first heaven, sun and moon, obsolete and unnecessary (Rev. 21:23). Isaiah had foreseen this day, when creaturely and mutable light sources will no longer be needed:

> No longer will you have the sun for light by day,
> Nor for brightness will the moon give you light;
> But you will have the LORD for an everlasting light,

And your God for your glory.
Your sun will no longer set,
Nor will your moon wane;
For you will have the LORD for an everlasting light,
And the days of your mourning will be over. (Isa. 60:19–20; cf. v. 1)

John's wording draws a small but significant distinction between the light-giving roles of God the Father and of Christ the Son. The Father is the ultimate source from which all truth flows ("the glory of God has illumined it"), and the Son is the agent who reveals the Father in his glory and truth ("its lamp is the Lamb"). These have been the perfectly complementary roles of Father and Son in revelation throughout the cosmic conflict of redemptive history, and they will continue to be so in eternity.[26]

Two results follow from the presence of the Lord as the constant light source among his people. "The nations walk by its light," and their kings bring glory into God's city (Rev. 21:24, 26). And because night never falls and no defiling intruder can slip into the city under veil of darkness, the city's gates never close but remain wide open to receive a glory that will constantly enrich its beauty (21:25, 27).

The imagery of the nations walking by God's light, which shines from the new Jerusalem, and bringing their wealth into the city is derived from Isaiah 60:3–5:

Nations will come to your light,
And kings to the brightness of your rising.
Lift up your eyes round about and see;
They all gather together, they come to you.
Your sons will come from afar,
And your daughters will be carried in the arms.
Then you will see and be radiant,
And your heart will thrill and rejoice;
Because the abundance of the sea will be turned to you,
The wealth of the nations will come to you.

26. See Matt. 11:27; John 1:4–9, 14, 18; 8:12; 17:6.

John does not literally envision Gentile nations outside the holy city, for the Gentiles whose names are written in the book of life are the city (cf. Rev. 22:27b). Those not inscribed in the Lamb's book have already received their apportioned inheritance in the lake of fire (20:15; cf. 21:8) and have no place in the new heavens and earth, of which the new Jerusalem is queen. The nations' influx into the city, bearing their glory and honor, vividly portrays the reality that this bride of the Lamb does and will include and embrace the elect from all the world's peoples. John saw a preview of this climactic gathering for worship in Revelation 7: "I looked, and behold, a great multitude which no one could count, from every nation and all tribes and peoples and tongues, standing before the throne and before the Lamb . . . saying, 'Salvation to our God who sits on the throne, and to the Lamb'" (7:9). That preview also makes clear that the glory and honor that are carried into the city are not intended for the new Jerusalem's consumption. Rather, they are brought into this final sanctuary, as were the gifts and sacrifices of the earthly sanctuary, to be offered to the divine King enthroned in it.

The absence of night is related to the fact that the city's twelve gates stand perpetually open, never needing to be shut against attack or intruder. Just as the new earth contains no sea, the region of lawlessness from which the beast had emerged (Rev. 13:1), so the new Jerusalem experiences no night, in which darkness could cloak evil deeds. (Hence sun and moon are not needed either as light providers or as time dividers, Gen. 1:14–18.) Not only will the holy city be shielded from the assault of external persecutors, as it is not now (11:2), but also it will be immune from infiltration by traitorous hypocrites. As in Revelation 21:8, the spiritually unclean, who practice idolatrous abomination and lying and are excluded forever from the city, are those who profess allegiance to Jesus the Messiah but who compromise in order to avoid suffering or achieve acceptance by the surrounding pagan culture (21:27; cf. the earlier discussion of 21:8). The light of God and the Lamb not only beautifies the city like a gleaming jewel but also secures the city's safety and purity forever.

The angel has one more perspective on the bride's beauty to show to John. This final camera angle focuses on images of the abundant

life, refreshment, and nourishment that the Lord will provide for his
people: the river of the water of life (Rev. 22:1) and the tree of life
(22:2). The most explicit biblical background to these aspects of the
new Jerusalem is Ezekiel's vision of the last days temple (Ezek.
47:1–12). Ezekiel saw water flowing from the eastward-facing thresh-
old of the house of God. As he watched the angel measure the river's
depth at thousand-cubit intervals, he observed that this strange river
reached ever-greater depths—without inflow from tributaries—the
farther it moved from its fount in God's house (Ezek. 47:3–5). The
river in the vision was unlike any that ever flowed in Palestine in another respect as well: when it flowed into the Dead Sea, it turned the
sea's heavily mineralized waters fresh, so that fish could thrive there
(Ezek. 47:8–10). The river's unusual features show the figurative or
symbolic form in which Ezekiel's vision is given. From the presence
of God, in the last days, will flow life-giving water—quite consistently
in the prophets an image of the Spirit of God, who cleanses and imparts life to the dead (especially Ezek. 36:25–27; 37:9–10, 14; see also
Isa. 44:3; John 3:5–6). Moreover, on the river's banks "will grow all
kinds of trees for food. Their leaves will not wither and their fruit will
not fail. They will bear every month because their water flows from
the sanctuary, and their fruit will be for food and their leaves for healing" (Ezek. 47:12).[27] Not only the quenching of our heart's thirst but
also the satisfaction of spiritual hunger and the healing of wounds and
woes proceed from the throne room of God. So now John sees the
river of the water of life flowing from God's throne, as clear as crystal. When he first saw this throne, he noted the pavement in front of
the throne "like a sea of glass, like crystal" (Rev. 4:6; cf. 15:2). Now
the stillness of the glassy sea, symbolizing God's sovereign tranquility,
flows into a crystal-clear river, symbolizing God's overflowing goodness, imparting life to all who in their thirst respond to his invitation
to drink deeply of the abundant life that only he can give. We have
heard this promise from God's lips earlier in this vision (21:6), and in
the conclusion it will reappear as a welcoming invitation to the thirsty

27. See also Zech. 14:8: "And in that day living waters will flow out of Jerusalem,
half of them toward the eastern sea [Dead Sea] and the other half toward the western sea [Mediterranean Sea]; it will be in summer as well as in winter."

person, to come and drink from this life-giving water that flows from God's throne of grace, as a free gift of grace (22:17). Jesus had told the Samaritan woman that he himself gives "living water" (John 4:10). In first-century Greek "living water" sometimes meant flowing water from a spring or river rather than standing water in a cistern, and apparently that is how she first understood Jesus' words (4:11). But Jesus was not speaking of physical water that could stave off thirst only for a time. He promised her water that would become in her "a well of water springing up to eternal life" (4:13–14). This is the water of the Holy Spirit's resurrection life, which John now sees in vision flowing from the throne of God and the Lamb.

John's vision traces the imagery of Ezekiel's eschatological temple even further back, to the beginning; for he sees "the tree of life" on both banks of the river. The tree of life stood in the center of Eden, the garden of God (Gen. 2:9), and after their foolish rebellion Adam and Eve were expelled from the garden specifically to bar them from access to the tree of life in their condition of spiritual fallenness (Gen. 3:22–24). In the new heaven and earth, however, the earth's peoples will again have access to the tree of life. The seventh and final benediction will show us how this can be: "Blessed are those who wash their robes, so that they may have the right to the tree of life, and may enter the gates into the city" (Rev. 22:14). We already glimpsed what this "washing of robes" entails when the elder interpreted for John the international assembly of blessed ones, who stood before the throne of God and the Lamb in white robes, washed and whitened in the blood of the Lamb (7:14).

As the trees in Ezekiel's vision continuously produced fruit and leaves beneficial to humanity, so John sees that the tree of life bears twelve types of fruit, one in each month, and that its leaves heal the nations. Recognizing the rich symbolism of John's visions, we understand that he is not implying that in the new heavens and earth there remain diseased nations, still in need of healing. Rather, drawing on the imagery of Ezekiel 47, the comment on the healing power of the tree's leaves vividly illustrates the next exultant declaration: "There will no longer be any curse" (Rev. 22:3). The sin of Adam and Eve unleashed curse on the earth, as well as on all their children

(Gen. 3:14–19). In the new heaven and earth, for the sake of the new Jerusalem bride of the Lamb, that curse will be reversed, erased forever-more. When death and Hades are thrown into the lake of fire, the na-tions who are inscribed in the Lamb's book of life, the citizen registry of the new Jerusalem, will have experienced healing.

Revelation 22:3–5 thus concludes the description of the bride with a summary of earlier aspects of the vision. "There will no longer be any curse" echoes and recaps the promise that when God dwells with his people and wipes away their tears, "there will no longer be any death; there will no longer be any mourning, or crying, or pain" (21:4).[28] John's earlier observation that the city contains no separate sanctuary edifice because the Lord God and the Lamb are the temple of the city (21:22) now receives fuller elaboration: the throne of God and of Lamb is in the city, God's servants wait on him in his presence, and they shall see his face (22:3–4). The "bond-servants" who will serve in God's presence are the nations who bring their glory and honor to present them in worship to the King of kings (22:3). Re-deemed by the Lamb's blood from all the world's peoples, they will offer the service of worship as "priests to our God" (5:9–10).

The brief statement, "they will see His face" (Rev. 22:4), under-scores the unimaginable wonder and joy awaiting all who are mem-bers of the bride through faith in the Lamb. Even Moses, with whom God spoke "mouth to mouth" and whose face radiated God's glory, could not see God's face and live (Num. 12:8; Exod. 34:29–35; 33:20). He needed to be shielded by God's hand from the overpowering splen-dor of God's glory (Exod. 33:22–23), just as Israel needed to be shielded by the sanctuary curtains and the high priest did not dare to enter the Holiest Place until the atonement cover on the ark was engulfed in smoke from the incense altar (Lev. 16:13). For the new Jerusalem in the new heaven and earth, however, there will be no more need for protection of God's people from his consuming holiness; hence John sees no temple in the holy city (Rev. 21:22). Seeing his face is deadly

28. The parallel is as unmistakable in Greek as in the NASB's English translation: "there will no longer be" is *ouk estai eti* in Rev. 21:4 and 22:3 (as in 22:5, regard-ing night; and a similar construction, with only a variation in verb tense, in 21:1 re-garding the sea).

danger to us now because we are defiled by sin, but then all our shame and guilt will be a thing of the past as we stand before him beautiful, in the robe of righteousness that he has given us.

The promise that God's name will be on the foreheads of his servants reminds us of the role of that name as a seal, marking believers as God's property and therefore assuring us of protection from his coming wrath (Rev. 6:17–7:3; 14:1). It is the overcomer's badge of honor to bear, as Jesus says to the persecuted Philadelphian church, "the name of My God, and the name of the city of My God, the new Jerusalem, which comes down out of heaven from My God, and My new name" (3:12). It is already true that believers' identity is bound up with our union with Christ; then it will be evident for all to see (Col. 3:3–4).

The vision closes, as it began, in resplendent light (Rev. 22:5). As John saw the holy city descend from heaven, it shone with the glory of God and its brilliance resembled a precious gem (21:11). He learned that the divine glory that illumines the city, mediated through the Lamb as lamp, will make sun and moon superfluous and banish the threatening darkness of night forever (21:23–25). These themes—no more night, no need of sun or created lamp, the Lord shining—are recapped in Revelation 22:5, with the further comment that the saints' ultimate destiny is not only priestly intimacy in service to God but also royal authority in union with Christ: "and they will reign forever and ever" (cf. Dan. 7:18).

The conclusion that wraps up the revelation of the bride (Rev. 22:6–9) reproduces the pattern at the finale of the judgment of the harlot (19:9–10):

(1) The revealing angel affirms the faithfulness and truth of God's words (22:6; 19:9).
(2) The angel pronounces one of the book's seven benedictions (22:7; 19:9).
(3) John falls at the angel's feet to worship the celestial messenger (22:8; 19:10).
(4) The angel rebukes John, "Do not do that. I am a fellow servant of yours and your brethren. . . . Worship God." (22:9; 19:10).

John's "brethren" are identified from complementary viewpoints in the two angels' words. The angel who revealed the harlot spoke of the brethren "who hold the testimony of Jesus" (19:10), whereas the angel revealing the bride describes them as "the prophets and those who heed the words of this book" (22:9).

The hallmark of the true bride, in contrast to the harlot, is that she worships no one but God and waits for no bridegroom but the Lamb. This church, composed of John and his fellow servants who hold to the testimony of Jesus and cling to the faithful words of God, now appears to be a small minority, defenseless in the face of the aggression of hostile government, the deception of pseudo-religion, and the seduction of euthanizing affluence. In fact, however, she is the King's beloved; and he is driving history to the consummation of their marriage, when her every enemy is vanquished and the Lamb's glory floods her life with light.

Epilogue: Promised Blessings and Instructions (22:6–21)

As we saw in our examination of the overall structure of the book (chap. 2), Revelation 22:6–9 not only concludes the vision of the new Jerusalem but also belongs to the epilogue, resuming themes introduced in the book's prologue:

(1) God sent his angel "to show His bond-servants the things which must soon take place" (22:6). This echoes the wording of Revelation 1:1.
(2) The promise, "Behold, I am coming quickly" (22:7), which will be repeated twice more in the epilogue (22:12, 20), has its counterpart on the prologue's "Behold, He is coming with the clouds" (1:7). It also echoes Jesus' announcements to the churches at Pergamum and Philadelphia—the first a threat and the second a promise (2:16; 3:11).
(3) The sixth benediction, "Blessed is the one who keeps the words of the prophecy of this book" (22:7 dej), corresponds quite closely to the first (1:3).

Thus at the book's end, as at its beginning, we are summoned to keep the words of this prophecy, clinging to them for dear life amid the flood of satanic lies swirling all around. This book is the testimony of Jesus (cf. 19:10), and it contains God's words, which are faithful and true. John also confirms how reliable the process of transmitting the message has been: "I, John, am the one who heard and saw these things" (22:8; see 1:1–2). Later in the epilogue Jesus will speak directly his testimony, to confirm his suffering churches' faith in his words (22:16). In a world where things are not what they seem, the only sure guide is the faithful word of the living God.

The angel's instruction to John, "Do not seal up the words of the prophecy of this book, for the time is near" (Rev. 22:10), is the opposite of the instruction given to Daniel (Dan. 12:4, 9). The sealing of Daniel's prophecy signaled that the time of its fulfillment was remote, standing in a different epoch of God's redemptive plan from the prophet (cf. Dan. 8:26). What John has seen, however, concerns the redemptive-historical epoch in which he is living—the span between the resurrection of Christ and his return, the 1,260 days between the enthronement of the woman's child and his return as the captain of heaven's cavalry. Because John stands with his hearers in the time in which the conflict of the ages has reached its critical pitch in the sacrifice of the Lamb and the expulsion of the dragon accuser from heaven, every individual needs to face immediately the sort of person he or she is today, without assuming a perpetual string of tomorrows in which change might occur. "Let the one who does wrong, still do wrong; and the one who is filthy, still be filthy; and let the one who is righteous, still practice righteousness; and the one who is holy, still keep himself holy" (22:11). This is a strange pairing of exhortations. Although we are not surprised to hear encouragement to persevere in righteousness and holiness, it is shocking for Scripture to urge evildoers to persist in their injustice and the defiled in their defilement. The background in Daniel 12:10, immediately after a text to which reference has been made when John was prohibited from sealing his book, helps us find our way: "Many will be purged, purified and refined, but the wicked will act wickedly, and none of the wicked will understand, but those who have insight will understand." The end time will make the division between the purified and insightful and the wicked in-creasingly sharp and irreversible. What Daniel saw in the future John sees in the present. The apparent exhortation to the wrongdoer and the filthy is more rhetorical than real, observing the behavioral out-come of their failure to discern that they live in the last days. The ex-hortation to those who have the wisdom to pursue righteousness and holiness is a genuine summons to persevering faith and obedience.[29] Opposite heart orientations and behavior patterns have opposite des-tinies, as will be clear when the Lamb who is the supreme judge comes.

The voice suddenly changes without notice, as the speaker's self-description makes clear that he is not a mere angel, unworthy of wor-ship, but the eternal God (Rev. 22:12–13). The titles used earlier by the enthroned One, "I am the Alpha and Omega, the beginning and the end" (21:6), are further explained by a third pair of opposites, "the first and the last." This set is drawn from the Lord's proclamations of his uniqueness as the only true and living God (Isa. 41:4; 44:6; 48:12). In Revelation we have heard it previously only on the lips of the triumphant Son of Man (1:17; 2:8), and it is he who is now speaking. The one and only, incomparable and eternal God, who stands sovereign at history's dawn and its sunset, is the One seated on the throne—and this one God is also the Lamb who became dead for his own, yet lives forevermore (1:18). His coming at history's midpoint was to accomplish redemption, and the coming he promises at history's end is to execute judgment: "Be-hold, I am coming quickly, and My reward is with me, to render to every man according to what he has done" (22:12). "My reward is with me" recalls Isaiah's promise to downcast Zion that the Lord will come to re-store his people and destroy their enemies (Isa. 62:11; cf. 40:10), which is followed immediately by the vision of the Lord marching home in righteous victory, the blood of his enemies staining his garments red like wine from the press (Isa. 63:1–6; cf. Rev. 14:17–20; 19:13–15).

The reward that Jesus brings imparts blessing to those who trust in his cleansing blood, as well as retribution for those who persist in evil (22:14–15). The last of Revelation's seven benedictions highlights the Lamb's atoning sacrifice and the privileges it bestows (22:14). The blessed

29. See Beale, *Revelation,* 1131–34.

are "those who wash their robes" and so have the right (*exousia*) to eat of the tree of life and to enter the gates of the final city-garden. Since John has heard the bride's fine linen wedding dress interpreted as "the righteous deeds of the saints,"[30] one might assume that "washing robes" symbolizes the strenuous pursuit of personal, subjective holiness. John's choice of language, however, points in a different direction. "Wash" (*plynō*) appears only once elsewhere in Revelation, in the elder's explanation of the international multitude dressed in white robes: "they have washed their robes and made them white in the blood of the Lamb." Citizenship in the new Jerusalem and free access to the tree that imparts eternal life are not wages earned through our self-improvement efforts. Rather, they are free gifts that flow from the sacrificed Lamb to those who humbly trust him, thirsting for the water of life that he alone supplies (cf. 21:6; Matt. 5:6). The bride wears fine linen, bright and clean, because this beautiful raiment has been given to her (Rev. 19:8).

Those whose recompense from the Lamb is exclusion from the city have only themselves—their desires and deeds—to blame (Rev. 22:15). This final warning rephrases the judgments announced twice in the new heaven and earth/new Jerusalem vision (21:8, 27), and the offenses listed here—sorcery, immorality, murder, idolatry, lying—all appear in Revelation 21:8. As we saw in connection with that verse, the primary purpose of this statement may well be not so much to comfort Christians with the assurance that their external enemies will be punished. Rather, it is to warn those who are superficially or hypocritically affiliated with the churches but who then capitulate to pressure and temptation from the surrounding pagan culture. Their eternal dwelling will not be in the city of God but in the lake of fire.

The concluding verses (22:16–21) reemphasize that this book is "the Revelation of Jesus Christ" (1:1) and "the testimony of Jesus" (1:2, 9; 12:17; 19:10). "Testimony" is highlighted by a threefold repetition of the cognate verb, "testify" (*martyreō*), each time with Jesus as its subject (22:16, 18, 20). The divine authority of the Christ who bears witness in this book calls its hearers to embrace its promises, accept its invitations, and be warned by its threats.

---

30. Another possible interpretation, though, is "[God's] vindicating acts on behalf of the saints." See chapter 12 on Rev. 19:8.

The faithful witness (Rev. 1:5; 3:14) identifies himself by name—
"I, Jesus"—and reminds us of the chain of transmission introduced at
the beginning of the book: I "have sent My angel to testify to you these
things for the churches" (22:16; cf. 1:1–2, 4). In Revelation 1:1 John
alone was mentioned as the human recipient of the testimony sent by
Jesus through his angel, but here the plural form, "to you" (*hymin*),
places him in the company of other New Testament prophets ("your
brethren the prophets," 22:9) who serve the churches by bringing them
God's word. Jesus' authority to judge and save, to promise and threaten,
is rooted in his identity as "the root and the descendant of David, the
bright morning star." As we saw in Revelation 5:5, the imagery of the
root of David is adapted from Isaiah 11:1, 10, in which God promised
to raise up a wise, just, and mighty king from the Davidic dynasty even
after it had been cut down to "the root of Jesse" (David's father) in the
exile to Babylon. The adaptation of this image in Revelation signals
the uniqueness of Jesus. He is not only David's descendant (*genos*), the
"shoot from the root" in the picture from Isaiah; but he is also David's
root, David's source or origin—even more deeply than Jesse was the
root from which David and his heirs had sprung. Thus these two titles
pose the mystery of his person in a way complementary to the dilemma
that Psalm 110:1 posed for Jesus' theological opponents: Is Messiah
David's son, or David's Lord (Matt. 22:41–46)? In that Holy Week dispute, and now in this triumphant self-disclosure at the close of Revelation, Jesus answers, "Both! I am David's Lord, the root from which
he and his royalty sprang. But I am also David's son, the offspring in
whom God's promise of endless righteous rule is finally fulfilled." Jesus
is the bright morning star foreseen by Balaam, the royal champion who
would arise from Israel to conquer God's enemies, including Balaam's
employer, Moab (Num. 24:17; see Rev. 2:28).

"Come" is the key term of Revelation 22:17, but to whom is this
invitation, command, or request addressed? "The Spirit and the bride
say, 'Come,'" and the hearer is instructed to do likewise. Is this a prayer
addressed to Jesus, who has twice promised, "I am coming quickly,"
in the preceding verses (22:7, 12)?[31] If so, it anticipates the fuller form

31. G. R. Beasley-Murray, *The Book of Revelation*, NCB (Grand Rapids: Eerdmans, 1981), 343–44.

of this prayer that will be found in Revelation 22:20: "Come, Lord Jesus." Yet in the closer context, the rest of Revelation 22:17, the thirsty one is exhorted to "come" and take the water of life as a free gift.[32] The enthroned One has promised to refresh the thirsty with this fresh and life-giving water (21:6), and Jesus had issued an invitation similar to this at the Feast of Tabernacles, using water to picture the Spirit: "If anyone is thirsty, let him come to Me and drink . . . rivers of living water" (John 7:37–39). So it is appropriate that the Spirit, symbolized as lamps in heaven (Rev. 4:5), and the church-bride, symbolized as lampstands on earth (1:20), now blend their voices to invite this world's thirsty ones to the water, holding forth the testimony of Jesus for as long as God's patience delays final judgment. The repetition of the invitation echoes a similar gospel offer in Isaiah 55:1,[33] confirming that the "comes" in our passage are evangelistic, inviting the world's peoples to repentance, faith, and life in this age of divine forbearance. The Spirit's mission is to make the bride into faithful witnesses among the nations, so he is not satisfied if the church merely hangs on by its fingernails under the pressure of a hostile culture. The bride's calling is to call out to the thirsty, "Come to my Husband, who gives heart-thirst quenching waters." Everyone who hears the voice of the Spirit and the church is to add his or her voice to their testimony.

Jesus testifies[34] to all who hear not only about the freeness of his grace but also about the inviolability of his words (Rev. 22:18–19). He pronounces severe sanctions against anyone who presumes to add or subtract from this book, echoing the prohibition of Moses against adding or taking away from the law of God: "You shall not add to the word which I am commanding you, nor take away from it, that you

---

32. Caird, *Commentary*, 286–87: "The first 'Come!' is addressed not to Christ but to all comers; . . . it is a summons both to join the ranks of the Conquerors and to enter into the Conquerors' reward."

33. Isa. 55:1: "Ho! Every one who thirsts, come to the waters; and you who have no money come, buy and eat. Come, buy wine and milk without money and without cost." This text is also alluded to in Rev. 3:18.

34. Many interpreters and translators believe that John is the subject of "I testify" (*martyrō*) and therefore the speaker of Rev. 22:18–19. The repetition of "testify" in Rev. 22:20, however, identifies "He who testifies to these things" (*ho martyrōn*) as Jesus, who is coming quickly.

may keep the commandments of the LORD your God which I command you" (Deut. 4:2; cf. 12:32; Josh. 1:7). The false prophet who presumes to add to the words of this prophecy, speaking where God has not spoken (Deut. 18:20–22), will have added to him the horrific plagues that have been visualized throughout the book, including the lake burning with fire and brimstone. The person who presumes to delete any of the words, evading Jesus' call to purity and endurance or scorning his promised blessings or threatened judgments, will discover that his share of the tree of life and the new Jerusalem have been deleted by God. This divine Witness is not to be toyed with! He jealously guards the integrity of his word, for it is through this word that he jealously guards his beloved bride from the devil's lies.

Jesus' final word of testimony in Revelation is a repetition of his promise to come quickly (22:20). John, on behalf of the church, affirms confidence in this promise: "Amen"—a Hebrew word meaning "it is firm, trustworthy," carried into Greek by the early church, and from there into the tongues of the nations as the gospel spreads and the church is planted among the world's diverse peoples. In this confident hope, we respond to Jesus' promise, "Come, Lord Jesus"—a translation into Greek of the early Aramaic-speaking church's eschatological prayer, *marana tha* ("Our Lord, come!"; cf. 1 Cor. 16:22). Nothing less than the sight of her glorious, risen Lord Jesus will release the church from its present sufferings into his kingdom of justice and peace, bringing our current endurance to its final destination (cf. Rev. 1:9).

A brief, closing blessing reminds us, John's hearers, that even before Jesus' triumphant bodily return from heaven, he has not left us orphans, defenseless before our mighty foes: "The grace of the Lord Jesus be with all" (Rev. 22:21). With such strong grace accompanying us each step of the way, Jesus' embattled people have every reason to anticipate with confidence our indescribable joy when "we will be like Him, because we will see Him just as He is" (1 John 3:2).

Conclusion

Revelation has shown us repeatedly that those who dwell with God in heaven constantly break forth in song, overwhelmed with joy and adoration by his perfections in himself and by his awesome achievements in creation and redemption. In Revelation 21–22 we have seen the wife of the Lamb, new Jerusalem, descend from heaven as the holy garden city of God. We have learned that all who belong to her will see their God face to face and serve him with gladness. We have witnessed a glimpse of history's climactic wedding and the beautiful home—new heaven and earth—to be created by the divine Bridegroom for his bride, his church. Surely here a song is called for, and "New Jerusalem" by Terry Talbot and Jamie Owens-Collins captures powerfully how the promise of our coming wedding to the Lamb fortifies the church to endure present testing in hope.

> Lord, make ready your queen now.
> She waits in hope, watching the clouds.
> Clouds of rain, washing her clean now.
> Soon she'll be seen
> Ready to have and to hold.
> *Stand, New Jerusalem,*
> *Dressed in white linen,*
> *Take his hand!*
> *Take his hand, you lovely bride of the Lamb.*
> The bride-to-be is waiting, clothed in purity,
> Getting ready for the wedding to begin.
> And now she sings her love song,
> Watching for the Son,
> And she knows, yes, she knows He'll come again.
>
> She hears of war and famine, as her Lord foretold,
> Sees the nations rushing blindly to their doom,
> But she lifts her head, rejoicing,
> Watching for the Son,
> For she knows the world will bow before her Groom.[35]

35. Terry Talbot and Jamie Owens-Collins, "New Jerusalem," from Jamie Owens, *Growing Pains,* sound cassette/CD. © 1976 *Bud John Songs, Inc. International Copyright Secured. All Rights Reserved. Used by Permission.

CHAPTER FIFTEEN

Conclusion:
What Should This Book Do to Us?

When we wrestle with Revelation, the obvious question to ask is "What in the world does this strange book mean?" (Or, "What out of this world does it mean?") Confronted with bizarre visions that are alien to our ordinary experience, it is natural and right that we set ourselves to the task of solving the puzzle, trying to understand, to the best of our ability, the content of the message that this book expresses.

It soon becomes evident that answering the question of meaning raises a prior question: "How should we read this book?" We cannot investigate what Revelation means unless we grasp what kind of literature it is and unless we find a strategy for interpretation that fits that kind of literature. Different literary genres deliver their payloads of meaning in differently shaped vessels. Each vessel is composed of common clay, the language that people share in common; yet each is also molded into a distinctive form in order to carry its communication content effectively. In Revelation we have noticed the prominence of symbolism, a pictorial vocabulary already prepared for John's message in the events and prophetic visions of the Old Testament. Knowing how to view these pictures is crucial to hearing what they say.[1]

---

1. See Dennis E. Johnson, "The Rules of the Road," *Tabletalk* 23.2 (February 1999): 8–10, 56–57.

If we are content when we think we have answers to questions of meaning and hermeneutics, however, we will stop short of the question that God wants us to ask whenever we read Revelation: "What should this book do to us?" Scripture is not a passive cadaver, waiting for curious medical students to dissect it in their quest for information. It is a living, double-edged sword that proceeds from the mouth of the triumphant Son of Man and pierces the thoughts and intents of our hearts. It is a hammer that shatters, a seed that grows, rainfall that never returns to its Giver without accomplishing the mission on which he sent it. Scripture has a job to do in us: "All Scripture is inspired by God and profitable for teaching, for reproof, for correction, for training in righteousness; so that the man of God may be adequate, equipped for every good work" (2 Tim. 3:16–17). Scripture's mission is not only teaching, enriching our understanding and expanding our knowledge, although it includes this. God sends his Word also to reprove us, showing us where we are in the wrong; to correct us, straightening us out and setting us on course; and to train us in righteousness, engraining deep within our hearts lovely patterns of integrity, kindness, and glad obedience. So it is right to conclude our study by stepping back from questions of interpretive theory and cognitive content to ask how God intends the Book of Revelation to change us, its hearers.

Revelation is, after all, written for a church under attack (see chap. 1, principle 5). We, no less than John's first hearers on the west coast of Asia Minor, are a church under attack. In some places in today's world the attack is as blatant and violent as it was in Pergamum, where Satan's throne was and where Antipas had proven his faithfulness as Jesus' witness by laying down his life for the word of God and the testimony of Jesus. Elsewhere the attack is as subtle as the spiritual stupor that had overcome the church at Sardis or the smug complacency that blinded the Laodiceans to their poverty of heart. The beast, the false prophet, and the harlot are still the dragon's weapons in his futile war against the saints, as they were in John's day, when they took the forms of the Roman Empire's politico-military strength, the imperial cult that worshiped Rome and its rulers, and the idolatrous lust for social acceptance and material luxuries.

See Your Situation in Its True Perspective

We perceive things three-dimensionally because our two eyes view objects from slightly different angles. Without these distinct perspectives supplied by two eyes and then mysteriously integrated by our brains, we would lack depth perception. Visually we would inhabit a two-dimensional world. Revelation's paradoxical portraits of the church's identity and present experience in the world provide the contrasting and complementary perspectives that we need to find our way through this life.

You are living between two worlds: the first heaven and earth, which are destined for destruction; and the new creation, to which you already belong as God's holy city, the bride now being beautified for her Husband. Jesus' Revelation to the churches through John is given to help you navigate the paradoxes built into the betweenness of your situation.

In the truest and deepest perspective, you are safe and secure, protected by the Lord God Almighty and defended by the Lamb who has overcome. You are the sealed people of God, marked with his name. Whatever may occur between today and the great day of the wrath of God and the Lamb, you know that on that last day, you will be able to stand without terror and with expectant joy. You are the measured sanctuary of God, jealously guarded by his Spirit from any defilement that would lead to his withdrawal from your midst. You are the two invincible witnesses of God. His enemies cannot silence you until you have completed your mission and delivered the testimony that he has entrusted to you in your generation. Even when death seems to have gained the upper hand and you lie in the dust or the city street, its victory will be short-lived.

Revelation is also brutally frank in revealing the call to follow Christ as a call to suffering and even death. The reality of harassment, rejection, arrest, beating, and martyrdom as the cost of Christian discipleship was no surprise to John's first hearers. Nevertheless they may well have been perplexed with the question, "Why must following the King of kings hurt so much, cost so much?" Jesus' answer to their distress is that by his death and resurrection he has already won the decisive battle against the dragon, expelling the accuser from the heavenly courtroom, so the church's present sufferings are symptoms of Satan's frustrated death throes, knowing that his time is short and trying to lash back at his conqueror. More than this, Jesus shows us that his victory over the enemy has blazed the trail for our victory. Just as the Lion of Judah conquered by being slain as a Lamb, so his witnesses overcome the dragon when we do not love our lives, even when faced with death. In regard to our heavenly, true identity in Christ, we are the measured and protected sanctuary; in regard to our daily, earthly experience, we are the unmeasured courtyard, exposed to trampling by the unbelieving nations.

Both poles of the paradox fortify us to endure in hope as we are called to live between the two worlds. If we close our eyes to Revelation's harshly realistic portrait of the church's life as one of suffering and martyrdom, we will be caught off guard when pain, social rejection, or even violent opposition break in upon our lives. Is it our intentional deafness to Revelation's call to expect and endure suffering that leaves so many comfortable Western churches and Christians ill-prepared to stand fast when life gets hard? Does this explain their disappointment with God when he does not deliver the tranquil life they expected and instead calls them to endure hardship—walking by faith, not sight? But if we focus only on the troubles and ignore Revelation's pictures of the church's security in the strong hand of God, the frailty of the church in the world and the evident might of its enemies will overwhelm our hope. When we view our experience and the condition of the church in the world through both of the lenses that Revelation provides, we are equipped to endure in sober hope.

> Though with a scornful wonder men see her sore oppressed,
> By schisms rent asunder, by heresies distressed,
> Yet saints their watch are keeping, their cry goes up, "How long?"
> And soon the night of weeping shall be the morn of song.
> The church shall never perish! Her dear Lord to defend,
> To guide, sustain, and cherish, is with her to the end.
> Though there be those that hate her, and false sons in her pale,
> Against or foe or traitor she ever will prevail.[2]

2. Samuel J. Stone, "The Church's One Foundation" (1866), in *Trinity Hymnal,* ed. Lawrence C. Roff, rev. ed. (Philadelphia: Great Commission Publications, 1990), 347.

See Your Enemies in Their True Colors

Revelation repeatedly reminds us that people and institutions are not as they appear to our eyes. We must look beyond the surface of the page to discern the realities that explain history's events and our experience. Revelation calls the church, Jesus' witnesses, to exercise wise discernment, lest we be taken in by an impressive image that masks an ugly and empty reality.

See the Beast. The power of government, symbolized in the beast, can accomplish great good, and Rome had come to the rescue of some of the Asian cities in time of need. It is no wonder that emperors, at least after death, were lauded in the eastern empire as "lord and savior." It is not surprising that the world's peoples offer the beast divine adulation: "Who is like the beast, and who is able to wage war with him?" But at bottom it is all illusion: Rome ultimately did not rule for the benefit of its client states or subjects but for itself; its apparently unconquerable military power and administrative network would ultimately prove too fragile to hold its far-flung domain together. Nor will any later world power that magnifies man (though driven by the devil) ever embody the justice and omnipotence that deserves our unqualified trust and adulation. Followers of the Lamb, who will rule the nations with justice and his rod of iron, must not be duped into worshiping state power as though it holds the keys to salvation. Neither should we quake in terror before a godless state. Though Revelation exposes the beast in all its grotesque violence, it also shows that the dragon's plot to destroy the church through the beast's world conspiracy is now thwarted by God's restraint and in the end will bring God's enemies to their doom. When the dragon, through the beast, seems to have the upper hand in silencing the voice of the martyrs, it is their victims who have conquered the aggressors by their faithfulness to the death for the gospel.

Do you find your hopes dashed by trends in government? Do you fix your dreams on the state to restore order and righteousness to a society spinning out of control? To be sure, government is God's servant, charged by him to uphold justice, and any semblance of order and uprightness in human courts of power is a blessing far better than our fallen race deserves. But Revelation reminds us of the ugly underbelly of even the best of merely human institutions, and its visions call Christ's servants to heed the psalmist's wise counsel: "Do not trust in princes, in mortal man, in whom there is no salvation" (Ps. 146:3).

See the False Prophet. Religious deception, symbolized in the false prophet, can delude many by appealing to impressive experiences, performing great signs rather than humbly teaching God's revealed truth, the testimony of Jesus. Satan can appear as an angel of light, and so can his lackeys. Civil religion seems so credible and satisfying, so affirming and nonconfrontational, so supportive of the social order and conducive to cultural harmony—as long as everyone docilely complies. Appearances and experiences, however, provide no sure guide to the way things are. No matter how much the earth beast looks like the Lamb, it is not to be trusted, for it speaks like the dragon.

How do you decide what is true in the spiritual realm? Countless undiscerning church members, whatever they may profess about the Bible as God's Word, in practice judge religious claims and spiritual reality on experiential criteria. Not only are they reluctant to put religious leaders to the test of the Word of God, as the Ephesian church did and the Thyatiran church did not. In their daily lives their confidence of God's love and their awe-filled fear of his holiness fluctuate wildly, floating on the ever-changing ebbs and flows of their moods and experiences: "I got a raise; God loves me." "My boyfriend left me; God has turned his back on me." Revelation tells us over and over: You cannot trust the way things look to you, and you cannot trust the religious trendsetters who peddle a palatable message that never assaults our pride, never throws us on our knees before the awesome majesty of a God whose fullness of holiness casts the elders of his heavenly council on their faces. Keep the words of the prophecy of this book. Hold fast to the word of God and the testimony of Jesus. This alone is your sure guide through a world swarming with pleasing and plausible lies.

In his chronicle of Narnia, *The Silver Chair,* C. S. Lewis tells of a quest entrusted to two children, Eustace and Jill, with the assistance of the Marsh-wiggle Puddleglum. Jill alone meets Aslan, the Lion who is Narnia's creator and rightful Lord, when the task is given to rescue an enchanted prince. Aslan gives her four signs to guide the rescue party through a world of illusion, with a solemn charge:

> "Remember, remember, remember the signs. Say them to yourself when you wake in the morning and when you lie down at night, and when you wake in the middle of the night. And whatever strange things may happen to you, let nothing turn your mind from following the signs. . . . And the signs which you have learned here [on the mountain] will not look at all as you expect them to look when you meet them there [down in Narnia]. That is why it is so important to know them by heart and pay no attention to appearances. Remember the signs and believe the signs. Nothing else matters."[3]

In a world of religious counterfeits and masters of spiritual sleight of hand, followers of the Lion of Judah will find our way only by holding fast to the true and faithful words he has given us.

See the Harlot. The idolatrous allure of material affluence and social acceptance, symbolized in the harlot, is perhaps the most lethal of Satan's stratagems against the followers of Jesus. After all, we have to make a living; and the more we make, the more we can give to missions—or spend on suburban niceties (a newer, bigger, louder, wall-filling, room-shaking electronic home entertainment system; a sport utility vehicle for weekend off-roading), for which we will certainly give thanks to God. Wasn't it unreasonable for the early church to ex-

---

3. C. S. Lewis, *The Silver Chair* (New York: Macmillan, 1953), 20–21. These signs function for Jill and Eustace as Scripture functions for the Christian, as Lewis's obvious allusion to Deut. 6:7 makes clear. Jill does not heed the Lion's command to embed the signs in her heart through constant repetition, so at a later point, when the search party is confused and disoriented and Puddleglum asks Jill to repeat the signs, she cannot recall them correctly and answers petulantly. Lewis comments: "As you can see, she had got the order wrong. That was because she had given up saying the signs over every night. She still really knew them, if she troubled to think: but she was no longer so 'pat' in her lesson as to be sure of reeling them off in the right order at a moment's notice and without thinking. Puddleglum's question annoyed her because, deep down inside her, she was already annoyed with herself for not knowing the Lion's lesson quite so well as she felt she ought to have known it" (85).

pect new converts to withdraw from the enjoyment and economically strategic networking of trade-guild parties merely because such parties happened to honor pagan deities or promote sexual license? And what if some ethical corners have to be cut to keep the Roman commercial network afloat—trade in human slaves, for instance? (What would be the counterpart in your workplace?) Is that not just the price of doing business in this dirty but lucrative world, the unfortunate downside involved in keeping the world's goods flowing in for Babylon's consumption? Surely Jesus would not ask his followers to jeopardize their financial security or impede their commercial advancement, merely over a few minor points of conscience. Or would he?

The laments of kings, importers, and seamen over Babylon's destruction sound like an eerie overture to the bipolar frenzy of those intoxicated by expanding technologies, overheated economies, and e-commerce. The manic explosion of dot-com faux wealth in the West at the turn of the third millennium sometimes seems to be tottering on the brink of implosion into deep depression, economic and psychological, for those who have gulped Babylon's cocktail. We trust our computers and the worldwide web that links them, but apprehension gripped the developed world as the fateful Y2K approached, a failure of technological foresight decades ago seeming to threaten life as we know it. The electronic information world survived virtually unscathed as January 1, 2000, passed into history. So now Babylon's lovers pour even more of their energy and hopes into cyberspace and information technology, turning a fine servant into a false savior. But Jesus' people must not be taken in by Babylon's cosmetics. However chic her current ensemble, at heart the harlot is a blood-sucking vampire, stealing people's life and joy, and consuming, not fulfilling, those who fall for her wiles.

See Your Champion in His True Glory

Whenever Revelation works on us as God intends it to, we trust, love, and fear Jesus more. The purpose of its graphic portrayals of the dragon's heavy artillery is not to haunt us with nightmares or keep us awake with night sweats. It is to direct our eyes and hearts away from ourselves, to focus instead on Christ, the seed of the woman who crushed the ancient serpent's head and now sits on God's throne. He is the faithful witness, so his word can be trusted implicitly. He is the Son of Man, invested with infinite and eternal authority, so his command is to be obeyed instantly and eagerly. He is the conquering Lion of Judah, who like his father David went out in the name of the Lord to fight the towering enemy of God's people—and conquered. He is the slain Lamb—for that is exactly how he won the victory—and those for whom he spilled his blood are not only freed from the devil's oppression and lethal domain but also purchased to belong to the living God. He is the captain of heaven's armies, riding into conflict against the forces of injustice and destroying them in his holy wrath, vindicating his suffering saints and repaying their killers in kind. His burning eyes pierce masks and search hearts. His two-edged sword wages war against all that defiles and destroys, whether in the culture at large or in his church. And he is no absentee ruler or distant champion: he walks among the lampstands, ever present with his churches in our joys and sorrows, our faithfulness and our failures. He is the Husband who loved his bride before the world was, who in his matchless love plunged into history and poured out his life to make her his own, and whose love now persistently pursues the process of beautifying her for the consummation of our great wedding.

When you think of Jesus the Christ, do you see him in all the ways that Revelation's images portray him? When you think that you have hidden your sins well from others, do you remember his eyes like flames? When fear grips your heart—fear for yourself, your family, or Christ's church—do you fight that fear with the picture of the rider on the white horse, against whom the devil's worst, last weapons are impotent? When you are confused, not knowing whom to trust or which path to take, do you hear the voice of the faithful witness ringing in your ears, "These words are faithful and true," and do you turn expectantly to his words to find your way? When the accuser, though disbarred from heaven, renews his prosecution against your conscience, do you stand with John in awestruck wonder, gazing at the slain Lamb who poured out his blood to wash you clean and robe you in his own fine linen, bright and clean, to make you—yes, you!—God's precious treasure?

341

Please do not be content to come away from studying the Book of Revelation merely with solutions to some of the puzzles that always troubled you in John's visions. Please, please, do not leave the Book of Revelation until it has etched more deeply into your heart its vivid portraits of your Savior and Lord and until you have grasped more deeply the difference that each portrait makes to your relationship with Jesus and your response to every trial that he leads you through—walks with you through—on your pilgrimage.

See Yourselves in Your True Beauty

"I love thy church, O God," a hymn writer sings, "her walls before thee stand, dear as the apple of thine eye, and graven on thy hand."[4] This is more easily sung than done, however—and even more easily sung in the abstract than done in the concrete. Churches made up of flesh-and-blood Christians are often unattractive and hard to love. Most of the seven churches of Asia Minor received some commendation from their Lord for one strength or another, but even their glowing qualities were mingled with flaws of various kinds: lovelessness, false belief, hypocrisy, toleration of lethal heresy, proud self-satisfaction, flagrant immorality, the adultery of idolatrous worship, and more. What groom could find beautiful a bride so covered with blemishes?

Yet Jesus does. Even to the Laodiceans, for whom he has no whisper of praise, he says: "Those whom I love, I reprove and discipline" (Rev. 3:19). Of course he is not blind to the blemishes, nor will he leave them untreated to mar his bride's complexion when our wedding day arrives. But Revelation shows the lengths to which the Lamb has gone and will go to make us the holy city in whom he will dwell forever. Christ loves his church and binds himself to her with bonds that no enemy from without and no failure of ours from within can sever.

In Revelation's final portrait, John ransacks human language and experience to find images adequate to convey the new Jerusalem's

4. Timothy Dwight, "I Love Thy Kingdom, Lord" (1800), in *Trinity Hymnal,* ed. Lawrence C. Roff, rev. ed. (Philadelphia: Great Commission Publications, 1990), 353.

splendor. Jesus calls us to see his church through his eyes and to have our hearts gripped by her beauty, as his heart is enraptured by his love for her. Who would have guessed that we could ever look so good to the Son of Man whose flaming eyes search minds and hearts? We are so stained with anger, lust, conflict, pride, division, confusion, falsehood, and failure. Surely with such a sordid record, not only as individuals but also as congregations, we are unworthy to serve at the wedding, much less be the bride in whom the Lamb delights! Yet the almost scandalous wonder of grace is that our God so loves us in our unloveliness that he pays the ultimate price to wash us clean from our defilement, to clothe us with his purity, the fine linen that he gives to make his bride lovely.

Do you love the church of which Christ has called you to be a member? For all its flaws and frictions, do you have hope that you and your brothers and sisters will one day shine brightly in the beauty of holiness? When your congregation or denomination seems to suffer one spiritual setback after another—"by schisms rent asunder, by heresies distressed"—are you tempted to give up on the organizational church and go it on your own? Do the so-called saints you rub elbows with on Sunday seem to be obstacles rather than aids to your friendship with Christ and your growth in his grace? Then look again at the church through Jesus' eyes, and in the bright light of her final destination. Jesus' eyes see all the churches' blemishes and bruises, yet our defects do not diminish his love for us or dim his eager expectation for the day when he will present the church to himself "in all her glory, having no spot or wrinkle or any such thing" but rather being "holy and blameless" (Eph. 5:27). When we glimpse the bride through the eyes of her Groom, it lifts our head in hope and calms our frustrated hearts for persevering love for one another.

Revelation is a book to be seen, so four of our seven concluding observations about what Revelation should do to us and in us have focused on the way it changes our perception of our experience, our enemies, our champion, and ourselves as his church. If these transformed perspectives grip our hearts deeply, they will transform our responses to trials and to other people.

Endure as You Suffer

The first-century churches to whom John wrote had endured persecution for their faith and, in one instance at least, a martyrdom ("Antipas my faithful witness," Rev. 2:13). In the next several centuries the Roman Empire's suspicion of this new religion would harden into virulent opposition, intimidation, and bloody aggression. That was only the beginning, for church history is strewn with the corpses of martyrs, slain at the hands of Muslims, Hindus, animists, Marxists, and even other Christians. This cost of discipleship seems far removed from the experience of most Christians in the West, but it continues to characterize the experience of many of our brothers and sisters throughout the world as the third Christian millennium begins.

This sobering reality calls us to two responses. First, it humbles us, putting into clearer perspective the relatively minor inconveniences that most of us endure for the sake of the name of Christ—perhaps some harassment at work, disrespect and marginalization from the news media, or (more painfully) alienation from friends or family. To be disowned by those who have loved us is genuinely distressing, but perhaps we can bear this deep sorrow with greater patience and grace as we remember that others who hold to the testimony of Jesus are facing prison cells, beatings, torture, and death. The Book of Revelation tells us frankly not to expect life this side of the new heaven and earth to be pleasant and problem free but to be prepared for sufferings large and small, and so to face them with hope and calm courage.

Second, Revelation's realistic summons to endure suffering for the faith calls us to support and identify with the church in those places where persecution is its most intense today. If violent persecution has not yet been our lot, is that any justification for failing to join our voices with the lament of the martyrs and the prayers of suffering saints, rising as incense before God's throne, appealing for relief from their and our enemies and vindication of our cause and Jesus' name? If, like the Laodiceans, we enjoy a more than comfortable supply of this world's goods, such sufficiency should move us not to smug self-reliance but to costly compassion, seeking opportunity to invest God's resources in the relief of his suffering children. Peter placed his readers' trials in worldwide perspective, reminding them of their solidar-

344

ity with the whole church as he urged them to fight back against the devil's efforts to intimidate them: "But resist him, firm in your faith, knowing that the same experiences of suffering are being accomplished by your brethren who are in the world" (1 Peter 5:9). We in the West, who enjoy a respite from physical persecution for the time being, should cultivate the same sense of global identification with the family of God in other places.

Stay Pure as Compromise Invites

At this time, spiritual seduction is a greater threat to the church in the West than are physical intimidation, coercion, and persecution. Economic security, material comfort, and social acceptance are idols alluring to many Christian hearts. In a culture that will not tolerate those whom it views as intolerant, postmodernism's polemic against transcendent truth and universal values (faithfulness, justice, compassion for the weak) begins to sound plausible as well as expedient. One gets along better in society if one agrees with the opinion makers that all things are relative, different folks need different strokes, and it's all a matter of varying tastes. That was true in the first century—as long as one didn't challenge the political supremacy of Rome. The same inoffensive tolerance works well in the twenty-first century if we do not want to alienate those who hold the power over our vocational or financial future. The next step is the question "If I have already given up the belief that Jesus is the Lord who has authority to distinguish truth from error, and good from evil, for my neighbor, coworker, or employer, does Jesus even have the authority to tell me what to believe and do?"

John's visions show us the appealing power of the devil's lies and the alluring guise in which the dragon comes to seduce us. Money and pleasure are such attractive idols, like the harlot in her scarlet and purple gowns, her pearls and gemstones. But the cup she offers, promising delight, contains an elixir of death. Jesus, the faithful and true witness, says so. The entertainment industry portrays purity as arrogant, odd, or offish. Do you believe it? Or do you believe Jesus when he says that genuine purity, not self-righteousness but the glad response of a heart set free by grace, is in his eyes the loveliest thing in the world?

Bear Witness as God Waits

People who perceive themselves as marginalized and oppressed minorities in the midst of a hostile cultural consensus are tempted either to compromise and assimilation or to withdrawal and isolation. When the culture aims the guns of persecution on us, we may be inclined to respond to the call to endure by keeping our heads down, making ourselves into small, hard-to-hit targets. When its attack comes with greater subtlety and allure, we may recoil from contact with people who could be sources of infection.

Jesus calls us in Revelation to a different response to our minority status. We must not compromise and assimilate in order to evade persecution or curry acceptance, but neither may we withdraw into a safe and self-contained ghetto. As the Lord's minority in the midst of a hostile world, the church is called to be Jesus' witnesses, fearless in engaging the culture because we are confident in his care for as long as our mission on earth lasts. Christ's call to endure is not a summons to grim, teeth-gritted obstinacy but to openhearted, openmouthed persistence in serving as the King's ambassadors to a foolish, needy, and undeserving world. Knowing that we ourselves are foolish, needy, and undeserving, we hold forth the testimony of Jesus in joy and love, for as long as God's patience waits. We know that through this witness he gathers in every one of his own, so the whole number of his true Israel—every one of them, from every one of the earth's peoples, nations, tribes, and tongues—will stand before his throne, gladly serving him. And we will see his face.

"Amen. Come, Lord Jesus."

A Concise Overview
of the Book of Revelation

Letters to Churches (1–3). Jesus is the glorious Son of Man, who is present by his Spirit in his churches (1:9–20). He knows their situation and their deeds as they are attacked by religious deception, persecution, and the seduction of pleasure, affluence, comfort, and conformity (2–3).

Seals (4:1–8:1). Jesus is the victorious Lion because he died as the sacrificial Lamb. He has authority to reveal the meaning of what will happen in history (4–5). At his bidding military conquest (white horse), war and bloodshed (red horse), and food scarcity (black horse), leading to death through violence, famine, and disease (pale horse) will punish the church's enemies until the end (6:1–8). Although his martyrs must wait awhile until their enemies are destroyed (6:9–11), God's justice will come (6:12–17). Through it all Jesus protects his covenant people, symbolized as a full army of twelve tribes (7:1–8), who are drawn from all the world's peoples, so that nothing will separate us from his love (7:9–17). When Jesus brings woes on earth's evil powers, it is in answer to his people's prayers for relief (8:1–5).

Trumpets: Warning Signals of Coming Judgment (8:2–11:18). Jesus will bring limited, providential judgments on the earth as signal blasts, foreshadowing the great judgment and calling earth's inhabitants to repent. These include the effects of war (burning of land, bloodying of sea, defiling of fresh water, darkening of sky by smoke, 8:6–12). Even worse, rebels will be tormented by demonically induced despair and death (9). But Jesus gives John the sure testimony that his patient waiting will not continue forever (10). In the meanwhile his witness church cannot be harmed until its task is done, and even its visible defeat (martyrs' death) is its victory (11:1–14). In the end the kingdom of the world will belong to our Lord and his Christ (11:15–18).

The Dragon and the Lamb: The Heart of the Conflict (11:19–15:4). The center of the Revelation gives an X-ray of the central conflict: Christ versus the dragon. The birth, death, and enthronement of the child of Eve/Israel have abolished Satan's authority to accuse believers (12:1–12). In his death throes all that Satan can do is to try to attack believers on earth (12:13–13:1) through persecution (sea beast, 13:1–10), deception (land beast, 13:11–18), and sensual pleasure (harlot, 14:8; 16:9; 17–18). The Lamb and his pure army are enthroned in victory on the heavenly Zion (14:1–5; 15:1–4), and the Lamb will bring his enemies to judgment for the death of his martyrs (14:6–20).

Bowls: God's Wrath Completed (15:5–16:21). The complete judgment previously foreshadowed in the limited, providential disasters of history (trumpets) will come on those who have served the dragon through the beasts and the harlot: neither earth, sea, water springs, nor sunlight will sustain life (16:1–9). The dragon's final conspiracy to gather the world's powers and peoples against Christ's church will result in the rebels' destruction (16:10–21).

The Harlot Babylon (17:1–19:10). The world's seductive power (harlot) has been supported by its coercive power (beast, 17); the source of her intoxication has been the death of Jesus' faithful witnesses (17:6; 18:6; 19:2). But the glamour of the beast's woman is a sham, and her luxurious wealth will be stripped from her in the full view of those who have loved the comforts she has offered (18:1–19:5). Jesus' bride will be vindicated (19:6–10).

Thousand Years, Last Battle, and Last Judgment (19:11–21:8). When the dragon, beast, and false prophets have gathered the world's powers to destroy the church (16:14), Jesus will defeat his enemies and cast them into the lake of fire forever (19:11–21; 20:7–10). Until that time, however, Satan has been bound, prevented from assembling this worldwide conspiracy against the church (for "one thousand years" = a long time), while the martyrs who have died on earth live and rule with Christ in heaven (20:1–6). The climax of Jesus' victory is the judgment of all people, in which rebels are condemned for the deeds written in their "record books" (20:11–15) and saints who are written in the Lamb's "registry book" are welcomed into the new heaven and new earth as the bride-city of God (cf. 21:1–8).

The New Creation and the Bride Jerusalem (21:1–22:21). Her enemies destroyed, the church will stand complete in flawless beauty as the bride of the Lamb, the temple of God, resplendent with his glory. Overcomers will inherit the new heaven and new earth (21:1–8) and will delight in God's presence forever. Even as the church cries out to her Husband, "Come, Lord Jesus" (22:20), his delay allows time for the thirsty still to come to him for the water of life (22:17).

Schools
of Interpretation

As the church has struggled to understand the Book of Revelation over the last nineteen hundred years, four main schools of interpretation have emerged: historicist, futurist, preterist, and idealist. Although the origins and relative antiquity of some views are debatable, the clear evidence available to us suggests that forms of historicism and idealism can be traced back into the Middle Ages or even to the patristic period. Nevertheless, though it is always wise to listen carefully to interpreters living near in time and cultural setting to the composition of a New Testament book, the correctness of the schools cannot be determined simply by determining which of the four is oldest.

If a commentary on Revelation written soon after the apostolic period (in the early second century, for example) were discovered today, it is conceivable that all four schools might claim it as confirming their various approaches. If such a commentary suggested that many of John's visions were coming to fulfillment in events that had transpired since his death, historicists and preterists would feel vindicated and idealists could claim the patristic commentator for their school. If it also expected that other visions would be fulfilled in days to come, futurists and historicists would rejoice, though for different reasons, and idealists and some preterists (those identifying the beast and harlot with Rome, not Jerusalem and apostate Judaism) would still feel their approaches reinforced by the ancient interpreter. It is only with the passage of significant time (several centuries) after John's reception of the

Revelation that the differences between the four schools with respect to the chronology of fulfillment would emerge. Generally speaking, historicism and idealism agree that the visions of Revelation symbolize the whole span of time between the ascension of Christ and his return at the end of history, although they differ on the relationship of the visions to what they symbolize and to each other. Futurism and preterism agree that the visions concentrate on a more limited time period, either immediately preceding Christ's second coming in the future (to us; futurism) or immediately following John's writing and therefore past (to us; preterism).

The schools also differ from each other regarding their interpretation of the symbolism of the visions. All agree that certain visions symbolize specific events in history: the first coming and resurrection of Messiah (Rev. 12:1–6) and his second coming (19:11–21). Historicism, futurism, and preterism, each in its own way, apply this principle to the visions generally, seeking to draw direct, one-to-one lines of symbolism and fulfillment between the visions and particular persons, institutions, or events in political, cultural, and ecclesiastical history. Idealism, by contrast, views more of the visions as symbolizing abstract trends or forces that may find expression in a variety of historical particulars without being limited to one. As one persuaded of idealism, I argued, for example, that the beast found expression in ancient Rome and that the principle of the deified state imposed by force will reach a manifestation of horrendous proportions in the brief time that the dragon will be loosed. But I also contended that since the beast has attributes making it a composite of all four beasts of Daniel 7, it transcends its particular historical incarnations and should not be equated with only one of them, much less with a single human individual.

Since premillennialists, who are almost invariably futurists, often stress the literal-where-possible principle in interpreting Revelation's visions, we might have expected a wide disagreement between futurism and the other views over whether Revelation's visions are symbolic in form or literal, physical depictions of the persons, institutions, and events to which they refer. However, futurists are as sensitive as those espousing other views to the symbolic form of John's visions, differing from the other schools not over whether the details of John's visions are symbolic but rather over what sorts of referents they symbolize. Futurists, like other interpreters, interpret the two witnesses of Revelation 11 as human beings, not olive trees or lampstands, even though that is what John says they are. Since the witnesses are humans, futurists agree with others that the fire that is said to proceed from the witnesses' mouths is not physical or literal. Even some of the better-known futurist interpretations treat John's visions as symbolic, not journalistic reporting. To interpret the locusts from the abyss as helicopters employed in Middle East air combat is no less symbolic than to interpret them as demonic spirits, unleashed to torment Satan's followers. It is symbolism that looks in a different direction from others for its interpretive key to the link between symbol and referent.

In this appendix I offer a brief description of the approach taken to Revelation by each of the four schools, with a brief assessment of the strengths and weaknesses of each.

Historicism

Historicism can plausibly claim to read Revelation quite straightforwardly as a series of sequential visions that symbolize, in order, the sequence of events that span the history of the church, from John's day to the second coming, millennium, last judgment, and the eternal state. Historicists recognize Revelation's symbolic mode of communication and expect the symbols of John's visions to refer to specific, identifiable developments—events, institutions, and movements—that are to unfold in the history of the church's life in the world, leading up to the return of Jesus. For example, commentators belonging to the Church of Rome during the late Middle Ages typically identified the emergence of the beast from the sea (Rev. 13) as the rise of Islam; Protestant theologians during the Reformation typically interpreted the harlot Babylon (17) as the Roman church and its papacy, which persecuted defenders of the true gospel. Some historicists viewed the locusts released from the abyss with the sounding of the fifth trumpet (9:7) as the Muslim invasions of Europe (e.g., the Moors in Spain). Jonathan Edwards was persuaded that he lived in the time between the sixth and the seventh bowls (16) and that the seventh bowl would be poured out in the nineteenth century.

Although historicists have not agreed on which events or time periods to identify with each vision, they are united by a common hermeneutic, built on two presuppositions. First, the literary sequence of visions in Revelation reflects the historical-chronological sequence of the events that they signify. The vision of the Son of Man and the letters that follow from it concern "the things which are," and the vision of the One on the throne and the Lamb begins the section of the book that reveals "what must take place after this" (1:19; 4:1). Thus it is reasonable to expect this principle to apply to the order of visions throughout the book. Because they believe that John saw his visions in the order in which their referents would occur, historicists would disagree with my emphasis on repetition and recapitulation, in which John's visions provide complementary and overlapping perspectives on the same events, time periods, and institutions. Second, John's visions symbolize specific, identifiable historical developments (as the samples above illustrate), so properly interpreting Revelation involves correctly correlating the visions with events that would occur centuries after John and his readers lived. As the few samples I have given suggest, historicists have been far from unified regarding how and where to draw the lines of connection between Revelation and the developments of later church history.

Historicism's strengths are that unlike some expressions of futurism, it takes seriously Revelation's address to the situation of John's first-century readers, at least in the early chapters. Unlike some expressions of preterism, it affirms that Revelation focuses the church's attention not primarily on events that are now long past to us but on the future, glorious appearing of our Lord Jesus. Like idealism, it recognizes that Revelation also interprets for the church throughout the ages what is transpiring between John's generation and the second coming, although historicism and idealism differ regarding how the symbols in John's visions relate to and interpret the church's experience in the world.

Historicism's weaknesses are its presupposition that the literary order of John's visions reflect the chronological order of historical events contradicts and disregards the clear (I think indisputable) evidence that we have studied, which demonstrates that John's visions do recapitulate each other. Seal 6 brings us to the end with the cosmic earthquake and the falling of the heavenly lights, yet in trumpet 4 the sun, moon, and stars are still in the sky; and the same eschatological earthquake reappears in the seventh bowl. The labor of the heavenly woman and birth of the Messiah (Rev. 12) carry us back to events that preceded the founding of the Asian churches (2–3). Its assumption that John's visions provide a symbolic agenda for the specific events of history for centuries and millennia to come virtually seals up the meaning of the book to John's first hearers as Daniel's sealing of his prophecy symbolized that its fulfillment would only come in a distant future. Thus historicism's hermeneutic transforms the book from an *Apocalypsis* (revelation) into an *Apocryphon* (veiled book), at least for the seven churches to whom it was first sent. The disagreement among historicists over the correspondence between visions and events (Does Islam arise as locusts in Rev. 9, or as beast in Rev. 13?) is symptomatic of an interpretive approach that lacks appropriate controls to rein in the interpreter's imagination. In particular historicism has underestimated the essential role of the Old Testament background—both the history of redemption (creation, fall, exodus) and the prophetic visions—in guiding our interpretation of Revelation.

Futurism

Futurism, as its name indicates, views Revelation's visions as concentrated on events still largely future not only to John's first-century readers but also to us twenty-first-century readers—events that will immediately precede the second coming of Christ. Some futurists have interpreted the letters to the churches not as addressed to first-century congregations but as symbolic of the condition of the church throughout seven successive historical stages, an interesting departure from the literal-when-possible dictum. Others, such as John Walvoord, George Eldon Ladd, and G. R. Beasley-Murray, believe that a long temporal gap of unknown duration stands between the condition of the first-century churches, as diagnosed in the letters of Revelation 2–3, and the "things which will take place after this," signified in the visions of Revelation 4–20. In most futurist readings of Revelation, the bulk of the book (4–19) discloses conditions during a time of intense trauma, the tribulation, which is identified with the seventieth week of Daniel 9:20–27 and is therefore expected to last seven years. At the end of the tribulation the beast, who is equated with the antichrist mentioned in 1 John, will be destroyed at Jesus' second coming. (Some futurists—pretribulational premillennialists—believe that Jesus will have returned "in the air" to remove the church from the world before the tribulation begins.) Futurists typically expect an earthly millennial political reign of Christ following Jesus' return and defeat of the beast (the premillennial interpretation of Rev. 20:1–10), followed by the last judgment and eternal state.

Futurists tend to concur with historicism's desire to interpret the visions by identifying them with specific historical events, institutions, and individuals. Most also view the literary order of John's visions as reflective of the chronological order of the historical events that they signify, acknowledging the feature of recapitulation only when compelled to by the text (e.g., Rev. 12:1–6). Futurism parts with historicism, however, regarding the period of time symbolized by Revelation 4–19. Whereas historicists see these chapters as mapping out the whole history of the church age from John's day until Jesus' return, futurists view them as portraying only the final generation before the second coming. And dispensationalist futurists would even place the tribulation outside the church age, as the resumption of God's agenda for national Israel after the rapture of the church from the world. Thus, for example, the harlot Babylon is not the Roman church, which persecuted the Reformers, and the beast is not necessarily the papacy. Rather, she symbolizes apostate Christianity at the end of time, based on a revival of the Holy Roman Empire—a politico-economic alliance variously identified as the European Common Market, Soviet communism, or some other soon-to-arise one-world alliance. The locusts from the abyss (Rev. 9) are variously interpreted as symbolizing an outbreak of demonic activity near the end (as I have done), or as symbolizing helicopters used in conflicts between Israel and its Muslim neighbors in the Middle East, or in some other way. Popular presentations of futurism often attach great significance to the reestablishment of Israel as a nation in 1948 as a signal that the world stands within a generation of the outbreak of the tribulation.

Futurism's main strength is that, unlike preterism, it rightly emphasizes that Revelation speaks extensively of a period of intense trauma for God's people, yet future to us, and calls Christians to look forward and fix our hope on the second coming of Christ as the climactic event in God's victory over Satan. In premillennial futurism the belief that Satan's ultimate defeat will occur at least a thousand years after Christ's return vitiates this strength, since this long delay of complete victory means that at his appearing Christ destroys only some but not all of our enemies. Nevertheless futurism rightly sees that Revelation realistically expects that ongoing suffering and even intensified suffering will characterize the experience of believers until the bodily return of Jesus brings relief to those who hope in him.

The weaknesses of futurism are that influential expressions of futurism (though not all futurists) tend to ignore the evidence of recapitulation in the visions of Revelation, concurring with historicism in equating the literary order of the visions with the chronological order of their referents. Futurists who interpret Revelation's symbols in terms of twentieth-century political developments in the Middle East have cut their hermeneutic free from the control of Old Testament prophetic language and imagery. In so doing they have interpreted Revelation's symbols no more literally than idealists would, but the futurist's connection between visionary symbol and its historical referent is even more subjective and less exegetically defensible from the standpoint of what John's readers could have been expected to understand. For example, neither the imagery of the ancient prophets nor the background of the first-century churches provides a basis for interpreting a locust swarm as a helicopter battalion. In general, futurism relates so much of Revelation to events still in the future at history's end that it fails to do justice to the statements in the prologue and epilogue that the book reveals things which "must soon take place" and the fact that John, unlike Daniel, must not seal his book because "the time is near."

Preterism

Preterists may be either amillennial (Jay E. Adams) or postmillennial (David Chilton, Kenneth Gentry) in their interpretation of Revelation 20. G. B. Caird, whose interpretive approach to Revelation as a whole is preterist, even contended that John expected a premillennial return of Christ and an earthly millennial kingdom to follow it.[1] The defining feature of preterism is not its understanding of the conditions on earth during the time period symbolized by the "thousand years" of Revelation 20. Rather, preterists of all millennial viewpoints share a common agreement that a large proportion of Revelation's visions were fulfilled in the early Christian centuries. Of paramount importance is Revelation's promise to the first-century churches that the enemies then persecuting them would soon be brought to justice by God's intervention. Thus the fulfillment of most of John's visions lay in the near future from his perspective but in the past (preterist) from our standpoint. Since Revelation 1–19 concern the struggle of the first-century church and promise the imminent defeat of its persecutors, Jerusalem and/or Rome, preterists hold that only Revelation 20–22 describe events still present or future. The thousand years symbolize either the entire age of the church between Christ's ascension and his return or a final phase of the church age in which the church will flourish and Christ's kingdom advance through widespread conversion and cultural reformation. Thus preterists lay great emphasis on the time references in the prologue and epilogue that emphasize that the events symbolized in the visions were to take place "soon" because "the time is at hand." Preterism exhibits sensitivity to the symbolic genre of Revelation and to the significance of Old Testament prophetic imagery for the interpretation of John's visions. Many preterists also give significant interpretive weight to the extrabiblical contexts of first-century Jewish history (Gentry), Greco-Roman religion and mythology (Caird), first-century persecution of Christians by Jews and Gentiles, and Roman imperial politics. The fall of the harlot Babylon is understood by some preterists as symbolizing

---

1. G. B. Caird, *A Commentary on the Revelation of St. John the Divine,* HNTC (New York: Harper & Row, 1966), 251.

the destruction of Jerusalem, seat of anti-Christian Judaism in A.D. 70 (Chilton, Gentry); others connect Babylon's destruction with the overthrow of the Roman Empire and the sacking of Rome by Visigoth and Vandal invasions in the fifth century (Moses Stuart, Adams, Caird).

Preterism's strengths are that it takes seriously the signals in the prologue and the epilogue that "the time is at hand" and that John's visions concern "things which must soon take place," not primarily events removed by many centuries from John and his hearers. Preterists typically give careful attention to the Old Testament background of Revelation's imagery and to the Greco-Roman historical and cultural context in which John's first hearers lived. Therefore preterism, unlike some expressions of futurism, does not arrive at interpretations that would have been alien and unintelligible to the first-century churches of Asia Minor. Preterists recognize that the beast from the sea (Rev. 13) is to be identified with the fourth, terrible beast of Daniel 7. Consequently most preterists identify the beast with Rome, the fourth major world empire since Daniel's time (following the Neo-Babylonian, the Medo-Persian, and the Hellenistic empires) and the power under which John's hearers had begun to endure sporadic persecution. Some preterists (Adams, for example) are sensitive to the literary feature of repetition or recapitulation by which Revelation's visions are related to each other as multiple perspectives on the same forces and events in the cosmic conflict between Christ and Satan. Thus preterism in its better expressions wisely draws a distinction between the literary order of John's visions and the chronological order of the events that they signify.

Preterism's emphasis on the fulfillment of John's visions in the near future (to John's readers), which to us is the distant past, leads some preterist interpreters to minimize the present and yet future applicability of Revelation. Chilton, Gentry, and others date the composition of the book prior to 70 (another issue that we will not address here)[2] and view all the visions through Revelation 19 as having been

---

2. See G. K. Beale, *The Book of Revelation*, NIGTC (Grand Rapids: Eerdmans, 1999), 4–27, for a summary of arguments favoring a late date (90s) and those favoring an early date (60s). Beale concludes in favor of the later date of composition, during Domitian's reign.

fulfilled in the destruction of Jerusalem by Roman armies under Titus. Others see both the beast and the harlot as perspectives on the Roman Empire, rather than anti-Jesus second temple Judaism. In one sense they are right, but viewing Revelation as largely fulfilled in the defeat of enemies long departed underestimates the spiritual conflict still confronting the church long after Jerusalem's destruction and Rome's fall. In identifying the beast from the sea exclusively with Rome and the fourth beast of Daniel 7, preterists overlook the implication of the fact that the beast from the sea is a composite of all four beasts in Daniel. The harlot Babylon likewise is portrayed in imagery that shows that she unites the arrogant sensuality of various ancient powers, Babylon, Tyre, and others. In other words, the adaptation and transformation of Old Testament prophetic imagery in Revelation shows that John's visions symbolize not a single pagan kingdom, whether in the ancient past or in the future, but the power of paganism exhibited in military force, religious deception, and economic affluence. Thus preterism shares the weakness of historicism and futurism in their common assumption that John's visions consistently symbolize specific, identifiable events or institutions in political, societal, and/or ecclesiastical history. Many of John's visions portray overarching spiritual forces and trends, which found expression for John's readers in the Greco-Roman culture in which they lived and which continue to appear in new but similar forms throughout this age of the church's sojourn in the wilderness, prior to our Lord's return.

Idealism

Idealism is sometimes called iterism or recapitulationism because it interprets Revelation as a series of repeated symbolic pictures of the church's struggle from John's day until the second coming, the last judgment, and the eternal state. Thus Revelation offers multiple images that provide different perspectives on the same great warfare, sometimes in terms of its behind-the-scenes heavenly sources and at other times in terms of their visible, earthly outworking in the experience of churches, countries, and cultures. Unlike the other three schools, idealism does not rest its interpretation of specific visions or specific features within the visions on an attempt to link these details in Revelation with specific events between the two comings of Christ. Thus, while idealism agrees with historicism (over against futurism and preterism) that the visions symbolize the conditions confronting the church throughout the entire church age, idealists part company with historicists' efforts to locate the judgment symbolized in the fourth seal or the fifth trumpet at a particular point in world history. Idealism agrees with preterism against futurism, affirming that John's visions reveal dynamics and developments in the spiritual conflict of the church in the world that were directly relevant to the experience of the first-century Asian churches. And idealism agrees with historicism and futurism against preterism, contending that the massive enemy forces symbolized by beast, false prophet, and harlot were far from defeated when Roman armies razed Jerusalem in the first century or when Vandals overran Rome in the fifth. Interestingly, Augustine—writing at the time of Rome's fall—is the earliest known idealist interpreter of Revelation.

Idealism sees Revelation's symbolism as heavily dependent on the Old Testament and expressive of the unseen spiritual warfare behind the scenes of public human history, to which politics, economics, armed conflict, and organized religious structures belong. The paradoxical element in the visions (the Lion is a Lamb, the defeated martyrs are the victors) reinforces the contrast between the true insight into the church's experience made available to John and his hearers from the heavenly perspective and the illusory appearances of the earthly perspective. Although idealists differ from each other in interpreting some of Revelation's difficult visions (as the members of each of the other schools differ among themselves), the explanations offered throughout this book are representative of the interpretive fruit borne by the idealist approach.

Having grown up in a church that taught a futurist interpretation of Revelation and having flirted seriously with preterism at a later point, I find idealism most persuasive because idealism offers interpretations that would have been intelligible to John's first hearers in their context, confronted by Rome's military and economic power and the growing influence of the imperial cult, which blended religious devotion with political loyalty to the state. Yet idealism sees behind the specifics of the early church's historical and cultural context to deeper spiritual forces and trends that would long outlive and far transcend ancient Rome, issues that confront twenty-first-century Christians just as they confronted our first-century counterparts. With respect to preterism's key verses, which affirm that the time is near and the events symbolized in John's visions would occur soon, idealism understands these in light of the New Testament's frequent affirmations that the last days dawned with the work of Jesus the Messiah (e.g., Heb. 1:1–2). Consequently no redemptive event stands between John's readers or us and the climax of redemption in Jesus' second coming from heaven to judge his enemies and bring his bride into the new heavens and earth. The nearness of the end, predicted in the prologue and epilogue, is the point that preterism presses against each of the other three schools. We need to remember, however, that Jesus' eschatological parables warned his disciples against a loss of hope when his coming may have seemed, in their perspective, to be delayed. Interwoven throughout the eschatological teaching of the New Testament are three strands. Christ will come sooner than people think, unpleasantly surprising many and delighting others by the speed of the relief that he provides; Christ will come later than people think, so his faithful servants must be prepared to endure even if he seems to be delayed; and the time of Christ's coming is not given to us to know.

Some presentations of idealism seem to me to have the weakness of oversimplifying the relationship between the vision cycles in Revelation. William Hendriksen and G. K. Beale understand the trumpet cycle, like the bowl cycle, as symbolizing judgment disasters accompanying the end of history. I am more persuaded, however, by the suggestion of Michael Wilcock and Richard Bauckham, that the limitation of the judgments connected with the trumpets and the interludes signifying the protection of the saints from wrath between the sixth and seven trumpets (as between the sixth and seventh seal) are intended to set the trumpets apart from the bowls. The trumpets give glimpses of the providential woes that will befall proud human powers throughout the age of the church's sojourn in the wilderness, from John's day until the return of Christ. They resemble the bowl judgments as previews and precursors to the total, final judgment signified by the bowls. But the trumpets are fulfilling their function as warning signals, for as such judgments fall there is still time to repent. When the history-ending disasters pour out of the seven last bowls, the day of repentance will have passed.

Occasionally idealist interpreters, overreacting (I think) to futurism's fixation on the final tribulation, minimize Revelation's clear expectation that Christ's return will be preceded by a period of brief but intense persecution for the church. Revelation shows in various ways that the church's present experience of persecution, although genuinely painful, is nevertheless limited by God's powerful restraint of the dragon and his minions. The two witnesses' enemies cannot destroy them until their testifying mission is complete, at which time the beast will conquer and kill them. The evil trio will deceive and gather the kings and nations to wage war against the Lamb and his army, the camp of the saints—but not until the dragon is released to resume the deceptive power he wielded over the Gentiles prior to Christ's death and resurrection. Idealism that pays careful attention (as we should) to all that Revelation reveals will not conclude that history will go on normally and then Jesus will return. Revelation presents a more complex picture: the kingdom advancing and gathering in the nations through the church's witness amid suffering; and then, just before the end, intensified and coordinated hostility of the non-Christian world against the church, which is rescued by the glorious return of Jesus our Defender.

Works Cited

Adams, Jay E. *The Time Is at Hand*. Nutley, N.J.: P&R Publishing, 1970.

Adams, Jay E., and Michael W. Carroll. *Visions of the Revelation*. Virginia Beach: Donning, 1991.

Athenagorus. *Embassy for the Christians*. Translated by J. H. Crehan. Ancient Christian Writers 23. New York: Newman, 1955.

Aune, David E. "The Form and Function of the Proclamations to the Seven Churches (Revelation 2–3)." *NTS* 36 (1990): 182–204.

———. *Revelation 6–16*. WBC. Waco: Word, 1998.

Babcock, Maltbie D. "This Is My Father's World" (1901). In *Trinity Hymnal,* edited by Lawrence C. Roff. Rev. ed. Philadelphia: Great Commission Publications, 1990.

Barrett, C. K. *The New Testament Background: Selected Documents*. 1987. Rev. ed. San Francisco: Harper & Row, 1995.

Bauckham, Richard. *The Climax of Prophecy: Studies on the Book of Revelation*. Edinburgh: T & T Clark, 1993.

———. *The Theology of the Book of Revelation*. Cambridge: Cambridge University Press, 1993.

Bauer, Walter, William F. Arndt, F. Wilbur Gingrich, and Frederick W. Danker. *A Greek-English Lexicon of the New Testament and Other Early Christian Literature*. 2d ed. Chicago: University of Chicago Press, 1979.

Baugh, S. M. "A Foreign World: Ephesus in the First Century." In *Women in the Church: A Fresh Analysis of 1 Timothy 2:9–15,* edited by Andreas J. Köstenberger, Thomas R. Schreiner, and H. Scott Baldwin, 13–52. Grand Rapids: Baker, 1995.

Beale, G. K. *The Book of Revelation*. NIGTC. Grand Rapids: Eerdmans, 1999.

Beasley-Murray, G. R. *The Book of Revelation*. NCB. Grand Rapids: Eerdmans, 1981.

Beckwith, Isbon T. *The Apocalypse of John: Studies in Introduction, with a Critical and Exegetical Commentary*. 1919. Reprint ed., Grand Rapids: Baker, 1979.

Bock, Darrell L., ed. *Three Views on the Millennium and Beyond*. Grand Rapids: Zondervan, 1999.

Brown, Francis, S. R. Driver, and Charles A. Briggs. *A Hebrew and English Lexicon of the Old Testament, with an Appendix Containing the Biblical Aramaic*. Oxford: Clarendon, 1966.

Caird, G. B. *A Commentary on the Revelation of St. John the Divine*. HNTC. New York: Harper & Row, 1966.

Card, Michael. *In the Beginning*. Sound cassette. Brentwood, Tenn.: Birdwing Music/Sparrow, 1989.

———. *Unveiled Hope*. Sound cassette/CD. Nashville: Covenant Artists/Myrrh, 1997.

Charles, R. H. *A Critical and Exegetical Commentary on the Revelation of St. John*. ICC. Edinburgh: T & T Clark, 1920.

Chilton, David. *Days of Vengeance: An Exposition of the Book of Revelation*. Fort Worth: Dominion, 1987.

Clowney, Edmund P. "The Final Temple." *WTJ* 35 (1972–73): 156–89.

Dio Cassius. *Roman History*. Translated by Earnest Cary. LCL. Cambridge: Harvard University Press, 1987.

———. *Discourses (xii–xxx)*. Translated by J. W. Cohoon. LCL. Cambridge: Harvard University Press, 1939.

Duguid, Iain M. *Living in the Gap between Promise and Reality: The Gospel according to Abraham*. Phillipsburg, N.J.: P&R Publishing, 1999.

France, R. T. *Jesus and the Old Testament: His Application of Old Testament Passages to Himself and His Mission*. Downers Grove, Ill.: InterVarsity Press, 1971.

———. "The Worship of Jesus: A Neglected Factor in Christological Debate?" In *Christ the Lord: Essays in Christology Presented to Donald Guthrie*, edited by Harold H. Rowdon, 17-36. Downers Grove, Ill.: InterVarsity Press, 1982.

Gentry, Kenneth L. *Before Jerusalem Fell*. Tyler, Tex.: Institute for Christian Economics, 1989.

Good, Michael. "Affluenza's Gonna Get You." *KPBS on Air* 29.11 (September 1997): 14–15.

Gundry, Robert H. *The Church and the Tribulation*. Grand Rapids: Zondervan, 1973.

———. *First the Antichrist: A Book for Lay Christians Approaching the Third Millennium and Inquiring Whether Jesus Will Come to Take the Church out of the World before the Tribulation.* Grand Rapids: Baker, 1997.

———. "The New Jerusalem: People as Place, Not Place for People." *NovT* 29 (1987): 254–64.

Hemer, Colin J. *The Letters to the Seven Churches of Asia in Their Local Setting.* JSNT Supplement 11. Sheffield: JSOT Press, 1986.

Hendriksen, William. *More Than Conquerors: An Interpretation of the Book of Revelation.* Grand Rapids: Baker, 1939.

Hoeksema, Herman. *Behold, He Cometh.* Grand Rapids: Reformed Free Publishing Association, 1969.

Hughes, Philip E. "The First Resurrection: Another Interpretation." *WTJ* 39 (1976–77): 315–18.

James, P. D. *The Children of Men.* New York: Knopf, 1993.

Johnson, Dennis E. " 'I Am': Intimations of Eternity in John's Gospel." In *The Gospels Today: A Guide to Some Recent Developments,* edited by Malcolm J. Robertson III and William L. Lane, 132–49. New Testament Student, vol. 6. Philadelphia: Skilton House, 1990.

———. "Jesus Against the Idols: The Use of Isaianic Servant Songs in the Missiology of Acts." *WTJ* 52 (1990): 343–53.

———. *The Message of Acts in the History of Redemption.* Phillipsburg, N.J.: P&R Publishing, 1997.

———. "The Rules of the Road." *Tabletalk* 23.2 (February 1999): 8–10, 56–57.

Jones, Peter. *Spirit Wars: Pagan Revival in Christian America.* Mukilteo, Wash.: WinePress, 1997.

Kline, M. G. "Double Trouble." *JETS* 32 (1989): 171–79.

———. "The First Resurrection." *WTJ* 37 (1975): 366–75.

———. "Har Magedon: The End of the Millennium." *JETS* 39 (1996): 207–22.

———. *Images of the Spirit.* Grand Rapids: Baker, 1980.

———. *Treaty of the Great King: The Covenant Structure of Deuteronomy.* Grand Rapids: Eerdmans, 1963.

Kümmel, Werner Georg. *The New Testament: The History of the Investigation of Its Problems.* Nashville: Abingdon, 1972.

Ladd, George Eldon. *A Commentary on the Revelation of John.* Grand Rapids: Eerdmans, 1972.

Lewis, C. S. *The Silver Chair.* New York: Macmillan, 1953.

Liddell, Henry G., and Robert Scott. *A Greek-English Lexicon*. 8th ed. New York: American Book Company, 1882.

Louw, Johannes P., and Eugene A. Nida, eds. *Greek-English Lexicon of the New Testament: Based on Semantic Domains*. 2 vols. New York: United Bible Societies, 1989.

Longman, Tremper III. *Literary Approaches to Biblical Interpretation*. Foundations of Contemporary Interpretation, vol. 3. Grand Rapids: Academie Books, Zondervan, 1987.

Mounce, Robert H. *The Book of Revelation*. NICNT. Rev. ed. Grand Rapids: Eerdmans, 1998.

N. E. Thing Enterprises. *Magic Eye: A New Way of Looking at the World*. Kansas City: Andrews and McMeel, 1993.

Osborne, Grant R. *The Hermeneutical Spiral: A Comprehensive Introduction to Biblical Interpretation*. Downers Grove, Ill.: InterVarsity Press, 1991.

Peterson, Eugene. *A Long Obedience in the Same Direction: Discipleship in an Instant Society*. Downers Grove, Ill.: InterVarsity Press, 1980.

Petronius. *Petronius: The Satyricon, and Seneca: The Apocolocyntosis*. Translated by J. P. Sullivan. New York: Penguin, 1977.

Poythress, Vern S. "Genre and Hermeneutics in Rev 20:1–6." *JETS* 36 (1993): 41–54.

———. *The Returning King: A Guide to the Book of Revelation*. Phillipsburg, N.J.: P&R Publishing, 2000.

———. *The Shadow of Christ in the Law of Moses*. Brentwood, Tenn.: Wolgemuth and Hyatt, 1991. Reprint ed., Phillipsburg, N.J.: P&R Publishing, 1995.

———. Unpublished series of structural and chiastic outlines on Revelation. Philadelphia, Westminster Theological Seminary, n.d.

Ridderbos, Herman. *The Coming of the Kingdom*. 1962. Philadelphia: P&R Publishing, 1975.

Roff, Lawrence C., ed. *Trinity Hymnal*. Rev. ed. Philadelphia: Great Commission Publications, 1990.

Roloff, Jürgen. *The Revelation of John: A Continental Commentary*. Minneapolis: Fortress, 1993.

Shepherd, Norman. "The Resurrections of Revelation 20." *WTJ* 36 (1974–75): 34–43.

Smith, Christopher R. "The Portrayal of the Church as the New Israel in the Names and Order of the Tribes in Revelation 7.5–8." *JSNT* 39 (1990): 111–18.

————. "The Tribes of Revelation 7 and the Literary Competence of John the Seer." *JETS* 38 (1995): 213–18.

Stark, Rodney. *The Rise of Christianity: A Sociologist Reconsiders History*. Princeton, N.J.: Princeton University Press, 1996.

Stuart, Moses. *A Commentary on the Apocalypse*. 2 vols. London: Wiley and Putnam, 1845.

Suetonius. *Suetonius*. Translated by J. C. Rolfe. Vol. 2. LCL. Cambridge: Harvard University Press, 1970.

Swete, H. B. *Commentary on Revelation*. 3d ed. 1911. Reprint ed., Grand Rapids: Kregel, 1977.

Tacitus. *Annals*. Translated by John Jackson. LCL. Cambridge: Harvard University Press, 1969.

Talbot, Terry, and Jamie Owens-Collins. "New Jerusalem." From Jamie Owens, *Growing Pains*. Sound cassette/CD.

Thiselton, Anthony C. *The Two Horizons: New Testament Hermeneutics and Philosophical Description with Special Reference to Heidegger, Bultmann, Gadamer, and Wittgenstein*. Grand Rapids: Eerdmans, 1980.

Vanhoye, Albert. *Structure and Message of the Epistle to the Hebrews*. Subsidia Biblica 12. Rome: Pontifical Biblical Institute, 1989.

Virgil. *Aeneid*. Translated by H. R. Fairclough. LCL. Cambridge: Harvard University Press, 1974.

Volf, Miroslav. *Exclusion and Embrace: A Theological Exploration of Identity, Otherness, and Reconciliation*. Nashville: Abingdon, 1996.

Wall, Robert W. *Revelation*. Peabody, Mass.: Hendrickson, 1991.

White, R. Fowler. "Reexamining the Evidence for Recapitulation in Rev 20:1–10." *WTJ* 51 (1989): 319–44.

Wilcock, Michael. *I Saw Heaven Opened: The Message of Revelation*. TBST. Downers Grove, Ill.: InterVarsity Press, 1975.

Wilken, Robert L. *Remembering the Christian Past*. Grand Rapids: Eerdmans, 1995.

Yeats, William Butler. "The Second Coming." In *Modern American and Modern British Poetry*, edited Louis Untermeyer. Rev. ed. New York: Harcourt Brace Jovanovich, 1955.

Zinsser, Hans. *Rats, Lice and History*. 1934. Reprint ed., New York: Bantam, 1960.

Index of Scripture
and Ancient Writings

26:64—51, 173
27:28—245
27:53—168n.17
27:66—104n.11, 283n.25
28:18—51
28:18–20—281n.19

Mark

1:2—62
1:15—184
4:9—69
4:23—69
5:5—152
5:13—152
6:39—123
8:38—51
9:1—153, 184
13—2
13:7–8—288
13:8—120n.7
13:10—126
13:14—190n.12
13:19—55
13:20—41n.23, 289
13:32—210
14:62—51
15:17—245n.8

Luke

1:10—142
1:17—195
1:52–53—92
1:68–71—107n.14
2:1—88n.35
2:32—288
4:18—288
7:24–27—62
8:31—187
9:26—51
9:39—152
9:52—62
10:18—148, 184n.8
12:8—85
12:35–38—84
12:35–40—289
12:36—92
12:37—92
12:39–40—84, 92, 233

14:15–24—264
14:35—10
15:12—308n.7
17:7–8—92n.42
18:7—289
18:7–8—41, 161
19:11—289
21:9–11—124
21:20–21—167
21:24—167
23:11—257n.24

John

1:1–14—272
1:4–9—318n.26
1:14—311, 318n.26
1:18—318n.26
1:29—106
1:36—106
2:19–21—311
3:5–6—320
3:6—74
3:19–20—230
3:33—104
4:10—321
4:11—321
4:13–14—321
4:35–38—209
5:25–29—293
5:28–29—282n.24, 291
6:32–35—78
6:48–51—78
7:37–39—329
8:12—318n.26
8:44—151
8:58–59—54n.11
10—135
10:16—186n.9
10:28–29—89
11:51–52—186n.9
12:13—134
12:31–32—281n.19
12:33—7n.6
15:1–8—74
15:21—71n.10
16:33—55, 165
17:6—318n.26
17:15—89

17:21–23—73n.11
18:32—7n.6
19:1–2—245n.8
19:34—53
19:37—53
19:39—73
21:19—7n.6

Acts

1—176
1:6–8—116
1:7—210
1:8—135n.29, 170n.19
1:9—51, 173
1:21—311
2:30–33—184
2:32–36—116
2:33–36—153
3:20–21—210
5:1–11—60n.17
5:32—170n.19
5:41—71n.10
7:56—85
8:32—106
9:4—60
10:30—257n.24
13:5—74
13:15–42—74
13:30—311
13:33–34—201n.2
13:34–35—227n.7
13:46—116
13:47—288
14:15–17—239, 288
14:17—229
14:22—55n.13
16:14—79
17:30–31—288
18:12–13—74
19:13–20—70
19:23–41—70
20:28—109n.16
20:29—71
20:30—71

Romans

1:1–6—26
1:17—221

12–19—17
12–20—160n.7, 269n.3
12–22—31
12:1—7, 75, 214, 219
12:1–2—267
12:1–5—32, 33, 176
12:1–6—179, 356
12:1–17—44
12:1–14:20—39, 40
12:2–5—153n.11
12:3—7, 14, 17, 180, 181,
 188, 214, 245, 248n.14,
 270
12:4—44, 181
12:4–5—277
12:5—52n.6, 59, 173,
 180n.3, 181, 186,
 201n.2, 268, 269, 272
12:6—19, 44, 78, 171,
 172, 182, 185, 244,
 286, 307
12:7—62n.19, 233n.13,
 277n.14
12:7–9—148, 186, 269,
 277
12:7–17—179
12:8—298
12:8–10—183
12:9—62n.19, 151, 176,
 181, 284, 286, 287
12:10—61, 284
12:10–12—153n.11, 184
12:11—9, 18n.17, 27,
 125, 129, 133, 134,
 165, 182, 186, 194,
 203, 215, 272, 290,
 293, 311
12:11–12—251
12:12—185, 206n.9
12:13–16—244
12:13–17—185, 278
12:13ff.—244n.6
12:14—19, 171, 182, 286
12:14–17—78, 172
12:15—284
12:15–16—172
12:15–17—130
12:16–17—286

12:17—18n.17, 57,
 81n.23, 170, 179, 181,
 186, 233n.13, 268, 275,
 277n.14, 327
13—12, 353, 355, 359
13:1—14, 58n.16, 99,
 171, 205, 226, 229,
 245, 248n.14, 251, 270,
 273, 295, 304, 319
13:1–2—188
13:1–8—304
13:1–10—45, 268
13:2—186, 187
13:3—190, 247
13:3–4—112, 191
13:4—230, 257, 258n.25
13:5—19, 44, 171, 172,
 182, 189
13:5–6—188, 229, 245
13:5–7—172
13:6—166
13:7—9, 43, 53n.9, 55,
 74, 164, 171, 186, 187,
 188, 193, 205, 215,
 233n.13, 248, 249, 251,
 252n.20, 277n.14
13:7–8—203
13:8—85, 88, 191,
 202n.3, 206, 299
13:9—10
13:10—194, 208
13:11–18—130, 268
13:12—112, 193
13:12–14—205
13:13—195, 232
13:14—191, 193, 230,
 285
13:14–15—195
13:14–17—203
13:15—251
13:15–16—196
13:16—129, 202, 225,
 285, 286, 298
13:16–17—74, 246
13:17—202
13:17–18—192
13:18—10, 16n.14,
 194n.23, 207, 248
14–15—200

14:1—89, 129, 156, 196,
 206, 248, 310, 323
14:1–4—106
14:1–5—11, 15, 149,
 204n.6, 215, 218,
 275n.11
14:2—201, 204
14:3—100, 201, 216
14:3–4—131, 203
14:4—212
14:4–5—202
14:5—203
14:6—62n.19, 210
14:6–7—164, 205
14:6–13—219
14:7—175n.23, 229
14:8—168, 205, 206n.9,
 210, 238, 245, 253, 254
14:8–10—62n.19
14:8–11—201
14:9—210
14:9–11—206, 296
14:10—206, 212, 213,
 214, 227
14:11—207
14:12—18, 56, 194n.23,
 207, 208
14:12–13—215
14:13—16, 27n.2, 126,
 134, 207, 208, 294
14:14—75
14:14–16—203, 210
14:14–17—149
14:14–20—131, 201, 219
14:15—62n.19
14:17–19—62n.19
14:17–20—210, 271, 326
14:18—213
14:18–19—228
14:19—206, 213
14:19–20—206
14:20—214, 227, 270
15–16—62n.19
15:1—7, 14, 36n.15, 37,
 47, 139, 162, 179n.2,
 206n.9, 214, 217, 222,
 223n.4, 236, 278, 304,
 306
15:1–4—204n.6, 218

383

APOCRYPHA

PSEUDEPIGRAPHA

ANCIENT CHRISTIAN AND CLASSICAL WRITERS